ALSO BY ELAINE SCIOLINO

The Outlaw State
SADDAM HUSSEIN'S QUEST FOR POWER
AND THE GULF CRISIS

PERSIAN MIRRORS

The Elusive Face of Iran

ELAINE SCIOLINO

THE FREE PRESS

NEW YORK • LONDON • TORONTO • SYDNEY • SINGAPORE

THE FREE PRESS

A division of Simon & Schuster, Inc.

1230 Avenue of the Americas

New York, New York 10020

DESIGNED BY KEVIN HANEK

MAP COPYRIGHT © 2000 BY ANITA KARL AND JIM KEMP

Manufactured in the United States of America

1   3   5   7   9   10   8   6   4   2

Library of Congress Cataloging-in-Publication Data

Sciolino, Elaine.

Persian Mirrors : the elusive face of Iran/Elaine Sciolino.

p.   cm.

Includes bibliographical references and index.

1. Iran—Politics and government—1979–1997. 2. Iran—Politics and government—1997– .

3. Iran—Social life and customs. 4. Sciolino, Elaine—Journeys—Iran. I. Title

DS318.8 .S35 2000

955.05'04—dc21   00-041103

ISBN 0-684-86290-5

The author gratefully acknowledges permission from the following sources to reprint material in their control: Arash Forouhar for the text of an unpublished poem by his mother, Parvaneh Forouhar. IBEX Publishers for a poem from "The Hafez Poems of Gertrude Bell," © 1995 by IBEX Publishers, Bethesda, MD. R. D. McChesney, the editor of *Iranian Studies,* for the text of poems by Ruhollah Khomeini found in "Five Mystical Ghazals by the Ayatollah Khomeini" in *The Journal of the Society for Iranian Studies: Selections from the Literature of Iran, 1977–1997,* special issue, volume 30, No. 3–4, Summer/Fall 1997. Universal Press Syndicate for the text from a Doonesbury cartoon of May 30, 1980, © 1980 by G. B. Trudeau. Zagros Press, Princeton, NJ, for an excerpt from The Iraj Mirja poem "Aref Nameh" found in "The Poetics of Hijab in the Satire of Iraj Mirza," in *Iran and Iranian Studies: Essays in Honor of Iraj Afshar,* edited by Kambiz Eslami, © 1998 by Zagros Press.

In memory of Maynard Parker

Contents

Contents

PERSIAN MIRRORS

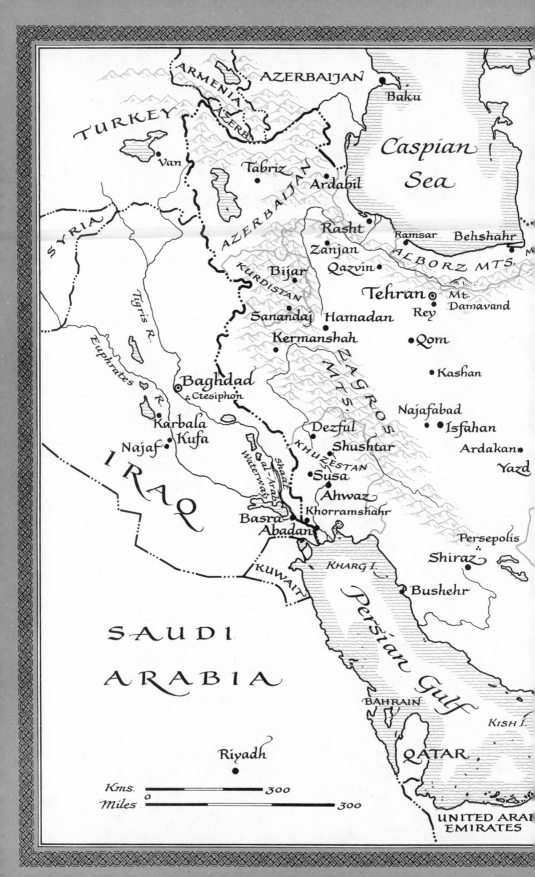

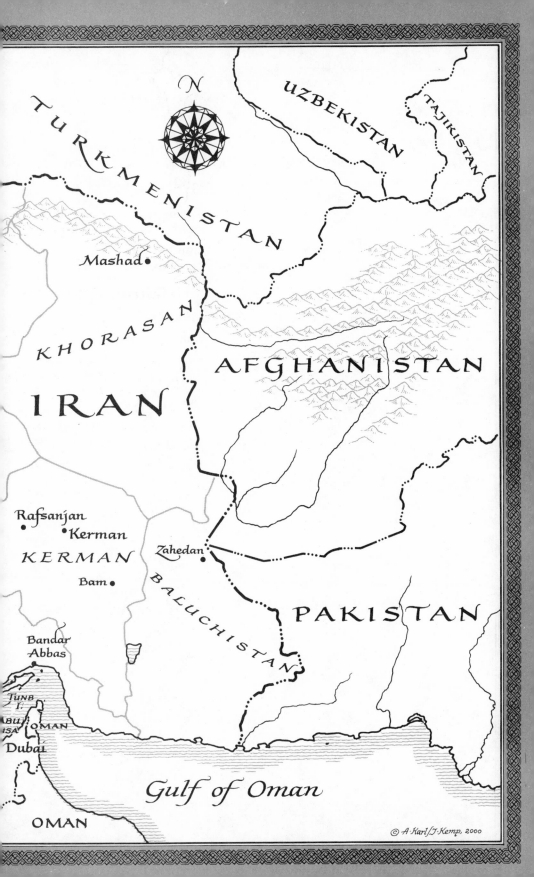

Reflections and Distortions

1 NEVER WENT to Iran for the nightlife.

I went for a revolution, a war, and an embassy seizure. And I kept going back.

For much of my career, I was what they call in the newspaper business a hard-news reporter. That meant I covered breaking events. I wrote about what I saw on the streets. I didn't do parties.

Yet here I was, late on a Friday night in the heart of Kurdistan province, at a raucous wedding party that didn't want to end. A young woman in a tight red dress and lipstick to match whipped a long pink chiffon scarf from her head to reveal waist-length curls. But it was her shoulders and hips that captivated the crowd. The shoulders and hips didn't stop rotating as she pranced hard on a concrete patio that had become a dance floor some hours before. She thrust her head back and her bosom forward, waving her scarf in the air as she beckoned others to join her.

The clerics had made the head scarf the national symbol of women's purity, and here was a lady in red, using it as a lure to pull others to dance with her. I couldn't quite figure out how she moved all those body parts in so many different directions at the same time. But all the rotating and thrusting and scarf-waving worked, and soon there were two dozen Kurdish men in balloon pants and waist-length jackets on the dance floor with her. They linked arms in a wide circle. Now it was their turn to sway and thrust and kick and prance for the crowd. It looked like a frenzied rendition of the hora.

Ayatollah Ruhollah Khomeini, the stern cleric who had fathered Iran's revolution a generation before, once said that "there is no fun in Islam." He would have been astonished at what he saw.

That evening, the dancing wasn't the only surprise. There was the way the women were dressed, and not just the young ones like the lady in red. We were in an open garden into which outsiders could peek, but here were two hundred women in mixed company breaking the law and revealing their hair—lacquered, teased, curled, dyed, twisted, braided, and frosted—in acts of vanity and defiance. Some of the women wore traditional Kurdish costumes, in jewel colors and layers of sequined lace bodices, flowered sashes, flowing satin skirts, necklaces of shiny plastic beads. One woman, who turned out to be the mother of the groom, resembled an aging fairy godmother: a gold lace skirt over petticoats, a gold satin vest, a gold chiffon blouse, gold-streaked hair, and matching gold earrings and bangle bracelets. The only accessory that was missing was a wand. Other women wore dresses not too different from ones I used to see in the cocktail lounges on the West Side of Buffalo, New York, where I grew up in the 1950s—trimmed with too much lace and too many rhinestones and revealing excess adipose.

Then there was the music. Iran's clerics had long since banned discotheques, nightclubs, bars, alcohol, coed sports, satellite dishes, gambling, and many kinds of music. The music here was so loud that it made small talk excruciating. It was so sensuous that, as often happens at weddings, it enticed guests onto the dance floor, even as they swore they did not know how to dance.

Finally there was the fact that I was welcomed that night not only as a visitor from afar, but as an American. I had never met the bride or the groom, but went along as the guest of a distant cousin of both. Iranians are passionate hosts, so it's not unusual for them to invite total strangers into their wedding parties. And an American visitor is a welcome emissary. Some guests had never seen an American before and wanted to take my picture. I was beckoned to the dance floor and offered endless glasses of tea. I was kissed by some of the women, over and over. I was asked to help with visas to America. The aunt of a distant cousin of the groom was so persistent in begging for visas for her two grown children, as if I held it in my power to issue visas, that after a while I used sign language to indicate that I couldn't hear what she was saying. And so it went, until 4:00 A.M., when the music stopped and the last guest went home.

When people ask me about Iran, two questions inevitably come up: Aren't you scared as an American? And don't you have to wear that black veil?

The answers are no and no.

Terrorists and veils. Veils and terrorists. That's probably what most ordinary Americans think about if they think at all about Iran. They remember the searing photographs of blindfolded American diplomats held at gunpoint as hostages. And they see the recurring images of dour angry women who swathe themselves from head to foot in yards of black.

Sure, there have been times in the twenty-plus years that I've traveled to Iran that I've been terrified. And on rare occasions I have donned the cumbersome and not very attractive garment called the chador.

But images can lie, as I saw at the wedding in Kurdistan.

Just days earlier, I had received a different reception as an American. July 1999 was the month of burning anger in the streets as students experimented with rebellion in a serious way for the first time since Iran's 1979 revolution. Six days of unrest that had started with student demonstrations degenerated into riots and bloodshed. Then they ended, with a day of nationwide pro-government marches and rallies, choreographed by the government, to praise the Islamic Republic and condemn its enemies, particularly the United States.

The Islamic Republic had withstood the challenge, but the fault lines had been exposed. On the day of the government rally, I watched from a street corner as thousands of angry bearded men and black-clad women screamed "Death to America" and punched the air with their fists. The student unrest had to be blamed on somebody, so why not the United States? To admit that the unrest was homegrown would be to admit that there was internal dissent and unhappiness with the Islamic system itself.

I had seen the same street theater many times before. This time the government-staged carnival was organized in at least two dozen cities and towns simultaneously, with nothing left to chance. Government workers and their families were "invited" to spend the night at their offices and offered a hearty meal as an incentive; soldiers were told to report to the demonstration in civilian clothes. All the players knew their roles by heart: the speakers at the podiums, the demonstrators in the crowds, and the security forces on the streets.

And I knew my role as a foreign journalist. I wore my laminated press card around my neck and openly took notes. I played Pied Piper to a line of plainclothes security officers with walkie-talkies who followed me wherever I went—into a grocery store and an optician's shop, to a newsstand and an ice cream vendor. The images on the television screens

3

beamed back to America sent a message of rage and hatred. Yet I felt perfectly safe. I knew the drill.

In my years as a foreign correspondent for *Newsweek* and as a diplomatic correspondent for *The New York Times,* I have traveled to some one hundred countries around the world. Many of them were inhospitable and hard to crack. In Iraq, the omnipresence of intelligence police in every village, factory, mosque, office building, and classroom made honest interviews excruciatingly difficult. In Saudi Arabia, I was denied entry to the public restaurants of my four-star hotel because I was a woman traveling alone. In China, I accidentally discovered yards of mysterious wiring while searching for an outlet for the modem of my computer; when I tried to get into my hotel room at an odd hour the next day I discovered the lock on the door had been changed. In Syria, it was even worse: I once asked the wrong question of the country's top religious leader and found myself in an unfurnished cell in the basement of a pleasant-looking villa that had been turned into a prison. My roommate was a Palestinian woman who obviously had been tortured.

But my expectations as a reporter have always been higher in Iran than in many other places. Iran is different. It may be hard to crack, but it is never inhospitable. As contradictory as it sounds, Iranians are both deeply suspicious of outsiders and extremely warm toward them. And it is that tension that allows for unexpected discoveries and endless possibilities.

No other country I have visited has seduced me the way Iran has. It is one of the most dynamic and exciting countries in the world, filled with surprises and complexity, sometimes even poetry and magic.

Imagine being able to live through one of the most important events of the twentieth century, a revolution that swept aside a powerful, repressive king who had sought power and prestige by linking his country to the industrialized West, replacing him with an old bearded cleric in a turban and cloak whose answer to the king's injustice was to wrap the country in a populist message of promise and smother it with an intolerant version of Islam.

Then imagine seeing this human drama play out over the years, as the people's yearning for a better life clashed with the clerics' prescription for keeping their souls intact. It was as if an entire country was playing a game of chess in which the rules had been turned inside out. The game started once the king was off the board and the bishop with his pawns had taken over. Both sides were trapped in the memory that the clerics' revolution had begun as a popular one. And everything was supposedly for the sake of the people. What brought me back time and again was not a story about politics or religion but a drama about human nature.

Even a generation later, the story of Iran's revolution isn't over. And I don't know the ending.

As the world's only modern theocracy, Iran is a contradiction, a traditional society wrestling to reconcile itself with the present. It offers living proof that a theocracy cannot thrive unchallenged where open thought is allowed, and that no government can keep out the rest of the world by decree. At the same time, Iran is also a place where many members of the theocracy themselves have become passionate proponents of the need for change. Iran's revolution may have destroyed an old order and created a new one, but a generation later a great battle is raging like nothing seen since its early days. It is a battle not over control of territory but for the soul of the nation.

Iran has become an exciting, daring laboratory where experiments with two highly volatile chemicals—Islam and democracy—are being conducted: in politics, in the press, in the cinema, in the bazaar, in the mosque, in the courtroom, in the universities, in the beauty parlors, in private homes, in the streets.

Much of the drama is playing out in public, as Iranians begin to lose their fear and assert themselves. Much of the drama also plays out in the shadows, behind the veils and shutters that open to an outsider only slowly. Over the years, Iran has revealed itself to me in fragments, and even then the fragments often don't fit together. It reminds me of what Robert Byron, the British travel writer, wrote about a trip to Iran in the 1940s: "The start of a journey in Persia resembles an algebraical equation: it may or may not come out."

This is not a book about the mysterious East. Nor is it a chronicle of the political, diplomatic, and military dimensions of Iran's revolutionary history. I have no prescriptions for how the United States should deal with Iran; there have been enough of those. I have no predictions for Iran's future; there have been enough of those too. I try here instead to offer a portrait of my own encounters with Iran, and with the Iranian people, in the hope it can illuminate whatever choices or predictions others make.

One of the first things tour guides tell visitors to the Carpet Museum in Tehran is that the finest carpets are knotted with matching skeins of silk, the more knots per inch the better. This book is not like a finely knotted silk carpet. It is a more like a rough tribal *kilim*, woven with bits and pieces taken from more than two decades of notebooks and memories and stories.

For that reason, I have divided the book into parts that reflect the journeys I have taken—the movements back and forth between public and private realms, the travels to remote parts of the country, the transitions over time. I have relied on material gathered both from trips to Iran since 1979 and from years of writing about foreign affairs from Washington and the United Nations. Every person in this book is real, although in a few cases, at the individual's request for anonymity, I have substituted fictional first names and omitted last names.

The Iran that I have seen is a nation that has chosen not to destroy the remnants of a 2,500-year-old empire but to preserve them for later. It is a place that long ago produced sensual romantic poetry that even the most austere clerics still read aloud, insisting it is about divine love, not the human variety. It is a country whose women—even some of its most religious women—adorn themselves with makeup and jewelry behind high walls, then cover themselves in black on the streets and struggle for their rights in the most creative and persistent ways. It is a state whose revolutionary system continues to defy those who proclaim its demise. It is a land whose geography, population, and quest for regional supremacy prevent it from being ignored, and that struggles, unevenly, for modernity and greatness.

One day not long ago, on a visit with a group of American tourists to the pale green Marble Palace built in the 1930s by Reza Shah Pahlavi, I came upon a place that captures the complexity of the country. It is a large reception room encased in thousands of tiny, angled bits of mirrors of a type used in many of Iran's mosques and holy shrines. In Islam, mirrors symbolize purity and the light of God. *Ayeneh kari*, these mosaics of mirrors are called. In the mosques, there are also mosaics, made with tiles. But the pieces of tile in these mosaics are separated by putty, which is used not only to keep the pieces together but also to fill in the gaps between them. The mirror mosaics have no putty; the pieces have to fit neatly into each other. There can be no gaps.

The glittering fragments, sometimes set at angles to each other like facets on a jewel, reflect light and distort images at the same time. In Reza Shah's reception room, we could not look in the mirrors and see our faces whole; we saw them shattered in pieces. For me, the mirror-mosaics are emblematic of Iran. Iran can be dazzling and light-filled, a reflection of its complexities; but it can also be cold, confusing, and impenetrable.

Iran has lured me and invited me in, over and over, for twenty years. But at the beginning of the twenty-first century, it is still the country of the mirror-mosaics, distorting reality and reflecting only parts of itself at any one time.

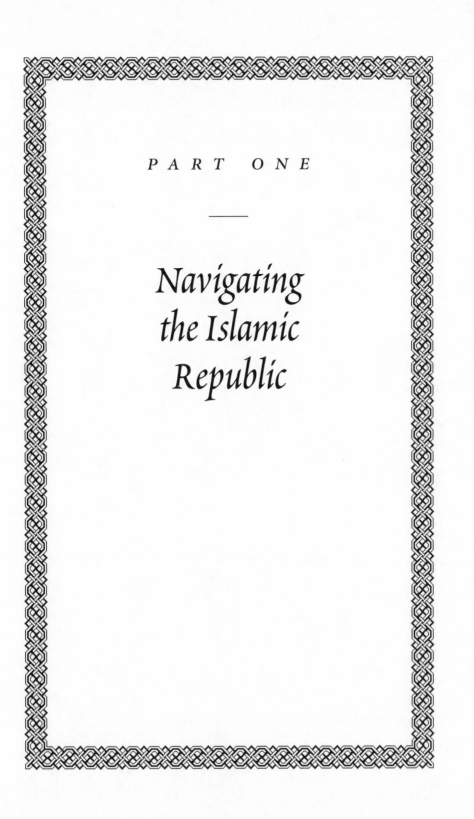

PART ONE

—

*Navigating
the Islamic
Republic*

Getting There, Getting In

1 HAVE NEVER LIKED flying into Iran in the middle of the night. But after too many trips to count, I now have the drill down pat.

It isn't easy to get there from the United States. Tehran is 6,337 miles from Washington, D.C., and no American carrier flies there. American economic sanctions, the absence of diplomatic relations, and common sense in the face of official Iranian hostility toward the United States preclude that.

Lufthansa is the most efficient way in: a seven-and-a-half hour overnight flight from Dulles to Frankfurt, a six-hour stay in a day room at the airport hotel, and a five-hour overnight flight that arrives at an ungodly hour in Tehran. Some people I know do the second leg on Iran Air, which is cheaper and whose aging American Boeing 747s are surprisingly safe. But Iran Air requires women to cover their hair with head scarves and serves no alcoholic beverages. I prefer to stave off the restrictions of the Islamic Republic as long as I can.

For security reasons, Lufthansa often changes the gate for Flight 600 to Tehran without explanation. The boarding pass lists one gate; the overhead monitor doesn't list the gate at all. The actual gate is usually somewhere else, sometimes in an isolated area down an escalator that is inaccessible to the duty-free shops and the luggage carts.

After unloading its passengers in Tehran, the Lufthansa plane loads new passengers and heads straight back to Frankfurt. The airline considers it too much of a hassle, and too dangerous, to stay overnight in Iran. A German businessman, a non-Muslim, was once sent to death row after being convicted of having sex with an unmarried Iranian Muslim woman, although his sentence was later reversed and he was sent home.

Even on Lufthansa, the metamorphosis begins before the plane lands. The liquor bottles are quickly stored and the Lufthansa playing cards collected. Passengers are given a warning to leave behind the miniature bottles of Jack Daniel's and Stolichnaya. A second warning is reserved for female passengers. "By the decree of the government of Iran, all female passengers are required to have their heads covered," the steward announces. "For your own interest we ask you to put on a scarf before leaving the aircraft." The dance of the veil begins. The women cover their heads and bodies. A woman sitting across the aisle in khaki pants, a low-cut black top, heavy gold necklace, gold bangle bracelets, big hair, and blood-red lips puts on a trench coat and a good knockoff of a Hermès scarf. A woman on the other side of me wraps herself in a black chador. I reach into my carry-on for a long, solid-colored, textured cotton scarf that doesn't need to be tied under my chin.

Mehrabad International Airport was once state-of-the-art, a showpiece of the Shah's campaign to transform Iran into one of the world's most modern and prosperous countries. Even today, despite the worn runways, the airport functions fairly well. Planes arrive and leave remarkably close to their scheduled times. There are Western as well as Eastern toilets. A twenty-four-hour prayer room welcomes the pious. A twenty-four-hour restaurant serves tea and pastries. A duty-free shop sells cheap souvenirs, flowery carpets, and good but not cheap caviar. In 1998 the airport opened a huge new waiting hall with fancy tiles, a carpet shop, and a small bookstore that sells books like *Facial Yoga: No More Wrinkles.* The giant government-protected Foundation for the Oppressed and War Veterans has a piece of the action. It runs a shop called Shahed (Witness) that sells televisions, VCRs, telephones, even refrigerators at prices below those in the shops in Tehran.

There is nothing revolutionary about the airport lounge for Commercially Important Persons, my immediate destination upon arrival at Mehrabad. Access depends on money, not on gender, age, nationality, sacrifice in the war with Iraq, or revolutionary credentials. In fact the only way to get in is with cash—$50 to be precise, which represents a month's salary for an average civil servant.

CIP, as the service is called, is a trip back in time. An airport official meets me on the tarmac, escorts me by car to a special area on the far side of the airport, and deposits me in a marble-floored lounge with recessed lighting and comfortable sofas. Waiters serve tea, cold drinks, and cream-filled pastries. Instrumental medleys from American musicals are interrupted by the predawn call to prayer. An English-speaking customs official takes my passport for stamping; a baggage handler fetches my luggage. The authorities justify the service on the grounds that it brings in hard currency and encourages foreign business executives to feel comfortable coming to Iran.

A photo of Ayatollah Khomeini stares down at me from the wall of the CIP lounge. He led a nation in revolution to rid Iran of places just like this. The revolution was supposed to empower and embolden the oppressed masses and make them independent of the dollar-carrying foreigner. It was supposed to disinfect the country of "Westoxication." The existence of the CIP lounge illustrates that things didn't work out as planned.

There was a time when going in and out of the country was enough to make me want to stay home. The baggage handlers and customs officials did not speak English; the passport control officers spoke barely enough to get by. It could take three hours to get through the checkpoints. I once counted three checkpoints for people entering the country—each representing different centers of power—and nine for people leaving. But it was the invasion of my privacy that got me most angry. Customs officers have dumped the contents of my suitcases on the floor, run their fingers through jars of face cream and leafed through books and manila folders of news clippings. Body searches—always by female guards in black chadors—could be rough and much too intrusive.

Iranians sometimes still suffer some of these indignities. Western magazines used to be what customs officials were after. Even a copy of *Newsweek* could cause problems. Then it was contraband CDs, cassettes, and videotapes. Bertrand Vannier, a French journalist for Radio France, and I once flew in on the same plane from Rome, and the customs officers confiscated his radio (which might pick up Revolutionary Guards communications) and his deck of playing cards (gambling is forbidden in Islam). Bertrand was given a receipt for both and told to retrieve them on his way out of the country. He was stunned that upon his departure, two weeks later, he was given back his goods.

Today customs checks for foreigners are rare. The last thing potential foreign investors want to deal with at 3:00 A.M. is a search of their suitcases. Even huge anti-American banners and looming portraits of Ayatollah Khomeini that once dominated the airport have been taken down, replaced by modest-sized photographs of Khomeini and his pale successor as Supreme Leader, Ayatollah Ali Khamenei. The only sign I continue to find offensive is one in yellow neon in the domestic terminal that reads, in English, "In future Islam will destroy Satanic sovereignty of the West."

Hadi Salimi, my friend and my regular driver, is always at the airport to meet me. Iranians can be rather formal, and it has never occurred to me to address him as anything other than "Mr." By day he has a full-time job maintaining a chemistry lab. After twenty years' service, his monthly salary is the equivalent of $50. But he can earn $50 a day, sometimes $75—in dollars—by driving foreign visitors. It is only when I see Mr. Salimi, smiling, in his jacket and knitted cap, that I feel that I have safely arrived.

Then, as we speed down the highway toward downtown, Tehran hardly seems like a worthy destination. It is a perfectly dreadful city that grew out of a barren brown plain, without even the saving grace of a storied past. "In the Middle Ages it was a savage place where people lived in holes," wrote Roger Stevens in his classic book on Iran, *The Land of the Great Sophy.* Tehran, he added, was "an obscure, ill-favored provincial town." It became the capital quite by accident. As dynasties changed over the centuries, Susa, Ctesiphon, Isfahan, Hamadan, Shiraz, Qazvin, Rey, Tabriz, Persepolis, and Mashad all served as capitals. In the latter part of the eighteenth century, Agha Mohammad, a Persian king of the Qajar dynasty, moved his court to Tehran because it was close to his native province of Mazandaran on the Caspian Sea, and to his tribal allies there. Only then did Tehran flourish, and were lavish palaces built.

Unlike the great ancient capitals of Baghdad or Cairo, Tehran has no river to bathe and cool it, to bring trade and commerce. Initially, it was built around a bazaar and a main mosque. Reza Shah, an army colonel who took over the government in 1921 and was crowned king four years later, expanded it with broad thoroughfares and a railroad as part of his single-minded campaign to modernize the country. During his twenty years in power, he also razed some of the most beautiful old residences, replacing them with structures every bit as monstrous as Stalinist designs. The oil boom of the late 1960s and 1970s then triggered a more ambitious building spree under Shah Mohammad Reza Pahlavi, who assumed power after his father was dethroned by the British and the Russians because he was thought to have pro-Nazi tendencies. The new Shah seemed determined to spend money as wildly and quickly as possible on high-rise buildings of no architectural importance. At the time of Iran's 1979 revolution, the population of greater Tehran was only about four million. Then came massive confiscations of property and the revolutionary dictum, "Land belongs only to God!" An order by Khomeini to bear more children, massive migration from the countryside, and disregard for building codes increased the population to nearly 12 million—almost one fifth of the country's population—creating a need for cheap housing and contributing to the city's dysfunction. It would be comparable to 50 million people living in New York City. A coffee table book of photographs of Tehran attests to its ugliness. The aerial shots show miles of squat, square, featureless buildings, mottled and gray with pollution.

The traffic requires a survival-of-the-boldest attitude. Nobody is timid and nobody yields the right of way and nobody stays in his own lane. Drivers routinely back down one-way ramps and drive the wrong way on one-way streets whose direction can change without notice. But everyone knows the rules, so when it seems as if an accident is all but certain, drivers move just enough to avert calamity. I often think that Tehran traffic is a useful metaphor for the country: individualistic, fluid, and yielding at the last possible moment. Even so, Tehran has one of the highest automobile fatality rates in the world.

After the revolution, the clerics renamed the streets after religious symbols, martyrs, and ayatollahs. (Ayatollah, which means "sign of God," is the title given to the most learned religious leaders in the Shiite Muslim world.) But in the minds of motorists, the names did not change. My favorite street in Tehran has always been Vali Asr Avenue, named for the revered hidden Imam (spiritual leader) of Shiite Islam, who, Shiites believe, went into hiding in the ninth century. A wide thoroughfare shaded with stately chenar trees, it cuts through the city from north to south. But for many Iranians, it will always be called Pahlavi Avenue. After all, it was Reza Shah Pahlavi who planted the trees.

I once asked Mr. Salimi what it was like to drive for a living. "The line in the middle of the road has no meaning," he said. "When you see the yellow light that tells you to slow down, people speed up. The women think the only purpose of the rearview mirror is to look at themselves. There is a written driving test, but if you say you're illiterate you only have to identify a few signs to get your license.

"Traffic," he concluded, "is worse than life."

"So you hate your job?" I asked him.

"I love my job!" he exclaimed, to my surprise. "It energizes me. On the road, I can get away with things."

The streets of Tehran are so clogged with cars—most of which are more than fifteen years old and lack exhaust filters—that Tehran has become one of the most polluted cities in the world, alongside Mexico City, Bangkok, and Jakarta. Tehran's location at the foot of the Alborz mountain range limits the free circulation of air. Radio and television announcements warn children and old people to stay home, schools can shut down for days, and it is not at all unusual to see people walking down the streets wearing face masks to keep out the bad air. I have often thought that one of the few benefits of the obligatory head covering is that at least it keeps women's hair cleaner.

Yet sometimes, in the early morning, after a windy night or a heavy snowfall, Tehran dazzles. The air is fresh and clean. The yellow-gray fog that has lain thick over the city lifts to reveal Damavand, one of the most beautiful mountains in the world. Sometimes I have come upon half-hidden treasures: an ornate nineteenth-century villa hidden behind a grimy brick wall adorned with exposed electrical wiring; or, near the bazaar, a winding street too narrow for my car; or an Art Deco house in gray stone that I longed to see painted South Miami pink; or a decades-old wishing well decorated with candles and framed portraits of Ali, the son-in-law of the Prophet, where people leave their dreams along with their 1,000 rial bills.

When I come to Tehran, I often stay at the Laleh International Hotel. The fourteen-story, 386-room concrete structure had been the Inter-Continental in the Old Regime, one of the top-of-the-line hotels built by Americans. Those were the days when Western businessmen crowded into Tehran seeking lucrative business deals. A Sheraton, a Hilton, and a Hyatt, with American decor and hamburgers on the menu, also had been built to make them feel at home. They all were confiscated, renamed, and Islamicized by the revolutionaries. Today the Laleh (which means "tulip," the symbol of martyrdom) is owned by the Ministry of Islamic Guidance and Culture, which also finds the hospitality business a good way to monitor the comings and going of Western journalists. But like the re-named streets, the big hotels are still widely known by their prerevolutionary names. I picked up my copy of the English-language *Tehran Times* one day to find a large front-page ad for a carpet merchant's annual sale at "Tehran's Esteqlal (ex-Hilton) Hotel."

I can plot the course of Iran's revolution by the changes I have seen at the Laleh. After the Shah left the country, his portrait and that of his wife that hung in the lobby were turned toward the wall; with the success of the revolution, they were taken down. The ayatollahs' plainclothes secur-ity guards replaced the Shah's plainclothes security guards. Milton Meyer, an American travel agent married to an Iranian, kept his business open in the shop off the lobby after the revolution and even after the American embassy was seized. Later, he moved his business across the street, and eventually he was arrested. In April 1994, he was sentenced to twenty-four months in prison and fined more than $200,000 after confessing, Iranian authorities said, to corruption and espionage charges.

The Mozaffarian brothers have kept one of their swank jewelry shops at the Laleh, a tribute to the staying power of capitalism in the Islamic Republic. Their prices are exorbitant—much higher than the bazaar—but that is the cost of shopping in the hotel. Whenever I enter the shop, they make me tea and sit me down and show me their museum-quality treasures. They are particularly proud of a necklace of matching dia-monds and emeralds made decades before by their father. In a country where university professors earn only a few thousand dollars a year, the necklace is priced at half a million dollars.

I met many of the Laleh's receptionists and waiters during the revolution. We lived through those heady and scary days when rival factions shot up the hotel looking for would-be enemies. For the most part, the staff stayed on, thankful to have jobs in a country whose revolution did not deliver prosperity. The men behind the reception desk are no longer allowed to wear ties, which are considered a symbol of the corrupt West. Some of them wear silk ascots instead, a modest rebellion.

In the early days of the revolution, it was still possible to get a drink in the hotel and the minibars were fully stocked as the hotel management tried to keep the Islamic Republic at bay. But armed Islamic zealots finally arrived at the hotel one evening and politely demanded access to the storage area in the basement. They had orders, they said, to destroy all the liquor in the wine cellar. In a fit of Islamic frenzy, they poured bottles of wine and champagne into the outdoor swimming pool. They opened thousands of cans of imported beer and pitched them into a service driveway. The manager of the hotel estimated the value of the lost stock at $325,000. That ended the battle.

Soon afterward, the Air France stewardesses were banned from sunbathing in the chaises longues near the five-sided pool. The pool was emptied of its water and closed. Later, masons came and installed a mosaic of tiles on the lobby wall. It welcomed all visitors with the words, "Down with U.S.A." The doormat was imprinted with a large American flag that visitors stepped on going in and out of the hotel.

Over the years, the Laleh became downright seedy. The carpets wore out, the bedspreads grew faded and torn. In the rooms, the air-conditioning system made so much noise that I opted for open windows and the sound of Tehran traffic. But that invited hungry, plump mosquitoes. The cockroaches became so comfortable that they didn't bother to flee when the bathroom light was switched on.

A few years ago, the Ministry of Islamic Guidance and Culture poured enormous sums into renovations. The occasion was the 1997 summit of the fifty-five-country Organization of the Islamic Conference, which attracted Muslim heads of state from all over the world. Iran was the host and wanted to show off. So the gray facade of the Laleh was painted white. The lobby was redecorated with gray and black marble, mirror-mosaics, polished brass, and crystal chandeliers. Gulf gauche, I call it.

New bedspreads, drapes, carpets, lamps, and air-conditioners were bought. The American flag doormat was replaced with ornate white stones decorated with stars. The tiles that spelled "Down with U.S.A." were removed and two red carpets were rolled out the front entrance. Framed posters were hung, not of mosques and mullahs (the generic term for members of the clergy) but of Iran's pre-Islamic sites. Pre-revolutionary Muzak tapes were taken out of storage—even an orchestral medley that included "Strangers in the Night" and "On the Street Where You Live." Ataollah Mohajerani, the Minister of Islamic Guidance and Culture, said at one point that three hotels could have been built for the cost of renovating this one.

Room service at the Laleh is a refuge from the restrictions of the Islamic Republic. I hate eating while wearing a head scarf; the ends of the scarf usually wind up in my plate. But I can eat all the caviar I want bare-headed in the privacy of my room—even for breakfast over scrambled eggs. And in Iran it's economical. Depending on the source, it can cost as little as $10 for one hundred grams of an excellent Sevruga. I keep it in my minibar.

When I do eat out, I can always get a table at the French Rotisserie, the culinary gem of the Laleh. With its caviar and blinis, its world-class wine cellar, and its view of the city and the mountains, it was once one of Tehran's finest places to dine. It stayed open throughout the revolution (though no longer serving alcohol), even when armed leftist militias used its windows for target practice and hotel employees had to douse the leftists with fire hoses. The restaurant moved to the first floor during the long war with Iraq and then closed for renovation. The Polynesian restaurant down the hall took its customers. Maybe it was for the best. My most vivid memory of the Rotisserie was the six-foot-long tapeworm I once got from eating rare beef tenderloin there.

Eventually, the Rotisserie reopened, and on a recent trip I decided to go back. Mr. Rasouli, one of the chief waiters, met me at the door. "Miss Sciolino?" he asked in disbelief. I was half disguised in my head scarf and we were both a generation older than when we had last seen each other. But Mr. Rasouli had served me at the same table, night after night, during the first year of the revolution. If we had been in the United States or Europe, we probably would have embraced. But this was the Islamic Republic, and he did the most daring thing he could: he stuck out his right hand for a handshake. We shook and shook.

The restaurant had been redecorated, but the management tried to preserve the old flavor. The metal chargers with the Inter-Continental logo were retained, as were the ashtrays. Even the menu was the same as it had been twenty years before: onion soup, steak au poivre (minus the cognac), trout meunière, and crème caramel. I asked Mr. Rasouli for the wine list. We both laughed. I ordered a Coke, which Mr. Rasouli poured into an Inter-Continental wineglass.

Mr. Rasouli was balder and plumper. But he retained his broad smile. I asked him how life had treated him over the years. "Hard," he said, simply. I waited for him to explain. "Life was great back then. The restaurant was full every night. I loved coming to work. Now I'm just counting the days until retirement." But he didn't want to spoil the moment of rediscovery. "I've lost all my hair!" he exclaimed, in mock horror.

After dinner Mr. Rasouli showed me where the redecorators had left the bullets embedded in the wood-paneled ceiling near the kitchen. "Remember, Miss Sciolino? We were standing right here when the shooting started. And the tear gas too."

Another waiter led me to a hidden cupboard in a storage room off the dining room. It contained dusty Inter-Continental brandy snifters from the old days. "Just in case," he whispered.

Ever since the beginning of the revolution, the Islamic Republic has tried with varying degrees of success to keep a leash on foreign and local journalists. I assume that the phone at my hotel, the cell phone I borrow or rent whenever I visit, and the local correspondent's phone and e-mail are tapped. I assume that my comings and goings are watched, not all the time, but enough to build a pretty good dossier. There have been times when unmarked cars with two men in the front seat would plant themselves outside the homes of friends I was visiting. During one particularly tense period, two cars with two men each parked in front of the apartment building of a friend for a month. One night an apartment in the building was burglarized, and the local police questioned the men in the cars. They identified themselves as officials from the Intelligence Ministry and ordered the police off the scene.

Technically, visits to shrines, universities, ministries, cemeteries, museums, and all travel outside Tehran require written permission from the Ministry of Islamic Guidance. Sometimes visits and appointments can be arranged privately; sometimes not. That means that whenever I visit Iran

I stop by the ministry soon after I arrive. The ministry has an enormous portfolio. It funds, censors, and approves books and movies. It gives and takes away newspapers' licenses. It distributes paper at subsidized prices to newspapers and journals. It runs conferences and exhibitions. It sponsors plays, concerts, and poetry readings.

I always bring chocolates for the women on the staff (lipsticks for the ones I am sure wear makeup). When he was the head of foreign press relations at the ministry, I would also bring books for Hosein Nosrat and for his deputy, Ali-Reza Shiravi. The trick with such officials is to persuade them to arrange the interviews I want. Sometimes permission to cover an event or take a trip is offered unexpectedly, and the opportunity has to be grabbed because the same one might not come around again for a long time. It is like eating New Jersey tomatoes in summer. You eat all you can because you won't see them for another year.

To understand why Iran's Islamic Republic endures, you have to meet Nosrat. This chain-smoking, fast-talking man in his forties is the best example of an Iranian bureaucrat. A former correspondent for the Islamic Republic News Agency, he had served as chief press aide at Iran's United Nations mission from 1994 to 1997 before returning to Iran to head the office in charge of foreign media at the Ministry of Islamic Guidance. (He returned to the United Nations in late 1999.) I first got to know Nosrat in New York. But it was in the Ministry of Islamic Guidance back home that he forever made his mark. He rid the foreign press office of aides who demanded money from journalists in exchange for interview arrangements. Unlike his predecessor, Nosrat spoke good English, was available at all hours on a cell phone, and was on a first-name basis with the best journalists in the American press corps. He wielded considerable power over foreign journalists and could hold up their visa applications just by letting them sit in his in-box. In the summer of 1999, when the Islamic Republic suffered through the worst street violence in its twenty-year history, he waited out the troubles before he approved the dozens of pending visa requests.

Nosrat still thought of himself as a journalist, not a bureaucrat. He took pride in his work and considered himself an expert on American journalism. His spacious office featured a Sony television, a VCR, a new computer, a large conference table, and tourism posters that captured "Persia," not "Islam." A TV junkie, he didn't watch Iranian television, but kept an eye on CNN all day long. He had spent so much time in the

United States that many of his reference points were American. In 1998, Iranians were fixated on the televised trial of Gholam-Hosein Karbaschi, the mayor of Tehran, and Nosrat explained that "for us, it's just like the O.J. trial was for you. You had to keep watching to see how it ended." By contrast, he said, Iranians were not at all interested in the reruns of President Clinton's impeachment hearings on local Iranian TV. "We already know the ending," he said. "The only people watching are those who want to improve their English." I wondered whether the clerical establishment would approve of the vocabulary they were learning.

Nosrat was industrious enough to secure funds to buy computers with Internet connections, and he reveled in showing me how he could call up *The New York Times* online. He devised a system of laminated press cards with photographs just like those of White House or Pentagon correspondents, except that for a woman to get an Iranian press card she has to pose for a photo wearing a head scarf.

Still, the ministry runs a dysfunctional system. The process of getting permission for an official interview or a trip is cumbersome. A secretary at the ministry has to type a formal request, get the requisite signatures, fax the letter to the person to be interviewed or the place to be visited, and wait for an official reply. The secretaries work only from eight-thirty in the morning until prayer time early in the afternoon.

Though some officials take my calls and make appointments without any formal authorization, others work through the ministry. Sometimes even private individuals with high profiles—the head of Iran's Jewish community and the editor of a monthly women's magazine, for example—required that the ministry arrange the appointments. It is a signal to the system that they are not meeting journalists secretly and have nothing to hide.

I like Nosrat because he levels with me. He doesn't believe in the Iranian system of *taarof* in which flattery and false modesty are used to make the other person feel good and to preserve a degree of social harmony. He has seen too much *taarof* in his life, and life is too short.

An interview with the family of Ayatollah Ali Khamenei, the Supreme Leader? "Impossible," raged Nosrat. A visit to Evin Prison? "Don't even bother to ask." A trip to Baluchistan province? "Too sensitive."

Sometimes I had to work around Nosrat, and in this effort, my best allies have been Iranian women, who are experts in finding ways around the constraints of the male-dominated system. Nosrat laughed out loud when I told him that for a story on the power women of Iran I wanted to be invited to the homes of the wife and daughters of Ali-Akbar Hashemi-Rafsanjani, who was then the President. When the women themselves invited me, he laughed even louder, as if to say, Okay, you got me.

For a while the ministry tried to assign minders to each visiting journalist, but the practice proved costly and inefficient. Eventually the ministry abandoned it—although from time to time Nosrat would suggest that I would get better access if I took along one of his aides. There was nothing preventing me from traveling throughout Iran on my own, without an official letter of introduction signed by Nosrat and stamped in green by the ministry. But Nosrat made clear that if I was to be stopped by local authorities and I didn't have written permission, he would not lift a finger to help me—and would probably not issue me another visa.

Nosrat's main priority was to try to keep journalists out of trouble. Once, when a strange-looking metal implement with wires that looked like a microphone was sent to my hotel room, he demanded that I deliver it to him immediately. It turned out to be a cell phone charger that could be plugged into the lighter of an automobile dashboard. (The owner of the cell phone I was renting had dropped it off without forewarning.)

Whenever I got into trouble, the first person I contacted was Nosrat. Like the time a policewoman came calling on me at my hotel in Sanandaj, the provincial capital of Kurdistan. I was summoned from my room to the lobby to find a dour middle-aged woman whose hands smelled of raw lamb. She was flipping through my passport, which I had been required to leave at the desk. She grumbled that her superiors had summoned her from her kitchen where she was making dinner. As she told me her story, she furiously recorded every page of my passport on sheets of plain white paper. Outside the hotel sat a large police van with two male policemen inside.

I produced three official letters of introduction signed by Nosrat and stamped by the Ministry of Islamic Guidance: one to his counterpart in Kurdistan, one to the governor of the province, and one to the security police. Then I called Nosrat in Tehran from my cell phone. "Hi, Hosein," I said. "I'm having a splendid time in Kurdistan. I'm sitting in the lobby with a lovely woman from the police. She has my passport and she's so interested in me."

Nosrat got it. "Oh, so it's question-and-answer time," he said. "Put her on the line."

Nosrat took over. Eventually the woman handed back the passport and left.

When I got back to Tehran, Nosrat told me how he had made a series of phone calls to figure out why I had been questioned. He told me that I had been lucky; it was not the Intelligence Ministry, just the security police. But then he told me how a conspiracy theorist might view my trip: My arrival happened to coincide with the worst unrest since the early days of the revolution, unrest that was officially blamed on the United States. I then went to Shiraz (ostensibly to have lunch with an ayatollah) at a time when a group of Jews from Shiraz had been arrested and accused of spying. I went to the Caspian Sea (ostensibly to write about oil) but then took a side trip to Behshahr (ostensibly to look for old wooden doors with colored glass), a place that in the Old Regime had been a Cold War listening post full of American spies. Then I went to Kurdistan (ostensibly to soak up local color and buy carpets) just after Turkey had conducted cross-border raids into Iranian territory.

"Of course you were looking for trouble!" Nosrat joked.

Nosrat prided himself on his ability to find creative solutions to problems. He told me a story about how, as a journalist in Eastern Europe in 1981, he had beaten all the odds and cornered Lech Walesa, then the head of Poland's Solidarity movement, in a hotel kitchen in Gdansk at eight in the morning. Walesa was in the middle of breakfast and had no choice but to give the Iranian wire service reporter an exclusive interview.

"I found him in a Gdansk chicken! I mean kitchen!" Nosrat told me.

Whenever I had a particularly challenging request of Nosrat after that, I referred to it as a Gdansk chicken. Not long ago I was having trouble getting a visa to enter the country and so I called Nosrat from Washington, hoping for some help with this particular Gdansk chicken.

"*Allo*," the voice on the other line said.

"Mr. Nosrat?" I asked.

"He's not here," he said.

"Is there a way to reach him?"

"No, he's sick," he replied.

I recognized his voice. But I felt I had to play along.

"Oh, my," I replied. "I'm calling from the United States."

"He's not going to be in the office for ten days."

"Ten days!" I exclaimed. "How serious is it?"

"I don't know."

By this time I felt I had to identify myself. The jig was up.

"Hi, Elaine," he said. "I recognize your voice."

It turned out he was not really sick, just trying to avoid another foreign journalist calling about a visa. He promised to process my visa the next day. The visa didn't come. I called again and again. Finally, I asked him how the Gdansk chicken was.

"Bad," he replied. Visa approvals were temporarily out of his hands. The Ministry of Intelligence was now vetting journalists' visa requests. My case eventually went all the way up to the President's office, and the visa didn't come through for another month. Security reasons, I was told later. In some quarters, *The New York Times* is still considered part of the international Zionist conspiracy.

Nosrat said he didn't believe in such things. But he also has an incredibly thick skin. One day in the summer of 1998 he and I were sitting in his office listening to the radio as the Parliament debated whether or not to remove Abdollah Nouri from his job as Minister of the Interior. Nouri was a close ally of Mohammad Khatami, whose enemies saw an opportunity to hurt the President by removing one of his key lieutenants. Nouri had been expected to prevail. Instead, by a vote of 137–117, the Parliament voted to remove him. I expected Nosrat to curse the Parliament. I expected him to start working the phones. He did not. He lit a Marlboro. He threw back his head and laughed, a hearty laugh that said, Let's move on.

"How can you be so calm about it?" I wanted to know.

"It's political life," Nosrat said. "You win. You lose. *Finito.*"

Nosrat saw the system for what it was—deeply flawed, but full of potential. He knew that this was just one battle in a long war, and that today's losers may well be tomorrow's winners. He was determined to stick with the Islamic Republic. Deep down, he was a believer.

CHAPTER TWO

Splendid Deception

There is perhaps some peculiar suppleness, some inherent flexibility in the
Iranian character which has enabled it to withstand shocks which would
have sent more rigid people reeling or would have broken their national
spirit.

— ROGER STEVENS, *THE LAND OF THE GREAT SOPHY*

These Persians are very strange people; they are ever on the watch to discover each other's intrigues, falsehoods, and finesses. A movement of the finger, a turn of the eye, is not left unnoticed, and receives an interpretation.
Yet each man invariably thinks that his own plots and intrigues are the
acme of human ingenuity, wholly unfathomable by the rest of mankind.

— LADY SHEIL, WIFE OF SIR JUSTIN SHEIL, THE BRITISH
AMBASSADOR TO IRAN, IN 1856

WHENEVER I THINK I understand Iran, it throws me a curve. That's
what happened on New Year's Day in 1999. Three parties, three curves.

The first day of *Nowruz*, the traditional Persian New Year, is a kind of
nationwide family get-together in which families visit each other's homes
throughout the day and into the night to eat, sit, and talk. It is the day that
is most universally celebrated throughout the country, the beginning of
thirteen days of joy surrounding the spring equinox.

The first party was an elegant buffet lunch and a lively political debate for about thirty people at the home of my close friend Fereshteh
Farhi, a microbiologist whose husband, Farhad Behbahani, is both a
chemist and a political writer. She is a middle-class, professional, secular
woman educated in the United States, but no alcohol was served. Farhad,
who is very religious, never would have allowed it in his home.

We sat in a large semicircle, balancing plates piled high with grilled fish, herbed rice, lamb stew, and a variety of salads. Flowers and sweets poured in; phone calls came from faraway relatives. The women took off their coats and scarves at the door, and I saw that most were dressed in tailored suits, tasteful jewelry, and high-heeled pumps. The men were in business suits, white shirts, and ties. In my black pants and sweater and sensible shoes, I felt underdressed. After lunch was picture-taking time in the garden by the pool. That's when the curve came. None of the women put on their head scarves. Here was a group of otherwise law-abiding, professional women, most of them middle-aged mothers, bareheaded in public! We were in full view of the neighbors' houses, smiling and posing. We might as well have been naked.

"Aren't you scared going out in public dressed like this?" I asked.

"This isn't public!" said Fereshteh. "It's our garden. It's our private space!"

Because the garden was outdoors, I considered it public space; for my friend, it was part of her private world.

After that party, I met my friend Sadegh and his wife and daughter, who brought me to an uncle's house for an early supper. Sadegh and his wife, Massoumeh, are American-educated professors at the University of Tehran. Their teenage daughter has never lived abroad but speaks excellent English. The curve came when mother and daughter put on full black chadors over their head scarves. And when we got to the uncle's house, the mother kept on her chador, gripping it tightly under her chin with one hand. Her sisters and female cousins poked fun at her and tried to pull it off when she wasn't looking. But because the party was not sexually segregated, they all kept their heads covered with scarves, their bodies in long, loose clothing, which made me feel as if I had to keep on my head scarf as well. Once again, in my black pants and sweater, I felt underdressed.

"You're shocked that I'm wearing a chador, aren't you?" Massoumeh asked me.

I was, but I was too embarrassed to say so, especially since I was the family's guest. "It all comes down to choice," I replied. "If you choose to dress like this, that's fine. I wish I had that choice to wear whatever I want." What I didn't say is that many outsiders regard the chador as a bad choice.

From there I went with my friend Farnaz to the biggest surprise of all: a late-night party at the home of a woman who supports herself and her unemployed son by running a gambling operation from her living room. It was an ordinary living room with sofas and chairs and end tables and a large round table covered in green baize in one of the corners. The table was the only equipment she needed for high-stakes card games that could net her thousands of dollars in one evening, every evening.

But this was the New Year, and the gambling operation was closed. Instead, the night was reserved for heavy drinking and dancing. I was there because I had been told I could meet Farnaz's friend, formerly named Mohsen, who had changed his sex—legally—and become a woman named Maryam. Maryam never showed up, but about forty other people did, and their demeanor and behavior were enough of a curve to startle any Westerner. The women's dresses were too short and too low-cut, their makeup too heavy, their hair too dyed and teased. The heavy-metal music was too loud, the cigarette smoke too thick. The drinking was too heavy, and by midnight, most of the guests were obnoxiously drunk. The children who had been dragged along were up too late, witnessing scenes on the makeshift dance floor that were too raunchy. Fellini would have felt right at home.

The star of the evening was an Iranian woman of about forty with long straight blond hair and a diaphanous white dress. Widowed with two young children years before, she had abandoned her children (they went to live with her parents) so that she could marry a man twelve years her junior who didn't want the burden of children. For the third time that day, I felt inappropriately dressed.

The surprises of that day remind me of a type of calligraphy done by my friend Golnaz Fathi, a brilliant young painter. Golnaz is one of the few women in Iran to have mastered what is traditionally a man's art. In 1997, when she was twenty-four, she was honored as the country's top female calligraphist. But she found the classic form too confining and began to improvise with a radical type of calligraphy called *siah mashgh,* "exercises in black." Her calligraphist's pen began to move in radically different directions on the page. The letters grew and stretched until the words no longer came together to form lines from poets like Hafiz or Saadi. In fact, the words meant nothing. The result was a storm of calligraphic curves.

So how to deal with all these curves? Over the years, I have developed a code of twelve rules that have helped me survive the setbacks and embrace the surprises of Iran.

RULE ONE: NEVER SAY NO TO AN INVITATION. Iranians by habit operate in two worlds, the public and the private. Traditionally just about
everything meaningful in both social and political life happens behind
closed doors. That is the way Iran has always been, whether its leaders
were kings or ayatollahs. The contrast is much sharper, however, under
the ayatollahs, who have set strict limits on what constitutes acceptable
behavior in public and sometimes even in private spaces. An outsider
can't just open the door and peer in. The only way to get the door to open
is to be invited in first.

I once went all the way to Bijar in Kurdistan to look for the famous
carpets that bear the town's name. I didn't find any. A carpet dealer in
Sanandaj laughed at me when I told him what I had done. "You can't just
go to Bijar for carpets," he said. "All the good ones are in private homes.
You have to get invited."

That was what my twenty years of visiting Iran has been: one long
struggle to get invited in—or to invite myself in. I've shamelessly asked
for invitations to mosques and churches and synagogues; to the homes of
clerics and to the homes of fashion designers; to Koranic classes and to
aerobics classes; to weddings and to funerals. Along the way has come the
delight of discovery. I have found real people with needs and desires even
as the Islamic Republic tries to make them faceless servants of orthodoxy,
and an outside world remains receptive to that stereotype.

It is common to meet people for the first time and have them invite
you to their homes for lunch or dinner. But "Come to my house for dinner" is the Iranian version of "Let's do lunch." It's not usually meant literally. The polite response is to reply, "I really don't want to be a burden,"
and then wait to see whether the invitation is extended again. After three
or four times, it is appropriate to accept. I, on the other hand, always accept as soon as the invitation is offered. It might be withdrawn and it
might not come again. I am, after all, a reporter.

RULE TWO: HOSPITALITY DOESN'T MEAN OPENNESS. Concealment is
part of normal life in Iran. Veils and scarves conceal women in public.
Both the bazaar and the mosque function as private clubs for the initi-
ated. The bazaar is not only the commercial heart of an Iranian city; it is
also a densely built community center—with mosques, public baths,
back rooms—that serves as a meeting place and center of communica-

tion. The mosque is not only a place of worship; it is also a vehicle for political mobilization.

Concealment makes Iranians very different from Americans. Americans live in houses with front yards that face out to the street. They sit on their front porches and watch the world go by. Iranians live in houses with front gardens hidden behind high walls. There is no connection to the street life outside. It is no accident that figures in Persian miniatures are often seen peering secretly from behind balconies or curtains or half-closed doors.

America's heroes are plainspoken, lay-it-on-the-line truth-tellers who love relating their life stories. For Iranians, Jimmy Stewart would be a chump. Self-revelation often is seen as a sign of weakness, or at least of self-indulgence. The only people who can be truly trusted are family. Iranians remind me of one of my Sicilian grandfathers, who used to curse the *stranieri*, the "foreigners," the outsiders who could not be trusted. My grandfather saw the world as a series of concentric circles with himself as the center, then the family, then people who had emigrated from his hometown, then Sicilians, then other Italians, then everyone else. Anyone in authority is to be avoided. *Gharibeh*, the Iranians call such outsiders.

Hassan Habibi is emblematic of the concealer who found success in the Islamic Republic. I first met him in Paris before the revolution, when Ayatollah Khomeini was in exile in France. Habibi said so little whenever I was with him that I didn't realize until much later that he even spoke French. Soon after the revolution he was named the spokesman for the ruling Revolutionary Council. I went to see him one evening and told him the job didn't seem like a good fit. "I am the silent spokesman," he said. "That's why they gave me the job." Twenty years later, he was a Vice President, with a big portfolio to accompany his closed mouth.

The award-winning filmmaker Abbas Kiarostami might talk within Iran about problems like censorship, but never outside. "Even if we have censorship in Iran, we should deal with it ourselves," he said in an interview that was appended to one of his films. "As my father used to say, 'If your head breaks, it is better that it breaks in your own hat.' Nobody can untie our knots or solve our problems. For that reason, I never speak about censorship outside of Iran, especially to foreign reporters."

RULE THREE: RULES EXIST TO BE CHANGED AND ALMOST ANYTHING CAN BE NEGOTIATED. The Islamic Republic is a fluid place where the rules are hard to keep straight because they keep changing. What is banned one day might be permitted the next. I've heard it said that Iranian political leaders are terrific chess players, always plotting their strategy ten steps ahead. To me they are more like players in a jazz band, changing the rhythm and the tempo and picking up spontaneous cues from each other as they go along. Knowing how to improvise is the only way to get things done—and sometimes even to survive.

In 1982, during the Iran-Iraq war, I went to Iran to interview the president, Ali Khamenei. (He later succeeded Khomeini as Supreme Leader.) His aides told me that my magazine, *Newsweek,* would have to publish every word he uttered during the seventy-five-minute interview. That was impossible for a magazine with space constraints, but as a courtesy, I spent hours with Khamenei's interpreter and chief aide to ensure that the translations were accurate and that the cuts did not distort his words.

After the interview was published, the official Iranian news agency ran an article in its English-language service under the headline: "Incorrigible *Newsweek* Mangles President's Words." "*Newsweek,* a foremost Zionist and imperialist publication, finally printed in its February 22 edition a highly censured [*sic*] and distorted version of the interview which Iran's President Khamenei had granted with the magazine's reporter," the article said.

As if that were not confusing enough, consider what happened next. A few weeks later, a large group of Western journalists—myself included—was invited to tour the war front. But when I presented myself at the Ministry of Islamic Guidance for credentials, the official in charge of our group said bluntly, "You again. Who let you in here?" So I was expelled.

The official asked me to move to a small, secure room where he pulled out a file with my name on it and rattled off the "lies" I had written about the revolution. But as expulsions go, it was pretty civilized. I was not arrested or put on the next plane out of the country. I was allowed to stay overnight to recover from jet lag. The official said politely, "You are our guest. You can enjoy our country, but you cannot work. We would kindly appreciate it if you would leave the country in the next twenty-four hours."

He added that even if he did allow me to stay, I couldn't go to the war front. Why, I asked. "Because ladies aren't allowed at the front."

"But I went to the front two months ago," I protested.

"Things were different then," he explained. "The rules have changed."

If Iran is a place of shifting lines, often the Iranians themselves don't know where the lines are. The lines might shift in different circumstances, at different times of the day or year. The lines of ideology can move. The lines of institutions, of heritage, of gender, of public and private spaces, of the economy, of the relationship with the United States— all are fluid. Even the lines of leadership have some give.

In such an atmosphere, Iranians learn early to negotiate between extremes. There are negotiations between the sacred and the secular, between the public and the private, between the traditional and the modern. "Iranians are like wheat fields," one saying goes. "When the storm comes, they bend; when the storm passes, they stand up again." Another goes: "Iranians are like water in a vase. If the vase is a globe, they become a globe; if the vase is long-necked, they become long-necked." The negotiations affect all areas of life—from gaining face time with a public official to avoiding a lashing for drinking alcohol to reclaiming land confiscated at the time of the revolution. In order to maneuver in a country of improvisers, I had to become an improviser myself, seizing opportunities wherever I found them and making mistakes and crossing invisible lines along the way.

RULE FOUR: BEING A WOMAN SOMETIMES MAKES THINGS EASIER. I hate to admit it, but my stealth weapon in working in Iran is that I am a woman. As a female reporter I have access to half of Iran's population in a way that men don't. I can enter beauty salons, lingerie stores, fashion shows, aerobics classes, swimming pools—private spaces that are closed to men. I can unveil and be in the presence of any unveiled woman and not violate any law or religious tradition.

For the most part, I don't feel that Iranian women are threatened by my presence. There is an unspoken bond among us that transcends culture, history, nationality, and language. It also helps that the women of Iran are steel magnolias, not shrinking violets. More than many women in the Islamic world, Iranian women occupy public spaces. Even as wives and mothers, they work, vote, drive, shop, and hold professional positions as doctors, lawyers, corporate executives, and deputies in Parliament.

I have been assisted over the years by a very special young Iranian woman in her twenties, Nazila Fathi, the sister of the calligrapher Golnaz Fathi. Educated in English translation, Nazila started out as a private English tutor until the journalism bug bit. Her small frame and delicate features are reminiscent of a Persian princess painted on a miniature. But they mask an iron will inherited from her mother, who taught her to regret nothing and find the way around closed doors. Nazila can recite entire conversations verbatim days later; she is truly gifted at simultaneous interpretation, and she is one of the hardest-working people I know. She is also a loyal friend. "I'm not a friend who would leave you in the middle of a trip," she told me once when we were stuck after a particularly arduous assignment in Shiraz and there was only one seat on the plane back to Tehran that night.

The onetime CIA agent Reuel Marc Gerecht wrote a fascinating book, *Know Thine Enemy,* published in 1997 under the pseudonym Edward Shirley, about a five-day secret sojourn in Iran. In it he speculated that "Western women can often loosen the lips, if not gain the confidence, of even devout Muslim males more quickly than Western men." He singled out Christiane Amanpour of CNN, Geraldine Brooks of *The Wall Street Journal,* Robin Wright of the *Los Angeles Times,* and me as "women not scared to project their femininity in the company of Muslim men." He added, "They would very likely not be allowed as deep inside a Muslim man's mind as an equally talented male observer, but they'd get through the heavily guarded front gate more quickly than even the most intrepid, clever, or duplicitous male colleague."

I have never met Gerecht, and in my review of his book for *The New York Times* I took exception to his point. How did he know what kind of femininity I did or did not project? I asked. Moreover, all four of us have been serious war correspondents. We know the Middle East. What made him think that none of us would be able to gain as much depth of understanding as a male reporter would?

Still, Gerecht was on to something, if not for the reasons he thought. It is not flirtation with men that is important, but sisterhood with other women. And it is those relationships with other women that have helped educate me about how to navigate in a country still dominated by men.

RULE FIVE: EVEN SEEING IS NOT BELIEVING. In his 1892 opus, *Persia and the Persian Question,* the British journalist and diplomat Lord George Curzon came up with a harsh, cruel, and classically colonialist description of Iranians. "*Splendide mendax* might be taken as the motto of the Persian character," he wrote.

A century later, Curzon is often considered a racist by Iranians and by scholars of Iran. And Iran is a very different place from the one Curzon discovered in his travels a century ago. But there is a kernel of truth in what he said. A number of Iranians I have met over the years know how to be splendidly deceptive. Even when the evidence is there for all to see, it could still be denied.

In 1995, I interviewed Reza Amrollahi, who was then the director of Iran's nuclear program. He said that his country's goal was to become less dependent on oil and that Iran had a concrete plan to build medium-sized nuclear reactors in the next twenty years—"something like ten of them"—if there was enough money and trained people. I wrote the story.

Two days later, he gave an interview to an Iranian newspaper saying that Iran was capable of building ten nuclear power plants in the next twenty years, but it had no such plan to do so. He also said that he had briefed *The New York Times* on the issue, but it had "distorted" his assertions.

I ran into the same problem two and a half years later, after I did an interview with Mohammad-Reza Khatami, the British-educated brother of Iran's newly elected President, Mohammad Khatami. I was writing a profile of the President and went to see his brother, a medical doctor, at his office at the Ministry of Health, where he was Deputy Minister. As we talked, he suggested ways that the United States could improve relations between the two countries. It was only fair to tell him in advance that his views merited a story. He seemed pleased. The story was published. Mohammed-Reza Khatami called me the next day. He was angry and denied that he had said any of the things I attributed to him. I reminded him that I had tape-recorded our conversation. "Even if I said those things, I deny them now," he yelled. "You shouldn't have printed what I said." In one of the Iranian newspapers the following day was a story in which he denounced me for inventing quotes.

The incidents illustrate that often what happens can be tolerated, but the exposure of what happens cannot. A friend of mine once told me, "Talk is more important than reality. Everyone knows that dogs pee in graveyards. But one of the worst things you can say to someone is, 'A dog peed on your father's grave.'"

RULE SIX: BEING POLITE IS OFTEN BETTER THAN TELLING THE TRUTH. Most of the Iranians I've met at least try to be polite when they are dissembling or stonewalling. Some prefer to invent stories rather than be rude and expose the whole truth. I asked Javad Larijani, a conservative member of Parliament and the head of Parliament's research center, about this one day. I wanted to know why the Parliament had never publicized its investigation of the country's giant foundations that ran vast swaths of the economy.

"There's a hidden reality, a hypocrisy that keeps the peace," Larijani told me. "It protects the dignity of the other. Architects don't build glass houses in Iran. If you don't speak of everything so openly, it's better. Being able to keep a secret even if you have to mislead is considered a sign of maturity. It's Persian wisdom. We don't have to be ideal people. Everybody lies. Let's be good liars."

Even my most trusted friends in Iran are accomplished in what I consider the art of lying. Over tea at a diplomat's house one afternoon, an American woman who had recently arrived in Iran modeled a full black robe and headdress that had been custom-made for her in Egypt. The headdress covered every strand of hair and part of her forehead; the sleeves came long and tight over her wrists. It was overkill. It told the authorities, "Not only do I accept your restrictions about women's dress, I revel in them." Nazila told her that it was lovely. "Maybe I should have one made for myself," she added.

"Why would you ever wear something like that?" I asked Nazila after the encounter.

"I wouldn't," she said.

"Then why did you make such a fuss about it?"

"It's *taarof*," Nazila explained. "It's exaggerated good manners that keep the peace. My mother always tells me I have bad manners because I usually don't do *taarof*. But in this case, I felt I had no choice. No harm was done."

Taarof is reflected in everyday Persian expressions of excessive politeness that when translated literally diminish the self in front of others: "I sacrifice myself for you." "I am your little one." "I am your slave maiden." "Step on my eyes."

I heard a great *taarof* story from Ali-Reza Shiravi, from the Ministry of Islamic Guidance. A Canadian journalist went into a store to buy a hat. The journalist went to pay for it, but the shopkeeper said, "Be my guest," indicating that the hat was a gift. The journalist insisted he should pay, but the shopkeeper insisted he should not. The journalist thanked the shopkeeper and left. A few minutes later, a policeman grabbed the journalist as a thief. The shopkeeper had turned him in.

RULE SEVEN: *IRAN IS NOT JUST THE ISLAMIC REPUBLIC. IT'S NOT JUST PERSIA EITHER.* Over the years I have discovered that Iran, even after a revolution in the name of religion, would not be simply an Islamic Republic. It would always be Persia as well. The austere spirituality of Shiite Islam meshes with the sensuous richness of Persia, even as the two clash. And Iran is even more varied than that. Yes, there is the Iran of austere Islam in the holy city of Qom. But I found another Iran in Shiraz, at Bagh-e Eram, or Garden of Earthly Paradise, a sprawling public garden filled with two-hundred-year-old cypress, pomegranate, salt cedar, and sour cherry trees, musk roses, coxcomb, and honeysuckle. I found a third Iran forty miles from Yazd at an abandoned caravansary where no one could see me slip off my scarf and jacket so that the breeze could touch my bare skin. And I found yet another Iran in Hamadan, at a mausoleum with a basket of yarmulkes at the entrance and the Ten Commandments mounted on a far wall. According to legend, Queen Esther, the biblical Jewish queen who saved her people from persecution in the fifth century B.C., and her kinsman Mordecai are buried there.

I have discovered that only half of Iran's estimated 65 million people are Persians. One fourth are Turks who filtered into the northwest Iranian province of Azerbaijan from Central Asia. Eight percent are Gilanis and Mazandaranis; 7 percent are Kurds; and the rest are Arabs, Lurs, Baluchis, and Turkmens. Only 58 percent of the people are native Persian speakers; 26 percent speak some sort of Turkish dialect. Most Iranians feel Iranian first, and their ethnic affiliation second. But it still startles me to visit Kurdistan and find people who speak only Kurdish or to enter the bazaar in Tehran and hear more Turkish than Persian spoken.

Even the climate and topography of Iran is a surprise to the uninitiated. Iran is susceptible to droughts and floods, sandstorms and snowstorms. It can be suffocatingly humid or desert dry. The weather can shift suddenly without warning. I once took a trip to the Caspian where I swam (on a women-only beach) in a bathtub-warm sea and then drove back to Tehran through snowstorms in the mountains. When people ask me if Iran has camels and deserts, I answer more deserts than camels. I also tell them that Iran has rice paddies, tea plantations, wetlands, wheat fields, and some of the best mountain climbing and snow skiing in the world. Try moving around Tehran when there's three feet of snow on the ground.

Many Iranians revel in their ethnic diversity, but not if they think it makes them appear backward. Of all the stories I have ever written in covering Iran, the one that sparked the most criticism within the country was not about political infighting or repression or the private lives of women. It was a story about Azeri cave dwellers in a tiny village in the northwest corner of Iran called Kanduvan.

I knew that there were cave dwellers in Turkey, but I had never read anything about cave dwellers in Iran. So when a friend in Tabriz offered to show me, I accepted. We found an odd honeycomb of caves hidden in the side of a deep valley. There, hundreds of Turkish-speaking herders live in the damp dwellings dug into the steep, strangely shaped cones of porous volcanic rock. They do not get many foreign visitors and keep to themselves. But one old man named Hassan recognized my friend. Hassan had sold vegetables and walnuts to my friend's father before the revolution.

In Hassan's cave, we sat on thin, brightly colored woven carpets that served as floor coverings. Bookshelves and closets were chiseled into the walls of tufa stone, which had been painted white. There was a refrigerator in one corner; mattresses were hidden behind a colorful curtain. Hassan and his wife even had a working television.

Most of the caves have at least minimal electricity tapped from the main electrical lines below and cold running water pumped up from a spring. The most difficult time, Hassan said, is the brutally long winter, when the people use makeshift heaters to burn dried manure, the same fuel they use for cooking. There are no telephones, local newspaper, mail delivery, or hot running water.

When I got back to Tabriz, I wrote a feature for *The New York Times*, describing daily life in the remote community. After the story appeared, a number of officials called my friend Nosrat at the Ministry of Islamic Guidance to complain. "People didn't like the story," Nosrat explained to me later. "They said it was humiliating, that it made us look backward. It's difficult for them to understand what was interesting about such a place.

"I told them," he continued, "'She went to Tabriz. This is what it's like near Tabriz. All kinds of people live there. Why should we be ashamed of it?'" Still, Nosrat did not put my story on Kanduvan into the daily foreign press digest he prepared for the ministry that day.

RULE EIGHT: IRAN IS FIGHTING SEVENTH-CENTURY BATTLES IN THE TWENTY-FIRST CENTURY. Iran's leaders haven't figured out what Islamic message to rely on in their struggle to build a modern society. Some insist on a strict version of Islam as they believe it was at its creation. Others want to interpret Islam to fit the modern era. All of this is colored by the Messianic nature of Shiite Islam, which predominates in Iran but which is in the minority in the rest of the Muslim world. Today, 99 percent of Iran's population is Muslim, of which about 80 percent are Shiites and about 19 percent are Sunnis. (The remaining 1 percent are Christians, Jews, Bahais, and Zoroastrians.) The Shiites split from the mainstream Sunnis in a conflict over who should succeed the Prophet Mohammad as Islam's political and spiritual leader when he died in A.D. 632. The Sunnis, whose name comes from the Arabic word for "tradition," argue that the leader should be selected in the pre-Islamic way: through consensus among the community's elders.

But a minority believed that Ali, the Prophet's pious first cousin and son-in-law, should replace him, because that's what Mohammad decreed. These dissidents became known in Arabic as the Shiites, or "partisans" of Ali.

The conflict intensified in A.D. 661, when Ali was stabbed to death while praying in Kufa, in Iraq. Then, nearly twenty years later, Ali's followers, led by his son Hosein, rebelled against the ruling hierarchy. Hosein had been forewarned of his martyrdom in a vision—but still he set out for Kufa. The forces of the Sunni Caliph Yazid stopped him on the sun-scorched plain of Karbala. During a ten-day battle, Hosein was stabbed to death as he held a sword in one hand and a Koran in the other. His male relatives and their supporters were shot with arrows and cut into pieces. Their severed heads were brought to Yazid in Damascus. The Sunni caliphs continued to reign.

For Shiites, the death of Hosein is the seminal event in their history. And because few Shiites came to Hosein's aid during the battle, their successors were left with both the burden of Sunni oppression and a permanent guilt complex.

But martyrdom and guilt are not the only pillars of Shiite Islam. Most Shiites recognize twelve historic Imams or rightful spiritual rulers.

The infant twelfth Imam "disappeared" in a cave in A.D. 874 and is believed to be not dead but somehow hidden. He will return one day as the Redeemer who will create the perfect, godly society. Until then, all temporal power is imperfect. Ayatollah Khomeini was always referred to as "Imam Khomeini," and although it would have been blasphemy to draw a literal connection with the twelfth Imam, the title certainly gave Khomeini additional authority.

Khomeini wore a black turban and was called a *sayyid*, indicating that he was a descendant of the Prophet's family. Night after night before the revolution, many people in Iran swore that they saw Khomeini's face—his turban, his eyes, his nose, his beard—in the moon. Then, against all odds, he brought down the King of Kings.

It wasn't just religion and tradition that triumphed in 1979. It was a long overdue popular revolution that just happened to have a leader in clerical robes at its head. Still, it was not surprising that in Khomeini's war against Iraq in the 1980s, Iranian fighters dreamed of redeeming the martyrdom of Ali and Hosein in that same land thirteen centuries before.

More than a decade after the end of that war, Iran is still engaged in a battle over interpretations of Islam. The struggle is not only between Shiites and Sunnis but within Shiism itself. Contrary to the perception outside Iran that religious truth is monolithic and that dissent is not tolerated, one of the defining traits of Shiism is its emphasis on argument. Clerics are encouraged and expected to challenge interpretations of the Koran, even those of the most learned ayatollahs, in the hope that new and better interpretations may emerge. It is a concept little grasped in the West, but it is critical to understanding Iran's current reformers and their leader President Khatami, who is the son of one of the most revered—and liberal-minded—of the ayatollahs in pre-revolutionary Iran.

RULE NINE: A TIME BOMB IS TICKING AND IT HAS NOTHING TO DO WITH EXPLOSIVES. Iran's clerics, like Muslim clerics everywhere, invoke the authority of the Prophet in explaining their positions and issuing orders. But, like interpreting the view from a fractured mirror, it is sometimes hard to figure out where those decrees will lead. That's what happened with the policy on procreation.

Early in the revolution, Ayatollah Khomeini encouraged his people to breed. The policy would create a generation of soldiers for God. "My soldiers are still infants," Khomeini explained. The policy worked better than even Khomeini could have envisioned. By 1986, the official annual growth rate was 3.2 percent—among the highest in the world.

When the war with Iraq ended in 1988, the ruling clerics realized that such a large birth rate was disastrous for the economy and reversed themselves. Sure, the Prophet Mohammad was on record as saying, "Marry and multiply, for I shall make a display of you before other nations on the Day of Judgment." But Ayatollah Khomeini was also on record in 1980 as saying, in a little-noticed statement, that Islam allows some forms of birth control as long as the wife receives the consent of her husband and the chosen method does not damage her health. The statement was used to revive the government's moribund national family-planning program. Later, Ayatollah Khamenei went further, proclaiming, "When wisdom dictates that you do not need more children, a vasectomy is permissible."

In the late 1980s, Iran's Health Ministry launched a massive nation-wide family-planning campaign and by the late 1990s, the population growth rate had been more than halved to 1.47 percent. But the trend had been set. At the time of the revolution, Iran's population was roughly 35 million. Today, it is approaching 65 million. And 65 percent of that population is under the age of twenty-five. The infants are growing up. Unlike their fathers, who lived the events of the revolution, most young people know it only through their history books. Many feel no particular love or hatred toward the Shah, or for that matter, toward Ayatollah Khomeini himself. But they know what they want: more jobs and fewer constraints on their personal lives. They can vote at sixteen, and that makes them a threat to the power of the clerics who had promoted the anti-contraception policy in the first place.

RULE TEN: IRAN IS THE BERMUDA TRIANGLE OF AMERICAN FOREIGN POLICY, SO DON'T LET YOUR GUARD DOWN. Iran's Islamic Republic is not a police state, but it is not a liberty-loving democracy either, at least not yet. Nowhere has that been more evident since the dawn of the Islamic Republic than in its political use of terror outside the country.

In fact, probably the deepest fear of Iran among decision-makers in Washington and among the American people is that Iran might sponsor terrorism against American targets, either in the United States or abroad. The seizure of the American embassy in Tehran in 1979 was the first but not the only time the United States was targeted. Shiite terrorists (believed by American and Israeli intelligence to have acted with Iranian support) were responsible for the bombing of the Marine barracks in Lebanon in 1983, in which 241 American servicemen died. In the 1980s, the holding of American and other Western hostages by Iranian-backed Shiite radicals in Lebanon culminated in the most embarrassing foreign policy scandal of the Reagan administration: the sale of weapons to Iran in violation of American policy and the illegal use of the profits to fund the contra rebels in Nicaragua.

Only some of the American hostages were freed as a result of the arms sales, but Iran eventually paid the captors between $1 million and $2 million to free each remaining hostage, according to American intelligence reports. Iran expected that economic and diplomatic rewards from the United States would follow, but by then the relationship was so sour that President George Bush decided against it, arguing that Iran should not be rewarded for doing something that should have been done years before.

Although Americans still fear that one day an Iranian bomb will blow up near the White House or on Wall Street, historically the most vulnerable targets of Iranian terrorism have been other Iranians. The attacks have tapered off in recent years, but opponents of the Islamic Republic anywhere in the world remain potential assassination targets.

One political assassination particularly affected me. For years, Abdol-Rahman Ghassemlou was the leader of Iran's Kurdish autonomist movement. He spoke passable English and Russian and took money wherever he could find it. I first met Ghassemlou in August 1979, when a civil war was raging in Kurdistan and the new revolutionary government in Tehran had not yet suppressed it. For five days I traveled through Kurdistan with Ghassemlou and his *pesh merga*—ready-to-die guerrilla fighters—as he met with his commanders. We bounced along in a jeep that seemed to have lost its springs, and we slept on the floors of safe houses. On the fifth day, a group of Kurdish women drew a bath for me and washed my clothes. I was lent a Kurdish wedding costume with a sheer red veil and a black velvet vest trimmed with gold coins to wear until my clean clothes dried.

"Miss Sciolino," Ghassemlou said when he saw me in full bridal regalia, "I think I'll just call your editors at *Newsweek* and tell them you got lost somewhere in the rugged Kurdish hills." We laughed. He sent me safely on my way the next day. I didn't see him again.

One evening ten years later, Ghassemlou and two other Kurds were meeting with officials from Tehran in a borrowed apartment in Vienna to negotiate an autonomy agreement for the Iranian province of Kurdistan. The police later found Ghassemlou shot dead, his body propped up in an armchair, a baseball cap placed in his lap. His two associates were also killed. Austrian authorities assumed that the officials from Tehran were the assassins.

RULE ELEVEN: IRAN IS IN THE MIDDLE EAST, BUT NOT ENTIRELY PART OF IT. Americans tend to think of Iran as a Middle Eastern country. But the word "Iran" comes from the word "Aryan." The people who settled in this region in the second millennium B.C. were Indo-European nomads who migrated from Central Asia in the east, not from the Semitic lands of the west and south. The Persian language is Indo-European, a distant cousin of English, French and Sanskirit. It is barely related to Arabic, even though it is infused with Arabic words.

Looking at a map doesn't solve the identity problem. Iran shares borders with Iraq, Pakistan, Afghanistan, Turkey, and three former Soviet republics: Armenia, Azerbaijan, and Turkmenistan. Iran is the only land bridge between the Caspian Sea and the Persian Gulf. Iran's intellectuals and politicians have long debated the direction to which they should turn: South to the Persian Gulf? West to Europe? North to the Caucasus? East to Asia?

Iran is the land of one of the world's oldest religions. Centuries before the birth of Christ, the prophet Zoroaster preached a message of monotheism, the central feature of which was a long battle between good and evil. (Good will ultimately win.) Judaism, Christianity, and Islam were influenced by the Zoroastrian belief in the devil and angels, heaven and hell, redemption, resurrection, and the last judgment. The word "paradise," which means "pleasure park of the king," comes from Old Persian.

Iran is also one of the world's few civilizations that, like Egypt, has enjoyed cultural continuity since ancient times. The boundaries of most other countries in the Middle East were defined in the twentieth century by European colonial powers. "Tribes with flags," is how the Egyptian intellectual Tahseen Bashir described them, insisting that Iran and Egypt are the only real countries in the region.

Even in its modern history, Iran has had an ambiguous relationship with the Arab Middle East. The issue is complicated by the fact that Iran is a Muslim country, but Muslim in its own way, and it has a small Arab minority.

Persia was the first—and fastest-growing—superpower of the ancient world. It started in the early seventh century B.C. as a small southern province named Parsa (now Fars). Hence the name Persia. It expanded through war, occupation, revolts, cruelty, and marriage, until under Cyrus the Great in the sixth century B.C. the empire stretched all the way from the Mediterranean to India. In victory, Cyrus was a tolerant ruler, allowing the Jews to return to Jerusalem after a long period of exile at the hands of the Babylonians.

His grandson Darius introduced a sophisticated administrative system, an empire linked by a 1,500-mile highway complex. Mail carriers used a relay system that became the model for the Pony Express, and the U.S. Postal Service adapted the original motto of the Persians: "Stopped by neither snow, rain, heat, or gloom of night." The empire also pioneered irrigation techniques, codified commercial laws, and created a universal system of weights and measures.

As a lasting testament to his reign, Darius built Persepolis, a magnificent new ritual city and capital on a vast, sunbaked platform in the desert, a place where the peoples of the empire could come to pay tribute.

But empires do not last. In 330 B.C., Alexander the Great conquered Persia, bringing the imperial age to a close. Centuries later, though, even after many other waves of conquest and foreign domination, Iranians feel passionately that they are a separate, special people. One of the reasons I feel the Iranian system works as well as it does is that Iranians have such a strong sense of a distinct national identity. Whoever they are and wherever they go, they want to speak Persian, read Persian poetry, eat Persian food, and debate Iranian politics.

RULE TWELVE: IRANIANS LIKE AMERICANS. Iranians view America as a land of demons and dreams, of unlimited power and unlimited promise.

Officially, America is Iran's worst enemy. Among its "crimes": fomenting a military coup in 1953 that restored Shah Mohammad Reza Pahlavi to the throne; bolstering him with billions of dollars in arms sales over the next quarter-century; tilting toward Iraq in the war against Iran; failing to resolve financial disputes dating from the hostage crisis; weakening the Islamic Republic with economic sanctions.

In February 1982 I toured the war-ravaged Iranian city of Dezful with Iranian officials eager to show how they had recaptured the city from Iraq a few months before. My Iranian guide pointed out a vast yard where a pregnant Iranian woman had been killed by a Soviet-made missile. After she was killed the neighbors came out and chanted, "Death to America," the guide said.

"If she was killed by a Soviet missile, why didn't they shout 'Death to Moscow'?" I asked.

"Because it is America who benefits by the war," he replied.

In other words, if you're America, you never win.

At the same time, the United States remains a fantasy Promised Land for many Iranians, the land of *Baywatch* and billionaires and an easy life in Los Angeles, where hundreds of thousands of Iranians have settled. Many Iranians, even those on very limited incomes, own illegal satellite dishes that give them instant access to American television. Even without satellite dishes, I have picked up CNN in Bushehr on the Persian Gulf because Dubai is so close. I once asked an eighteen-year-old middle-class high school student who had never traveled outside Iran how he came to speak such colloquial English and he replied, "CNN."

American CDs, videos, and computer programs are pirated and sold on the streets for a fraction of their price in the United States. E-mail is more widely available in Iran than in many other Middle Eastern countries. A friend once bought software on the black market for $10 that would have cost $1,500 in the United States.

Even after Bill Clinton imposed an economic embargo on Iran in May 1995, American goods did not disappear. They just got more expensive. Under Iranian customs regulations, Iranians entering the country are allowed to bring in one appliance, which has led to a lively importation of refrigerators, washing machines, and dishwashers. During a visit to the holy city of Qom I found a shop selling knockoffs of Wrangler blue jeans just down the street from the main shrine, one of Iran's holiest sites.

Almost every Iranian I have ever met has a relative living in the United States. And even those Iranians who rail most about American policy seem to genuinely like Americans. At the height of the American embassy seizure in 1979 and 1980, the same Iranian demonstrators who chanted angry slogans about the "den of spies" in the mornings followed me down Ferdowsi Avenue in the afternoons asking me to help them get visas or contact their relatives in Los Angeles or Dallas.

I saw that love-hate attitude again years later on a slow-moving German-made ferry on a 110 degree day in the middle of the Persian Gulf. In Iranian eyes, one of the worst American "crimes" was committed in July 1988, a month before the end of Iran's eight-year war with Iraq. An American naval cruiser, the USS *Vincennes,* had mistaken an Iran Air civilian airliner for a hostile military aircraft and shot it down as it flew over the Persian Gulf, killing all 290 people on board. Every year since, the Iranians have ferried families of the victims and journalists to a ceremony at the point twenty-five miles into the Persian Gulf where the plane hit the water.

I went along one year, and a group of young women in chadors, whose relatives died in the crash, discovered that I was an American. But instead of venting anger, they shyly touched me and wanted to have their pictures taken with me. I was the first American they had ever met, and they were endlessly curious. Did I like Iran? What did I think of the coverings that women have to wear in the breathtaking heat? They thrust pages from their notebooks and pieces of Kleenex at me. They wanted my autograph.

I like to tell Iranians that I am American. The information lights up their faces. For years, I also wore as a badge of honor the fact that I was on the plane that brought Ayatollah Khomeini from France in February 1979. It opened doors. And then one day it began to work only occasionally. I told someone I had been on Khomeini's plane.

"So it was your fault," he said.

CHAPTER THREE

The Improvised Revolution

*The Sovereign, The Pivot of the Universe, The Sultan, His Auspicious
Majesty, His Royal Majesty, The King of Kings, The Royal Possessor of
Kingdoms, His Majesty the Shadow of Allah, The Khaghan.*

— THE HISTORICAL TITLES OF THE SHAH OF IRAN

The Jewish agent . . . The American snake . . . The idiot boy.

— DESCRIPTIONS OF THE SHAH BY AYATOLLAH
RUHOLLAH KHOMEINI

𝓕OR THE AYATOLLAH with the fierce eyes, it was a midnight flight to
paradise. He would lead his people in an earthly revolution. Or he would
die a martyr with a ticket to heaven.

For me, it was an adventure of terror and excitement. I was flying on
a plane that might be shot down. I was riding the biggest story of my life.
I was also beginning a twenty-year odyssey through Iran.

At 1:00 A.M. on February 1, 1979, Ayatollah Ruhollah Khomeini,
forty-seven of his closest followers, an all-male, all-volunteer crew, and
141 journalists boarded a chartered Air France Boeing 747 jet in Paris for
the five-hour flight to Tehran. The plane took off even though it did not
have permission from Tehran to land. It flew half empty so that Air
France could carry spare fuel in case the plane had to head back to Paris.
The ayatollah left his wife behind. On his orders, no Iranian women or
children were on board. It was too risky. The only other woman I can recall being on the flight was my friend Carole Jerome from the Canadian
Broadcasting Corporation. In a sense we journalists were the ayatollah's
first hostages. In fact, we probably made the plane a lot safer. Carrying

representatives of foreign networks, magazines, newspapers, and wire services, it was less likely to be shot down.

There was nothing ceremonial about the day of the departure. Journalists stood for hours in the damp bitter cold of Khomeini's French garden, waiting for their plane tickets. His aides taped on apple trees handwritten lists of different news organizations that had made the cut. Journalists went from tree to tree with flashlights, cigarette lighters, and lit matches looking for their names. After I found mine, a young Iranian took five one-hundred-dollar bills from me and handed me a ticket. Even then, I didn't believe the plane would take off.

On the half-filled plane, Khomeini and his entourage settled into first class; the journalists were sent to coach. There was no alcohol on board. I was required to hide my hair under a scarf.

Khomeini seemed comfortable, even serene, during the flight. Shortly after takeoff, he climbed the circular stairs to the first-class lounge and turned it into a place of prayer and rest. Dressed in a white nightshirt and skullcap, he knelt on an Air France blanket, said his prayers, and fell asleep easily on the floor.

I couldn't sleep. I kept thinking, how in the world did I get here? I wasn't an expert on the Middle East. In graduate school I had studied eighteenth-century French history and my only exposure to things Persian was reading Montesquieu's *Persian Letters,* a dialogue in which two imaginary Persians traveling in France send home their critical observations. The social satire was all about France and not at all about Iran.

The only time I had gone to the Middle East was to cover a royal wedding. As a junior correspondent for *Newsweek* in Paris, I went to Jordan in June 1978 to cover the wedding of King Hussein to Lisa Halaby, now known as Queen Noor. A week later, I was in Beirut covering the aftermath of a massacre during Lebanon's long civil war.

But I wasn't yet a war correspondent. On returning to Paris, I wrote about things European: the fall of the dollar, the boom in escargot farming, the deaths of two Popes. My colleague Arnaud de Borchgrave was the Graham Greene–like figure who covered wars for a living. A permanently tanned, Belgian-born count, Arnaud got up before dawn, read eighteen newspapers a day, and kept an office and a full-time secretary in the Paris bureau even though he lived in Geneva. Yet this once, I was the one on the plane.

*　　*　　*

Khomeini had slipped into France four months earlier on his Iranian passport. He had come from Iraq, where he had lived for thirteen years. The Shah first imprisoned Khomeini in 1963 after he opposed the Shah's plan to redistribute land to the peasants, the granting of voting rights to women, and the shielding of American servicemen from criminal prosecution in Iranian courts. Then, after putting Khomeini under house arrest, the Shah expelled him. Khomeini settled briefly in Turkey, before making a new home in the Shiite holy city of Najaf in Iraq. In the fall of 1978, with protests against his rule intensifying, the Shah asked Saddam Hussein to expel Khomeini as a way of diminishing the extraordinary influence he wielded from so close to home. Saddam Hussein obliged. Khomeini wanted to go to a Muslim country, but Kuwait refused him entry and France was willing to admit him without a visa. There was another attraction as well, according to Ibrahim Yazdi, one of Khomeini's key aides, a naturalized citizen of the United States who had taught at a small college in Texas and who later became Foreign Minister. "Paris was a politicized city," Yazdi said, with a large, potentially supportive Iranian community. So the ayatollah ended up in Paris.

His followers rented a small house in Neauphle-le-Château, a sleepy village in a picture-perfect valley twenty-five miles east of the French capital. They installed four telephones and two telex lines. French workmen dismantled the Western toilet and installed a more familiar Eastern one, which consisted of a low porcelain fixture over a hole in the floor that led to the plumbing. The Shah had no objection to Khomeini's new place of residence. He calculated that it was better to have the old man in a Western country where his activities could be carefully monitored and where the Western press would see him up close and expose him for the backward man whom the Shah felt he was.

I was alone in the office in Paris late one night in October 1978 when a telex machine started clicking. The message was for Jonathan Randal, the intrepid correspondent for the *Washington Post*, whose parent company also owned *Newsweek*. Was there a story in the ayatollah's arrival? his editors asked. At that time I didn't know exactly what an ayatollah was. But when Jon offered to take me with him to meet an Iranian said to be close to the ayatollah that Saturday afternoon, I said yes. We met Sadegh Ghotbzadeh at a café in a shopping mall on the outskirts of Paris.

Ghotbzadeh was on his way to see the ayatollah, and offered to take Jon along. "Too bad you don't have a head scarf," Ghotbzadeh told me. "You could have come." This was no time to protest that this was France, the country of individual freedom. A story was a story. I raced around the mall and I found a big black silk chiffon scarf with red flowers. It cost $75. We drove to Neauphle-le-Château, where we were invited to listen to Khomeini's sermon—at a safe distance. I listed the scarf on my expense account under miscellaneous. I still wear it sometimes when I interview ayatollahs.

In those first few days, few supporters and almost no journalists visited Khomeini. Those supporters who did come brought along mattresses, rugs, sleeping bags, and even lawn chairs to make themselves comfortable. Some carried tape recorders to preserve the sermons or to send cassettes of them back home. Some slept in their cars, much to the annoyance of the neighbors.

When Khomeini appeared, as he did twice a day, his supporters shouted *Allahu Akbar*—"God is Great." I saw the old man as a sideshow, a human interest story, a powerless figure who sat cross-legged on a carpet, facing Mecca, his hands open to the sky, under an apple tree in a French garden lush with rosebushes. His black bushy arched eyebrows and hooded eyes made him look as sinister as people in the West made him out to be.

Khomeini said that the Shah must go. He said it over and over, to thousands of Iranian pilgrims who came to pay court and to hundreds of foreign journalists hungry like me for a story. He spoke in riddles, mumbled as he talked, and didn't smile. His followers lamented his situation—an exile, a transplanted Persian, having no access to a mosque. Eventually the Iranians rented a huge blue-and-white-striped tent, which they pitched on the lawn and called a mosque.

A large sign in English and Persian outside Khomeini's headquarters proclaimed, "The ayatollah has no spokesman." That really wasn't so. Khomeini had a number of aides who talked in his name. For obvious reasons, my colleagues and I called the clerics "the turbans" and the Western-educated laymen "the neckties." The neckties divided up the press corps and tried to convince us that Iran under an Islamic Republic would be a freedom-loving democracy wrapped in the precepts of the Koran.

Ghotbzadeh was assigned to *Newsweek*. A broad-chested man with swarthy good looks, he was one of Khomeini's closest aides, "like a son," the ayatollah told me later. Ghotbzadeh had briefly attended Georgetown University, carried a Syrian passport, and had been banished from Iran years before because of his political activities against the Shah. He used an elegant apartment in the sixteenth *arrondissement* lent to him by a friend as a command center for the Shah's opponents in Europe. He did not drink alcohol, but he did wear well-tailored three-piece suits and ties, and smoked a pipe. His favorite place to meet was La Closerie des Lilas, a Left Bank hangout once patronized by Hemingway and Fitzgerald.

It was Ghotbzadeh who steeped me in Iranian politics, even if he seemed to know little about Islamic law. And it was Ghotbzadeh who flirted with me, even as he lectured about the strict sexual morality that would exist in an Islamic Republic. "Sadegh, you said fornication between unmarried adults would be prohibited in an Islamic Republic," I joked once, turning him down as politely as I could.

"But this is Paris," he replied in his silky voice. "And there is no Islamic Republic here."

It was the mildest and the idlest of flirtations. Ghotbzadeh soon fell passionately in love with Carole Jerome, who later told the story of their romance in a touching memoir.

It was also Ghotbzadeh who arranged my first private interview with Khomeini. I was required to submit my questions in writing—a process that makes any journalist queasy because it makes follow-up questions more difficult to ask and gives the interview subject a chance to prepare answers in advance. So I kept the questions vague. When the day arrived, I waited five hours in the damp cold outside Khomeini's house. There was no Persian hospitality here.

Eventually, Ghotbzadeh admitted me into the ayatollah's house. I was wearing a loose-fitting Missoni knit dress that would probably not be allowed on the streets of Tehran today. I was told to take off my coat, cover my head, and take off my shoes, Persian style. No matter that the floors in the foyer were cold and damp. I was escorted into a small, unlit room, unfurnished except for rough tribal carpets that clashed with the garish pink-and-blue-flowered wallpaper. No independent interpreter or photographer was allowed.

As I entered the room, Khomeini was already seated cross-legged on the floor, his hands folded in his lap, next to a fireplace and leaning against the wall. I was positioned a safe fifteen feet away. He didn't shake my hand. He didn't even stand to greet me. Ghotbzadeh did the translating. During the forty-five-minute interview, Khomeini smiled only once, when his young grandson ran into the room and jumped into his lap, prompting the ayatollah to warmly embrace him. And I caught the ayatollah looking at me at one point. We probably viewed each other in the same way: as a curiosity. I was, after all, the first woman and the first American to interview him.

Khomeini mumbled in Persian in a barely audible monotone. He accused the Shah of destroying the economy, giving away the country's oil to the industrial powers, reducing agricultural production to provide a market for American goods, subjecting the military to foreign leadership, massacring thousands of dissenters, and destroying freedom of expression. He didn't seem to believe he would go back to Iran, at least not for a while. But that didn't mean he wanted to stay in France. Khomeini stayed in the village, determined not to be tainted by what he believed was the corrupting influence of Western culture. His goal was to stay in France only as long as it took to find a Muslim country closer to home. Syria was one possibility, Algeria another. The Shah would have to be out of power before he would try to return home, he said.

In other words, Khomeini didn't have a master plan for the future. Rather, with the help of his aides, he improvised. Day by day, ideas were formulated, assignments were given, committees were appointed. His answers about what his government might look like evaporated into an Islamic mist as he called himself the symbol of the people. "I talk their language, I listen to their needs; I cry for them," he told me.

I interviewed Khomeini again—for a shorter time—just a few weeks later, when the fall of the Shah seemed imminent. This time, Khomeini was more than just a media curiosity. Once again Ghotbzadeh did the translating.

"What will your role be in a future Islamic Republic?" I asked.

"I will not have any position in the future government," Khomeini said. "I will not be the President or the Prime Minister. I will be some sort of supervisor of their activities. I will give them guidance. If I see some deviation or mistake, I will remind them how to correct it."

"So would you describe yourself as the future strongman of Iran, the ultimate power?"

"You may assume so."

I asked him again to explain precisely how the new system would work. He became irritated. Maybe he didn't know. Maybe the answer wasn't part of the prepared script. Maybe he was getting fed up with the spoon-feeding by his advisers. "I've already answered your question," he said sharply.

And with those words, he stood up and left the room.

To some outsiders, Khomeini seemed a throwback to Iran's medieval past. But the truth is that he embraced the use of modern technology in order to get his message out. A red-brick garage attached to one of the two houses rented by Khomeini was turned into a communications center. Heated by a small space heater, lit with a single light bulb, the garage became the duplicating room, where students made hundreds of cassette tapes of the ayatollah's pronouncements. From the house they were transmitted by telephone to Iran's thousands of mosques and then to the bazaars—the two ready-made networks for spreading revolution. Once on the streets of Iran, Khomeini's message resonated with a population that had grown disenchanted with the rule of the Shah.

A king survives as long as he is successful, an Iranian saying goes. In other words, everyone loves a winner. And the Shah had come to look like a loser. Part of the problem was that the fifty-year-old Pahlavi dynasty did not have deep roots. It was so weak that it was nearly toppled in 1953. Two years earlier, the Iranian Parliament had voted to nationalize the British-owned Anglo-Iranian Oil Company, which dominated the development and sale of Iranian oil. The twenty-seven-year-old Shah, facing rising domestic discontent, appointed the nationalist Mohammad Mossadegh as Prime Minister. The British government, with the support of all the major oil companies, responded with a global boycott of Iranian oil. Mossadegh amassed more power for himself, and he and the Shah struggled over control of the government. In August 1953, when the Shah attempted to dismiss him, Mossadegh's followers took to the streets and forced the Shah to leave the country, raising fears in the new Eisenhower administration that Iran might get pushed too close to Moscow. America was not prepared to "lose" Iran as it had "lost" China four years earlier. So the CIA and the British orchestrated a coup that ousted Mossadegh. "I owe my throne to God, my people, my army, and to you!" the Shah told Kermit Roosevelt of the CIA. In the Iranian retelling of the story over the decades, the coup came to be seen as America's original sin in Iran, as the Shah came to be seen as an American puppet.

In the twenty-five years that followed, the Shah created a system of government based on political repression, patronage, state control over private organizations, dependence on the United States, and increasingly autocratic rule. Drunk with oil money, he spent recklessly as he pursused a grandiose vision of Iran as one of the world's great nations. But he was unable to share power, even with his most trusted advisers.

By the time the Shah tried to adapt, it was too late. The most traditional elements of Iranian society were turning against him. The thousands of mosques offered secure places to meet and plan protests. The bazaar was abandoning the Shah as well. The *bazaari* were conservative, deeply religious, and important financial backers of the religious establishment; they had long resisted the Shah's concessions to foreign interests and had opposed his moves to secularize the country. Then riots in Qom in January 1978 touched off a cycle of mourning ceremonies and unrest in dozens of cities and towns. Clerics railed against the Shah in their sermons. The *bazaari* became willing converts, giving money to the families of demonstrators killed by the military and financing strikes and demonstrations. University students, from secular Marxists to deeply religious conservatives, joined in. By November, striking workers had paralyzed the economy.

Never loved, no longer feared, the Shah became isolated. Depressed, suffering from a cancer that he tried to keep secret, he lost the will to govern. He put his government in the hands of a caretaker Prime Minister, Shahpour Bakhtiar, and fled the country. At the airport on January 16, 1979, the Shah broke down in tears as his officers seized his hand and kissed it. He headed for Egypt on a Boeing 707 with hundreds of pieces of luggage, including a box filled with Iranian soil. It was supposed to be a "vacation" of undetermined duration. He never returned.

Iran Radio's announcement of the Shah's departure set off an orgy of exultation. People throughout the country held spontaneous demonstrations of joy, distributing sweets and fruits, making bonfires with piles of his photographs, and cutting the Shah's picture out of bank notes. In Tehran, they tore down an enormous bronze statue of Reza Shah, his father, on horseback. The head of another statue of the Shah's father was used as a soccer ball. In cities like Ahwaz and Khorramshahr, the military stepped in, killing and wounding civilians.

But in Tehran, the military commanders who had not already left their posts understood the new political reality. The 400,000-man army and the large police force were not equipped, trained, or organized to crush a popular internal rebellion. The commanders did nothing to stop the crowds. From then on, Iran was like a headless body, awaiting the arrival of the ayatollah.

Halfway into the flight to Tehran with Khomeini, Ghotbzadeh stood on the front row of seats, faced the crowd of journalists, and told us he had some bad news. "We have received a warning over the airplane radio that the Iranian air force has orders to shoot us down," he said. Nevertheless, he added, the plane would continue on its course and try to land.

I had never questioned whether to get on the plane. Neither had my editors at *Newsweek* in New York. I did not have the responsibility of a husband or children yet and I did not think much about death in those days. Like other young foreign correspondents, I was still a vagabond, searching for the story that could be the center of my work.

My destiny, it turned out, was the revolution. Even then, I knew I had to go. My editors at *Newsweek* in New York agreed, although one did suggest I think twice because I might be raped. I reminded him that men could be raped too. Actually, the danger was worse than either of us knew. Years later, I learned that a number of the Shah's generals, including General Amir-Hosein Rabii, the commander of the air force, had devised a plan to shoot down Khomeini's plane. (A less drastic option, included in the plan, was to divert it to a remote part of Iran where the ayatollah could be put under arrest.) The generals took the plan to Zbigniew Brzezinski, the American National Security Adviser, seeking American approval. Brzezinski brought it to President Carter. The President, Brzezinski later told me, "wouldn't have anything to do with it." But that didn't mean the Carter administration rejected the idea that the Iranians do it themselves.

Brzezinski went on: "The United States is not in the business of assassinating people. The question that is legitimate to ask is whether the U.S. is in the business of preventing other people from assassinating their own countrymen." There was nothing to stop the Iranian officers from moving against Khomeini. But, said Brzezinski, "One of the problems with Iranians is that they often talked more than they did anything." In the end, the Shah's generals did nothing.

Journalists are always being manipulated, and they sometimes wittingly or unwittingly become part of the story. In retrospect, it isn't unreasonable to think that this was one case where our presence may have changed history. Was our presence on the plane a factor in Carter's decision? Would the Shah's troops have been more likely to shoot down the plane if Peter Jennings, then a correspondent for ABC in London, had not been on board? Brzezinski insisted that our presence made no difference in the American decision. "The issue simply didn't arise," he said. Could I really believe that? Even today, I don't know. What really mattered is that in the end the Iranian air force did not shoot us down, and we rode the ayatollah's plane into history.

When morning came, I saw Damavand mountain from my window. On the ground, dozens of the Shah's troops were waiting for us on the tarmac. The massive plane dipped and turned as it struggled to circle the airport at low altitude. Slowly, three times around. And then, without warning, after twenty-five long minutes, the plane touched down in the gray-pink haze of Tehran's morning sky. When Khomeini awoke, he did not rush to the door. The journalists were ordered to get off first. Just in case. But there was no gunfire, only a roar of chants, shouts of joy from the crowds who had come to greet their leader.

While we were still airborne, Jennings and the ABC crew had been allowed to the front of the plane, and Jennings had sat down next to the ayatollah. As the plane entered Iranian airspace, Jennings asked the obvious question and Ghotbzadeh dutifully did the translating: "Ayatollah, would you be so kind as to tell us how you feel about being back in Iran?"

"*Hichi,*" the ayatollah replied. "Nothing."

"*Hichi?*" Ghotbzadeh asked him. Even he seemed incredulous at the response.

"*Hich ehsasi nadaram,*" the ayatollah said for emphasis. "I don't feel a thing."

A generation later, Iranians are still debating what Khomeini meant. Did he really feel nothing? Or was he exercising what Shiite Muslims call *taqiyah*—dissimulation—in which one's true feelings are hidden for some other purpose?

In fact, as I got off the plane a few minutes later, I saw a hint of a different explanation. Khomeini did something that did not seem to come easily to him in public: he smiled. After fourteen years in exile, Khomeini was home again.

More than one million people were on the streets of Tehran to greet him. At the airport terminal, hundreds of men pushed and jostled, even trampled, each other for a chance to touch the ayatollah. At one point they pushed so hard against a locked glass partition, with me and hundreds of others on the other side, that I was terrified it would not hold.

In his first public statement, Khomeini assured the crowd that Islam would prevail over the monarchy and the corrupt values it had imported. "Final success will come when all the foreigners leave," he announced. "I beg God to cut off the hand of foreigners and their helpers." I was told years later that cutting off the hand of somebody was an Iranian expression that meant preventing interference or blocking access. But at the moment when Khomeini uttered those words, I stopped taking notes.

Then Khomeini left the airport in a blue Chevrolet Blazer and headed for Behesht-e Zahra cemetery to honor the "martyrs" killed over the years by the Shah's secret police. The crowds swarmed over the motorcade, scrambled atop his car, and made the route impassable. He had to climb into an Iranian air force helicopter, made in America just like the Blazer and the Boeing 747. American technology was helping to bring him home again.

Meanwhile, there I was, trapped at the airport, a young American journalist on my first major foreign assignment, an Islamically correct scarf on my head, in one hand a portable typewriter, in the other an Adidas bag that contained a shortwave radio, a change of clothes, one hundred rolls of film for the *Newsweek* photographer on the ground, a guidebook to Iran, and $20,000 in cash. Alone, in a crush of frenzied Iranian men.

"Sadegh!" I called out to Ghotbzadeh, who had also been left behind. Ghotbzadeh, I knew, was a can-do revolutionary. When Air France would not accept Iranian currency to charter Khomeini's plane, Ghotbzadeh flew to Germany to get hard currency, arriving at the office of a French middleman days later with a suitcase containing more than $100,000 in deutsche marks. During the first months of revolution, he would become the head of Iranian radio and television, using them as power centers to whip up anti-Western fervor and fanaticism, and then Foreign Minister, trying to explain to American television audiences why their diplomats were being held hostage.

Over time, Ghotbzadeh would become disillusioned with the revolutionary excesses and broken promises. Filled with ambition, he would turn against Khomeini, complaining bitterly that the principles of Islam were being ignored and that Khomeini's men were destroying the nation. But Ghotbzadeh was a big talker, even on closely monitored international telephone lines, and Iran is a nation of good listeners. In 1982 a plot to overthrow Khomeini would be uncovered (at least that is what officials said), and in a closed courtroom Ghotbzadeh would be found guilty of treason. The old ayatollah, in turn, would do nothing to save the man he considered "like a son." Khomeini had an extraordinary ability to conceal his emotions and to absorb emotional pain, members of his family told me. They said he had not cried when his own older son, Mustafa, died mysteriously in 1978. Later Khomeini said of his second son, "If they had taken my baby Ahmad, and killed him, I would not have said a word."

Ghotbzadeh would be put before a firing squad and executed.

But on the day of Khomeini's return, Ghotbzadeh was still in the ayatollah's good graces, and he was my protector. He grabbed my arm and pushed me onto a bus full of Khomeini's lay disciples. They were the remnants of the nationalist movement against the Shah, some very secular and others very religious, who had been educated in London and Paris and dressed in suits and ties. They would emerge within weeks as the core of Khomeini's first government. They did not "cut off the hand" of the American in their midst or rail about the crimes of America. Rather, Persian style, they welcomed me, offered candies and boiled eggs in celebration, and pointed out the landmarks of the city.

On the streets of Tehran, many women were bareheaded, and I took off my head scarf. A handwritten cloth banner bore the words—in English—"Welcome to the journalists coming with the ayatollah."

A few days later, a woman swathed in black spat out the word "whore" as I passed by, my head uncovered.

Welcome to Iran. Welcome to the revolution.

It took only ten days to make a revolution.

At first the government the Shah had left behind vowed to fight any attempt by Khomeini to form a government. Long columns of Chieftain and Scorpion tanks and military vehicles, heavy-duty trucks and jeeps fixed with machine guns were ordered into the streets, where they shot at followers of Khomeini who tried to stop them. But the ayatollah paid no attention to the warnings. He appointed a provisional government. He called on the army to join him and assured Iran's religious and ethnic minorities that an Islamic Republic would allow them to live in peace.

Within days, millions of marchers were on the streets, protesting against the Shah's government. Then, on Friday night, February 9, 1979, a massive crowd attacked the Doshan Tapeh Air Base outside Tehran and seized its guns and ammunition. The Shah's Imperial Guard fired back at air force cadets and civilian technicians loyal to Khomeini. The battle lasted throughout the next day, and as word of it spread, thousands of Khomeini's supporters built flimsy makeshift barricades throughout the capital. They lined up old cars, timber, garbage bags, tires, boulders, pieces of metal and concrete, even their living room furniture.

Khomeini threatened all-out war. And the Shah's army cracked.

Army tanks came at dawn on Sunday. But the Shah's troops wound up battling each other. So did gangs of ragtag soldiers whose uniforms—or partial uniforms—gave no clue to their real allegiance. Young soldiers loyal to Khomeini stuck carnations into their rifle muzzles and refused to fight as they rode by in flatbed trucks waving Khomeini's portrait. By the end of the day, the army had declared its neutrality and ordered its troops to their barracks. The caretaker government collapsed. At least five hundred people were killed.

I drove around the streets of Tehran that day in a red Mercedes that belonged to my interpreter, a young British-educated Iranian woman of Indian descent named Nindi. We didn't talk to anyone. There was too much to watch, as the Old Regime's formidable, Western-equipped military went over to the ayatollah's side. At one point the radio called for professional wire cutters to bring their equipment to the prisons to help set the inmates free.

Amid the chaos, the Mercedes didn't seem out of place, even with all the tanks and the trucks filled with young men carrying weapons. Nindi wore jeans and a sweater; I wore the same Missoni dress I had worn to interview Khomeini in France three months before. Neither of us wore head scarves.

In graduate school, I had studied European history and even after signing on with *Newsweek* was researching a doctoral dissertation on Louis-Sébastien Mercier, a French journalist and utopian who wrote about daily life at the time of the French Revolution. In the roiling streets of Tehran that day, I realized I'd probably never finish that dissertation.

It was a time of telephone death threats and random shoot-outs, a time when Americans were blamed for the crimes of the Old Regime and anti-Americanism ran high. Many of the foreign journalists were veterans of the Vietnam War. But some American journalists were so terrified of the shooting and the tear gas that they hid their passports and concealed their identities. One of my colleagues, a veteran of both Vietnam and Beirut, pretended to be French. He took to wearing a beret and a press pass from the Elysée Palace in Paris and refused to speak to his colleagues in any language but French.

One day a dozen militiamen came tearing through the Inter-Continental, shooting out windows, pounding on the doors, and looking for spies. *The New York Times* correspondents used the mattresses from their beds to cover the windows. I sat in the bathtub in my room until the shooting was over. Another day a mob of gunmen invaded the American embassy. It was liberated within a few hours, but not before three people, including two of the invaders and an embassy waiter, were killed. The embassy staff managed to destroy its most secret files and $500,000 worth of sensitive communications equipment, and burn hundreds of thousands of dollars in cash.

One night my close friend David Burnett, the photographer for *Time*, and I were stopped as we were leaving a restaurant. Two self-appointed "Islamic guards" carrying G-3 rifles pointed their weapons at us. "You have been drinking alcohol," one said.

"No, no, there wasn't any," I lied.

"Breathe," he replied.

We breathed into his face, in the first of many Breathalyzer tests I would have to take at gunpoint. They let us go and then went into the restaurant to smash some bottles.

On another evening, my taxi driver for the day got so scared by random shooting that he left me behind. I hitched a ride with two affable young engineers who had joined Iran's general strike months before. They were now guerrillas, and they showed off the hand grenades, revolvers, and rifles hidden under the front seats. At a roadblock the next evening, I asked the young guerrilla who had stopped me to please point the muzzle of his gun in the air. To reassure me, he motioned that the safety catch was on, pointed the rifle straight at my belly and pulled the trigger several times to prove it wouldn't fire. He laughed. I wrote the lead sentence of my obituary in my head.

And then, within days, the free-form chaos that had gripped the streets of Tehran ended. The old man who had sat under the apple tree in France had prevailed.

Once he seized power, Khomeini was free to reveal himself. He spoke directly to his people and made clear what his government would be: an Islamic Republic, nothing else. But Khomeini also seemed to be making it up as he went along. He had said many times that he had no interest in any political position himself. Instead, he became an authoritative, authoritarian father figure. His rule would be that of the *Velayat-e faghih*, the "rule of the Islamic jurist." The principle, as stated in Iran's newly adopted Constitution, made the revolution's leader an all-powerful religious guide or Supreme Leader who would have ultimate authority in the absence of the infant twelfth Imam. Supreme Leader turned out to be a much more powerful position than any other.

Perhaps, in retrospect, it should have been clear. In 1970, Khomeini had lectured on religion and political law to students at the Shiite Center in Najaf in Iraq, and these lectures were later published as a book, *Islamic Government.* "Since Islamic government is government of law, it is the religious expert and no one else who should occupy himself with the affairs of government," he said. "There is no room for opinions and feelings in the Islamic Government system."

Yet the creation of Iran's revolutionary government was haphazard, said Ibrahim Yazdi, one of Khomeini's lieutenants. Yazdi recalled years later that when he handed Khomeini a political framework titled *Islamic Government,* Khomeini crossed out the word "Government" and replaced it with the word "Republic." He wanted a state governed by Islamic principles, but not a system that looked like it was dominated by one person: that might recall a monarchy. His ambivalence laid the groundwork for the political dilemma that would confront Iran a generation later.

"Revolution is not a dinner party," Mao Zedong once said. "It cannot be advanced softly, gradually, carefully, considerately, respectfully, politely, plainly, and modestly." Iran's revolution was no more a dinner party than China's. The terror came quickly. The revolution brought hunger for "revolutionary justice" with swift show trials without lawyers.

One cold night in February 1979, women covered in black and wielding butcher knives and meat cleavers surged around the two-story schoolhouse where Khomeini had made his headquarters. They screamed for the execution of the Shah's generals. "We want to kill!" they cried. "Bring out the murderers." Inside the schoolhouse, four of the

Shah's top generals were seated around a large table for interrogations. Journalists were invited to ask questions. Yazdi, who played the role of Grand Inquisitor, translated their answers. A firing squad executed the generals on the roof of the building that night.

Every day I opened the newspapers to find photos documenting the hangings and shootings of drug dealers, prostitutes, officials of the Old Regime, Kurdish and Arab rebels, and all those who could be considered "counterrevolutionaries."

In the newspapers there seemed to be a certain delight in showing close-ups of corpses, strings of people hanging from makeshift gallows, blindfolded men tied to posts. It also seemed as if no one was in control. Some killings were carried out by clerics and guerrilla groups not directed by Khomeini. He often seemed passive in the face of them, unwilling to stop what many Iranians felt was a natural and necessary bloodletting. One of the first generals to be executed was General Rabii, the air force commander who had gone to Brzezinski with the plan to shoot down Khomeini's plane.

Yet Khomeini seemed to have at least one standard for judging events: their usefulness in consolidating his power. When hundreds of zealots seized the U.S. Embassy and the dozens of Americans inside it on November 4, 1979, the hostage-takers assumed it would be an anti-American sit-in lasting a few days at most. Even Ayatollah Khomeini's initial instinct was to liberate the embassy. "Who are they? Go and kick them out," Khomeini said of the militants to Yazdi, then the Foreign Minister, in the first hours of the occupation. But, as Yazdi recalled later, Khomeini changed his mind after he saw the masses of enthusiastic demonstrators in front of the embassy. Realizing that this was a chance to galvanize new fervor, he announced that the captors had launched "the second revolution, greater than the first."

The hostage crisis would last 444 days. Khomeini found it useful to keep relations with the United States in permanent crisis, which in turn helped him purge the liberals from the regime and to Islamicize and radicalize his government.

Many of Khomeini's associates were surprised by the methods he used to consolidate power. One such aide was Mehdi Bazargan, a genteel, French-speaking Islamic liberal with impeccable revolutionary credentials who served as Prime Minister in the Provisional Government created just after the revolution. Bazargan lamented the swift, secret trials and executions, opposed the Islamic Constitution as undemocratic, and tried to forge good relations with other countries, even the United States. Two days after the American hostages were seized, the student militants holding the embassy condemned Bazargan for "sitting down with the American wolf"—specifically, Brzezinski—at a conference in Algiers the previous week. Bazargan immediately resigned, saying bitterly, "I was always the last to know what was going on." Later, he told me he blamed himself for not seeing Khomeini as the authoritarian leader he would become. "We should have known better," he said. "The evidence was there all along."

I heard about the embassy takeover on French radio in my Paris apartment and happened to have a valid Iranian visa in my passport. I knew I had to get on a plane right away, but it didn't seem like a big deal. The embassy had been taken once before and had been liberated after a few hours. My main concern, I told my editors at *Newsweek,* was not how dangerous Tehran might be. It was whether there would still be a story by the time I got there the next morning. I sure got that wrong.

This time, arriving at Mehrabad Airport felt unreal. My own embassy was under siege, and the diplomats I would have turned to in times of trouble were hostages of the host government. Yet the airport was so normal. The passport official found my visa in order and wished me a good stay.

The impact of the embassy seizure had not yet sunk in. The embassy property, larger than Rockefeller Center, attested to the unique position the United States had enjoyed with the Shah. Its dozen buildings included a big but ugly chancery building, a warehouse, an enormous commissary, a football field, a swimming pool, a parking lot, a cultural center, tennis courts, an elaborate rose garden, and landscaped wooded lawns dotted with fountains and intersected by winding paths.

But its bulk and seeming permanence were no match for the single, well-planned act of hatred and rage with which the hostage-takers shattered the image of American prestige in Iran. The immediate provocation for the hostage-taking was a decision by the Carter administration to allow the deposed Shah to enter the United States for medical treatment. In protest, a group of young Islamic militants, many of them university students, occupied the embassy.

In those first days, the embassy became the focal point for thousands—sometimes tens of thousands—of Iranians eager to vent anger at the United States. But the scenes of these crowds broadcast around the world told only part of the story; there were also hints of ordinary life amid the orchestrated hatred. The embassy became Tehran's top tourist attraction, a place to take the kids for a living civics lesson, meet friends, grab a snack, or watch free street theater for an hour or two. Enterprising street vendors sold boiled eggs, baked beets, fava beans, sticky cakes, coconut slices, ice cream, color photos of the ayatollahs, fur hats, vinyl shoes. My all-time favorite banner was: "Iran was like a kidney for America. With the help of our leader Imam Khomeini, we have severed this vital link." My all-time favorite slogan was shouted by a vendor: "Death to Carter. Eat eggs."

And just a block away Iranians went about their business. People went to work, shopped, dined out, and visited relatives on weekends; students went to school. In time, even the demonstrators became so weary—or perhaps so hoarse—that they withheld their shouting and cursing until the cameras started rolling. When pencil pushers like me and still photographers arrived, the demonstrators sometimes only punched the air with their fists in silence.

And then one day, the hostage crisis was over. The hostages had outlived their usefulness and after long and complicated negotiations were sent home. The world of which Iranians thought they were the center had changed, sometimes in ways they had neither anticipated nor wanted. Yes, the crisis had helped Ayatollah Khomeini consolidate his revolution. And certainly it had humiliated America. But it also had forced Jimmy Carter to freeze Iran's assets, break diplomatic relations, put aircraft carriers on alert, change his reelection strategy, and order a rescue mission that failed, leaving eight servicemen dead. All of this damaged relations with the United States and frightened the international community in ways that left it unsympathetic when, during the hostages' captivity, Iraq invaded Iran and triggered eight catastrophic years of war against the new Islamic Republic.

Even so, the ayatollahs defied the doomsayers and endured. The revolution built a domestic policy around national pride, religious fervor, and self-sacrifice and a foreign policy independent of both the United States and the Soviet Union. It used every crisis to exterminate or marginalize enemies, and to strengthen the system of direct clerical leadership. It built a powerful government based on the Shah's institutions while simultaneously creating parallel revolutionary ones. So garbage got picked up; traffic tickets got written; telephone bills got sent out; mail got delivered. The two most powerful unofficial structures of Iran, the mosque and the bazaar, survived intact.

Terrorist bombings and assassinations only strengthened the resolve of those leaders who survived. The war against Iraq became the glue that held Iran's revolution together and, in the minds of its people, excused the new regime for demanding so many sacrifices. Khomeini's decision in 1988 to stop the fighting snuffed out his dream of propagating his revolution throughout the Muslim world. That decision shifted the course of Iran's own revolution, but it did not kill it.

Then, less than a year after the war ended, Khomeini was dead. Visiting the ayatollah's tomb years later, I recalled the frenzy of his funeral, when mourners tipped over his coffin and Khomeini's frail corpse slipped out of its white shroud and was passed along by the crowd. The crowds moved forward toward the sarcophagus with such force that paraplegics were pitched out of their wheelchairs and crushed; dozens of mourners suffered heart attacks.

More than being a brilliant theoretician of revolution, Khomeini had been smiled on by circumstance. Iranians of all classes and levels of religiosity had been searching for change. In that atmosphere, he became all things to all revolutionaries: a democrat to the liberal nationalists and the intellectuals, a devout man of God to the clerics, a believer in free trade to the bazaar merchants, a standard-bearer of economic justice to the leftists and workers, a protector of family values to fathers and mothers, a savior to the nation.

Khomeini is often seen from the outside as a fierce, rigid leader who never budged from a fixed position and was determined to drag Iran back to the seventh century. That is what we in the United States focused on. But in truth, he was a highly political master improviser, particularly supple when the survival of the Islamic Republic was at stake.

There were little things—like caviar. At first the Islamic Republic ruled that the sturgeon was a fish without scales and therefore its flesh and eggs could not be eaten. But then the loss of hard currency began to be felt. So Khomeini changed his mind. Sturgeon and caviar were relegitimized.

There were big things too. One of Khomeini's major concessions dealt with the Islamic nature of the state itself. In 1988 he declared that the state had the right to suspend Islamic laws (even observance of the five principal pillars of Islam) if the preservation of the Islamic order was at stake. Of course, the Constitution had to be changed accordingly, showing once again that Khomeini and the Islamic Republic were not rigid followers of their own self-made rules. Like all revolutions, this one was made by mortals.

Not just a victory of religious piety and justice, this was also a revolution of the dispossessed—and a realignment of those who possessed. But by the late 1990s, Khomeini's cult had faded. The photographs still hung in most government offices; the billboard portraits still appeared in some town squares. But it was a struggle to keep alive the memory of a stern old man who preached a message of self-denial and vengeance.

One day early in 1999 I went looking for the legacy of Khomeini in Iran's holy city of Qom. At 435 Moalem Street, not far from the main shrine, I found the yellow-brick house where he had lived in the 1960s and again after the revolution. Visitors were rare, and the house was open to the public only a few hours a day. In the courtyard, the fountain was dry; the Iranian flags were soiled; the plants needed water. The house itself was a warren of small rooms with musty carpets layering the floors. A room that looked as if it might have been Khomeini's library was locked behind glass doors.

A cleric in a crooked turban and a stained robe tight around his belly told Ali-Reza Haghighi, an acquaintance from the Ministry of Islamic Guidance who accompanied me, that there was no one to answer any questions.

On the way out I asked the guard, who was twenty-seven, what it meant to him to guard the house where Khomeini had lived. "Khomeini means nothing to me or my life," he said. "The mullahs promise; they don't deliver. There is no country here." The guard said he had neither time nor energy to ponder the meaning of his proximity to history. He had a wife and two children to support. He even worked another full-time job as a night watchman. So I asked him what would make him happy. "I want a house of my own," he said. "I want a car, a good car to take trips in."

I was in Iran that spring, twenty years after Iran's revolution, to watch the nation celebrate. Not for the ten days of government-organized festivals memorializing the ayatollah's return, but for *Nowruz,* the Persian New

Year. *Nowruz* is the celebration not of any Islamic event, but of something older than Islam itself, something rooted deep in Iran's heritage and sense of national dignity: the sense that somehow, they, as inheritors of the Persian empire, are located at the center of the universe. Everyone who had ruled Iran before the ayatollahs had adapted to that legacy.

Initially, the revolutionary purists of 1979 tried to stamp out the ancient festivities surrounding *Nowruz,* which date back more than 2,500 years, to the time of the religious leader Zoroaster. The purists call the celebrations "superstitious" and "anti-Islamic."

But the people of Iran prevailed. Despite the official disapproval, *Nowruz* festivities have grown louder and more ambitious each year since the revolution.

What I found on my trip in 1999 is that even the most religious Iranian families thoroughly clean their houses and buy new clothes for their children at *Nowruz.* They set their tables with a mirror, a goldfish in a bowl, colored eggs, and seven items whose names begin with the letter S in Persian. The difference between religious and secular families is telling: the pious put a Koran on the table, the secular a copy of the works of the fourteenth-century poet Hafiz. Banks, government offices, and schools are closed for as many as fourteen days. Most newspapers do not publish. Most people do not work. On the thirteenth day of *Nowruz,* people pack lunches and go out with their families—to the countryside, to the mountains, to the sea, even to the landscaped dividers between the highways—for a nationwide picnic.

Nowruz in 1999 was actually a very special New Year, because, for the first time since Iran's revolution, the Interior Ministry issued a safety advisory and officially allowed the festivities to proceed. On the Tuesday evening before the New Year, known as *Charshanbeh Suri,* I watched with fascination and horror as children and teenagers in an apartment complex I was visiting built seven raging bonfires in the courtyard and then proceeded to jump over them in a symbolic purification rite meant to replace illness with health. "My yellowness to you and your redness to me," they chanted as they jumped. Astonishingly, their clothes didn't catch fire, although a number went home with singed eyebrows. Trick-or-treating, fireworks, bottle rockets, Roman candles, sparklers, and other small explosives were also de rigueur.

The reformist newspaper *Khordad* praised the festivities as an authentic manifestation of nationalism that countered the cultural invasion of the West. But others did not approve. In Mashad, six people were sentenced to eighteen months in jail and 228 lashes of the whip for disrupting public order and goading people to dance in the streets. The conservative newspaper *Jomhouri-ye Islami* called the ritual dangerous and "a superstitious tradition promoted by the Shah's regime." Ayatollah Khamenei, the Supreme Leader, condemned the fire jumping and criticized the Ministry of Islamic Guidance for "making a mistake" in allowing the public celebration to proceed.

But the facts could not be denied: a generation later, the secular coexists with the Islamic in revolutionary Iran. And the Islamic Republic is faced with a choice: reinvent itself or face the wrath of its population. Amid prayer and sacrifice and praise for martyrdom, there is a yearning, indeed a demand, for Roman candles and picnics.

CHAPTER FOUR

The Mullah Wore Beautiful Shoes

What the nation wants is an Islamic Republic. Not just a Republic, not a democratic Republic, not a democratic Islamic Republic. Do not use the word "democratic" to describe it. That is the Western style.

— AYATOLLAH RUHOLLAH KHOMEINI AFTER HIS
RETURN TO QOM IN MARCH 1979

We are at the key phase of the transition toward an Islamic democracy in Iran. No one should hide behind the principles of the 1979 revolution, or use them as a cover for ousting political rivals. Everyone must respect and recognize differences.

— PRESIDENT MOHAMMAD KHATAMI IN A SPEECH
TO THE NEWLY ELECTED TOWN COUNCILS IN
FEBRUARY 1999

*J*UST AFTER SUNDOWN in the desert city of Yazd, three dozen women and children sat on the carpeted floor of an upper-class home, kissing and joking as heavy platters of food were laid before them on a plastic checkered tablecloth. It was time for *eftar,* the nightly ritual of breaking a dawn-to-dusk fast during the holy month of Ramadan.

The food was typical Persian fare: saffron rice, grilled chicken, lamb stew with herbs and scallions, fruits, dates, halvah, and sweets. But this was no ordinary *eftar.* It was an intimate meal with relatives of the newly elected reformist president, Mohammad Khatami: his mother, three of his sisters, and a gaggle of cousins, grandchildren, and friends.

In itself, an invitation to the home of a powerful family in the public eye is unusual in Iran, where private lives are fiercely guarded and trust of outsiders comes slowly. Fatemeh Khatami, the President's older sister and the head of the women's organization in the nearby town of Ardakan, explained that I had been invited because "hospitality is one of the pillars of our religion." But I knew there was more to it than that. In fact, the invitation was a political gesture. Iran has changed drastically since the early days of the Islamic Republic, and President Khatami had been elected in 1997 as a champion of social reform. Iranians knew that. But the outside world didn't know how far to trust this man. So the Khatami family seemed to think it important to reassure the world that the new President was both approachable and modern.

Because the women and men at the *eftar* were not all close blood relatives, the women and girls did not remove their chadors. But even the traditional garb could not hide the face of the guest of honor: Sakineh Ziai, Khatami's mother, smiling broadly and draped in a black and white print. She was wearing makeup. Pencil-thin black eyeliner. A layer of foundation. A bit of blush. And was that lipstick on her lips? At one point, her chador dropped from her head to reveal a jet black pageboy, dangly hoop earrings, a thick gold necklace, and the look of a woman who knew she had been born beautiful. So the conversation at the women's table turned to good looks. "My mother was a great beauty in her youth," said one of President Khatami's other sisters, Maryam, a schoolteacher in Yazd. "She is very aware of her looks. So she wears a little makeup, not when she goes out in public but in private social gatherings like this. We like to say that God is beautiful and appreciates beauty."

The table talk was full of praise for President Khatami. One woman wanted to send him a kiss. "I wish you were part of our family so you could kiss the President for me when you go back to Tehran," she said to me. Over fruit and pastries in the television room, the group became so boisterous that when the talk turned to family, I was asked to show photographs of my two daughters. Maryam jokingly offered to marry off her nine-year-old son, Mohammad, to one of them. In a later telephone conversation, she added a punch line for the joke: "If your daughter wants to marry my son, she has to wear a chador. My husband is very rigid."

But months later, Hosein Nosrat, my friend at the Ministry of Islamic Guidance, told me that Khatami had not been pleased with articles I had written about his family for *The New York Times*. He had taken exception to the publication of a photograph that Khatami's mother had given me. He said that the President had banned other media interviews with his family. I wasn't surprised that a picture had caused trouble, assuming Nosrat was talking about a photograph of Khatami in his uniform as a second lieutenant in the Shah's army.

"No, not that one," said Nosrat. "His office said he didn't like the picture of himself with his daughters. He thought he looked messy. He thought the house looked messy. I told his office to forget it."

The complaint about what I had written was more serious. "You described the hair and makeup of the President's mother and the President's wife," Nosrat said. "You should know better. You don't write about these things here."

I later learned from a friend of the family that the President was even more angry with his mother than with me, apparently for talking about makeup and beauty. Sakineh Ziai was so offended that she didn't speak to her son for days, the family friend said. Finally, Khatami apologized to her, proving just how tough an Iranian mother could be, even if she wore a veil and her son was the President.

But this was not just a family spat. On some level, Khatami must have felt exposed, even vulnerable, by the public presentation of his family in the Western media. He wanted to be seen by the outside world as welcoming and open, but the revelations cut both ways. Such articles could be used against him at home.

How else to explain the presence of the pink rose on the day in January 1998 that I interviewed Zohreh Sadeghi, the First Lady? There we were, in her headquarters in one of the Shah's former palaces. Suddenly she interrupted herself to comment about the flower arrangement on the table that divided us. Sticking up in the middle of the bowl of yellow, purple, and white flowers was a single pink rose. On closer inspection, it had a tiny microphone attached to it. "There is a microphone here!" she exclaimed. "Is somebody listening to what we're saying?" I didn't doubt that she was surprised, and the official interpreter omitted the comment from her simultaneous translation. It turned out that in the hallway outside, three men with headsets were recording the interview. It was just for the archives, they said.

The two incidents—Khatami's anger and his wife's surprise—spoke volumes about the tenuous nature of political power in the Islamic Republic, and showed how tricky any interaction with the press can be. These days, Iran's politicians worry about how their actions and words will be received by rivals and by public opinion, which in Iran consists of fragmented audiences with different and even conflicting agendas—the clergy, merchants, students, war veterans, women, ethnic groups. Portrayals of private lives are particularly dangerous territory. Many leaders, like Ayatollah Khamenei, simply refuse that kind of access. (Once, during an interview with Khamenei in 1982, I asked him to describe his childhood and education. He told me such questions were a waste of time.)

If all this sounds familiar to Western ears—that supposedly powerful politicians fear becoming hostage to the caprices of the press—it is worth considering how surprising it is that Iranian politicians fit this mold too. Over the years, many Americans have come to think of Iran's theocracy as a terror-based totalitarian regime like those set up by revolutions in Russia and China earlier in the twentieth century. In fact, Iran's revolution has set up something quite different. It isn't a democracy in a Western sense, of course. But within the tight intellectual limits of the theocracy set up by Ayatollah Khomeini, there is substantial rivalry for the loyalties of the Iranian citizen—a citizen who votes, and who is gaining more choice about whom to vote for. The fact that politicians worry so much about press coverage is proof.

Iran, in fact, has become a country with an open-ended political game, in which the stakes are enormous. As reformers challenge old-line clerics—in part by appearing more transparent and accountable to constituents—the rules of political conduct and the secret understandings that used to determine decisions are being questioned. But Iran is not yet a place where transparency and accountability are the rule. Instead, anyone who dares to innovate can find himself tripped up by a tough and messy style of domestic infighting with origins a lot older than the Islamic revolution.

Iran has a hundred-year history of dabbling with democracy and pluralism, as well as a long parliamentary tradition. Early in the twentieth century, Iranian leaders and politicians experimented with the ideas of a law-based state, and wrote a progressive Constitution. Even the Islamic Constitution ratified in 1979 reflects concerns over public accountability and transparency.

Once the clerics were in control, they found it hard to keep their people restricted to a rigid view of what Islam allows. Over the years, new ideas bubbled up about how to interpret the faith. Interest groups began debating them, in ways that have begun to have some of the trappings of a pluralist democracy—if not yet through official, mass-member political parties, then certainly through political groups that have begun to function as parties. Later, odd things began happening in key institutions such as the Parliament and the courts, which conservatives tried to use as vehicles for maintaining their hold over society, but where the Islamic Republic itself could also be put on trial. It began as a process not to overthrow the Islamic system but to reform it from within, to strike a balance between secular and religious worlds and between democratic and undemocratic principles. The outcome was not at all clear.

The origin of tension within the system lies in the nature of the Islamic Republic itself. What exactly is an "Islamic Republic" anyway? Its founders in 1979 certainly didn't agree on a definition. The code of Islamic law, the sharia, had been around for quite a while, of course. Several Muslim countries—most famously Saudi Arabia but also, to a lesser degree, countries like Pakistan and Malaysia—were governed by Islamic principles. But a whole political system run by Islamic "guardians"? This was something new.

In its original form the Islamic Republic sounded like a straightforward theocracy, in which elections served to ratify the decisions made by the clerics, much as meaningless Soviet referendums once confirmed decisions already made by the Politburo. When Ayatollah Khomeini called for a referendum to determine the level of popular approval for an Islamic Republic, the people were asked not to choose between various options, but to vote either yes or no to the simple question of whether an "Islamic Republic" should replace the monarchy. According to the official tally, 98.1 percent of the voters said yes.

The task of defining an Islamic Republic was left to the drafters of the new Constitution, who included people of different political persuasions. They argued fiercely over the relationship between Western-based secular law and Islamic law, the role of Iranian culture alongside Islamic culture, and the distribution of power between the President and the Parliament. But the framers couldn't agree, and instead of resolving the conflicts, the Constitution embraced contradictory elements—at once democratic and authoritarian, secular and religious. The entire government—with a President, a Prime Minister (abolished later with a Constitutional change), an elected Parliament, and a judiciary—was put inside a theocratic structure whose ultimate authority would be a man of God holding control of the state's enforcement machinery, the police and military.

"Islamic principles" were explicitly recognized as the basis for the country's legal system. The role of interpreting these principles was left to the conservative Guardian Council, an overseeing body of six clerics and six legal experts. That body was powerful enough to reject candidates for the presidency and the Parliament, and to strike down legislation passed by the Parliament.

The most creative—and drastic—innovation was the concept of the Supreme Leader. Khomeini had lectured about the rule of the ideal and just Islamic jurist years before, and as the constitutional debate raged in 1979, the position was added after the first draft was written. In the revolution's first years, when Khomeini held the position, it was an unshakable pillar of the Islamic system. But a generation later it had become a lightning rod for democratic reformers who questioned its power and jurisdiction.

Since Khomeini's death, the Supreme Leader has been appointed for an unlimited term by a clerically dominated but popularly elected Assembly of Experts, which also has the power to remove him. He controls the national police and the security agencies. He appoints the chiefs of the military, the Revolutionary Guards, the judiciary, national television and radio, and the ostensibly charitable foundations that control hundreds of companies and industries. He names the principal members of the Guardian Council. He sets the direction and tone of the country's domestic and foreign policy. The President, by contrast, has responsibility for the cabinet, the government bureaucracy, and the economy, and for carrying out foreign policy.

In Khomeini's time, the Supreme Leader had dictatorial powers. As the "founder" of the Islamic Republic, Khomeini used his authority in ways that went far beyond the Constitution. Yet he was also an astute politician who was careful to distance himself from the forces and personalities that competed for power in the revolution's aftermath. The situation changed with Khomeini's death. His successor, Ayatollah Khamenei, did not share the founder's aura. Even constitutional amendments that gave his office more power could not assure his dominance. Khamenei himself complicated the situation with his inability to stay out of partisan politics. As a result, he undermined his own credibility and that of his office.

The stranglehold of the Islamic state also began to fail in the realm of ideology. The official and rather rigid version of Islam propagated by the state had created a backlash: a new breed of Islamic thinkers willing to challenge the official political orthodoxy on theological and ethical grounds. They took their inspiration in part from the much older commitment of Shiite Islam to argument and debate among the clerics. And this new challenge began to resonate ever louder once society itself began to change with the end of the Iran-Iraq war, the death of Khomeini, and the rise of a new generation.

Take, for example, Abdol-Karim Soroush, one of Iran's most brilliant political and religious scholars. He is a dangerous man for the Islamic Republic these days, because cloaked in his philosophical language is a clear message: the need to replace Islamic dictatorship with Islamic democracy. He was dismissed in 1995 from his university teaching position and has been repeatedly attacked and prevented from lecturing by the *Ansar-e Hezbollah* or "Helpers of the Party of God," club-wielding thugs believed to be funded by extremists inside and outside the government. "If you do not preach the official interpretation of Islam, you will not be allowed to go to a mosque to preach," he once explained to me. "You will not be allowed to teach at a high school or a university. This official interpretation is an achievement—a negative achievement—of the revolution."

I once asked Soroush to define the Iranian state. The answer eluded him. "The state is Islamic," he said. "It is a republic. It is a mixture of both. It is neither of them." Yet he survives and I continue to talk to him. Obstreperous clerics and lay intellectuals may find themselves isolated and imprisoned. But there is no system of gulags in the Iranian theocracy, nor is there excommunication. However hemmed in they are, their religion guarantees them a right to their point of view.

Firmly in the conservative camp was Ali-Akbar Nateq-Nouri, an outgoing, mid-ranking cleric who had been the Speaker of the Parliament from 1992 to 2000. Over glasses of sour cherry juice in an ornate reception hall in the Parliament building one day in 1998, I asked him what he thought of Soroush's idea that clerics should not be running the state. He laughed so hard that he spat out the juice he had not yet swallowed.

"If I believed in the separation between religion and the state, what am I doing here then?" he asked. In fact, Nateq-Nouri wanted to put more clerics into government. "Yes, more clerics!" he exclaimed. "Our presence proves that government is not separate from religion."

The Mullah Wore Beautiful Shoes

*   *   *

So the Islamic Republic remained an odd entity. It tried to gain legitimacy through the use of democratic forms: referendums and elections, and a promise to build a freer, more just society. It was consolidated when there was a leader—Ayatollah Khomeini—with enough charisma, vision, and credentials to compensate for the fact that his revolution didn't come with a wiring diagram. But after Khomeini's death, there was no single person strong enough to resolve differences or to rule alone—certainly not Ayatollah Khamenei, Khomeini's successor as Supreme Leader. So new ideas were forced into the open, demanding resolution in the open.

Never was this clearer than in the May 1997 presidential election. Nateq-Nouri was running and he was expected to win. He had the endorsement of the conservative Militant Clergy Society, which included most of the leading politicized clerics; the clerical leaders of Friday prayers from most big cities; the majority of Parliament; and a number of key cabinet members and bazaar merchants. He enjoyed the implicit backing of Ayatollah Khamenei. All that support brought with it the power of state-run television and a well-organized political machine with the resources to get out the vote: the nationwide network of mosques.

I went to see Nateq-Nouri five months before the election. He was so confident of victory that he told me who he would put in his cabinet. "Specialists, believers, competent, healthy, and honest Muslim people!"

At first there were only two other candidates, both of them weak. Neither represented the dissatisfaction bubbling up among an increasing number of reformers. So after a considerable amount of prodding, Mohammad Khatami, the head of the National Library and a former Minister of Islamic Guidance, entered the race. The son of a prominent cleric and a supporter of the revolution in 1979, Khatami owed his emotional and spiritual allegiance to the religious world in which he was raised and trained. But he had studied various concepts of law and representative government, and he was able to combine worldliness and intelligence with a gift for politics and campaigning. For Iran's Islamic Republic, he was a fresh face, and the perfect candidate to reach out to the disaffected segments of society.

It wasn't just anyone who could run for President. All candidates had to have the tacit acceptance of Ayatollah Khamenei and the official approval of the Guardian Council. In 1997, more than 230 candidates put their names forward; only four were not struck down, among them Nateq-Nouri and Khatami.

Khatami demanded assurances from the top that it would be a fair fight. "When Khatami wanted to run for President he went to the Leader and shared his ideas and said, 'If you think it's possible and society will tolerate my ideas, I'll become a candidate,'" Khatami's American-educated younger brother, Ali, told me after the election. "'But if you don't see that possibility I won't. I don't want your personal endorsement, but I want a free and fair election.' And Khamenei said, 'Whoever wins, I will support him.'"

At the start, Khatami hardly looked like a threat. The assumption was that the clerical system would not allow anyone but Nateq-Nouri to win. But there was space for political competition, and the campaign that followed had some echoes of an American election: tough, nasty, confusing, and full of alliance-building, horse-trading, and mud-slinging.

Khatami was supported by the oddest of coalitions; it included two factions that functioned like mini-political parties, the Servants of Construction and the Militant Clerics' Association (not to be confused with the conservative Militant Clergy Society). The Servants of Construction included technocrats and businessmen who favored a smaller role for the state in the economy, more foreign investment, and better relations with the West. They were aligned with Rafsanjani, the outgoing President, who was ineligible to run for a third four-year term. The group threw its support behind Khatami late, only after it could not come up with a candidate of its own. The Militant Clerics' Association was behind Khatami's nomination from the start. It consisted of left-wing supporters of state control of the economy and included among its ranks several of the militants who had seized the American embassy in 1979.

Khatami took his message directly to the people and ran a Western-style campaign: he traveled in a simple Iranian-made car or by bus. In interviews he talked about his hobbies—table tennis and swimming—his favorite philosophers, and how he wished his wife knew how to drive. He appealed to women, young people, and intellectuals with pledges to create a civil society, promote the rule of law, fight "superstition and fanaticism," break the political monopoly of the right, and create more jobs and better educational opportunities.

The lofty discourses about tolerance and the rule of law were tempered by Khatami's wry sense of humor. "Who is the boss in your house?" an interviewer from *Zanan,* Iran's boldest women's magazine, asked. "Naturally my wife has a more important role than I," he replied.

Khatami also got a boost from a series of televised presidential debates. The state-controlled television barely covered Khatami's campaign. But when the debates were broadcast, they could not help Nateq-Nouri compete against Khatami's open style and intellect. A friend watching on a construction site in Shushtar noted that the entire workforce—from construction workers to senior supervisors—was won over by the reformist.

In fact, Khatami had a basic advantage. Nateq-Nouri was regarded as part of the clerical establishment, and the establishment had lost much of its credibility. And the fact that Nateq-Nouri acted as if he had already been elected turned off many voters. "Why is the television showing him every hour on his trip and broadcasting an anthem written especially for him?" one reader asked in a call-in complaint column in the leftist daily *Salaam.*

Despite all this, it became apparent in the final days of the campaign that this election was a real contest—one that would help define just what an Islamic Republic is. By this time, there was little that the conservatives could do. Authorities in the Intelligence and Interior ministries worried that any effort to rig the election would set off uncontrollable demonstrations. The notion that elections might be rigged was not outlandish. Indeed, there were rumors that a well-known and powerful ayatollah had gone to Qom to put in the fix. In the end, both Khamenei and Rafsanjani pledged that the election would be free—and this, in turn, inspired a larger turnout than had been expected. People realized that their votes might actually count.

I knew this would be a different kind of election when a young friend took to the streets to campaign for Khatami. For days after work she handed out leaflets to shoppers and pedestrians. She even dragged her relatives to the polls on election day—among them her father, a retired civil servant who had served under the Shah and had never voted before in his life.

In the end, nearly 80 percent of those eligible voted, the highest percentage since the early years of the revolution. (By contrast, the turnout in the American presidential election in 1996 was 49 percent.) The turnout made large-scale fraud unthinkable.

More than twenty million people—70 percent of those who voted—cast their ballots for Khatami. Khatami captured the vote of the young, the women, the intellectuals, and the middle class. He won among voters of extremely different political views and economic and educational backgrounds. He even did well in small towns and villages where citizens generally do what their religious leaders tell them to do.

As Khatami's mother told me at the *eftar* dinner, "It is said my son's election was a second revolution."

Indeed, the election of Khatami as President exposed fault lines that were present at the creation of the Islamic Republic. His call for tolerance and the opening of public spaces invigorated an intense reform movement among many clerics and religious and secular intellectuals; they began to experiment, to take chances, and to challenge the most fundamental tenets of the state. The restrictive measures that had worked in times of revolution and war no longer fit a dynamic society where the people had come to want the fruits of peace. What resulted was a struggle between conservatives determined to preserve unity and stability and reformists equally determined to make the system more transparent and accountable. More significant, Iran began to debate how to let go of a controlled political system without descending into chaos.

The central question became: Will the people be allowed to govern through an elected President, an elected Parliament, and a freer press while still holding to the vestiges of clerical rule? Can elements of democratic politics become integral parts of the Iranian political system even as a relatively closed club of deeply conservative clerics and entrenched lay revolutionaries continue to wield tremendous power? What the election touched off was a fierce guerrilla style of politics, full of remarkably intense and intellectually creative surprise attacks and waged on a variety of battlefields—much of it in public.

Iran's President, who was fifty-four when he was elected, invites comparisons to Nelson Mandela, Vaclav Havel, and Bill Clinton. Khatami is a larger-than-life figure with the ability to defy the odds and stick it out during times of crisis. Like Clinton, he has the ability to compartmentalize problems and smile through the bad times. And he seems on a permanent campaign, constantly selling himself and his message to a public that can turn apathetic and weary, no matter how much it yearns for change. During my first meeting with the President in January 1998, I found myself blurting out that if he and Bill Clinton sat down with each other, they would probably hit it off beautifully.

If Khatami played a musical instrument, it would be Clinton's: the saxophone. The Iranian President is the political equivalent of a jazz musician. He knows how to improvise, to listen to voices around him and then pick up the theme as if he had invented the solo, to negotiate and blur the lines and move on to the next stage, even if he doesn't know exactly what that stage will be.

Khatami is charming, so much so that it is tempting to think of him as a Jeffersonian democrat masquerading as a cleric. But this is no masquerade. He is one of them. He is a midranking cleric known as a *hojjatoleslam,* and he wears a black turban that identifies him as a descendant of the Prophet Mohammad.

Many of the attitudes Khatami has brought to the presidency—tolerance, duty to country, nationalist feelings, the absence of any sense of victimization—derive from his own upbringing. Behind a wall in Ardakan stands the spacious mud-colored house with a stone terrace where Khatami was born. His mother was the daughter of a wealthy landowner; his father a famous cleric. As an ayatollah, Khatami's father became the leader of Friday prayers in the provincial capital, Yazd, and one of the country's most beloved religious leaders. He was so revered that he also held the Shah's repressive state system at bay. Sitting many years later in the house in Yazd where she lives with one of her daughters, the President's mother told me this story: Years before the revolution, the Shah's security police summoned Ayatollah Khatami for questioning. "But as he entered, all the employees and the visitors bowed to him and kissed his hand," she recounted with a laugh. "The authorities told him to go home."

The Khatami family enjoyed a comfortable life not uncommon among well-to-do clerical families. In addition to the large residence in the center of town, they owned a summer house a few miles away with a lush garden of pomegranate trees and an enormous, deep pool—for water storage, but, more important, for swimming. The President's sister Maryam was particularly eager to present her family as both enlightened and well off. "We had no restrictions on anything," she said. "We could spend as much money as we wanted." Her brother Ali, a businessman who lived in Fort Lee, New Jersey, for a year and a half while getting a master's degree in industrial engineering in Brooklyn, put it more bluntly: "My mother came from a rich family. Very rich."

Khatami learned tolerance from his father. Ayatollah Khatami allowed his children to listen to news on the radio and read banned books while they were growing up, which helps to explain his son's political dexterity. At one point after the revolution, a group of fervent believers came to the ayatollah with a list of people in Yazd who had collaborated with the Shah and therefore should be arrested. Ayatollah Khatami told them, "Then arrest me too, because I didn't do more to oppose the Shah."

As a boy, Mohammad Khatami talked of becoming a doctor, but his father wanted him to become a cleric. So Khatami, as a teenager, dutifully went to study religion in Qom. There he became a disciple of a firebrand preacher named Ruhollah Khomeini and a close friend of his son, Ahmad. There would be other connections. Khatami's brother Mohammad-Reza married a granddaughter of Khomeini; Khatami's future wife was the cousin of the wife of Khomeini's son, Ahmad. Khatami's sister Maryam married a widely respected cleric who had been a close aide of Khomeini's during his exile in Paris. Connections like these are extraordinarily important within the clerical class.

But Khatami also persuaded his father to allow him to study philosophy at the University of Isfahan, where he was exposed to ideals of freedom and civic responsibility that he believed could be incorporated into Islam. Although many clerics obtained exemptions and avoided serving in the Shah's military, Khatami fulfilled his two-year mandatory military service as a junior lieutenant in the army.

Khatami never spent time in the Shah's prisons and played only a peripheral role before the revolution, as the head of Iran's Islamic Center in Hamburg, Germany. Soon after the revolution, though, he was elected to Iran's first Parliament from his hometown of Ardakan and was appointed, then dismissed, as head of the giant Kayhan Publishing Company. For ten years after that, Khatami served as Minister of Islamic Guidance. In his first several years in the job, he enforced the regime's strict censorship. But in the last three years he eased restrictions on films, music, art, and literature. He reinstated awards for the best books and created a press arbitration council to help mediate accusations against journalists and writers.

In 1992 the Parliament forced Khatami to resign. In an impassioned resignation letter, he complained of threats and ill will. His efforts to create "a superior culture" for Iran were a "weighty responsibility" that, he said, had become too heavy for him to carry. He was banished to the National Library in Tehran and for five years faded from public view.

But there Khatami developed a passion for the computer, envisioning a time when Iranians in remote villages would log on to networks for information contained within library walls. He also wrote two books that sealed his reputation as a forward-looking thinker. *Fear of Waves*—a phrase taken from a Hafiz poem—is a collection of essays in which he argues that even though Islam is superior to Western thought, it is no longer responsive to modern life, especially when it comes to "one of the basic needs of human beings: freedom." As a result, he wrote, the West has more economic, political, military, scientific, and technical power. Khatami's other book, *From the World of the City to the City of the World,* is a conventional survey of several Western philosophers, including Plato, Aristotle, Machiavelli, Hobbes, Locke, and Rousseau.

In his election campaign, Khatami continued to work within the system. He extolled the Iranian revolution and endorsed the Islamic Constitution and the idea of the Supreme Leader. He said he approved of the rules governing dress for Muslim women. On the other hand, he argued that the way to make the system relevant for the people was to create an open civil society that reconciled the sacred and the secular. Once in office he extended individual rights and basic freedoms and called for the rule of law. Nothing less than the survival of Iran's Islamic Republic, he argued, was at stake.

I knew Khatami was different the first time we met, during a chance encounter in January 1998 at the Presidential Palace. His shoes gave him away. "If you want to figure out someone's politics, look at his shoes," Nazila once told me. She was right. Shoes often reveal class, wealth, religiosity, and Westernization. Khatami wore beautiful shoes. Simple, finely stitched black leather shoes with laces, not the *nalein* or rough slippers favored by Iran's ruling class of clerics. The shoes complemented the crisp gray pin-striped robe and matching black cloak and turban. So did the string of small turquoise-colored prayer beads dangling in his left hand.

Khomeini hadn't worn beautiful shoes. The first time I saw him in Paris, he was wearing blue plastic sandals. Indoors, he left them at the door and conducted business in his socks. So did his aides. A pair of Khomeini's sandals, brown and worn, have even been placed in a tiny shrine to his memory at his house in Tehran.

By contrast, Khatami seemed worldly. If Khomeini represented the triumph of the clerical over the temporal, Khatami stood for a reconciliation of the sacred and the secular, the traditional and the modern.

Actually, I hadn't gone to the Presidential Palace that day to see Khatami. I was looking for his chef de cabinet, a portly cleric in his late thirties named Mohammad-Ali Abtahi, whom I had been unable to reach by phone. Having decided to just show up, I called him from the phone at the security station. "I just tried to call you," he said, full of hospitality and regrets. "I would have been able to meet you right now."

"That's great," I replied. "I'm downstairs."

It shouldn't be so easy to get into official buildings in Iran. The country has a history of terror attacks, and even the holiest Islamic sites have not been immune. Security is usually tight.

But Iran is also a place of face-to-face lobbying, cajoling, begging, and, more and more frequently, bribing, to secure favors. Abtahi couldn't lose face by refusing to see me after he had told me he was available. So I was body-frisked by a pair of energetic chador-clad women, forced to relinquish my handbag, camera, tape recorder, and wristwatch, and sent up a broad, elegant staircase into a sunny circular room where visiting dignitaries are received. After an hour of conversation, Abtahi abruptly stood up and said, "Come and meet the President."

There in the hallway was Khatami. He escorted me back into the reception room. He did not shake my hand, but unlike Khomeini, who had sat far away and turned his gaze from me during our interview in France years earlier, Khatami pulled up a large armchair, sat close, smiled broadly, and looked me straight in the eye.

He had once been a journalist himself, he said, and asked me how I had come to cover Iran. I told him I had been based in Paris when Ayatollah Khomeini arrived there in 1978. Khatami threw his head back and laughed. "*Khanoum* [Ms.] Sciolino," he said, "you look too young to have been in Neauphle-le-Château with Khomeini." I know full well that I have a face to match my age, and that the head scarf is not exactly an age-defying accessory. And I had never heard that kind of talk from a serious mullah before. Simply stated, Khatami is a charmer.

Khatami spoke passionately, sometimes in English, about the need for women's advancement and the need for a "dialogue among civilizations." He admitted that he might fail in his attempt to bring reform to Iran. "Politicians only speak to the superficial level of the spirit," he said.

"There is a need to have more in-depth dialogue, with a deep meeting of minds among peoples. This is my hope. But maybe I'm not capable of carrying it out."

And he went off on a long sentimental riff. "We say we love all the people in the world and we want them to love us in return," he said. "Resentments should be turned into kindness and love." I thought of one of Mario Cuomo's best lines about politicians: "We campaign in poetry, but when we're elected we're forced to govern in prose." Khatami is that rare politician who campaigns in poetry and tries to govern in poetry.

I saw Khatami's dynamism firsthand many times after that. After a speech to the graduating class at the all-women's Al Zahra University in Tehran in 1999, young women greeted him with applause and two-fingered whistles. They shoved to get close to him, squealing and reaching out to touch his cloak. They begged him to sign autographs and pose for pictures. When the crowds dispersed, he even posed for a picture with Nazila and me, although he took one step back and looked away from the camera just before the shutter clicked. It wouldn't do him any good to be photographed too close to an American journalist, I guessed.

Still, Khatami stopped for a chat. He asked me in Persian, as he had before, whether my Persian language skills were improving. Then he asked me if I had learned how to cook Persian food. That question was beyond my language ability, so Nazila stepped in. "Oh, Mr. President, she's a great Iranian cook!" she exclaimed. "She knows how to cook *ghormeh sabzi.*"

Ghormeh sabzi, a subtle dish of lamb, herbs, and lemon, is considered one of the hardest Iranian dishes to prepare. It takes hours and is easy to ruin. In fact, I don't know how to cook it. The question about cooking had sounded condescending to me, and I told Nazila afterward that we should have asked Khatami if *he* knew how to cook it.

But when I told this story to some of my female Iranian friends, they told me I was being unfair. They told me the President had been struggling to make small talk and find some common ground. They told me that he was the first leader in the Islamic Republic to talk seriously about women's rights. They told me stories about their own fathers who didn't know how to make *ghormeh sabzi* either, indeed, who never cooked at all, but sent their daughters as well as their sons to college and insisted they get good jobs. But I stuck to my position. The Iranian women I knew were among the strongest, toughest, most inventive women I have ever met. How could an open-minded cleric like Khatami still think of women as the keepers of the hearth? Then something my friend Farideh Farhi, Fereshteh's sister, said made sense. "You don't understand something about Iranian culture. We take our food and our language very seriously. They are the most important components of Iranian identity." Language and food. That made sense. As someone who took my Italian identity very seriously, I could relate to that. And I realized how once again I had seen only one facet of the mirror.

Khatami's charm does a lot to explain his popular appeal. But it isn't always enough to prevail. The main impediment to his success may be the Islamic system itself. The President is one player among many, and in his executive role Khatami is sometimes hampered by the powers the system assigns to others. Chief among them is Ayatollah Khamenei, with whom Khatami has an extraordinarily complex relationship.

The two men have a lot in common. Both are clerics, only a few years apart in age. Both are committed to upholding the powers of the Supreme Leader and the Islamic Republic. Both are men of ideas and claim descent from the Prophet. In addition, clerical families in Iran are like a private club, and the Khamenei and Khatami families have been close. Khamenei, as a teenage student of religion in the holy city of Mashad, was a devoted disciple of Khatami's father. Khamenei later made special trips to Ardakan to visit Khatami and his relatives, who in turn stayed with the Khameneis when they traveled to Mashad on pilgrimages.

But Ayatollah Khamenei, the son and grandson of clerics, is not a fun-loving sort. Or perhaps his position prevents him from loosening up. One of his most famous religious rulings as Iran's Supreme Leader was to ban music lessons—this despite his own experience early in his career in Mashad, where he wrote poetry, appreciated painting, played the stringed *tar,* and sang.

Khamenei has expressed views on all sorts of subjects. For example, *Sobh,* a radical right monthly magazine, once published his answers to a list of twenty-nine questions on social morality. He never said that his answers were fatwas, or official religious decrees, but others treated them as if they were. A sampling:

What color clothing may women wear? "Women should avoid colors that attract attention."

May women wear makeup? "It is permissible to wear makeup but women must cover their makeup in the presence of men who are not close relatives."

May men shave? "Shaving a beard is forbidden, but trimming it is allowed."

May women ride bicycles or motorcycles? "Women riding bicycles or motorcycles would spread corruption and so it is banned."

But in the competitive world of Iranian politics, even Ayatollah Khamenei cannot always muster full obedience. A religious leader in Iran is judged by the sagacity of his writings and the approbation of his peers. By these criteria, Khamenei has fallen short in the eyes of many. He was not even an ayatollah when Khomeini died, although he was quickly given the title when he was promoted to Supreme Leader. From the start, he was out of his depth. He had been President from 1981 to 1989 but lacked the religious credentials, the intellect, and the fire of Khomeini.

Still, Khamenei had golden revolutionary credentials. According to some reports, he was one of the original band of young theology students in Qom who first rallied to Ayatollah Khomeini's call for religious revolution in the 1960s. He became a loyal confidant of Khomeini, leading the movement against the Shah in Mashad and helping to organize secret cells. He spent three years in prison and one year in internal exile. He was tortured; his beard was shaved and his turban removed to humiliate him. Ironically, it was pressure from President Jimmy Carter that forced the Shah to free Khamenei in the late 1970s. One of his strongest supporters was Khatami's father.

After Khomeini's return to Iran, Khamenei was appointed the first head of the Revolutionary Guards, the military force initially envisioned as an alternative to the regular army. He wrote press releases and gathered intelligence on plots against the new regime. He became a member of the secret Revolutionary Council that governed Iran immediately after the monarchy was toppled. In 1980, he became Friday prayer leader in Tehran, in effect becoming the capital's spiritual guide. Throughout the war with Iraq, he chaired the Supreme Defense Council that determined war strategy. On June 27, 1981, he was giving a fiery speech at the Abuzar mosque near Tehran's vast bazaar when a bomb hidden inside a tape recorder exploded, costing him the use of his right hand. He has been in pain ever since. But he recovered enough to be elected President later that year and held that position until Khomeini's death.

When I interviewed Khamenei in 1982, he said that no one man could ever replace Khomeini as Supreme Leader, predicting that instead a council of three or five religious leaders would have to rule. He certainly didn't portray himself as a candidate for the job. Indeed, in a rare unguarded conversation just months before Khomeini's death, Khamenei confided to a foreigner, "I'm not qualified to be Supreme Leader. It's not the proper place for me."

But the group of clerics whose role was to choose a successor to Khomeini thought differently. The stability of the Islamic Republic was more important than charm or brilliant religious thinking, and so sixty out of its seventy-four members voted for Khamenei. He was a clear departure from the inventive and improvisational Khomeini. Still, Iran remained what it was: a vastly complicated, subtle, and challenging society no matter who was in charge.

During celebrations in February 1999 for the twentieth anniversary of the revolution, Khamenei's aides acknowledged as much when they pointed out how his image had softened. He hosted a meeting with athletes and actors. He publicly discussed his passion for soccer and how he had stayed up late to watch Iran beat the United States in a World Cup match the previous June. He was shown in television footage strolling in a flower-filled garden, smiling. In the background soft music played. The man who had once studied music and then banned music was now using music to try to get the people to like him.

But it was easy to see that these exercises in public relations were really a result of Khatami's challenge to Khamenei's authority. In the battle over the shape of the Islamic Republic in the twenty-first century, Khatami had come to represent those forces who believe that lively public discourse will open up the political system and that cultural isolation is neither possible nor desirable. Khamenei—at least in his public pronouncements—represented those who want to keep the country Islamically pure, walled off from the West.

Their differences were on display in their public statements. More than once, Khatami attacked the state of Israel as a "racist Zionist regime," but suggested that Iran would not impose on the Palestinians its own views about a peace settlement. Khamenei seized every opportunity to condemn the state of Israel and rail against the Middle East peace process and the Palestinians for signing a peace agreement. Khatami wanted to find ways to forge a positive relationship with the American people, if not necessarily with the American government; Khamenei reflexively condemned the United States, calling those who seek a rapprochement "simpletons and traitors."

The reality was that despite their differences, the two clerics needed each other if Iran's fluid political system was to function. Khamenei had power on paper—and the keys to the security apparatus—but Khatami had the support of the people. They didn't openly attack each other, for that would have undercut the myth of the unity of the ruling elite. And their relationship was flexible as well, for each was mindful that their views could change with political circumstances. At times, they seemed to work together, one pursuing the cause of reform and the other struggling to prevent factional conflicts from spinning out of control.

Their peculiarly symbiotic relationship was on clear display when Khatami gave an interview to CNN in January 1998 in which he expressed his desire to break down "the wall of mistrust" with the United States through cultural exchanges. Nine days later, Khamenei branded the United States "the enemy of the Iranian nation" and "the Great Satan," but pointedly referred to Khatami as the "respected President" and dismissed their differences as "a tone of speech and difference of taste."

Khamenei's praise for the President on a personal level quieted those conservatives who charged that Khatami was undermining the achievements of the revolution. But his diatribe against the United States reinforced the mind-set in the Clinton administration that Iran's leadership was not yet united or predictable enough to modify its hostile attitude toward the United States. So much for Khatami's larger goal of predictability, rationality, and accountability.

However much Khamenei and conservatives stand in Khatami's way, though, I have become convinced that the real challenge to Khatami's rule and the reform movement in Iran is only partly political. I saw that one morning in Yazd. Khatami stood before four hundred clerics, teachers, *bazaari*, politicians, disabled war veterans, and professionals. He preached a radical message—tolerance. "The majority does not have the right to act like dictators," he said. "The minority must have the right to express its opinion as well."

A woman in a chador leaned over and whispered to me—in English, "He is making a counterrevolution. It's about time."

But outside the hall, as I waited with the Iranian press corps for our bus to leave, an elderly woman came up to our group to ask what all the commotion was about. When we told her who we were, she screamed at us. "Write about poverty!" she said. "Tell the President how poor the people are. He doesn't know." She thrust a plastic bag holding a kilo of potatoes into my face and said, "I paid eight hundred for this little bag. Last year they cost only four hundred." She pinched the potatoes for me to see for myself. "Look how small they are," she said. "Tell *that* to the President."

The two speeches—by Khatami and by the woman with the potatoes—captured for me the main lines of debate in Iran at the turn of the century. The first was part of the intense, often angry debate about the rule of law and the creation of civil society, that is to say, what the Islamic Republic will look like in the future. The second represented a much more universal and fundamental dialogue: "How do I feed my kids?" It is a question that still begs for an answer in Iran, whether it is asked of Khamenei or Khatami.

I sometimes wondered whether Khatami would end up like Mehdi Bazargan, the revolution's first Prime Minister. Khomeini criticized Bazargan for being too weak, when he really was too much a believer in the rule of law. "It has been my role to be a liaison between modern culture and social science on the one hand and tradition and Islamic belief on the other," Bazargan had told me on a bus the day of Khomeini's return to Iran. "We will be guided by tolerance, freedom, equality, and justice."

But then I thought of the differences. Bazargan was a transitional figure, a fervent opponent of the Shah who came into power not through the will of the people but through the will of Khomeini. He had no organization behind him during a period of chaos and terror after the revolution. Khatami came to power with the support of powerful factions from different ends of the political spectrum and, more important, the mandate of the people at a time when revolutionary fervor had waned.

Perhaps it was more to the point to wonder if Khatami should be compared to Mikhail Gorbachev and Boris Yeltsin, who believed that if Russians got a freer political system, economic prosperity would naturally follow. The woman with the small potatoes probably knew little about global economics. But her rant suggested that there were Iranians who would settle for a China-style solution instead: fix the economy first and let political liberty take care of itself later on—if ever.

There are, of course, enormous differences between the unfolding evolutions of Russia and China and the process now playing out in Iran.

But all three have now had to face the question of how to make ideologically driven societies practical enough to feed their people and free enough to satisfy individual yearnings for liberty.

In finding his own answer to that question, Khatami became convinced that for much of the country the Islamic Republic had lost its legitimacy. He believed that transparency in the political system was the key to curbing corruption and promoting economic growth. If only he could create a tolerant civil society governed by the rule of law, the system would prosper and endure.

But was he steering fast enough? The Iranians who voted for Khatami wanted a new kind of leader; but they wanted jobs too. Two decades earlier, many of them had made a revolution not only in the name of Islam, but for the cause of improving their lives, and those of their children. And they were tired of waiting.

PART TWO

Private Lives,
Women's Lives

CHAPTER FIVE

Leaving the Islamic Republic at the Door

There was a Door to which I found no Key,
There was a Veil past which I might not see . . .

— *RUBÁIYÁT* OF OMAR KHAYYAM, TWELFTH-CENTURY
PERSIAN POET

We used to drink in public and pray in private. Now we pray in public and
drink in private.

— POPULAR JOKE IN TEHRAN

"Y EK! DO! SEH! *Chahar! Panj! Yek! Do! Seh! Chahar! Panj!*"
The teacher barked out the numbers in Persian. The women were out of formation, and she was determined to drum some discipline into them before she dismissed them for the day. No, this was not basic training. It was an aerobics class in a private home in north Tehran.

In fact, it felt far more comfortable in that room than outside in the street, where the rules about what a woman could do were different. Here, as in many other private spaces in Iran, was a safe, legal place where women could literally strip off their Islamic dress, be themselves, admonish each other, and laugh together without the prying eyes or standards of the morals police.

Private space is one of the true wonders of Iranian society, but one of the hardest for an outsider to figure out. There is a range of refuges from the theocracy's strict rules, from private homes to private salons and clubs to semipublic facilities set aside for women or men—or even to remote bits of the outdoors where the morals police just don't go. The availability of these refuges is one of the reasons the Islamic Republic endures.

There are not enough of these refuges, and the ones that exist are invaded from time to time by the state. But because of them, ordinary Iranians need not feel oppressed all the time. Personal expression, it turns out, is entirely possible in Iran. You just have to be careful when and where you engage in it, and you have to be ready for nasty surprises when the rules change. So seeking out and defining the refuge of private space has become one of the necessary skills of life in Islamic Iran.

The aerobics studio is a good case in point. More than a dozen leotard-clad women lay on black mats spread out on the hardwood floor. They panted and sweated to the beat of dance music sung by an Iranian expatriate, whose music was banned in Iran and who was living and working in Los Angeles. The cassette tape had been smuggled into Iran, along with the latest pirated videos of American films. The aerobics drillmaster was Ladan, a twenty-two-year-old former gymnast whose long brown curly hair streamed down her back. The ninety-minute workout was rigorous, even by American standards. When it was over, all the women let out a long, loud collective whoop acknowledging their hard work.

Two years before, Maryam and Mina, two sisters in their forties, had pooled several thousand dollars of their savings, gutted part of the vast walled house they shared, and built a state-of-the-art aerobics studio. They installed ballet barres, ceiling-to-floor mirrors, lockers, and a sound system, and bought Iranian-made stationary bicycles, treadmills, and other exercise machines. A license from the Ministry of Health authorized them to engage in bodybuilding, aerobics, and yoga classes. Government inspectors made periodic visits to ensure that the premises were safe and that nothing that could be construed as un-Islamic was going on.

"We decided when we turned forty that we wanted to do something for our country and something for ourselves," said Maryam, a twice-divorced painter and mother of two. She and her sister rejected the idea of opening an art gallery not only because they thought the bribes to city authorities would have been too high, but also because an art gallery would have been a public space for both men and women in which women would have had to keep their heads and bodies covered. "Ours had to be a fun project that would help other women and not violate the Islamic codes," said Maryam. "This is what we came up with."

What they built is not only a place of exercise, but also a place of repose, decorated with huge bouquets of purple iris and yellow daffodils. There is a separate space for weight training and nutritional analysis and a tiny kitchen in which to make tea. On the day I visited, a platter of chocolate-covered creampuffs was laid out to celebrate a client's birthday.

Mina, who is two years younger than her sister, told me how depression has spread like a contagious disease among her generation. "When I turned forty, the sadness that came was a passing thing," she said. "But for some women the depression stays. A lot of my friends say, 'I wasted my youth raising kids and now I'm worth nothing.' There are so few places for women to go to meet other women. I can't move heaven and earth. But I can do this."

At the end of the class, Ladan, the instructor, said she would dance for me. Technically, dancing is prohibited in the studio. The authorities have given permission for athletic exercise, which is considered healthy therapy; not dancing, which is entertainment.

Ladan was dressed in a low-cut belly shirt, tight red and white paisley pedal pushers, big gold hoop earrings, and athletic shoes. But the dance she chose was pure Persian. She turned down the lights and put on the sinuous music. She thrust out her small breasts, revealing her slightly rounded belly and her navel, threw back her head, and put her arms over her head. She parted her wide lips in what I can only describe as an orgasmic smile. Then she moved, swaying and undulating her way around the room. She outlined the curves of her body with her hands and beckoned the audience to her.

It was a moment of sheer sensuality like others I have been invited to see from time to time in Iran. Men can be wonderfully erotic when they show their skills in traditional dances that have survived, despite the Islamic Republic. But for women, there is an additional dimension of freedom. So much of a woman's body is covered in public, so much is forbidden and repressed, that when the veil falls, even for a moment, there is a heightened sense of excitement. The women whistled through their teeth and hooted at Ladan as if she were a male stripper. Then, when the music stopped, Ladan and the other women put on their head scarves and the coats they call *roupoush* (outerwear) and left their refuge for the public space of the street.

This is how the Islamic Republic survives, and how its citizens survive in it. Inside coexists with outside. Private with public. Freedom with restrictions. The Islamic Republic can be left at the door—up to a point.

Iranians can adhere to perfect Islamic codes of behavior on the outside and yet behave much differently when the doors are locked and the drapes are drawn. But it isn't quite so simple in practice. The limits of behavior are complicated because the rules are often nonexistent or changing or left open to interpretation. Iranians can therefore live in violation of what they think the rules say and get away with it most of the time. But they have to be prepared to pay the price when the state suddenly decides not to look the other way. So there are intrusions, and there is no pattern to them.

As a reporter, and as a visitor, I find myself fascinated and confused by the distinction between public and private life that Iranians have learned to make. Sometimes, even today, I can't keep the two straight. For me, private space can mean any space where I can take off my head scarf and relax, but even that is not a precise definition. Given the constant fear of intrusion, I have been amazed to see how people manage to lead what has looked to me like normal lives behind closed doors, even though their behavior clearly violates the moral standards set by the state. Watching the way Iranians cross back and forth between private and public behavior has made it even harder for me to figure out where the lines are. Over the years, I have tried to define a number of spaces that offer varying degrees of protection and escape. But it isn't easy.

Take, for example, the time friends invited me to tag along to a wedding reception in a large villa with a swimming pool and a beautifully landscaped garden. There were two hundred guests and mountains of food. Vodka, wine, and beer were being served in silver pitchers placed haphazardly on end tables, both to conceal the fact that they contained alcohol and to make it easier to dump the contents into the rosebushes should the morals police show up.

About ninety minutes into the party, I saw several shabbily dressed bearded men wandering among the guests. Without warning, they announced a threat to arrest everyone for immorality. The women ran for their head scarves and coats. Some of them rushed a coat rack that fell on top of me. Most of the guests took their belongings and left quickly. Members of the rock band threw their instruments and then themselves over the wall to the neighbor's garden. The remaining guests took refuge in the house.

Rumors spread quickly: the bride's father hadn't paid enough in advance to the Komiteh, the neighborhood morals police, to ensure that the party would be undisturbed; the music was too loud and had attracted attention. The father argued with the intruders. He persuaded them to take him to jail but to leave the guests alone and let the party continue. He would later be put on trial and forced to pay a stiff fine.

At first, the bridal couple sat dazed on their thronelike chairs. They seemed not to notice that their guests were leaving and that the mountains of food were left untouched. Then suddenly, the bride and groom disappeared as well. The story spread that they were too hurt and humiliated to say goodbye to their guests. But the groom's younger brother was unfazed. A party was a party. After the Komiteh left, he persuaded the band to come back. He and about a dozen friends danced throughout the night.

Anyone can feel the tension between publicly banned and privately allowable behavior in this story. But to try to draw a coherent lesson about where that line is—what is permitted and what will be punished—is to invite frustration.

The roots of the distinction between the public and private are found in both Iranian and Islamic culture, in which inner spaces of human privacy and choice are supposed to be inviolable. The Koran clearly states, "There is no compulsion in matters of faith." The sanctity of private space also builds on something even older: the home. As in many societies, the Iranian home is supposed to be a sanctuary immune from intruders. But historically there is more: an Iranian home had two parts, exterior public rooms that were furnished simply and belonged to the men, and interior private rooms that were decorated with the good carpets and ornaments and belonged to the women. Men had a role in public; women ran the private space. This division of labor coincided with the idea that women were to be enjoyed by their men only in private, and that public life was for men. So the women needed a sphere of life to operate and control.

Even today, Iranian social life is rooted in the family and the home. In fact, it is more so now than before the revolution, because so much of what used to be considered normal social intercourse is forbidden in public. Friday, the Muslim day of prayer, is also a day to visit family members—at home. Unlike most places in the Middle East, where men go out with one another on weekend nights, men in Iran are expected to take out their families. Nazila and I were once driving along a main street in Shiraz at about 11:00 P.M. When we saw hundreds of families picnicking—in parks, in squares, on the median strips—I asked Nazila what the occasion was. "It's Thursday night, of course!" she said. Of course. Thursday is the equivalent of Saturday in the West.

For many Iranians, family ties, which have always been strong, unraveled after the revolution as breadwinners were forced to emigrate to distant places in search of work. But for others, family ties became stronger, as parents and grown children were forced by economic circumstances to live in the same apartment, or at least nearby, in order to pool resources and share chores. There is a political side to this too. People who were considered enemies or even suspect by the revolution took refuge not with friends but with family.

In principle, the Islamic Republic observes the sanctity of the home. Article 22 of the Constitution clearly protects the "reputation, life, rights, homes, and jobs" of individuals from outside invasion. Ayatollah Khomeini reminded government employees of this dictum early in the revolution. "If you by mistake and error enter a personal house or personal place of work of somebody, and there you are faced with weapons or tools of corruption or other deviant material such as drugs, you do not have the right to disclose this information to others," he said. "And you do not have the right to arrest or beat the house residents and owner, for this is going beyond God's bounds."

But actual practice is a different matter. The home is protected from outside invasion under the Constitution only if laws are not broken. The Islamic Republic routinely violates private spaces if there are suspicions of drinking, dancing, or gatherings of unrelated men and women. Much of this intrusiveness stems less from Islamic purity than from greed: the low-level police and self-appointed cultural vigilantes who patrol the streets and knock on doors usually are willing to resolve the matter with a payoff rather than an arrest.

That makes the intrusions into private space all the more shocking, because they suggest that the Islamic Republic and people operating in its name do not take the rules they have written seriously. And that is why, in July 1999, there was universal condemnation of vigilantes and security police who invaded a University of Tehran dormitory and beat up students, demolished property, and stole the students' possessions after the students began protests against censorship. Still, even if the clerics disapprove of the vigilantes' behavior, they don't punish it severely, and that allows it to continue.

One of the unexpected beneficiaries of the restrictions on public behavior is the takeout restaurant. Something as simple as going on a date to a movie or a public park can be risky. So many people just stay home at night. Those who can afford it order takeout and watch pirated videos of American films or foreign television programs beamed in on illegal satellite dishes.

Billing and cooing isn't the only thing Iranians feel free to do in the privacy of their homes. The home protects those who give the outward appearance of being part of the Islamic system, but behave differently—some would say hypocritically—indoors. A friend who lives in an apartment has a bearded neighbor who works for the government and whose family is extremely religious. The apartment had been confiscated years before from one of the Shah's bureaucrats and was given rent-free to the new tenants, presumably because of their piety. Yet the husband can be heard late at night cursing Khomeini. The family plays the banned music of Googoosh, a wildly popular Iranian female singer at the time of the Shah. The daughter takes piano lessons. And the family has never returned the videos of American movies it borrowed from my friend.

In all this talk of refuges from the intrusiveness of the morals police, I should make one thing clear: one of the reasons Iranians still manage to do what their government doesn't want them to do in their private lives has to do with the nature of the government itself. When it comes to using the citizenry to inform on its neighbors, Iran is not like the former Soviet Union or Saddam Hussein's Iraq or Mao's China. Certainly, the Islamic state has tried to stamp out moral infractions and has employed cadres of vigilantes. But the Islamic Republic is not very organized or centralized. It is a collection of fiefs rather than a monolithic state. It generally has not forced its average citizens to inform on relatives and neighbors. It never developed a sophisticated system of rewards and punishments to promote reporting.

There is also something about Iranian culture that makes circumventing the government easier to condone. Culturally, Iranians don't like to snitch. Sure, they snitch if they see an advantage to it, but centuries of dealing with authoritarian rule have contributed to a deep distrust of authority. Many Iranians observe a code of silence rather than turn in neighbors who break the rules. In the battle between a duplicitous system based on unreasonable state rules and a resourceful people intent on living the way they have always done, the people have the upper hand.

I used to think that the safest refuges in Iran were the homes of diplomats who enjoy immunity under international agreements. But the Islamic state intrudes even into these private spaces, from time to time. This is, after all, the country that seized the American embassy.

And there was the Gust affair. In 1996 a dozen security police from the Intelligence Ministry burst into a dinner party for six prominent Iranian writers and intellectuals hosted by Jens Gust, the German embassy's cultural and press attaché. The young diplomat was not allowed to call his embassy; the guests were interrogated and jailed for the night. The police videotaped the scene: Iranian women with their heads uncovered and bottles of alcohol that had been served. An Iranian female friend was heartsick that the government now had ammunition to use against her.

So much for diplomatic immunity.

Iran's Foreign Ministry apologized afterward to the Germans, but that must have been cold comfort for Gust. He was reprimanded by his ambassador, then temporarily reassigned to Bonn. He never came back.

I thought of the Gust affair when, months later, I was dining at the home of a young male diplomat and he invited me and another guest to swim in the enormous pool on the property. It was a brutally hot evening, and a tempting offer. Then I wrote the headline in my head: "American Journalist Arrested for Immoral Behavior." I thanked my host for his hospitality and left him and his friend to swim without me.

Other diplomats have been more insistent about swimming. One ambassador liked to meet his guests at the door in his swimming trunks and take them immediately to the swimming pool. It was the one place he felt he could talk openly, for he suspected that his house was bugged. But it was not long before even the pool in his private garden was compromised. A high-rise apartment building was going up nearby, and the high floors offered an unimpeded view of the pool. One day when the ambassador's nephew invited some young Iranian friends to swim, the construction workers from the apartment building stoned them with building blocks.

Despite the intrusions, I have met many people who have transformed rooms of their private homes into creative spaces. One is Shahrzad Hajmoshir, a clothing designer, artist, and antiques dealer who was divorced in the early years of the revolution and then opened her home for business. Today, from her house on a winding dirt road in the hills north of Tehran, she collects authentic brightly colored tribal costumes that she restores and sells. If the garments are too torn to restore, she salvages the good pieces and uses them in original creations.

Hajmoshir's home is an oasis to which I have escaped from time to time. She serves tea made from grated quince in cranberry-colored glasses as incense burns. Just about everything in her house is for sale—the samovars, the two-hundred-year-old doors, the Turkmen hats, the Qajar embroideries.

But the clothing and art businesses aren't enough. Hajmoshir also has turned herself into a yoga instructor and gives private lessons. Yoga has given her the spiritual peace to overcome the frustrations and the limitations she endures in the Islamic Republic. Like many other women who have discovered peace in their private spaces, she has never thought seriously of leaving the country she loves. "I love being with original things and I find myself here," she said. "If you find yourself, you can be happy where you are. Life passes. Your children grow up and leave. But I am Iranian. I love my country. Where else would I want to go?"

Hajmoshir's one act of defiance is that she walks on her land bare-headed. I asked her if she is afraid that someone will see her. "This is my property, my space," she told me. "No one from the outside has the right to invade it or look at me. If you feel harmony in life, everything is in balance. I'm close to the sky and the land. Why should I be afraid?"

Unafraid and innovative are perhaps the best ways to describe how Iranians—particularly women—have expanded the meaning of home. Another such woman is the beautiful blond singer Pari Zangeneh, who has turned her home into an auditorium. Zangeneh was one of the most popular folksingers in Iran before the revolution. She hid behind big sunglasses, having lost her sight in a car accident. Nowadays, if she can't perform unveiled in public spaces or in mixed company, why not do it for women in her living room?

When the revolution came, many Iranian singers were denounced as corrupt and "Westoxicated." Some of the best fled the country. But Zangeneh's music didn't die and she didn't move away. Over the years, she used her villa in north Tehran to give private singing lessons and to perform.

Then, quietly and unexpectedly, Zangeneh was granted official permission by the Ministry of Islamic Guidance to expand her space and perform in concert. Women lined up for hours to buy tickets. Scalpers sold them for ten times the official price. One night, a hundred women gathered behind the closed doors of a small theater hall in central Tehran to hear her. No men were allowed. The sound of her voice might be too arousing. (Indeed, an American male friend of mine who had heard her sing before the revolution told me, "She can lead men to dreams.")

Zangeneh brazenly took off her head scarf and coat. Her blond hair was piled high on her head; she wore an elegant black suit. She sang old familiar songs for her fans, songs filled with love and longing, not religion. "I want to go hunting, hunting deer," she sang. "Where is my gun? Where is my gun, my beloved Leili?" She encouraged the audience to clap, a gesture rejected by some clerics as an effete import from the West.

I heard about the concert and went calling on Zangeneh shortly after. I sat sipping coffee served by a manservant as I waited for her in a library filled with sunlight that she could not see. A Norma Desmond–like character, she made her entrance in a long black robe and gold backless sandals, led into the room by a female aide. She seemed desperate to hold on to the past, and asked me if I found her beautiful.

"Every night for eighteen years people wanted me to perform," she said. "It happened last week. I stood on my feet and sang for four hours. The crowd was overwhelming. Everyone said I looked the same. I felt no distance from the past. And I felt the future."

In Zangeneh's case, the rule-breaking within the confines of the home had begun to pay off. In other cases, it has not, and never will. Probably the rule that Iranians break more than any other at home involves consumption of alcohol. It is the Koran that bans Muslims from drinking wine and gambling. "Avoid them," one verse says, "so that you may prosper. Satan seeks to stir up enmity and hatred among you by means of wine and gambling, and to keep you from the remembrance of God and from your prayers."

But Iran in fact is a wine-making country, perhaps the oldest in the Middle East. Some of the most beautiful paintings in the palace show long-haired maidens pouring wine from jugs. Persian poetry is infused with praise for wine. Hafiz wrote about it in the fourteenth century, and today even clerics still recite the poems, in their case insisting that Hafiz's "wine" is not an alcoholic drink that causes intoxication but a divine experience that causes mystical rapture. A typical poem goes like this:

O cup-bearer, set my glass afire
With the light of wine! O minstrel, sing:
The world fulfilleth my heart's desire
Reflected within the goblet's ring
I see the glow of my love's red cheek,
And scant of wit, ye who fail to seek
The pleasures that wine alone can bring!

Wine-making didn't stop with the revolution; neither did drinking. There are just too many good grapes grown in Iran. Alcohol simply has gone underground. A huge industry in homemade wine, vodka, and beer has sprung up. Scotch of indeterminate origin, often with counterfeit labels, is smuggled in from Turkey and Dubai. As long as they do so quietly, non-Muslims are allowed to make alcohol for religious services and personal consumption. One of my heavy-drinking Iranian friends told me a joke as he poured me a drink that I really did not want. "Islam promised to teach us self-sufficiency," he said. "We succeeded. We became self-sufficient in producing alcohol."

I've been told by Iranians who used to live in the United States that their drinking actually increased dramatically after they moved back home. "I didn't drink before the revolution," a friend told me after dinner one night at his home in Hamadan, as he poured me a glass of his homemade mulberry schnapps. A retired engineer, he spent his nights watching satellite television, playing cards with friends, and getting drunk. "I was the only one of four brothers who didn't drink."

"So why do you drink?" I asked.

"Khomeini drove me to drink," he said, laughing. Then he turned serious, adding, "It's the loneliness, the depression."

He escorted me into his front garden, to an area where no flowers grew. Under six inches of dirt were dozens of bottles of distilled alcohol that he had made. He took me to his basement; it looked like a three-room chemistry lab. One room had huge vats for making vodka, which could be flavored with berries, apricots, cherries, pears, or plums. In another room he made wine.

He didn't sell the liquor he made. And even though he drank, he didn't drink very much and probably would not have fit the American definition of a heavy drinker. His problem was that he had too much time on his hands. Making and bottling drinks has become his hobby. His next project, he explained, would be beer. It would be difficult to store but easy to make in his big cellar: take a big bucket, mix nonalcoholic beer with sugar and yeast, and after a week bottle it. A month later it would be ready.

For women, one of the most important private spaces available is the beauty salon. I used to wonder why Iranian women bother to get their hair done, since they have to cover it up on the street. But they have their reasons. The first is that much of Iran's social life takes place behind closed doors and they want to look good around their family and intimate friends. The second is purely psychological. Just because women have to wear scarves doesn't mean they don't want to look and feel beautiful on the street. The third reason is that getting one's hair done regularly is not a luxury; it is an act of rebellion. It tells the authorities, you can make me cover my head but you can't stop me from becoming more beautiful. Khomeini once tried to ban all beauty parlors, labeling them "dens of corruption." In the end, all he accomplished was to put male hairdressers (and female barbers) out of business.

I have a favorite beauty salon in Tehran. It is simple, with fake flowers and worn furniture, but welcoming, with offerings of cookies, fresh fruit, and tea. The air is usually full of cigarette smoke (women, particularly married women, like to smoke in Iran). Customers begin lining up at eight in the morning and are often still crowding in at eight at night. The clients are mostly middle-class women struggling to simultaneously make ends meet and feel good. There is a small sign on the front window, but the curtains are drawn and the door is locked. You have to be buzzed in. No men are allowed. The salon is a legal establishment licensed and regularly inspected by Iran's Ministry of Health, but the owner, who has run the business since the mid-1970s, asked me not to write its name or exact neighborhood. Don't give outsiders an excuse to meddle, she said.

The salon offers haircuts, coloring, blow-dries; facials and massages and makeup treatment; manicures and pedicures; and every type of hair bleaching, tweezing, and wax removal imaginable, including for underarm and pubic hair. It takes about five hours to get a bride fully coiffed, painted, depilated, manicured, creamed, and perfumed. The cost is equivalent to almost two months of an average government worker's salary.

I never have seen so much attention paid to body hair as I have in Iran. Iranian women are known for their heavy mustaches and eyebrows, and religious women do not remove their facial hair before their wedding days. But for secular women, it is different. There is even a special system of removal of facial hair widely used throughout the Middle East in which a beautician uses a heavy sewing thread to remove the hair with friction against the face. Pain is part of the process. A Persian saying goes, "The pain of your upper lip is less than the pain of your mother-in-law's words." Another is, "Kill me, but make me beautiful." There are even jokes about facial hair. Question: "Why do men grow mustaches?" Answer: "To look more like their mothers."

I like the beauty salon because, like the aerobics studio, it is a space where women have permission to take off their head scarves and relax.

In a category all by themselves are the lingerie shops. These too are women-only refuges with drapes blocking the windows. And good lingerie is not cheap. One shop in a small shopping alley in north Tehran sells sets of silk and lace bras and bikini pants from England starting at $100. "Our best customers are the wives of the *bazaari*," said the saleswoman, as she looked up from her reading, Mario Puzo's *Fools Die*. "Even when they're fat. The *bazaari* women may cover themselves in black and show only one eye. But they spend a lot of money on jewelry and clothes. They do whatever they can to look sexy for their husbands."

The morals police once inspected a lingerie shop, hauled off the manager, and confiscated dozens of boxes of bras that showed a female model wearing one. But take away the display of a woman's body and something as intimate as a bra can be sold openly on the street. Every weekday outside the German embassy in the middle of Tehran stands a male street vendor who hawks cheap Iranian-made bras, punching the cups with his fist to prove how durable they are.

There are still other refuges in Iran that are run, paradoxically, by the government. The Hejab (Islamic Dress) Club, a huge state-run sports facility for women in the heart of Tehran, provides athletics for the Islamic masses. It is unlike the chic aerobics studio in north Tehran, but it is still a place where ordinary women can engage in athletics—in this case basketball, karate, squash, judo, fencing, tae kwon do, marksmanship, and field hockey—far from the gaze of men. The club also offers full-service medical examinations, even access to a psychotherapist. The cost is low, but still beyond the budget of many women.

Because it is government-run, there are strict rules. "You can't go inside dressed like that," a young, sour-faced woman in a black chador barked at me as she blocked my entry into the cavernous building one day. "Take off your lipstick and cover your head better."

Once inside, I found an enormous swimming pool in a suffocatingly overheated room that reeked of chlorine. In it, two hundred women ranging in age from fifteen to seventy-five and dressed in colorful bathing suits and caps took lessons and practiced their strokes. A dozen female lifeguards kept watch. No bikinis here, but a lot of body fat and see-through Lycra. (A young friend who turned up in a bikini was told that bikinis were too revealing and could contribute to lesbianism.) Other women used the club's sauna and whirlpool. "You see, the rumors that women wear black chadors to swim is not true," said Zahra Mousavi, the head of the club's swim team, dressed in a pink polo shirt and short-cropped denim shorts. It is only at public, mixed-sex beaches that women are required to swim with their heads and bodies covered. What surprised me even more, given the vigilance of the guard outside, is that some women casually walked around the locker rooms totally naked.

Men have their own swimming pools and sports clubs. Indeed, saunas are where guys go after work to unwind with their friends. Men have a much greater choice of clubs than women—from government-run militarylike clubs that give deep discounts to civil servants to the opulent Naranjestan Club, built of marble and travertine.

Iranians also find refuge in the great outdoors, especially in the three small mountains north of Tehran—Tochal, Darakeh, and Darband. The air is always cleaner and cooler there. Young couples, old couples, civil servants, diplomats, all use the mountains as a place of release, beyond the watchful eye of the Islamic Republic. On weekends the paths are clogged with people, but before sunrise and on weekday mornings they are nearly empty.

A young Iranian woman I know goes camping with a coed group of friends in mountains where the police do not go, deep in Mazandaran province near the Caspian Sea. For days, they sleep in tents and cook food over campfires. It is an act of both liberation and desperation. In reality, the mountains are not private at all, and if the campers were to be caught, they could be arrested, fined, and perhaps lashed. But the longing to feel free makes it worth the risk.

Although snitching is generally frowned upon in Iranian society, there is some nevertheless—haphazard and episodic. In some instances, this makes the possibility of betrayal particularly unsettling, if more remote. Iranians just don't know what to expect, or from whom to expect it. It doesn't happen very often, but parents can never predict when a teacher might ask their children whether their mother wears a chador, or whether their father drinks. And it can work the other way around—with teachers fearing that their young charges may inform on them. A young man who teaches religion in a public school told me that some of his preteen students worried openly that their fathers would go to hell because they didn't fast during Ramadan, as would their mothers because they didn't hide their hair at home in the company of men who were not close blood relatives. These boys were so open about their concerns they even questioned the teacher's piety. "One day I was wearing my gold wedding ring and the topic of that day in class was the appearance of men in public," he recalled. "The boys found a religious saying that told men not to wear gold and if they wear gold while they pray, their prayers are not heard. One boy asked me, 'Sir, why didn't you take off your gold ring for your prayers?' I had to come up with a cover story, so I said, 'My son, last night was my wedding anniversary and I wore my ring. But I forgot to take it off.' You see, we are forced to lie all the time."

The teacher's comment about lying echoes a theme that many Iranians find in the disconnect between public standards and private behavior. The lying, the compulsion to beat the system in the name of freedom, the insecurity that comes from not knowing when the state might intrude into a private space all create anger. The feeling is just under the surface, but it can explode unexpectedly.

I saw it while driving with a young married couple from the Caspian Sea to Tehran in a snowstorm late one night in the New Year season. Just a few days earlier, Ayatollah Mohammad Yazdi, then the conservative head of Iran's judiciary, had given a sermon warning the overzealous not to invade people's private spaces in the name of Islam. "No one can violate the people's personal sphere without a legal permit thus causing insecurity; this includes their homes, their cars, and their offices or places of business," he said.

But prices were high and petty corruption seemed worse than at any time since the revolution. The poorly paid security forces needed money for new clothing for their children for the New Year. Our car was stopped by three security officers in uniforms of indeterminate origin. They ordered an inspection of the car. We complied. Then they demanded proof of marriage from the couple with whom I was driving. The man was ready to show them their identity papers. But it was too much for his wife. Though normally serene, she just couldn't take it anymore. "You have no right to search our car!" she screamed at one of the guards. "Ayatollah Yazdi said it himself. Didn't you hear him?"

"Ayatollah Yazdi has no control over this road," the guard sneered. "Now show me your papers."

The husband handed over the papers. We were allowed to drive on. But the wife was still raging. "After all these years someone has to stop them!" she screamed at her husband. "Sheep! Sheep! My mother and her generation were like sheep, letting people like this come into our lives whenever they wanted. I won't be a sheep!"

CHAPTER SIX

Sir, Have You Ever Beaten Your Wife?

*Persian women since 1907 had become almost at a bound the most progres-
sive not to say radical in the world. That this statement upsets the ideas of
centuries makes no difference. It is the fact.*

> — MORGAN SHUSTER, THE AMERICAN FINANCIAL
> ADVISER TO THE IRANIAN GOVERNMENT IN THE
> EARLY TWENTIETH CENTURY

*Islam made women equal with men; in fact, it shows a concern for women
that it does not show for men.*

> — AYATOLLAH KHOMEINI, ADDRESSING WOMEN IN QOM
> ON MARCH 6, 1979

*Khatami is talking about the rule of law. Everyone is talking about the rule
of law. We will only have the rule of law in Iran on the day that women are
treated the same as men under the law.*

> — SHIRIN EBADI, HUMAN RIGHTS LAWYER AND THE
> FIRST FEMALE JUDGE DURING THE OLD REGIME

AZAM TALEGHANI is not a sheep.

A mother of four in her fifties, she is so traditionally Islamic that she
wears black on black—a black chador, with black hose and sensible black
shoes. She is an open, generous sort, with a sharp sense of humor and an
inability to be on time. Her bad back (and probably her being over-
weight) causes her to waddle slightly when she walks. Her passion is so
great that she can ramble on and on well past midnight, but she uses only
her right hand to gesture because her left keeps her chador firmly in place
under her chin. Once when I arrived at a conference in Cyprus minus my

suitcase she offered to lend me part of her wardrobe. "You look better in a scarf anyway," she said.

But Taleghani has both pedigree and name recognition. She is the daughter of the late Ayatollah Mahmoud Taleghani, who was one of the most celebrated and progressive clerics of the twentieth century and was almost as important as Ayatollah Khomeini in his day. Soon after the success of the revolution, Ayatollah Taleghani warned of a return to despotism, as he opposed the intrusion of the clergy into politics and Khomeini's vision of the all-powerful Supreme Leader. Massive demonstrations in Taleghani's name in Tehran shortly after the revolution threatened to plunge the country into chaos. Khomeini summoned Taleghani to Qom, and he emerged from their meeting a humbled man. I saw him on television, his face pale, his eyes studiously avoiding the camera, as he declared his unconditional loyalty to Khomeini. Afterward, Khomeini gloated that Taleghani was "sorry for what had happened." The demonstrations for Taleghani subsided and he kept quiet about politics until his death the following September. The official line was that he had died in his sleep. Some of his supporters claimed that the electricity and phone lines to his home had been cut on the night of his death and that he had been poisoned.

Azam Taleghani is not the silent type. Her father had taught her how to think—and to argue. "Women have many skills and potential for growth, but even they themselves don't realize their skills and their rights," he would tell her. Even though she first started wearing a chador when she was six, she threw it off in a fit of rebellion as a young woman, daring to go out in public unveiled. Years later, she reveled in recounting how she debated the issue with her father, who told her she had to make up her own mind. Eventually—years before the Islamic revolution—she made the choice to return to the veil. She also turned to politics. Her clandestine activities distributing literature against the monarchy landed her in prison for two years, and helped win her a seat in Parliament after the revolution, where she incurred the wrath of many clerics by speaking out against the stoning of women.

Now Taleghani earns money from a small clothing-making operation in Tehran, whose headquarters also serve as a classroom for a Koran-reading and -interpreting night school—for women only. For nearly twenty years she published an outspoken weekly newspaper called *Payam-e Hajar* that challenged the clerical—and patriarchal male—interpretation of Islam. From the moment I met Taleghani in her classroom one evening, I liked her. She was suffering from a dreadful cold, but obviously didn't believe in antihistamines or bed rest. So she coughed and wheezed and blew her nose loudly as her students stumbled through the dense Koran reading in Arabic, offering textual analysis in between. Even though it was late, she invited me to stay as she slurped down a medicinal soup of herbs. Her mission with her informal school, she explained, was simple: "to give women the intellectual tools to flourish in the Islamic Republic." She didn't like it at all that the brand-new seminary in Qom, Mofid University, had a student body of five hundred men and no women. That's why she had started training women herself.

Then, in 1997, she shook up the status quo even more. She tried to run for President.

"I didn't want to become President," Taleghani confessed that evening. "I didn't have any claim on the job. What I wanted to do was seize an opportunity, to crystallize the issue in the mind of the nation."

Taleghani is one of the new power women of Iran—a small, elite group with impeccable Islamic credentials, loyal daughters of the revolution who have entered the fluid, treacherous battlefield of Iranian politics to negotiate ever so carefully for change. Fearless, she had been repeatedly threatened by vigilantes loyal to the conservative clerics. But when she decided to run for President, Iran's clerics had no choice but to take her seriously.

The role of women has always been one of the most vexing issues for the Islamic Republic. Just as race is the great problem for American democracy, gender is the fault line of the Islamic world, as women struggle at different stages and at different speeds both to push beyond the confines of the veil and to use the veil to enter the public domain.

Given the harsh treatment of women in much of the Islamic world, it is understandable that Iran's clerics would seek to rehabilitate their country's image around the world by celebrating the centrality of their women. Women make up 25 percent of Iran's labor force and half of the university population. They drive their own cars, buy and sell their own property, and run their own businesses. They keep their own names at marriage. The roots of these rights date from the constitutional movement of the early twentieth century, when women began to demand

more rights, and later from the rule of Reza Shah, who expanded education and employment opportunities for women.

Most important, women vote in elections and hold political office. In
1999, when Iran held the first town council elections since the revolution,
some Iranians told me that they voted for certain candidates simply because they were women. (In the city of Qazvin, eighty miles from Tehran,
for example, a 25-year-old woman came in first.) But women in political
life have a long way to go. In 2000, a smaller percentage of women were
elected to Iran's 290-seat Parliament than had been four years before, and
women have yet to enjoy a significant presence in the decision-making
circles of government.

Unlike many other Islamic countries, Iran has an active family planning program, and birth control is widely available. Women are out on
the streets early and late; they catch buses and communal taxis to school
and work at 6:00 A.M., and they shop for food at 3:00 A.M. in twenty-
four-hour supermarkets. In countries like Saudi Arabia and Kuwait, most
of these rights are denied to women.

Despite the Western perception of Iranian women as backward and
oppressed, Azam Taleghani and others like her are very much of the
modern political world. The declaration of Taleghani's candidacy forced
a serious debate on a key provision of Iran's Constitution, which said that
only a *rajol*—a respected person of consequence—could run. In Arabic,
the word is masculine, but Taleghani argued that in Persian its meaning is
not so clear. So Taleghani went knocking on the doors of religious scholars in Tehran and Qom who had been drafters of the 1979 Constitution,
seeking opinions on whether she might be considered a *rajol*. They debated for hours over endless cups of tea. Eventually, she came to her own
conclusion: she was, indeed, a *rajol*.

"Some of the clerics said that women absolutely could not become
President," she told me. "But one ayatollah said that men and women,
and, I'm sorry, even hermaphrodites could become President."

Some ayatollahs argued that in theory women could become judges,
clerics, or even Supreme Leader, but that the presidency was different.
Others, claiming ignorance, said they could only set aside the matter for
later. One ayatollah declared that women should be invisible from public
life altogether. "Word got around Qom that Miss Taleghani, the daughter
of the late Ayatollah Mahmoud Taleghani, was asking these questions,"
she said. "While I was at the home of one ayatollah, the phone rang. It

was another cleric who said, 'Please tell her the word *rajol* means man and only man.' That proved I had caused quite a stir!"

When one ayatollah said that such a high-level, high-pressure job "destroys women and puts too much pressure on their nerves," that was too much for Taleghani. As a young mother, she had spent time in the Shah's prisons and even now remains the primary caregiver for one of her children, who is severely disabled. "I pointed out that running a household, earning a living, and raising children is not exactly an easy job," she said.

In the end, the Guardian Council disqualified Taleghani from running, as it disqualified most of the potential presidential candidates. Still, she looked on the exercise as a success. "I was told I wasn't a religious and political personality and that was why I couldn't run for President," she said. "But it was a victory. I was not disqualified because I was a woman. That proves that a woman can run for President."

Her battle was not over. She tried to run for Parliament in the 2000 elections—as she had tried every election cycle since her first term in Parliament—but was again rejected by the Guardian Council. The assumption was that her rejection was not because of gender but because of her long affiliation with the Freedom Movement co-founded by her father to oppose the monarchy half a century ago. Despite the expansion of Iran's political landscape, members of the movement were banned from running for public office.

When I first came to Iran, black-clad women like Azam Taleghani all seemed the same: scary, unsmiling servants of the ayatollahs. Monireh Gorji, the only woman in the Assembly of Experts that wrote the Constitution in the summer of 1979, was a model revolutionary woman. She told Iranian women that their freedom would come only through Islamic law. "I am the slave of God," she mumbled from behind the black garment that hid even her chin and mouth.

But over the years, I have come to realize that a sustained and creative ideological war is being waged by Iranian women, whether they wear black chadors or Western dress topped with a small kerchief. I also have realized that I have something in common even with the sour-faced women who bodily frisk me at airports and the entrances to government buildings. We are all working women, many of us working mothers. So I smile at them and ask about the health of their families; I shake their hands; I show them pictures of my kids. Eventually they start smiling back. Their battles mirror the battles of women everywhere: to balance their public and private lives and attain a better quality of life for themselves and their children.

As sweeping as it was, the revolution did not wipe out the Westernized, secularized society built up by the Shah, in which women had begun to play an important role. Many secular professional women fled the country; many others lost their power and jobs; some even lost their lives. But many stayed behind. They had fought for more equality and legal rights and they were not about to relinquish their hard-won gains. They forged an uneasy peace with the new rulers, continuing to function as doctors, lawyers, academics, writers, and businesswomen.

The rights enjoyed by the professional, Western-educated female elite of Tehran under the Old Regime might not have meant much to the majority of lower-class religious women who had never stopped wearing the veil. But many of these women came into the public sphere through another avenue: the revolution. Ayatollah Khomeini, in an act that illustrates just how complex his tactics were, chose to politicize these women. In the early days, he encouraged them to leave the confines of their homes and take to the streets—with or without the permission of their husbands and fathers. And so they did, by the thousands, putting on their black chadors to confront the Shah's army. They were joined by many secular women who demonstrated against the Shah's dictatorship. When it was over, both groups of women expected to assume a less subservient place in society. The secular, Westernized women expected that their emancipation and professional opportunities would expand as society became more democratic; the religiously oriented revolutionaries expected that society would become more pious, but in a way that would respect women as the equals of men.

When that didn't happen, many women felt betrayed. They began to rebel, quietly, against the constraints. As the economy contracted, as they lost their husbands and sons in the war with Iraq, they often had no choice but to go to work. The clerics discovered that they simply could not exclude women, particularly younger women, from government, employment, and education. Mohammad Khatami's sweeping victory in the 1997 presidential election—the contest in which Taleghani had sought to run—was due in large part to the votes of women, who believed his pledges to elevate their legal and social status and give them a key role in the civil society he envisioned.

It stuns me to see women daring to be outspoken, whether it is a peasant woman arguing with a bank clerk or a female deputy in Parliament arguing for passage of a piece of legislation. Perhaps it is that women are not as harshly treated or punished for wrongdoing as men; perhaps it is that they are not taken as seriously as men or considered as much of a threat. Or perhaps the traumas Iran has suffered since the revolution have in some way jarred loose the feminine imagination, allowing previously powerless women to become more powerful if only because they need to be. During the Iran-Iraq war, for example, women in chadors pressured the Parliament to change the law that gave custody of the children of a war casualty to the dead soldier's family, not to the children's mother, and the law that gave survivor benefits to fathers rather than to widows.

The reality, of course, is that Iranian women have an uphill struggle. Despite their gains, women do not serve as judges or religious leaders. Adultery is still punishable by stoning to death. Polygamy is legal. In a divorce, fathers control custody of sons over the age of two and daughters over the age of seven. A girl can be tried for a crime as an adult at the age of nine (a boy at fifteen). Although the practice is officially discouraged, girls are allowed to marry at nine. (At the age of fifty, the Prophet Mohammad took Aisha, who was said to be nine years old, as one of his wives.) Women inherit only half of what men do. Men can divorce their wives at will, but women need to prove that their spouses are insane, impotent, violent, or unable to support the family. A woman needs her husband's permission to start a business and sometimes even to get a job.

Married women cannot get passports or leave the country without the written permission of their husbands, as was the case under the Shah. Rape is more often than not blamed on the woman. A woman's testimony in court has half the weight of a man's. Women can be arrested for jogging or bicycling or swimming in sexually integrated places, and for exposing their heads and necks and the curves of their bodies in public. Women are not even allowed routinely to share the same physical space with men of the same profession. Nazila and I once traveled with the Iranian equivalent of the White House press corps on a trip with President Khatami. Except for the two of us, the other reporters were men. We all flew on the same plane, rode on the same bus, and stayed at the same hotel. But at mealtime, the men sat at one long table while Nazila and I were ushered to a separate one.

Women have begun to use their growing political clout to press for more rights, more important jobs in government, and the same pay, work benefits, and promotions as men. Like Taleghani, the women leading the charge are products of the revolution. They have been joined by educated younger women who feel they deserve the same rights as men. (Since the revolution, literacy among women has soared from less than 50 percent to 70 percent.) Paradoxically, these women have been aided by secular professional women who struggle on the fringes of society to reclaim the rights the clerics have taken away. Together, these women share a common goal. They want something much more fundamental than sisterhood. They want power.

Following Khatami's election, the most powerful woman in Iran's government—on paper at least—was Massoumeh Ebtekar, a steely symbol of his promise to promote women into high-profile positions. Khatami had been elected with the help of the left, and the left needed to be rewarded, or at least neutralized. So he named one from its ranks to his cabinet. A mother of two with a doctorate in immunology, she was appointed at the age of thirty-six as Vice President for the Environment, the first woman to hold cabinet rank in the Islamic Republic.

Unlike Taleghani, who is unadorned, down-to-earth, and speaks only Persian and Arabic, Ebtekar is Islamically elegant, wears high-heeled boots and pin-striped coats with matching hoods under her chador, and speaks near-perfect, American-accented English. Ebtekar quickly became Khatami's showpiece woman. She has met with foreign journalists and environmentalists to explain how Iran is struggling to improve Tehran's dismal air quality and to prevent further pollution of the Caspian Sea from oil development. She has chaired environmental seminars for the United Nations and the World Bank. She has accompanied the Foreign Minister to the annual World Economic Forum in Davos, Switzerland.

But Ebtekar is a woman with a past, one that does not appear on her official résumé. I had heard a rumor and thought I knew her secret. I confronted her one day in 1998 with second-rate-movie lines. "Mrs. Ebtekar," I said, "I think we've met before. I remember your face."

She gave me a puzzled look. "You were once very famous in America," I continued. Then I asked her whether she was ever known as Mary.

Ebtekar took a long breath. Her dark eyes stared through me, betraying quiet anger. "I was," she said sharply. "But I don't bring those issues up."

In 1979, as an eighteen-year-old freshman at what is now Amir Kabir Polytechnic University, Ebtekar was the face and voice, the official interpreter and spokeswoman, of the militants who occupied the American embassy. Hiding her hair under a kerchief and using an anglicized nom de guerre, she became an object of anger and curiosity with her regular appearances on American television during the 444-day siege.

The hostages had called her Tiger Lily, after the name they knew to be hers—Niloufar Ebtekar. Niloufar is an old Persian name that means "water lily." Somewhere along the way she became Massoumeh—an Islamic name that means "innocent woman."

Night after night Mary had listed the "crimes" of America against Iran and denounced the hostages as "spies" who should be put on trial if the United States did not turn over the deposed Shah. Asked by an ABC News correspondent one day whether she could see herself picking up a gun and killing the hostages, she replied: "Yes. When I've seen an American gun being lifted up and killing my brothers and sisters in the streets, of course."

This teenager was one of the first examples Americans saw of the Iranian revolutionary woman, and her combination of veil and vitriol contributed to the tortured relationship that followed. Standing with other journalists outside the embassy gates in Tehran day after day during the hostage crisis, I wondered about her identity. Her American-accented English suggested long exposure to the United States. But if that was the case, how could she not understand how despicable her words would sound there?

Indeed, I now know, Ebtekar had lived in a middle-class suburb of Philadelphia for six years, attending an elementary school in Highland Park while her father was a doctoral student on an engineering scholarship at the University of Pennsylvania. Back in Tehran, she majored in engineering and banded together with fervently religious students to demonstrate against the Shah.

Her loyalties to Khatami dated from those early years of the revolution. When Khatami became head of the Kayhan Publishing Company in 1981, he named Ebtekar editor-in-chief of *Kayhan International,* the English-language edition of the daily newspaper *Kayhan.* Later, she received a Ph.D. in immunology and participated in government-sponsored programs for women.

I asked Ebtekar about the wisdom of the embassy takeover. She offered no apology; she made no excuses. "I wouldn't think that it would be logical for any nation to look back and see any part of its revolution or its movement as negative," she said. "That was the best direction that could have been taken." She said the embassy was seized to preserve what she called "the values" of the revolution. "It wasn't a plot," she said. "It wasn't a ploy. It was a natural reaction. I can say that."

There is an Iranian word, *porrou,* which means *beyond chutzpah.* And in an extraordinary display of it, Ebtekar blamed the United States for causing the embassy to be seized. "The action was a natural consequence of decisions that had been taken by the Americans," she said.

At that point, she had had enough.

"Our time is up," she said. She pointed to my tape recorder. "Turn this off."

Then she pulled me aside. "Please do not write much about these things," she said dryly, as if the personal history of someone as public as a cabinet minister should remain private. She asked for my complicity in her secret, and I politely but firmly refused.

I couldn't understand why Khatami, whose mantra was the rule of law and who came as close as any Iranian official had to apologizing for the hostage crisis, would have chosen a woman like Ebtekar as the Islamic Republic's first female cabinet member. There were so many other qualified women around, serious, outspoken women with agendas for change.

One such woman is Taleghani; another is Faezeh Hashemi, the daughter of Iran's former President Rafsanjani, and herself a strong promoter of Khatami's platform of reform. In her thirties, Faezeh has been the head of a sports federation for women, a member of Parliament (until she was defeated in 2000), and, until it was banned, the editor of a lively daily newspaper called *Zan* (Woman). There is nothing soft or sentimental about her. She is arrogant and brusque, daring and foolish, sometimes all at the same time. Women respect her or reject her, but I never found anyone who doesn't know who she is or who feels neutral about her.

Faezeh refuses bodyguards, drives without a chauffeur, barks at her two children, and grew up wanting to be a boy. She puts blond streaks in her hair and sometimes forgets appointments. She wears blue jeans and sneakers under her chador, even though she has been criticized for wearing Western dress. She rejects the "feminist" label because, she said, it suggests "special privileges for women." Married at seventeen to a man chosen by her parents, she doesn't believe in romantic love before marriage because, she said, "love before marriage usually doesn't last." But she does believe in women proposing marriage to men and in getting married young. "One of the problems we have in this country is women wait too long before they get married," she said. "A girl is mature at thirteen or fourteen. If she waits too long, she won't have many suitors. And her expectations will get higher—too high."

The first time I visited Faezeh at her apartment in Tehran, she arrived at the door barefoot, dressed in a red terry bathrobe, her wet hair wrapped in a towel. She took me on a tour, even showing me her bedroom where the ironing board was stacked high with a pile of clothes. And in a country that condemned "Westoxication," she allowed her daughter to fill glass cases in her bedroom with nearly two dozen Barbie dolls, even a Barbie dollhouse and a pink convertible.

Faezeh has an ambitious agenda: to use the framework of Islam to keep women healthy. Specifically, she is determined to get women—particularly young women—physically active again through sports programs in order to fight the insidious low-level depression that has come to affect much of the country's female population. Even the conservative newspapers acknowledge that rising depression among women has contributed to the 2,500 suicides in Tehran each year. One women's monthly cultural magazine laid out the reasons: "Family problems such as addiction of the spouse, difference of age, lack of mutual understanding, polygamy, lack of interest in family affairs, lack of love, premature marriage, and excessive sensitivity toward the taboo of divorce are the most important reasons that lead to suicide among women." The article also cited studies indicating that the degree of a woman's piety made no difference in her decision to commit suicide, even though suicide is forbidden under Islam.

"If women are not active, they will become susceptible to disease and depression," Faezeh said. "And sports can fill the empty times for young women. It gives them the strength and courage to be taken seriously. And it will keep them away from addiction, corruption, and mischief—and will help prevent suicide."

This stance is more controversial than it may sound to the Western ear. Women's sports virtually disappeared with the Islamic revolution, because the clerics banned men and women from training and competing together. In addition, some religious hard-liners consider exercise for women to be both frivolous and immoral. At one point, bands of men beat up female bicyclists in a park outside Tehran and a group of ayatollahs denounced bike riding, boating, running, and horseback riding for women as sexually provocative.

Faezeh argued back, insisting there was nothing un-Islamic about activities like bicycle riding. The debate that followed led to the creation of a separate bicycle path for women in the park. She insisted that all female athletes wear Islamic dress, which mollified some of the mullahs, but meant that Iranian women could not compete in most international sporting events.

But Faezeh has a larger battleground than athletics or even mental health. Her real goal is to get more political power for women. "Socially, artistically, athletically our women are doing better, but in politics women haven't made much progress," she said. "Men don't have to prove themselves to be chosen for high positions, but women always do."

She is acutely aware of her own political vulnerability. "The clerics are very powerful in this country," she said, sounding not at all like the daughter of one of the country's most powerful clerics. Her father, she added, is always telling her to keep her opinions to herself, or at least let surrogates do the talking for her. Instead, in August 1998 she started her own newspaper, *Zan*, a women's newspaper with an attitude. Operating from a beautiful marble-floored mansion rented from a wealthy *bazaari*, the paper argued against such practices as stoning to death and the unequal valuation of women's lives in case of death or injury. It criticized a rule requiring female students at public universities to wear the full black chador, interviewing students who complained about the strict dress code. It sought out women's views in surveys, concluding in one, for example, that more than 97 percent of women wanted the right to be spectators at soccer matches, which had been denied to them until recently.

But *Zan* had a short life span. First, Faezeh came under fire over a cartoon in which a husband appealed to a robber to shoot his wife instead of him. His argument: under Islamic law the compensation the thief would have to pay the family would be half what he would have to pay for killing a man. Faezeh was accused of ridiculing one of the primary principles of Islam. Then, Faezeh became even more brazen, publishing excerpts from a New Year's message from Farah Diba, the Shah's widow, to the Iranian people. It was all part of Faezeh's campaign to challenge conventional thinking about what constituted acceptable public discourse. The two items were considered acts of counterrevolution and the paper was shut down, although Faezeh herself was never brought to court the way other newspaper publishers have been.

Faezeh's staunchest supporter throughout her ordeals has been her mother, Effat Marashi, whose message to her daughter's enemies was clear: "I asked God to take revenge." Marashi said that the silence of her husband, the former President, when Faezeh's newspaper was closed, was "tormenting" her. He kept telling her to keep quiet, she added. Obviously, she did not obey. "Faezeh was being persecuted," she said.

I first met Marashi when Rafsanjani was President, and her boldness did not surprise me. Over tea and pastries one evening in the living room of her modern but surprisingly modest house, she sounded more like a militant feminist than the wife of an Iranian cleric-politician. "Every Iranian woman should become educated and use her knowledge to work outside the home," she told me. "Women have been deceived, cheated. It's like this all over the world. It's time for them to go out and be active in society, to gain their own rights. There is no need to stay at home and do the housework."

Indeed, the battlefield in which women are the most disadvantaged is marriage. As in most Islamic countries, marriage in Iran is not a contract between equals but an acquisition of property: the wife by the husband. Issues such as wife beating are scarcely ever talked about, and there are no statistics on how prevalent it is. Shelters for battered or homeless women do not exist.

One woman who has begun to talk about such issues is Shahla Sherkat, whose provocative monthly women's magazine, *Zanan,* was a model for Faezeh Hashemi's feminist journalism. Sometimes I could not figure out why *Zanan* had not been shut down. Perhaps the authorities didn't consider the magazine much of a threat because its circulation was small and Sherkat never took them on directly. But there were subtler ways to pressure her. One time, she lost a government subsidy for newsprint, forcing her to buy it for several times more on the open market. When *Zanan* published a cover story featuring Rakhshan Bani-Etemad, one of Iran's top female filmmakers, dressed in a colorful print scarf, fashionable sunglasses, and a garment that exposed her wrists and bangs, the issue was swiftly confiscated from the newsstands.

Sherkat ran the magazine with a tiny budget, a staff of five, and a mounting debt. "I do this for two reasons," she told me once. "I love it and I'm insane. I have two children and I always say *Zanan* is my third child. If one day the magazine stopped publishing, it would be as if I would never see one of my children again. I don't belong to myself anymore."

Zanan has run articles with headlines like, "Why Should Only Women Be Receptionists?" and "Is Your Baby Sitter Your Husband's Doll?" Sherkat showed me an article that she had recently edited on Iran's burgeoning prostitution industry. It included an interview with a married man who owned a shop in the bazaar and was a patron of the streets frequented by prostitutes.

"Why have you come here?" the man is asked.

"Ask my wife. Whenever I go home she smells of food. When I want to talk to her she says our kid has an exam and she has to study with him. I'm fed up. I'm a human being. I haven't married a cook. I want a wife, a woman who smells good and wears nice clothes."

"If you give your wife extra money she will wear perfume and good clothes."

"No, I'm a *bazaari*. I make good money but even if I gave my wife five million rials she would buy meat and chicken and vegetables."

"Why don't you tell her these things?"

"Do we have the time? Either I'm not home or she's taking care of the house."

Another article titled "A Triangular Love" dealt with the little-discussed issue of polygamy. Khosrow Sinaee, a well-known documentary filmmaker, had been "happily married to two painters for twenty years," the article said. He and his first wife (who is Hungarian) lived together for ten years and had two children before they met the Iranian woman who would become his second wife. It was the first wife's idea. "The three of us realized that we could not live without each other," the second wife told the interviewer. The two wives divided the housework. The second wife bore the husband two more children and did all the shopping and errands. The first wife kept house and took care of the garden. The second wife declared that she could not choose between her husband and the first wife. "I cannot tell which one I love more," she said.

Many readers were shocked. Stories were always circulating about traditional Iranian men taking more than one wife. But here was a secular intellectual giving legitimacy to the practice. The article mentioned nothing about sexual feelings between the women but still, some readers thought the arrangement sounded like a ménage à trois. Sherkat defended the article, saying, "I'm against polygamy, but if there are some people who have made this choice freely, we shouldn't judge them."

Sherkat added that it would be wrong to assume the relationship was a ménage à trois. Rather, she saw the article as a kind of feminist statement, because the women expressed more love for each other than the husband they had in common. "The man was on the margins," she said.

For me, the most chilling article ever published in *Zanan* was a cover story titled, "Sir, Have You Ever Beaten Your Wife?" It included interviews with men who beat their wives and with women who had been physically abused.

The matter-of-fact flatness of the interviews gave the story its power.

"Sir, have you ever beaten your wife?"

"It happens."

"What for?"

"We had problems."

"Where were your children when you were beating your wife?"

"They were there. . . . Of course, it's better if they don't see."

Another interview, this time with an abused woman:

"What was the excuse this time?"

"The fight began and I swore at him. He became angry and started beating me. He beat me so much that my daughter had to pull me away from him."

"What do the children do when he beats you?"

"They cry and shake like scared chickens. . . . I have gone to court three times. They tell me that maybe it's my fault."

Sherkat explained that she was barraged with criticism after that article appeared. She had gone into the most intimate private space in Iran—the bedroom—and exposed its secrets. "People came into my office and said, 'Now, are you happy to write about what happens in the bedroom?' Some people said there is no such thing as wife abuse. Others admitted these things happen but said it's better not to talk about them."

Complicating the problem of wife abuse is the difficulty women often have in getting a divorce. Almost every woman I know in Iran has a friend or relative with a horror story to tell. Even though the standard marriage contract gives women many rights on paper, they are extraordinarily difficult to enforce. The Iranian family court is a hothouse of double standards and male vengeance. A woman might have to wait years to persuade a male judge (the Islamic Republic considers women too emotional to be judges) to grant a divorce.

The most transparent window into the way the Iranian system of divorce works is an extraordinary documentary film, *Divorce Iranian Style,* co-directed by the Iranian anthropologist Ziba Mir-Hosseini, who is herself twice divorced. Produced with the cooperation of the Ministries of Justice and of Islamic Guidance, the film takes the viewer into a tiny Tehran courtroom presided over by a wry, white-turbaned judge whose primary mission is to persuade couples to stay together, since divorce is considered abominable in the eyes of God. I watched a video of the documentary in Iran with a young, educated upper-middle-class couple and their single male friend. Just as surprising as the documentary itself were their reactions to it.

The documentary portrays women as active players in their fate, alternately using logic and emotion, anger and humor, deception and charm to achieve their common goal: liberation from their marriages. In one case, a woman tries to convince the judge that her husband is crazy, testifying that in thirty years of marriage he has refused to let her answer the phone "even if it rings a hundred times." "This man has made my life hell," she says. The judge tells her to make herself attractive so that she can get back into his good graces.

In another, a sixteen-year-old named Ziba, who was married off by her parents at the age of fourteen, wants more than freedom from her loveless marriage to a man two and a half times her age who smokes, works late, and hangs out with "rascals." She has lost her virginity and wants her husband to give her the $10,000 *mehriyeh* so that she can go back to school. (*Mehriyeh* is a kind of dowry pledged by the husband at the time of marriage in case of divorce that the wife has the legal right to collect even if the marriage has never been consummated.) The case goes to an informal sort of arbitration in the living room of a relative in which her uncles serve as mediators. Although she is the only woman in a room full of older men, Ziba boldly struggles to make her case. "Why won't you grant me my legal rights?" she asks. "Wasn't I a virgin?"

"Ha!" exclaimed the husband of my friend as we watched. "She's such a bitch. All she wants is money."

His friend agreed. "Her family is treating it like a business deal," he added.

The court also handles child custody cases and the documentary shows the plight of Maryam, who has remarried for love and is ordered to turn over her four-year-old daughter from her first, loveless marriage to her former husband. He already has custody of their older child, an eleven-year-old girl. At one point during the proceedings, the clerk of the court, a woman, puts in her two cents. "She's ruined her children's lives just for lust," she says. "It was lust, lust, lust."

But Maryam is despondent. She lies, shouts, sobs, pleads, and throws herself on the mercy of the court. "I'll never give you the child!" she cries, holding her younger daughter. "You could at least give me one of them! For the sake of your own children, let me keep this one. . . . I'll go mad! Please, sir, for the sake of the child." Unmoved, the judge tells her, "You remarried, and when you remarry you lose the child."

The two young men watching the documentary were as unmoved as the judge. "What phony crying," said the family friend. "She should have stayed with her first husband if she really wanted the kids. He had a job. He wasn't a drug addict. He didn't beat her. There was nothing major wrong with him."

My young female friend was incredulous. "Would you want to be with a woman who didn't love you?" she asked. "How come you as a man have the right to fall in love with a new woman—a blonde maybe—and divorce your wife? Why doesn't a woman have that right?"

Her husband tried to calm her down. "You're taking sides, you're taking sides," he told her. "You think the woman should have custody? What about the man's rights?"

The harshness of the courtroom infects the court clerk's young daughter, who comes to the court every day after school to wait for her mother. In one scene, the girl climbs into the judge's chair when he goes off to pray. Pretending to be the judge, she opens a file, bangs the table for silence, and delivers a devastating monologue, ordering the imaginary wives before her to go back and obey their husbands. But later she tells the judge that she will herself never get married. "I've seen what husbands are like," she says.

For Mehrangiz Kar, a secular lawyer whose practice focuses on women and family law, the documentary is an accurate, but sanitized, depiction of reality. Most judges are not so enlightened, she said. "Even if the husband insults his wife or beats her, the judge demands a witness," Kar told me one day. She described one case that had been going on for three years in which the husband brutally beat his wife and she wanted a divorce. "But he comes to court and says, 'I love my wife. If she divorces me, I'll die.' The judge tells them over and over to try again."

Even the most minor changes in the law are difficult to attain. For several days in December 1996, I watched a rancorous debate in Parliament about whether the wife's *mehriyeh* should be adjusted for inflation. Those deputies who opposed the move argued that it would set an inflationary precedent for all debts and thus create widespread economic instability. At one point, Abbas Abbassi, a conservative male member of Parliament, said: "A woman who gets married at a young age is highly valuable to her husband. And as she becomes older, her value depreciates. So it is not right to adjust upward for inflation because she is worth less."

The female members of Parliament were outraged. "He believes that women are created to be used by men, that they are just secondhand goods that should be in men's service," Soheyla Jelowdarzadeh, who is also an engineer, shot back. "This is against the Koran!" Eventually, the female deputies prevailed and the measure passed by a comfortable margin. They considered it a major victory.

Even more fundamental than the problem of divorce for women is the problem of sex. Islam forbids all sex outside marriage. Adultery can be punished by stoning, although technically four witnesses to the "crime" are needed. Even secular parents expect—or at least hope—that their daughters will remain virginal until marriage. But neither they nor the Islamic Republic can prevent men and women from socializing, dating, and having sex outside marriage. Birth control is legal; abortion is not, except to save the life of the mother, but that doesn't stop young women from getting pregnant and having abortions in small, underground clinics run by doctors who sometimes offer surgical hymen reconstruction as well.

There are occasional voices in the Islamic Republic that have encouraged couples to make use of a uniquely Shiite way around the fornication ban: temporary marriage. Temporary marriage, or *sigheh,* originated during the lifetime of the Prophet Mohammad. Prostitution was widespread, and *sigheh* was a way to give names to children born outside of marriage, who would otherwise be considered no better than slaves. The Sunni Muslims banned the practice; the Shiites did not.

Historically, *sigheh* was practiced most frequently among pilgrims and clerics in the holy cities of Mashad and Qom. Pilgrims who traveled had sexual needs, it was argued; *sigheh* was a legal way to satisfy them. In his two-volume 1892 opus on Iran, *Persia and the Persian Question,* Lord Curzon described his shock at the widespread practice of *sigheh* among pilgrims in Mashad, where, he said, "a gigantic system of prostitution, under the sanction of the Church, prevails."

Clerical use of temporary marriage is more complicated. It is hardly ever talked about, although the cultural anthropologist Shahla Haeri, in her groundbreaking study of *sigheh, Law of Desire,* cited interviews with clerics who offered a number of explanations. One proclaimed that because God banned alcohol, he allowed temporary marriage. Another said that some clerics exercised a "hypnotic influence" over young women, becoming both their spiritual and sexual tutors. Still another said that he believed that *sigheh* contracts had increased among clerics since the revolution. He told the story of a highly educated cleric who became headmaster of a boarding school for girls in Qom. The headmaster's wife became suspicious of his socializing with his students and took him to court. He was ordered to temporarily marry eleven of the girls. "The headmaster's wife, who had appealed to the court expecting justice, found herself a temporary co-wife to eleven teenagers!" Haeri wrote.

The *sigheh* ritual is simple. A man and a woman agree to a marriage contract. The contract can last for as little as a few minutes or as long as ninety-nine years. In some cases, the woman is paid. The couple can be creative in structuring their contracts, putting in writing how much money will be paid, how much time they will spend together, and what services will be provided. A cleric generally registers the contract with a written order, but the couple can write the contract without witnesses or formal registration. The union is not recorded on identification cards. Only virgins need their father's permission.

Children born of a *sigheh* marriage are considered legitimate and entitled to a share of the father's inheritance, although in practice it can be difficult to register the father's name on the child's birth certificate, force fathers to pay child support, or enroll children with no birth certificates in school. Although it is less common, nonsexual *sigheh* has been used by unrelated men and women who want to live or work in close quarters.

Even though *sigheh* is on the books, it was not talked about much in public until a stunning sermon by President Rafsanjani during Friday prayers in November 1990 at the University of Tehran, the country's main public forum for launching political statements. It was there that the President tried to revive it as an acceptable—and necessary—arrangement, particularly for young people. He called sexual desire a "God-given" trait that needed to be fulfilled. He condemned Iranian culture for dictating that young people had to be deprived of sex until they were twenty-five or thirty years old and had made a home for themselves. "We know that when a child reaches fifteen, when he or she becomes sexually mature, a serious desire forms in his or her body," he said quite openly. The solution was not to be "promiscuous like the Westerners," but to obey the law. "God has not said that this need cannot be met. . . . God and religion have practically and simply resolved the problem."

In his own way, Rafsanjani was also arguing that the use of temporary marriage would further the rule of law by wrapping the practice of extramarital sex in an Islamic cloak. It would end the common practice of arresting—and often fining and lashing—couples who were not married and charging them with immoral activities. If young people were too embarrassed to go before a cleric, they could even make the contract privately between themselves, Rafsanjani said. "No court has the right to prosecute anyone, whoever they may be, if they have indulged in temporary marriage," he said. "This is the law."

Rafsanjani's sermon touched off a rancorous debate. Thousands of demonstrators protested against him in front of Parliament. Some women argued that the government should financially support war widows and poor women, not encourage them to enter into temporary marriages. After all, the practice favored the man. He could take as many temporary wives as he wanted and up to four permanent ones; a woman in a permanent marriage could not take a temporary husband. He could break the *sigheh* contract at will; she could not.

From time to time, I heard stories of *sigheh* relationships. I once met a woman whose father was in construction and had to travel a lot. Only years later did her mother learn that in one of the cities where her husband worked he had temporarily married a peasant woman and had two children with her. An Iranian businesswoman I knew became the *sigheh* of a married man until his divorce came through and they could be permanently married.

Years ago, a Turkish journalist friend of mine, Cengiz Candar, was offered a *sigheh* contract by a well-known ayatollah who even suggested a temporary wife for him: me. Cengiz and the cleric were together late one evening when Cengiz phoned me at my hotel. I had interviewed Khamenei, who was then President, that afternoon; Cengiz had an appointment to see him the following day and wanted a sense of what he had said. Years later, Cengiz told me the rest of the story: "When I got off the phone, I told the ayatollah about our conversation. He said, 'I don't want to block your real intention. If you're interested in something else, it's perfectly okay. It's legal.' He was joking and saying, 'I give you my blessing.' I told him, 'No, no, it's not that kind of relationship.' He said, 'Come on. You are a Turk; she's an American. You're a Sunni and you don't have this system, but Shiism provides these kinds of opportunities. Don't be shy!' After a few minutes he left so that I could implement my real project if I wanted to!"

Despite the legality of *sigheh* in the Islamic Republic, it is unpopular among young people and that is not likely to change. It has nothing to do with religion. It has to do with long-held Iranian traditions. Most Iranians I know regard the practice as little more than legalized prostitution, for *sigheh* is a public advertisement that a woman is not a virgin. And for many Iranian families, that makes her unmarriageable. Even illicit sex is considered better than *sigheh*—as long as the sex is kept secret.

Although Mohammad Khatami captured much of the women's vote in his campaign for the presidency in 1997, I did not see much evidence that the legal situation of women had improved much during his tenure. Khatami's political agenda—the creation of a civil society, the need for tolerance, and the rule of law—did not train the spotlight on women. Women's rights per se would have to come later.

"Everyone's forgotten about women's rights in Iran," Kar, the lawyer, told me one day in her office. "We're seeing a political war between two factions of the system. All the arguments about freedom have overshadowed women's rights. Women as women have been forgotten. Women need a separate space for themselves in this thing called civil society."

Kar ranted about Islamic dress, calling its enforcement "violence against women." She ranted about how girls could be married off or prosecuted for crimes at the age of nine. She ranted about how women's prisons had become a training ground to initiate teenage girls into a life of crime. She ranted about the failure of the government to create women's shelters. She ranted about how she is not allowed by the court to represent a group of male prisoners who had been accused of homosexual activity because she would have to talk about male sexual organs and the details of the homosexual act. "The rule of law means nothing for women," she ranted. "There are so many battles, so many battles," she said. "I am so tired."

"Why don't you just leave?" I asked her. I knew she had family in the United States.

Suddenly, Kar's demeanor changed, and she smiled broadly. "I love it here!" she said. "I would feel lost in a country like America. Nothing belongs to me there. My life is here."

In her case, it was a brave choice indeed. In April 2000, several months after that conversation, she participated in a conference in Berlin about Iran's reform movement. The conference was disrupted by protesters, including one woman who stripped to her bra and panties and another who did a hip-rotating dance—bareheaded. Back home, Iran's state-run television broadcast the incident and accused conference participants of "decadent" activity. Kar was among those arrested and held for questioning. Even a seasoned lawyer like Mehrangiz Kar was not immune from the country's capricious system of justice.

CHAPTER SEVEN

The Chanel Beneath the Chador

What are these unbecoming cloaks and veils?
They are shrouds for the dead, not for those alive.

— MIRZADE-YE ESHQI, EARLY TWENTIETH-CENTURY
IRANIAN POET

The most precious ornament for a woman is the Islamic covering.

— POSTER AT SHIRAZ AIRPORT SHOWING THE FACE
OF A WOMAN COVERED IN BLACK EXCEPT FOR HER
EYES AND NOSE

You cannot enforce the hejab *with clubs and weapons.*

— ABDOLLAH NOURI, FORMER VICE-PRESIDENT AND
FORMER MINISTER OF THE INTERIOR

*I*T WAS HER WEDDING DAY, and the bride wore a form-fitting white gown and a sheer veil. She was determined not to ruin her hairdo. So she defied the law and did not cover up when her groom took her out in a swan-shaped paddleboat on a crystalline lake hidden in the woods near the Caspian Sea. A hired cameraman videotaped the scene: the sweating groom in an ill-fitting suit paddling as hard as he could, the bride smiling sweetly as she drank a bottle of Iranian cola in the thick, humid, summer air.

The wedding season in Iran had begun, and just a few days before, the police had issued warnings about proper behavior. "The public presence of a bride dressed in a transparent gown showing her figure or without the necessary Islamic head scarf is forbidden," said the statement. Violators would be prosecuted.

This bride didn't care. She stayed with her groom on the lake for an hour. When the newlyweds got back to shore, I saw that she was a rebel of sorts, a pretty enough woman who looked no more than eighteen, wearing too much makeup, showing too much cleavage, and ill-accessorized in black patent leather platform shoes. She put on a long white chador and her moment of freedom was over.

Many of my Iranian women friends criticize me for focusing so much on what women wear. But the reality is that since the beginning of Iran's revolution, by far the most relentless struggle for control of public space has been over women's dress. More energy has been spent on this social issue than any other, and there are profound political consequences. Women, after all, are a large part of the constituency for reform. They test the limits with colorful clothing or painted toes or visible bits of hair, then retreat in the face of episodic mass arrests. The battle is fought on different levels: between women who try to wear less and men who believe that women should wear more; between women who feel comfortable with veils and women who consider veils to be backward. The issue is serious enough that in just about every store, every taxi, every bus, every public building, particularly in neighborhoods and cities in which a large percentage of women try to bend the rules, there are warnings that " *bad-hejab*" (badly covered) women will not be served.

The leaders of the revolution must have known from the start that the dress code would be the most difficult rule to implement. Yet *hejab* (literally "curtain"), which is defined as any dress that follows Islamic principles, is the most visible symbol of the Islamic Republic's power, and so it will be the last to go. I sometimes think that Iran will have some sort of relationship with Israel before it allows its women to go bareheaded.

The *hejab* is also something that I have to deal with personally. When it comes to dress, Iran in some respects is even stricter than Saudi Arabia, where foreign visitors like me can get away with a flimsy hat. But if I want entry in Iran, I have to cover up, and I have to decide whether and how much of a political statement I want to make with the degree of my coverage and the color and shape of my dress.

For the Islamic Republic, the rules about dress are laid out in the Koran: "Say to the believing women that they should lower their gaze and guard their modesty. . . . They should draw their veils over their bosoms and not display their ornaments." They can go bareheaded only in front of other women, their husbands, fathers, sons, nephews, servants, and children small enough to "have no sense of the shame of sex." A rule requiring all women to appear in public in Islamic dress was written into the country's penal code, but the Koranic verse that defines it is subject to interpretation.

The Islamic Republic didn't invent the veil, of course. Even before the advent of Islam, the practice of veiling probably existed among the Zoroastrians. From the sixteenth century on, a kind of all-enveloping Islamic veil was worn, although it was not black and its style varied according to region. Eventually, well-to-do women of the cities and the court—certainly not a majority of women—took up veiling and secluding themselves from public view. The black chador seen on the streets today probably made its entry in the late eighteenth century—among the upper classes.

In the countryside, women have always worn veils, usually lively prints that protect their heads from dust. They often wear scarves with veils over them, wrapping and gathering them at their waists to free up their arms and to make the garments less cumbersome. In fact, the consensus among modern and traditional, secular and religious women in Iran is that if women were given a choice, the majority would probably choose to cover their heads in public in some way.

Choice—to wear or not to wear the veil—has been an issue for decades. In 1935, going even further than Turkey's secular modernizers, Reza Shah issued an edict that declared the wearing of traditional dress (for both women and men) an offense punishable by a prison term. The army and police roamed through villages to enforce the law, tearing chadors off women and handing out free Western-style suits to men. Reza Shah also banned men from wearing turbans. Mustaches were allowed but beards were forbidden, even for clerics.

To reinforce his message, Reza Shah brought the Queen Mother and the royal princesses, unveiled, to a graduation ceremony at the Women's Teacher Training College in Tehran in 1936. The king told all Iranian women to follow their example and "cast their veils, this symbol of injustice and shame, into the fires of oblivion."

Not all Iranian women saw it that way. To many, the veil was a source of protection, respect, and virtue. In her 1992 memoir, *Daughter of Persia*, Sattareh Farman Farmaian, the daughter of a Qajar prince, recalled her mother's bitter reaction to Reza Shah's edict: "He is trying to destroy reli-

gion. He doesn't fear God, this evil Shah—may God curse him for it!"
Some women refused to leave their homes, some because they didn't
want to be seen bareheaded in public, others to protest the decree. One of
those women was Ayatollah Khomeini's wife, Khadija Saqafi, who, according to relatives, went without a bath for a year rather than venture to
the public bathhouse unveiled. But that was only one view. The elderly
mother of a close friend of mine called the announcement of Reza Shah's
edict "one of the best days of my life."

During the revolution in February 1979, women could go bareheaded
in Iran, but within a month, Khomeini ordered all women to wear Islamic dress. At first, Iran's women resisted. I walked through the streets of
Tehran as thousands of women marched—bareheaded—to protest
Khomeini's order. Men hurled stones, bottles, and insults. Soldiers fired
shots in the air. The American feminist Kate Millett showed up, branding
Khomeini a "male chauvinist" and marching with Iranian women. She
was expelled.

Still, Khomeini was politically supple enough to sense the strong opposition to his sweeping dictum. He had called the floor-length chador,
the garment that covers all but a woman's face, "the flag of the revolution." But then he backed down, saying he had meant only to suggest how
women should dress.

Eventually, however, head covering prevailed. The regime ordered
women who worked in ministries and universities to cover their heads.
Restaurants and hotels put baskets of scarves near the entrances. The
mother of a friend met me for tea one day early in the revolution in the
lobby of the Inter-Continental Hotel. She was wearing a maroon-colored
knit hat that covered much but not all of her hair. I was bareheaded. A
waiter handed my friend's mother an eggshell-blue card that said, "Sister,
following Islamic laws helps keep the place of women in society so high.
Please respect the rules and let us have the pleasure of serving you." She
was furious and argued with the waiter. Her head was covered, she said.
He said only a scarf would do. She refused. We left. And that was the wave
of the future. By the beginning of 1982, three years after the revolution, all
women were forced to cover up in public space—Iranians and foreigners
alike.

Iran's women, being subtle and adaptable, came to think of the veil as
something more complicated than just an imprisoning garment. The
writer Farzaneh Milani argued in her book, *Veils and Words,* that "veiling

has functioned more like a code that allowed anyone and everyone to vent their private aspirations, fears, dreams, and nightmares. An emblem now of progress, then of backwardness, a badge now of nationalism, then of domination, a symbol of purity, then of corruption, the veil has accommodated itself to a puzzling diversity of personal and political ideologies." For many women, the Islamic dress became a tool to be used to their advantage, a way into public spaces. It gave them the right to be present in public spaces—to work in offices, to attend college, to drive, to walk on the streets. "The veil gives women the license to do things," my friend Farideh Farhi, the political scientist, once told me. "They can cross borders with it."

Still, the *hejab* was undeniably a symbol of the forced will of the Islamic state. So resistance to it became part of everyday life. Since the revolution, there have been degrees of acceptable coverage. It took a while for me to figure out that what an Iranian woman wears often defines her politics and her level of piety. If a woman wants the most anti-regime dress of all, she will first put on any kind of clothing that looks stylish, and then accessorize it with a kerchief that reveals hair. Sunglasses, see-through hose, jean jackets, bright colors, makeup, and colored nail polish send clear, even subversive messages to the authorities. Teased or frosted hair is one way to protest the head covering; another is the gravity-defying trick of showing as much hair as possible without the scarf falling entirely off the head. Sometimes I have found women's use of makeup and the choice of hairdos grotesquely exaggerated. That's what happens when something is forbidden.

A more Islamically acceptable covering is a loose-fitting, drab-colored longish coat called a *manteau* (after the French word for coat) or a *roupoush* (which literally means "outerwear" but has come to mean "uniform"). It is worn over a long skirt or pants, with a hood called a *maghnaeh* that covers the head and neck but leaves a hole for the face. The trend began in the 1980s, when, amid pressure for more cover, women started wearing raincoats indoors and calling them "Islamic dress." The advantage of the hood is that unlike an ordinary head scarf, it ensures full coverage. And it doesn't slip. That may be one reason that schoolgirls in state-run elementary schools must wear them; outside of school girls can get away with going bareheaded until they are about ten or eleven, especially if they look younger. As for the coat, it can be stylish. It is sold in crepe, silk, polyester, wool, rayon, or cotton. It comes plain or with epaulets, gold buttons, lace, sashes, or sequins; single-breasted, double-breasted, unbelted, loosely belted, hooded, collared, or zippered. It can resemble an oversized Thierry Mugler trench coat, a voluminous Issey Miyake kimono, or a classic London Fog. Some enterprising seamstresses ran profitable *manteau*-making businesses out of their homes. I once found a tailored pin-striped Ralph Lauren coat-dress at a second-hand shop in my home town of Buffalo that became my colleague Nazila's power suit.

The unassailable uniform, of course, is the classic black chador. More than anything else, it symbolizes the Iranian revolution. Some women wear it out of conviction; others out of opportunism. Massoumeh Ebtekar admitted in an interview in *Zanan* that she began wearing the full chador only when she assumed the position of Vice President for the Environment in 1997. She wanted to represent her country with the "ideal" covering, she said.

In Qom shortly after the revolution, I saw a scene that chilled me: three women in black chadors, their faces hidden behind gauzy black cloth. They could see out, imperfectly, I guessed, but outsiders couldn't see in. "Death out for a walk" was the way the nineteenth century French writer Guy de Maupassant once described women in chadors. He could have been in Qom with me that day.

Unfortunately, there is no scientific survey measuring what percentage of women wear chadors. In parts of the Arab world, the long black veil worn by some women at least has sleeves. But in Iran, the chador is a garment sewn of two pieces of fabric with no buttons or hooks that is thrown over the head, falls to the ankles, and is normally held in place by a hand under the chin. Except, that is, when carrying an object like a baby. Then the chador is held in one's teeth. The dry cleaning slip at Tehran's Laleh Hotel translates the word chador literally as "tent." Some people call the women who wear them *kalagh siahs*—black crows. It's astonishing how many black crows there are.

The veils send a double image of the ideal Iranian woman. Women are supposed to be shrouded wives and mothers; they are also supposed to be warriors of Islam. Some of the most powerful images of the revolution and the war with Iraq showed women in chadors carrying machine guns. The images were reminiscent of an earlier time, in 1911, when hundreds—some said thousands—of women marched from behind their walled courtyards into the office of the President of the Parliament, then pulled out revolvers from beneath their chadors, demanding that the Parliament not give in to the Russians, who were claiming the right to certain properties in Tehran. The Parliament was destroyed by a Russian-backed coup the following week, but the women had made their point.

During the revolution and the war with Iraq in the 1980s, however, the existence of veiled and armed women—"nuns with guns," we journalists called them—was largely a myth. A film produced by a German television crew during the war with Iraq showed soldiers teaching women in layers of black how to use weapons. The women rolled on their bellies as they wrestled with old muskets. The propaganda was too much even for Ali-Reza Tabesh, President Khatami's nephew, who showed the film to me years later. "Did you see that?" he asked. "She was holding the gun backward! That was a smart cameraman!"

As in other areas of social conduct, the rules regarding dress can change without warning. Some clerics regard *hejab* as a vague edict on modesty for both men and women; others give a strict interpretation; still others seem to bend with the circumstances. One ayatollah told a friend of mine who had inquired about the dress code that "it's very important to cover the head and the skin under the neck." But, he added, "This is only important for pretty women. You don't have to worry about it."

During a visit to Qom shortly after the revolution to interview Ayatollah Kazem Shariat-Madari, the female Iranian interpreter working with me wore a sweater, jeans, and a head scarf. Wearing a head scarf was not yet obligatory, but she wore it out of respect for the ayatollah. I was wearing—badly—a chador. "Where's your chador?" the ayatollah asked her. "I respect you and so I am covering my hair," she replied. "But there is nothing in the Koran that requires me to wear the chador."

At first, he looked at her quizzically. But Shariat-Madari was an easygoing sort of ayatollah. "Okay," he replied, smiling. "You made your point."

Schools are particularly whimsical when it comes to dress codes. "When I was in seventh grade, our dress and handbags were checked every morning and if we were not wearing the *maghnaeh* we were not allowed in," Nazila told me one day. "If they found mirrors in our bags we could get expelled from school. They kept changing the rules. In eighth grade, we were not allowed to wear jeans, only black, brown, or dark blue pants. In ninth grade, white socks and backpacks were banned. Backpacks were considered too Western. But now white socks and backpacks have been rehabilitated."

I have never found the chador particularly comfortable, practical, or safe. It gets caught in escalators. It drags along the ground collecting dust. It makes it hard to climb stairs. It is hot in summer. Try taking notes or straphanging on a bus while holding a chador firmly under your chin, or in your teeth.

Many Iranians have nothing but disdain for women who choose to wear the chador. A scathing attack came decades ago from the poet Iraj Mirja in his 1921 satirical epic *Aref Nameh*. In translation it reads:

> *Pardon me but are you some onion ball*
> *A garlic in chador or praying shawl?*
> *You who're the mirror of God's Divine Splendor,*
> *A turnip sack of undetermined gender?*
> *Bound at both ends when down the lane you careen,*
> *Not like a lady—maybe aubergine?*

By contrast, some people find veiling erotic. An entire industry sprang up in the nineteenth century devoted to erotic photography of semiclothed but veiled Middle Eastern women. There is one well-known nineteenth-century photograph of the wife of a carpet merchant from Isfahan shown in a veil that covers her hair, ears, throat, shoulders, and the right side of her torso. She also wears a knee-length slip and calf-length stockings. But her entire left side—from her breast to her hip—is naked. A diplomat friend who was single and male and lived in Iran told me he found the process of unveiling women arousing. "It's like opening a Christmas package," he said. Indeed.

Certainly there is something unsettling about taking off the scarf after wearing it for so many hours on end. I get so conditioned to keeping my hair covered in Iran that whenever I take off my head scarf in an outdoor space like a church courtyard or an embassy garden where bareheadedness is allowed I feel as if I am doing something unlawful.

The first time I wore a chador was as a member of the press corps accompanying Ayatollah Khomeini to Qom early in the revolution. I customized a black and white print chador with a piece of elastic to secure it on my head and a zipper to keep it closed. That gave me the ability to take notes. Then I discovered a novel use for the chador: bathrobe. In my hotel, the only bathroom on my floor was down the hall. It was tiny, and I didn't want all my clothes to get wet when I showered. So I wore nothing down the hall except my quick-drying rayon chador.

Within a couple of years of the revolution, customized chadors with pieces of elastic sewn in became common. Or they could be fastened with straight pins on the side of the head, just as the Catholic nuns of my childhood wore their wimples before Vatican II allowed nuns to unveil.

The black chador undercut Iran's official campaign to look modern in the eyes of the world. When he was ambassador to the United Nations, Kamal Kharrazi, who later became Iran's Foreign Minister, asked Iranian women not to wear chadors on official business there. Fatemeh Hashemi, the elder daughter of President Rafsanjani (and Faezeh's older sister), followed the ambassador's request, appearing chador-less in some meetings at the United Nations in 1995. To Iranian eyes, her large royal blue scarf tied with a bow, fake Gucci handbag, and long black coat trimmed in black satin lapels and black-and-white-checked cuffs were a political statement of just how modern she could be, though she undoubtedly looked extremely Islamic to New Yorkers.

Fatemeh took an even bolder step months later when she invited me to an official dinner in Tehran. A white-gloved honor guard saluted a parade of women swathed in black as they hurried inside. But once there the women handed their chadors to a female servant. Beneath the black, the women were clearly ready for a party, with lacquered hair, careful makeup, and stylish clothes. One wore a black taffeta party dress with a plunging neckline and a big black bow at the shoulder; another, a form-fitting black suit trimmed in fake zebra.

This event, it turned out, was for women only. Fatemeh herself dispensed with her chador, and her head scarf and coat as well, and stood revealed. With her perfectly tailored lime green and white Chanel-style suit, pale hose and pumps, and a single strand of pearls, she looked, well, modern.

The theme was underscored by the guest of honor, Hamideh Rabbani, the daughter of Afghanistan's former President, Burhanuddin Rabbani, who had recently been ousted by the fundamentalist Muslims known as the Taliban. Over caviar and grilled fish Rabbani held the audience spellbound with tales of horror about women under Taliban rule: how they could not leave their homes to go to work, how they could not send their daughters to school, how they were denied medical care in hospitals. Fatemeh gasped. Iranian women had it so much better, she said. "The image of Iranian women is so distorted around the world," she lamented. "How unfair it is." It was not an act.

To the outside world, the unveiling by Fatemeh in front of a female foreign journalist may seem insignificant. But I saw it differently: as part of a mission by women who now had the connections and the skills to re-claim their place in society. Still, the boundaries of dress could be dan-gerous to cross. "Do not write too many details—what my hair looks like or the shape of our bodies," she said to me at the evening's end, as her guests said affectionate goodbyes and wrapped themselves again in black to reenter the public space of men. Two days later, in her office, we nego-tiated what could be written. Her suit, her pearls, her hose, her shoes could be described; the shape of her body and the color and length of her hair could not. "Don't talk about hair," she said. "That's going too far."

Even for women like Fatemeh, who has worn the chador since child-hood, it is a difficult garment to wear. During a sixty-second goodbye to a group of male doctors in her office one day, she performed a sort of Is-lamic dance of the veil, even if her scarf, worn under the chador, prevented her hair from showing. She pulled the chador forward on her head. It slipped back. She pulled it down again and secured it at her waist. It slipped. She pulled it down again. She held it under her chin with her right hand. It slipped, this time exposing the top of her khaki-colored coat and black and white scarf underneath. The chador almost fell off her left shoulder. She pulled it down again. It opened. She closed it and pulled it down again. She tugged on the scarf underneath. She held the chador under her chin with her right hand. She pulled it down again. She held one side, then finally both sides of it with her left hand under her chin.

As a foreign visitor, I had my own ongoing battle to fight with the veil. Once in early 1982 I flew into Tehran from Rome wearing a gray Borsalino hat over my head scarf. I never had had to cover my head before in the Islamic Republic, but the rules had changed. This was a small protest. It didn't work. The Passport Control officer ordered me to take off the hat.

"The hat gives me more coverage than just a scarf," I argued.

"Take it off," he said.

"It's my national dress," I protested.

He was not amused. He said he would not stamp my passport if I didn't take off the hat. I took it off.

Forcing women to dress in a certain way also gives the enforcer a sense of power and keeps women off guard. When I turned up at the trial of Gholam-Hosein Karbaschi, then the mayor of Tehran, in the summer of 1998, I was initially denied entry. I was wearing a green head scarf and loose gray pants under a long patchwork tunic covered by a loose jacket with multicolored appliqués. So it was not a question of coverage. It was a question of color. I was wearing too many colors.

"Where does it say in the Koran that a woman can't wear colors?" I asked the security guard blocking my entry. "Where does it even say that a non-Muslim has to dress like this at all?"

The guard was not in the mood for a discussion of the Koran. "You can't go in like that," he said, and moved on to the next person waiting for entry.

It took more than an hour for Ali-Reza Shiravi, my escort from the Ministry of Islamic Guidance who was responsible for getting me in, to accomplish the task. A year later, I understood a bit more about why I had been turned away. It was not just the colors. It was also that in some Iranian eyes, I looked bizarre. Once when I was traveling with Shiravi to a rural area, he and the driver, Mr. Salimi, laughed when I showed up wearing a purple coat and a yellow scarf. "Purple is the worst color you can wear," Shiravi explained. "It's like orange. It's a peasant's color. Peasants wear a lot of colors and prints inspired by nature with flowers and trees. It doesn't matter for them whether the colors match or not. City people wear more somber, elegant colors."

"So that day in the courtroom, I looked like a peasant?" I asked.

Shiravi and Mr. Salimi burst into howls of laughter.

I found the dress code for women particularly onerous at the beach. Once, Nazila and I found ourselves at a private beach restricted for foreigners on Kish Island in the Persian Gulf. The beach was an isolated anomaly in revolutionary Iran, intended as a place where non-Muslim non-Iranian men and women could sunbathe openly and securely in their bathing suits. Even though Nazila is both Iranian and Muslim, the guard let her in after I told him I didn't feel comfortable alone.

I needn't have worried. Three young Iranian men who had come from the public beach just the other side of a barrier were already there.

They refused the caretaker's request to leave. They wanted to sit in the sun, they said. They wanted to collect shells and coral. "I'm Iranian and it's my property," one of them said simply.

The caretaker turned to us. "It's your decision if you want to stay," he said. When we said we would, he looked horrified. "Are you going to take off your clothes?" he asked, and looked even more horrified when we said we might. So that left Nazila and me, sitting on plastic lounge chairs on a delightfully sunny day, gazing at a crystal clear sea, swathed in long robes, head scarves, and socks. The hell with it, I told her. We ripped off the layers of clothing covering our bathing suits and ran into the water. It was then that we discovered that we had more than three men staring at us. Carloads of young men had a perfect view from a hill nearby.

Nazila likes to say that if the authorities want to find fault with your dress, they will, no matter how covered you are. She told me about once trying to cover an event at the shrine where Khomeini is buried. She was dressed in a black scarf and ankle-length coat but not a chador. Not a strand of hair was showing. "Four times the security women came up to me," she recalled. "Once they complained that my hand was showing. I didn't know what I was supposed to do with that! Once they said they didn't want to see me while they were praying so I had to sneak into a corner where they would not see me. And twice they thought I was standing too close to a crowd of men. My feeling was that they could not stand a woman who was not like them."

So *hejab* can be not just a lever of power but a means to humiliate. Nazila told me a story of showing up for a two-hour English exam when she was fifteen, wearing a coat that the dean of the school considered too short. "She pulled me by my *maghnaeh* and wouldn't let me take the exam. She ordered me to rip my coat and then rip my pants underneath so that I could never wear them again. I begged her to let me take the exam. She refused. One of the older students called my mother. She rushed to the school but they wouldn't let her in. My mother stood outside and yelled at them, 'If you don't let me in, I'll kill you!' The dean waited until there were only fifteen minutes of exam time left. Then she let me in." They hadn't reckoned with Nazila's intelligence. She got an A minus.

Humiliation is often motivated by class, carried out by lower-class morals police—both men and women—against higher-class Westernized women. A friend of mine was once stopped by the morals police because she was wearing pants and a parka that covered only her hips. But she was not wearing makeup; her head was covered with a small cotton scarf; she didn't dye her hair and a few gray strands were showing; she was wearing the cheap blue plastic sandals favored by the poor. "The notion of a 'bad-hejab woman' is a loose, Westernized woman," she recalled. "I was just badly dressed. He was totally confused. And so he gave up."

Many women interpreted Khatami's election as President to mean that they could loosen up in the way they dressed. So more hair began to show in Tehran than at any time since the early years of the revolution. A lot more makeup too. The President's mother and his wife wore makeup, so why not other women?

I have seen that easing in the rules at the Laleh Hotel. For years, the security guard there would greet me politely every day in Persian with the same message: "Fix your *hejab,* madam." I would smile and tell him I was not a Muslim. In early 1998, months after after Khatami's election, he just said hello. So, I even dared to shed the appliquéd raw-silk coat I normally wear (already a stare-getting getup) for a pantsuit. No one seemed to mind that I had legs. Then I tried it on the streets. There were no consequences.

For years, I asked people in authority whether women—foreigners in particular—could wear hats. I never found a religious scholar who could cite a specific ban in the Koran against hats for women. And I never got a consistent answer. Former President Rafsanjani's wife, Effat Marashi, once told me I didn't even have to wear a scarf. "If it were up to me, I wouldn't have forced you," she said. "Non-Muslim women can go out any way they want in our religion. They should dress just the way they always dress."

"May I go around Iran with no scarf, then?" I asked.

"You may," she giggled. "But you wouldn't."

By contrast, President Khatami's wife, Zohreh Sadeghi, took a harder line. "Our culture requires the scarf," she told me when we met. "Usually it is unacceptable that foreign women wear hats."

Foreign tourists visiting Iran also began to test the limits. On a tour I took with some Americans in the fall of 1998, the guide made the mistake of telling our group that women did not have to wear the poorly sewn, ankle-length polyester coats handed out to us at orientation. Some women donned their husbands' shirts over pants. One woman began wearing a floppy canvas hat from one of those fishing-and-camping catalogues. And she got away with it. Some of us even dared to go bare-headed on the tour bus, which caused major rubbernecking.

Nazila's sister, Golnaz, who was with us, kept her black scarf tightly tied under her chin. "Why don't you take it off?" I asked her. After all, I had seen Golnaz at private parties dressed to kill.

"I can't," she replied. "I'm Iranian. You can. You're not."

"Doesn't that make you angry?"

"It's sad that I cannot choose what to wear," she said. "But I save my anger for bigger things. If I get angry every minute of my life, I won't survive."

I began to conduct my own unscientific experiment. I began wearing a black, round-brimmed straw hat made in Italy and covered my neck with a scarf that matched my long black and white rayon dress. The combination gave me perfectly acceptable Islamic coverage. Some people smiled; others stared; others pretended not to notice.

I wore the hat to breakfast in the Laleh's coffee shop. "Very nice, your hat," the waiter told me.

I wore the hat to Persepolis. "I want to wear a hat," a woman told her husband as they passed by.

I wore the hat to an interview with Mohammad-Ali Abtahi, the cleric who was President Khatami's chef de cabinet. "You look . . ." he said, stopping himself in mid-sentence.

I wore the hat to the offices of the reformist newspaper *Neshat.* "You're a counterrevolutionary," joked Mashallah Shamsolvaezin, the editor. Hamid-Reza Jalaeipour, the publisher and chief columnist, had a different take: "As a sociologist, the hat tells me the atmosphere here is very secure."

I wore the hat to the Ministry of Islamic Guidance, where my friend Hosein Nosrat acted as if it was perfectly normal that I came dressed that way. In Islam men are not supposed to look at a woman so I guess he figured he shouldn't notice that anything was different.

One time I showed Nosrat a photo of my daughters. He had been trying to persuade me to bring them to Iran for a visit, and in the photo, they happened to be wearing hats and long skirts. That was all the ammunition he needed. "They can dress like this!" he said. "No problem."

Many Iranian women have launched their own revolution over dress—a revolution of the toes. There is nothing in the Koran that says that women have to cover their feet, and indeed, traditional women in Iran routinely expose their feet. So anti-*hejab* women began to paint their toes, first in white and pink, then in blood red, then in shades of purple and brown and gold.

Of course, it would be foolish to trust the new freedom that allows women to go bare-toed. Sure, there are fewer arrests of women for *bad-hejab* these days and fewer lashings to endure and fines to pay. But there are some. At one point, the reformist newspaper *Sobh-e Emrouz* reported that a woman and two of her daughters were attacked and injured by security forces for their *bad-hejab* as they emerged from their Koran-reading class. Ayda, the sixteen-year-old daughter, was quoted as saying that the security forces began threatening and cursing them until a group of bystanders intervened on their behalf. They told the security forces that if the women had done anything wrong, they should be arrested, not insulted. The paper said that the three women were eventually released. But during the scuffle with police, the women's handbags were "lost."

So there remain reasons to follow the rules. One big one is that other Iranians can get into trouble when one uses dress as a way to make a political statement. A room service waiter can lose his job, for example, if he enters the hotel room of a bareheaded woman. A tour guide can be hauled in for questioning for allowing tourists to take off their scarves.

Late one evening over tea in her apartment, I asked Faezeh Hashemi whether she ever wanted to go out bareheaded and let the wind blow through her hair. She paused for a long time. "Maybe when I was younger," she said. "But it's been years since I felt that way. Maybe that's why I wanted to be a boy when I was growing up."

Her words reminded me of a fascinating story I once read in a Tehran newspaper. It told of a seventeen-year-old girl named Leila, who cut her hair short and disguised herself as a boy. She ran away from her home in Kermanshah in western Iran and took a bus to Tehran. When she ran out of money four days later, she sought refuge in a police station. "I disguised myself as a boy because I always wanted to be a boy," the newspaper quoted her as saying. "Boys are freer than girls. I am very happy that I did what I did."

Girls dressed as boys get off easy. Not surprisingly, it's harder the other way around. In July 1999 a man in Mashad was given twenty lashes for wearing eye shadow and plucking his eyebrows. The following month a young man of eighteen dressed in a flowing overcoat and scarf was arrested in a park in Mashad. He told police that the cross-dressing allowed him to go out in public with his seventeen-year-old girlfriend without being noticed by the vice police. On the other hand, men disguising themselves as women are nothing new in Iran. After Abol-Hassan Bani-Sadr was ousted as President in 1981, the regime claimed that he fled the country by shaving off his mustache and disguising himself in a chador. Bani-Sadr insisted he had worn an air force military uniform, but when he arrived in France, his mustache was gone.

What seems incongruous to me about the rules is that the regime allows representations of unveiled women to be shown in the public space. Photos of bareheaded foreign women regularly appear in the newspapers. In 1998 one paper carried a photo of a group of angry Afghan women in exile—unveiled—their fists raised, protesting the excesses of Taliban rule. It used to be possible to print such images of Iranian women; early in the revolution Tehran's newspapers ran photographs of women marching bareheaded with their fists raised, to protest the order that they wear Islamic dress.

Today the Shah's palaces, transformed by the Islamic Republic into government-run museums and government offices, are full of paintings of unveiled women. A palace in north Tehran that is used by the presidency to receive important foreign visitors displays Western paintings of peasant girls and aristocratic ladies with exposed hair, neck, and shoulders. The *Joy of Wine* fresco inside the seventeenth-century Chehel Sotun Palace in Isfahan shows a woman in a gold-trimmed rust-colored robe, her gold cap revealing her right ear and some of her black hair. She is reclining, and holds a large flask of wine in one hand and a cup in the other.

In 1999, Tehran's Museum of Contemporary Art mounted a show of the best of its Western paintings and sculptures purchased under the Shah. Early in the revolution, a bronze statue of a woman watering plants at the main entrance was altered with a crude bronze scarf to cover her hair; it reminded me that the Catholic clergy in Italy used to alter Renaissance marble sculptures to cover exposed penises with fig leaves. Now, in this show there appeared a Picasso, *Peintre et son modèle,* a 1927 abstract painting. And indeed, it showed the angular figure of the painter and his curved model—with two pendulous breasts, a navel, and a vagina in clear view. The clerics allowed the show to proceed unimpeded, or more likely the museum director had just smuggled the painting in.

I have often asked women friends what would happen if on International Women's Day every woman opposed to compulsory veiling marched bareheaded in the name of choice. Some women say it wouldn't be a big deal because most Iranian women in Iran would choose to keep on their scarves and chadors—either out of choice or out of fear. Some women say they have bigger battles to fight, such as equal rights in matters of employment, divorce, inheritance, and child custody. Some say they have even learned to have fun with the *hejab,* constantly testing the limits. Others say that there would be no safety in numbers. They predict that women would be arrested, beaten, even killed en masse. Sometimes I think that the era of the forced head covering has passed, but that no one really knows how to deal with it. It seems that even those in power know that the policy of forcing women to wear *hejab* has not created believers. If anything, it has added to cynicism and the questioning of Islam itself. Still, when it comes to dress, fear appears to be all that is needed to keep women in line—at least for now.

It isn't just women's dress that is complicated. Negotiating the space between men and women is also hard work. The existence of the *hejab* is apparently not enough to separate men and women, and male-female relationships work themselves out in public spaces in irrational ways. There is no clear-cut definition of a sexually integrated public space. Women may be segregated from men in government offices, but are squeezed close to them in the buildings' overburdened elevators. Men and women are required to use separate entrances at airports, but they sit next to each other on domestic flights. Buses are segregated (women ride in the back), but communal taxis are not. In fact, men and women can sit so tightly packed in taxis that there is a popular expression for going on a date: going for a taxi ride.

Even public toilets can turn out to be integrated. I once was directed to a public toilet at a mosque in Sanandaj not knowing that it was unisex. There was no artificial light inside and it was hard to see. I was about to open the door of a stall when I spotted the head of a man over the top of the door. He turned to look at me, nonplussed, as he urinated.

Even worse than not knowing when to stand near a man is not knowing whether to shake his hand. There isn't a specific law or a line in the Koran about handshaking, but a ban on handshaking is part of the defined distance between men and women. Only the most Westernized

Iranian men reach out to shake a woman's hand. In fact, it is considered impolite for a man to reach out first. That is always the woman's prerogative. It is also considered impolite for a man not to accept the outstretched hand of a woman. So it took a while for me to figure out how to function. I have never shaken the hand of a cleric, although I have to admit that when I met President Khatami for the first time I was tempted to stick out my hand to see what would happen.

I find the no-handshaking rule particularly distasteful at the Foreign Ministry. Here is a collection of men who know the rest of the world and are supposed to have mastered the rules of diplomatic protocol. One evening, Hamid-Reza Asefi, the official spokesman at the Foreign Ministry, and I got into a debate about Iran's tortured relationship with the United States. Asefi is no diplomatic ingenue. He told me all about his background, his doctorate from the University of Essex, his stints as ambassador to East Germany and France. As we parted, he gestured as if he was going to shake my hand. Then he pulled back. "How long will it be until you can shake my hand?" I asked him, laughing. He paused, and then closed up. "I have never done such a thing," he said curtly.

Mohammad-Ali Abtahi, Khatami's chef de cabinet, was more gracious about the handshaking question. At the end of a particularly lively conversation one evening he put his hand on his heart as he said goodbye. So I said to him, "I wish I could shake your hand the way I would with any man outside Iran, but I know you won't. So I'll shake your hand with my heart."

"I do the same with you," he said, smiling. It was a moment of extraordinary intimacy. Yet he hadn't broken the rules.

I always shake the hands of foreign diplomats in Iran but sometimes even they hesitate. One evening a diplomat from a Western embassy met me in the lobby of my hotel and I reached out to shake his hand. He recoiled as if my hand was covered with sores. I kept my hand out and said sweetly, "George, you shake my hand. We have to show everyone that's how we do it where we come from." He shook my hand and apologized. He had been so conditioned about handshaking that he had to be reminded it was okay.

Then one evening after dinner I got the sense that things were changing. Nazila's father, Jaafar Fathi, drove me back to my hotel, got out of the car to open my door, and shook my hand in front of the porters and bellmen. I forgot where I was for a moment. I moved closer to kiss him on both cheeks, the way I do when I say hello or goodbye to him at their home. "Don't do it!" he warned in a booming voice. Yet at Mehrabad Airport, people who are not close blood relatives kiss hello and goodbye all the time.

Over the years, I have found that even the most traditional and religious Iranian women chafe at the intrusion of the Islamic Republic into their private space, particularly when the intrusion is enforced by men they don't know. Take twenty-year-old Leila, for example. An assistant in my favorite beauty salon, she has thick, braided, thigh-length black hair, a chiseled profile, and a slender frame. Because she comes from a very religious family, she never wears makeup, plucks her heavy eyebrows, or removes the hair that darkens her upper lip. All that will have to wait until her wedding day, when the other employees in the shop where she works will spend the entire day making her beautiful. Leila told me that her father, a gatekeeper at a school, was so conservative that he forbade her to have her photograph taken, even if she was swathed from head to toe in the black chador she always wears on the street. Her fiancé, a soldier doing his compulsory military service, would also disapprove. Leila didn't know why there had been a revolution or a war with Iraq. She didn't understand exactly why she had to chant "Death to America" every day when she was in school. She did know, however, that she didn't feel free.

But what does freedom mean for someone like Leila, who prays five times a day, who obeys her father and fiancé without reservation, and who has no intention of abandoning her Islamic dress? She defined it for me one day: "I'm a very religious person and I always wear a scarf and a chador over it. But when some stranger comes up to me and says, 'Lady, fix your *hejab*,' it hurts me. Because inside I know I am very religious. Who is he to tell me I'm not?"

PART THREE

The Spiritual, The Mystical

CHAPTER EIGHT

Beloved of the Night

Night is with child, hast thou not heard men say?
Night is with child! What will she bring to birth?

— HAFIZ, FOURTEENTH-CENTURY PERSIAN POET

Is it not passing brave to be a King,
And ride in triumph through Persepolis?

— *TAMBURLAINE*, CHRISTOPHER MARLOWE

AMIR MAHALLATI has an air of elegance about him. He always stands erect, his shoulders thrust back, his head slightly tilted upward, like the spear-carrying warriors chiseled in limestone at the ancient ruins of Persepolis. His beard is carefully sculpted to frame his smooth, lean, almond-colored face. His pale linen leisure suit does not reveal who he is: a former ambassador of the Islamic Republic to the United Nations and, more important, the son of one of Iran's most prominent and beloved ayatollahs.

On the day we met in his hometown of Shiraz, Mahallati was in love—with the poets of Persia.

Shiraz is by far my favorite city in Iran. Tehran, more than five hundred miles away, is more cosmopolitan, with its twenty-four-hour supermarkets and lively street life. But it is a city of unrelenting ugliness, gridlocked streets, and choking pollution. Isfahan, the onetime capital of Persia in central Iran, is more classically beautiful, with its perfect proportions and the dazzling bulbous domes of its many mosques. But it is a city of political intrigue and backstabbing, and I have never met a merchant there who didn't overcharge me.

Shiraz, by comparison, is a city of moderation, calm, and good sense.

It may be overcrowded with the hundreds of thousands of Iranians who migrated there during Iran's long war with Iraq, and it may be polluted and hot in the summer. But Shiraz opens to rich, rolling farmland, with a good highway that leads straight to Persepolis less than an hour away. Shiraz is not a place of religious pilgrimage, reflecting instead the glories of pre-Islamic Iran. So the Islamic Republic has largely left it alone, pouring money into cities like Mashad, Qom, and Isfahan. Shiraz is a place of roses, nightingales, rich people who smoke opium, and some of the best wine-producing grapes in the world. It is impossible to go to Shiraz and not feel the power of its beauty and the magic of its poetry. Some Iranians consider Shirazis lazy. I find them mellow and good-natured.

I had arranged to meet Mahallati early one morning on a street outside Shiraz's best hotel. He arrived at the designated time, in a beat-up Iranian-made Paykan automobile that offered no reprieve from the one hundred degree heat of a humid July day. We set off for what he called "a good beginning to understand Shiraz": the tomb of Saadi, the beloved thirteenth-century poet.

From then on, Mahallati talked of love. "Saadi is the Shakespeare of Iran. Period," he explained along the way. "There is no such thing as Eastern love or Western love. Love is love. And love in the mind of both Saadi and Shakespeare is the same."

Mahallati stopped at the gate leading into the tomb. "From the tomb of Saadi of Shiraz, you can smell love," he said, translating the inscription at the entrance. "A thousand years after his death you can still smell love."

Inside the gate is an elevated tombstone of brown-speckled marble. Suddenly, Mahallati turned dead serious. "Touch the stone and send Saadi a prayer," he ordered. Then he closed his eyes and fell into a trance, moving his lips and sending a prayer to Saadi's spirit. I did what I was told, closing my eyes and saying a prayer. I found the volte-face jarring. But it captured the two distinct worlds in which Mahallati navigates, the sacred and the secular. He does it with the ease of someone who has learned how to steer early in life.

Then Mahallati shifted back into the world of the poetic. He delighted in showing off his knowledge. He rushed over to a wall with a verse in dark blue tile. "Oh this is really beautiful!" he exclaimed. And then he recited the poem:

"I remember when I was a young boy, when I was with a caravan passing through the desert early in the morning. When the sun rose I noticed a person who went crazy going nowhere. I caught up with him and asked him, 'What's wrong with you?' 'I listened to nature and noticed all the birds, all the animals, all the beings praying, and that scene drove me crazy. I realized I was less than they, and that was a shock.'" Then Mahallati explained. "He was crazy in love. It's the extreme love that drives you crazy."

And then we heard a recorded voice on a loudspeaker singing a song of Saadi. "This night has no morning. How many thoughts went through my mind and I cannot sleep. Why does this night have no end?"

"It is hair-raising when I hear something as touching as this," Mahallati said. We moved into a garden, and he rushed over to a flowering bush. "*Mahbub-e shab,*" he announced. "It means 'beloved of the night.' It gives out a strong perfume only after dusk. It has a very interesting logic. In the day people are pragmatic, not poetic. In the day you have to work and sweat. You can't fall in love during the day. Only after dusk does your imagination start working. And then romance takes over. The perfume is so intense that it doesn't let you sleep at night. It pushes your dreams in such a way that you can't stay in bed. You want to embrace the beloved. If you leave Iran without smelling the beloved of the night, you have missed half of Iran."

I heard the sound of nightingales, a fast furious sound as if a dozen were chirping in reply. "Amir, are those real birds? Or is it a recording?" I asked. I realized too late that I had broken the spell.

"They're real, of course," he replied flatly. "Why do you think otherwise?"

Nearby I spotted a group of young boys. They were blowing on plastic whistles that made the sound of nightingales.

Next on the itinerary was the tomb of Hafiz. "This is the heart of all Iran," said Mahallati when we arrived.

Hafiz, whose given name was Shamseddin Mohammad, was a fourteenth-century Sufi (mystic) and Iran's great medieval lyric poet. Because he was so learned about the Koran, he was given the name "Hafiz," which means "he who remembers [the Koran] by heart." The poet's alabaster tombstone, engraved with two of his best-known verses, rests beneath an eight-pillared tiled cupola with an intricate dome tiled in turquoise. Acres of meticulously landscaped gardens lush with flowers embrace and protect it with a sensuality that is absent from the crowded streets outside.

The tomb is a peaceful, venerated place, where Hafiz's poetry is set to music with classical Iranian instruments. The ubiquitous call to prayer of the mosque is left far behind. Iranians of all classes, occupations, and ages line up every day in the late afternoon, to pay homage and to see into the future.

Mahallati tried to explain the difference between Saadi and Hafiz. "Saadi traveled to so many countries and married several times," he said. "Once he went to Syria and found a man who gave him room and board. The price was that he had to marry the man's daughter, who was, shall I say, not the most beautiful. Finally Saadi accepted. Then he divorced the woman and escaped. Saadi was a horizontal man: Hafiz was different. Hafiz traveled the spirit. Hafiz was a vertical man."

That didn't mean that Hafiz was an ascetic, Mahallati explained. "Hafiz had a lover," he said. "Her name was Shakheh Nabat. Whenever you want Hafiz to read your fortune you have to swear to Shakheh Nabat. You say, 'O the Hafiz of Shiraz, you who are proud of your beloved Shakheh Nabat. I swear you to Shakheh Nabat to tell me a fortune I would desire.'"

It was time to read my fortune. For centuries Iranians have practiced a delightful ritual in which Hafiz makes predictions. Petitioners say a special prayer to Hafiz and ask questions about their future. Then they open a book of his poetry randomly. The answer is on the top of the right-hand page. At Hafiz's tomb, it's not necessary to bring along a volume of his poetry. Outside the gate, a man holds a caged parakeet. For a fee, the man gives the parakeet a seed and the bird chooses one of two dozen bits of folded blue and green paper on which Hafiz's answers are written.

Mahallati bought me my fortune. Hafiz wrote in couplets, but Mahallati rendered a free interpretation, adding his own lines along the way: "I congratulate the owner of this fortune. You are like a crown over the best people in the world. You can be the mistress of your field. People will follow your orders and you will be blessed. Keep a written prayer of love with you at all times. Your heart is capturing something special. Since you have good intentions, keep them."

Nazila, who was with us, remarked, "According to Hafiz, everyone is master of the universe!"

"And why not?" asked Mahallati. "For Hafiz, life is not a zero sum game."

For Mahallati, poetry is a part of the soul of his country. "I can stop anyone at random on the street and ask him to recite Saadi or Hafiz," he said. "You couldn't ask an American to recite American poetry, could you?"

He certainly got that right. I couldn't imagine stopping people on the main street of any American city and asking for recitations of Walt Whitman. But even though Americans don't routinely recite poetry, we do sing songs. Perhaps Irving Berlin and Rodgers and Hammerstein are our Saadi and Hafiz.

Then Mahallati excused himself to look for a pay phone. I offered him my cell phone. "Your wireless has too many wires," he said. He said he wanted to keep his call private; cell phones are routinely monitored by various institutions of the state.

The call took a long time, and while he was gone I asked Nazila whether she was being sarcastic when she said that Hafiz believed that everyone is master of the universe. "Not at all," she said. "Hafiz is the poet of promise. He promises love, wine, and good times. He is the critic of hypocrisy, and sees power operating through hypocrisy. All Iranians identify with him. It's because of this attitude that we have survived all the miserable times in our history."

When young Iranians study Hafiz in school, they follow the same mystical, metaphorical understanding as the clerics who recite his poetry. On a previous visit to Iran, a tour guide had explained to our group, "When Hafiz writes about wine, some people say it's about the truth, about God. But sometimes he means wine from the bottle. Once when all the wine shops were closed, Hafiz complained, and they were reopened again."

As I have encountered Iran over the years, I have found two important components of the Iranian soul: love of poetry and love of country. No other people I know takes its poetry so seriously. And few countries have such a deep-rooted and long-lasting sense of national pride. Even the revolution and the creation of the Islamic Republic could not eradicate that unique sense of Persianness that goes hand in hand with the poets who extolled the virtues of beauty, love, and bravery.

Indeed, if poetry is a connection with the beautiful and the magical, it also is, as Nazila said, a means of survival. Wherever I travel in Iran, I hear poetry recited. Iranians are famous for their ability to memorize the Koran, and Koran recitation contests are popular and highly regarded by the clerics. But I often feel that if there were to be a contest between Koranic recitations in Arabic and poetry recitations in Persian, the poetry recitations would win out.

Just the week before this visit to Shiraz, I had found myself on one of Iran's massive oil drilling rigs docked in the Caspian Sea. In the captain's quarters a volume of Hafiz was sandwiched on a shelf between manuals on navigation. "What's the book of Hafiz doing here?" I asked the captain.

His look told me he thought I was asking him why he took food and water with him when he went to sea. "Hafiz is part of life," he said. "You can't be without Hafiz."

A few months before that, Nasser Hadian, a friend who is a political science professor at the University of Tehran, spent Christmas Day with me and my family in Washington, D.C. Nasser is American-educated and once enjoyed a flourishing academic career in the United States. He and his wife, Shirin Parvini, a pharmacologist, lived well. But Nasser gave it all up to go home. He said he couldn't stay away from Iran any longer.

My husband, Andy, was incredulous. How could you give up a tenure-track college teaching position in the United States to go back to Iran? he asked Nasser.

"The poetry," Nasser said. "The mystical poetry. I missed the sound of the poetry." To prove his point, he took a copy of Hafiz from one of my bookshelves and read poems to us in Persian.

I found a creative interpretation of Hafiz in a well-appointed, smoke-filled apartment in north Tehran late one evening. In terms of refreshments, there was nothing out of the ordinary for a party of that type. In the back room a small group of men and women in their twenties were smoking marijuana. In the living room two dozen more were getting quietly drunk on moonshine vodka. The mother of the host kept a lookout at the front door for the morals police. Dinner was served at midnight. What was exceptional was the music. In one corner, a young man named Houtan played a classical guitar and sang in a voice so tender that he had earned an unusual nickname: the Elvis of Iran. The crowd sat transfixed as he sang the songs he had written: renditions of Hafiz, set to Spanish flamenco music.

Simply put, poetry for Iranians is religion, a religion as powerful as Islam. The tension between the two is spelled out in the Koran, which railed against the poets of the time who wandered in a world of illusions. "And as to the poets, those who go astray follow them," one line goes. "Do you not see that they wander in the desert of bewilderment? And that they say much that they do not do?" But the Koran also approves of poets who "have faith in God and do good deeds."

For many Iranians, the fluidity, the layers of interpretation, the magic and the mystery of their poetry keep them going, the same way prayers do for others. I saw the magic one evening at the home of Reza Seyed Hosseini, the preeminent translator of French literature into Persian. I asked him to explain why poetry is so important to Iran. He tried to explain it in scholarly terms. His wife interrupted with a more emotional response. "As children every night in winter, we would gather around my father and he would read poetry to us. My father would open Hafiz and say, 'There will be a secret hand to solve your problem.' I truly believe in what Hafiz tells me."

"My mother believes in Hafiz too," said Golnaz, her daughter-in-law and Nazila's sister. "She reads Hafiz every night for guidance." Then Seyed Hosseini closed his eyes and began to recite, caressing the words and carrying us away with the music and the passion of the verses.

I found poetry in the oddest places. On a drive back to Tehran from the Caspian Sea one morning, Nazila, Mr. Salimi, and I stopped for breakfast at a teahouse that beckoned us with strings of colored lights. It was the Iranian version of a truck stop: a small grocery store attached to a slightly larger place to eat. The plastic tablecloths were sticky. The cheap cups and saucers were chipped. We ate what was available: tea, scrambled eggs, flat bread, a feta-like cheese, and big chunks of onion. Honey was scooped up fresh from the hives out back. The black flies loved the place.

I asked the owner about the old wooden abacus he used to calculate our tab. He showed me how it worked, flicking the beads fast with his fingers. "Take it, it's yours," he said.

I know that Iranians don't really mean it when they tell you to take something that is theirs. But I have always wanted an abacus. So I offered to buy it. He refused. In the end, we struck a deal. He gave me the abacus. I gave him a black vinyl overnight bag imprinted with the logo of *The New York Times*.

Then the deal-making needed to be celebrated. An old barefoot, bald-headed man who lived in the teahouse produced two wooden flutes. He said he wanted to play for us but that he was shy. We took our cue and urged him on. He was still too shy, he said.

So Mr. Salimi began to recite the *Rubáiyát* of Omar Khayyam. I had known Mr. Salimi for years, and he had always struck me as a strictly literal type. So I was both startled and delighted to find out that Mr. Salimi recited poetry. I reminded Mr. Salimi of the Persian saying, "You only know someone after you've traveled with him."

"Everybody knows Khayyam," he said, his face beaming. "Khayyam believed that life on earth was short. That's why he wrote about love." Mr. Salimi told the story of his father-in-law, who loved Khayyam's poetry so much that when he died the family tried to bury his body close to Khayyam's tomb in Khorasan province.

Finally, the old man got up his nerve. He put the larger flute between his lip and gum on the left side of his mouth and began to play and sing local love songs from Mazandaran province. "You are such a beautiful lady," he sang. "Your brow is high. Your eyebrows are arched. Whoever takes you will never age."

He sang and sang: medieval poems set to music, modern songs made famous by female singers of the Old Regime but banned by the Islamic Republic. Within a few minutes, trucks and a passenger bus pulled up and the teahouse was full.

Someone said that one of the truck drivers, a ruddy-faced man with a strong Turkish accent, was also a singer. "No, no, I don't have any energy!" the truck driver protested, and walked out of the room. He was cajoled back. "I can't sing without whiskey!" he then said. We fed him chocolates and tea instead.

"I'm on top of the highest mountain," he sang in his local dialect. "Don't give your daughter away! I want to marry her! Don't give your daughter away until I pick up my cotton crop. Then I'll come and marry your daughter. The water stops running. The moon is in the sky. The night is very long. And I must wait."

The audience applauded. One by one the drivers and passengers left. And we continued on our way back to Tehran.

Poetry is so universal that even Ayatollah Khomeini apparently loved Hafiz. The austere Khomeini was known to have had a strong mystical streak and to have read the images of wine and love spiritually, as longing and love for God. After Khomeini's death, his son Ahmad released poems said to have been written by his father. They were mystical verses in classical Hafiz style.

Good news, O meadow bird: spring has come again
The season of drinking and kissing and hugging has come again.
The term of withered fading and sadness has ended
The days of dallying with the beloved have come again. . . .
To celebrate a beauty's curly tresses
Wine bearers, wine shops, singers, and dancing have come again.
Should you pass the schoolhouse door, tell the sheikh that
A tulip-cheeked beauty to teach him has come again.
Close up the shop of abstinence for this happy season
For my heart's ears hear that the song of the lute has come again.

O Saqi, open the door of the wineshop for me;
Make me heedless of lessons, discussions, asceticism, and hypocrisy.
Lay a strand of your curly hair in my way;
Free me from learning, the mosque, teaching, and prayers.
Singing like David, bring me a jug of wine;
Make me heedless of worry over status and its ups and downs.

"Human fallibility aside, it is difficult to imagine Ayatollah Khomeini actually doing all the things he seems to long to do in his *ghazals* [sonnets]," wrote the scholar William Hannaway, in a commentary accompanying his translation of the poems. He suggested that someone as committed to both the form and the substance of Islam as Khomeini "would find classical-style mystical poetry a convenient vehicle to express his mystical feelings."

The poems reflected the mystery that shrouded Khomeini, even in death. Some Iranians didn't believe that Khomeini had written the poetry at all.

If poetry is one of the pillars of the Iranian identity, then another can be found nearly forty miles to the northeast of Shiraz, at Persepolis, the magnificent ritual site that was built by Darius the Great, one of Persia's most illustrious kings, more than 2,500 years ago.

The ruins there range from the meager to the magnificent. Some of the pillars are nothing more than short stumps, some not even that, just concrete planters with nothing in them except gravelly dirt in which nothing can grow. But then, amid the fallen columns and blocks of stone are sumptuously carved doorways and window frames and relief carvings on a monumental staircase to record the 256 peoples who came to pay homage to their emperor. At its creation, Persepolis had running water, a complex sewer system, a postal service, and highways connecting it to other cities of the Persian empire.

But when the Islamic revolution took control of Iran, Persepolis posed a problem. Over the years, it had become a symbol not just of Iranian identity, but of worldly power and royal grandiosity. Just eight years before, in 1971, Shah Mohammad Reza Pahlavi held an extravaganza at Persepolis to celebrate the 2,500th anniversary of the Persian empire and the thirtieth anniversary of his reign. The Shah envisioned it as a modern-day Congress of Vienna, to which kings and presidents and prime ministers would come to discuss the challenges facing them.

In preparation, the royal Imperial Guard waged war against the poisonous snakes that infested the desert. Shiraz was cleaned up too: the prison was painted, shopkeepers were given new jackets, birds in cages were hung on lampposts, and power stations were built to supply air conditioners, television sets, refrigerators, and telephones.

The affair attracted thirteen presidents, ten sheikhs, nine kings, five princes, two sultans, and an assortment of lesser dignitaries and hangers-on. A vast silk-lined tent that housed the apartments of the Shah and his wife was decorated by the house of Jansen in Paris with red-velvet drapes and gilded chairs. It was surrounded by smaller tents, all with marble bathrooms, sitting rooms, refrigerators, and even ironing boards for the maids. Elizabeth Arden created a new line of cosmetics named Farah, after the Shah's wife. Lanvin designed the court's uniforms, Baccarat the goblets. Maxim's of Paris led the team of chefs and caterers. Except for caviar that was served in quails' eggs, the food and wine were flown in from Paris as well. In the end, the effect was more French than Persian.

Estimates of the cost ran as high as $200 million—all so the Shah could say, as he was reported to have told a friend in Paris, "The descendants of Charlemagne came to Persepolis to pay homage to the son of a corporal."

From his exile in Iraq, Ayatollah Khomeini used the occasion to attack the monarchy. "It is the kings of Iran that have constantly ordered massacres of their own people and had pyramids built with their skulls," he declared. "Islam came in order to destroy these palaces of tyranny.

Monarchy is one of the most shameful and disgraceful reactionary man-
ifestations." Khomeini argued that Iran's kingly legacy was inauthentic.
The only true identity Iranians should have is their Islamic one.

When he came to power in 1979, Khomeini expunged the trappings
of royalty and eliminated the glorification of kings. He replaced sensuous
richness with spiritual austerity. I turned up for an interview with Prime
Minister Mehdi Bazargan one day as movers were carrying out carpets
and boxes of china and silver. The scholar Abdol-Reza Houshang Mahdavi, who was working at the Foreign Ministry at the time, recalled the
day the clerics came and removed the carpet from under his feet. "I
watched them throw priceless French and Dutch paintings out the window into pickup trucks, just like logs," he said. "They even took down my
dark yellow curtains. They said they looked too much like gold."

The artwork and crystal chandeliers that weren't destroyed or hidden
away were sold. The clerics stamped the words "Islamic Revolution" on
the postage stamps bearing images of Persepolis and other pre-Islamic
sites. They renamed streets after mullahs and martyrs. They rewrote the
national anthem. Even the crown jewels were locked up.

Nothing was too petty to be removed. Khomeini especially hated
lions. A lion wearing a crown and carrying a sword beneath a sun had
been used as the official symbol of the Pahlavi dynasty. Khomeini gave a
speech one day criticizing as un-Islamic the government workers who
continued issuing passports and writing on stationery with the Pahlavi
symbol. So work stopped at the ministries because no one dared to write
on the official stationery. For months, no passports were issued. Eventually, a new symbol for the Islamic Republic was created: a tulip-shaped
mirror image of the word "Allah."

As for Persepolis, it became a suspect site. For years after the revolution, it lay fallow, attracting few tourists and little government money.
"One cannot find a single reasonable king during all the monarchial dynasties," Khomeini had said in 1985. So it wasn't surprising that he never
visited Persepolis or that he and the other clerics didn't quite know what
to make of the place. During the war with Iraq, the army turned the
Shah's tent city into barracks for recruits. The evergreens planted by the
Shah grew so tall that they blocked the view of the ruins from the road.

Then in December 1988, just a few months after the end of the Iran-
Iraq war, Ali Khamenei, who was then President, visited Persepolis. He
thanked those responsible for preserving what he called "these historic

sites." He praised "the art, elegance, and the superb ability" that had created Persepolis, adding that even after all these centuries, they "still remain a marvel to mankind." But for Khamenei, Persepolis was great only
as an architectural feat that reflected man's ability to create. Otherwise, it
was a symbol of Iran's dark imperial past, what he called the "cruel greatness" of Persia's expansionist emperors driven by the motto on the stone
inscriptions: "One has become the ruler of many." In other words, the
artistic miracle of Persepolis was worthy of praise, but the kings who ordered it built were to be condemned. It was left to Khamenei's successor
as President, Ali-Akbar Hashemi-Rafsanjani, to rehabilitate the place.

That happened in April 1991, when Rafsanjani too made a stop at
Persepolis, and used the occasion to become the first clerical leader to
embrace the kingly legacy of Iran. Rafsanjani was a state-builder, and he
was determined to restore Iran to a position of power in the region, even
if he had to bend principles to do it. He came from a family of merchant-
farmers from Nough, near the southern Iranian town of Rafsanjan. The
family business, the Rafsanjan Pistachio Producers' Cooperative, was the
largest pistachio enterprise in the country. While other clerics wrote great
tomes interpreting the Koran, Rafsanjani wrote a favorable biography of
Amir Kabir, the nineteenth-century nation-building Prime Minister and
reformer.

From the early days of the revolution, Rafsanjani favored pragma-
tism over religious absolutism. I saw that firsthand in early 1980 during
the hostage crisis when Maynard Parker, an editor of *Newsweek,* and I interviewed Rafsanjani, who was then a member of the Revolutionary
Council. He justified the seizure of the American embassy, but his heart
didn't seem to be in it. Unlike Khomeini, he seemed filled not with hatred
and rage, just frustration. He wanted to get on with the business of governing—and with the business of business.

At a time when other Iranian leaders demanded the return of the ex-
iled Shah, Rafsanjani said he had a simpler solution: "If the Shah dies,
that would help," he told us. Shortly afterward, the Shah did die of com-
plications caused by cancer, but the hostage crisis went on. Not everyone
on the Revolutionary Council was as eager as Rafsanjani to get back to
business.

In 1991, the moment had arrived for Iran to give Rafsanjani's practical approach a try. He saw in Persepolis something other than monarchy:
the importance of heritage and national dignity. By now, the war with

Iraq had been over for three years. The religious rhetoric of the clerics had lost the power to inspire. So Rafsanjani—like the Shah before him—decided to re-create a glorious past based on the greatness of Persia's empire. "Standing in the middle of these wonderful centuries-old ruins, I felt the nation's dignity was all-important and must be strengthened," Rafsanjani said. "Our people must know that they are not without a history."

By the time I went to see Persepolis for myself several years later, its glory had faded. Near the entrance, hundreds of Iranians picnicked with their children in grassy patches near the royal tents built for the Shah's extravaganza. I was stunned to see that the tents were still standing. They had been well built, with concrete floors and thick wooden frames covered in red, blue, and tan rubberized canvas. The graffiti on the walls captured the shifting political sentiments of visitors. "Death to the traitor Shah" had been crossed out, replaced with the words, "Salute to the Shah." "Rafsanjani and Khamenei are donkeys," said another. The caretakers at Persepolis didn't even bother to paint them over.

A generous tip to one caretaker opened the main tent, revealing a room with red cut velvet on the walls, voluminous red fabric ballooning from the ceiling, gold-trimmed mirrors à la Versailles, more than a dozen crystal chandeliers, and an elevated stage. But there were no door handles of gold, no expensive carpets or silver or crystal. They had been carted away by revolutionary looters long ago. The bedrooms were still there: one for the Shah, another for his wife, a number of others, all with soundproof doors and bulletproof glass windows. The windows had bullet nicks in them. "When the military took over they used to bet whether they could break the windows," the caretaker said. The windows held.

At the main entrance a short drive away, more than four hundred people, mostly young families and newlyweds, filed in for the new "sound and light" show. The moonlight cast long shadows and turned the gray stones yellow. There were no mosquitoes that night. The day had been desert-hot, but the night belonged to the cool, clean breeze. Did I imagine smelling the scent of the magical *mahbub-e shab*?

Dozens of security police wandered on the set and through the crowds. Spotlights were trained on the pillars and carvings. Voices representing the ancient kings told the story of Persepolis over a crackling sound system that had seen better days. It was hard to figure out who was who and what the point of the presentation was. The recorded sounds of horses, dogs, chickens, and birds didn't help. Drums rolled when Alexander the Great set fire to Persepolis. Then the voice of God boomed across the ruins. He spoke of resurrection into heaven for the good and damnation for the wicked. There was not a word about Islam, the Prophet, or the Koran.

A strange intense crying pierced the silence, a sound so loud that it drowned out the show. At first I thought it was part of the act. But the sound continued, off-cue. It sounded like a dozen babies. Then I thought it must be cats. The sound got closer, then suddenly stopped. It was only later when I was reading a book on Persepolis that I realized what had been making the sound: a pack of wolves howling, probably from the nearby hills. I thought it a fitting metaphor: the majesty and permanence of Persepolis threatened by wolves.

"I have good news," Amir said. "My father has invited you to lunch." We had finished our tour of the tombs of the poets in Shiraz, and Mahallati was outlining where we would go next.

Our next stop was the private library of Ayatollah Majdeddin Mahallati, the father of my host. With thirty thousand books and manuscripts stacked deep on old wooden bookcases it is the largest private library in Shiraz. Dusty photographs of some of the most famous clerics of Iran looked down at us.

From there we went to a small building where many of the Mahallatis—most of them clerics—are buried. The Mahallati family had been the leading religious family in Shiraz for two centuries. Amir Mahallati would probably be buried there someday. He pointed out the grave of his paternal grandfather, a learned ayatollah.

I had heard about this grandfather. Early in the revolution, he had been too outspoken and was quickly silenced. "Wasn't this the grandfather who opposed the rule of the clergy?" I asked.

Mahallati clearly felt uncomfortable answering. But he didn't want to lie either.

"My grandfather saw what was going on and took some distance," he said. "He saw the summary executions of people without trials and he said, 'This is not Islam.' He took some distance, yes, some distance."

Next to the room of tombs is a shrine. It is a small room of extraordinarily intricate mirror-mosaics, not just clear glass mirrors pieced together but also mirrors in blue, green, red, and yellow, raised and angled in a dozen different shapes to make the room look even more dazzling and mysterious. "There is a saying, 'You don't pray in front of a mirror,'" Mahallati said. "That's because you are supposed to be so humble that you lose yourself. But with broken mirrors you don't ever see a complete face. You see but you don't see. It goes beyond reality."

When he visits the United States, Mahallati is exotic, the gadfly ex-ambassador son of an ayatollah who gives lectures around the country about the mysteries of Persia. At the tombs of the poets he had shown me his romantic poetic side. Now he was playing the role of the dutiful son. "I'm sure when you meet my father, you will tell him how much you like his library and his mosque," he said.

The ayatollah's house is a reflection of the man. He once had enjoyed great power, and had retained a position of prestige. A large grape arbor covers the entrance into the charming courtyard filled with rosebushes. Inside the house, there are no photographs of other clerics, living or dead, which suggests that the ayatollah felt secure enough—in the privacy of his home, at least—not to align himself with others. There are two couches in the living room, which suggests a touch of the Western, since traditional families usually sit on the floor. The house is a comfortable place, with a greenhouse on one side of the dining room, stained glass windows on the other, and air-conditioning. I was told later by a friend from Shiraz that the fact that this high-ranking cleric had invited me, a non-Muslim woman, to join him in a meal was a stunning act, "the epitome of modernity."

We didn't eat on the floor, but at a round table. Over a lunch of lamb, rice, and vegetables served by a manservant, the ayatollah spoke of poetry, not of Islam. He recited the poems of Iran's greatest epic poet, Abol-Ghasem Ferdowsi, not the verses of the Koran. "Two things are my favorite," the ayatollah said from memory, "a young companion and an old wine. The young companion takes away all your sorrows, the old wine gives richness to your life."

The ayatollah added that he was speaking metaphorically, of course, the way Hafiz and Saadi did. Still, his son did not like the way the conversation was going.

"Tell my father how much you appreciate his library," the son said. So we moved the conversation to old books. The ayatollah told me about the library and about the religious school where he and some of his former students taught. He told me about the other institutions he had created in Shiraz, all with grassroots fund-raising: an Islamic charity that provides social security payments to the poor, free housing units for families that have lost their breadwinners, and a mosque in the center of town. The conversation shifted to other topics: the fact that his own father had been such a learned ayatollah that he had taught Ayatollah Khomeini; the high morality of young people in Shiraz; the enduring popularity of Hafiz.

I asked the ayatollah about an often-told tale that he had rescued Persepolis from revolutionary zealots who came there with bulldozers in 1979. His version was a bit less heroic. As he told it, Sheikh Sadegh Khalkhali, the notorious "hanging judge" of the revolution, came to Shiraz with a band of thugs. He gave an angry speech demanding that the faithful torch the silk-lined tent city and the grandstand that the Shah had built.

"In the beginning of the revolution, everybody was trying to run his own show," the ayatollah recalled. "Everybody had weapons. Prisoners were freed. There was no law and order. My father, who was a grand ayatollah, and I stopped people from killing, looting, and taking money out of the country until, thank God, order was restored. Some people wanted to destroy historical places. We had to stop them. I heard the news that Sadegh Khalkhali wanted to set fire to Persepolis. So people went after him with stones."

"Did Khalkhali escape?" I asked.

"Yes, with stones thrown at him and shouts for him to go away." As for Persepolis, Ayatollah Mahallati added, "It's the oldest, strongest symbol we have."

I knew I could not let the lunch end without asking the ayatollah about his magnificent grapes. Shiraz, after all, once produced the finest wine in the country. But after the revolution, Shiraz became better known as the Australian and South African name for wines made from grapes that were similar—but not identical—to their Iranian cousins. Shiraz is now the most commonly planted grape in Australia. A cleric from Shiraz once told me a story about how Charles de Gaulle, during a visit as President of France, had loved the wine of Shiraz so much that he took cases of it back home.

I told the ayatollah about my Sicilian grandfather, and how he grew grapes in our backyard and made wine there every summer, white one year, red the next. The ayatollah ordered his manservant to cut some grapes for me. A platter of tiny, round amber-colored grapes arrived.

"Oh yes, the wine," said the ayatollah, matter-of-factly.

I couldn't tell from the tone whether he was praising it or condemning it. As a learned ayatollah, he certainly wasn't serving it or drinking it. But his son had grown even more uncomfortable about this topic. He interrupted again.

"I think you are late for your departure," he said dryly. I said goodbye to the ayatollah, who gave me a string of worry beads the same shade of gold as the grapes. The son drove Nazila and me straight to the airport.

On the flight back to Tehran, I thought about how the clerics and kings of Persia had something else in common: their deep sense of national pride. With it came a desire to prove their superiority over the Arabs, whose armies had overrun Persia in the seventh century and ruled for nearly a millennium. The Arabs may have brought Islam to Iran, but they also imposed Arabic letters onto the Persian, and injected Arabic words into the vocabulary.

Arabic became the language of religion, because the Koran was written and Muslim prayers were said in Arabic. But conversion to Islam came slowly. "The surrender was never complete," wrote Sir Roger Stevens, a former British ambassador to Tehran, in his 1962 book, *The Land of the Great Sophy.* "The Iranians were not in their hearts ever fully reconciled to fusion with Arab Islam; they accepted the tenets of the new religion but gave it an individual, nationalistic twist."

It sometimes seemed difficult for the Islamic Republic to reconcile itself to the fact that the language of Islam is not Persian, but Arabic. I was amused by a speech that Ayatollah Khamenei gave one day to an international conference on the Persian language. He noted that Islam was introduced to Iran in Arabic, but added that it was "promoted" through Persian. Arabic is a particularly difficult language to learn, and many students resent the fact that they have to study it at all. (Seven years of Arabic are required of all Iranian students.) The vast majority never master the language and thus have no idea what the clerics are saying when they recite the Koran from pulpits or television screens. So much for the "thought control" of the ayatollahs so often imagined in the West.

The American academic Terence O'Donnell lived for fifteen years on a farm in Iran, and he recounted in his delightful memoir, *Garden of the Brave in War,* the banter between him and his servant Mamdali every morning. Mamdali, wrote O'Donnell, would "knock on the dressing room door and ask the question, 'Are you an Arab or an Iranian?' If I was naked, I would answer that I was an Arab and he would wait outside the door, whereas if I was clothed, or partly so, I would reply that I was an Iranian and he would come in with the coffee. This, of course, was a joke reflecting the old Iranian view that Arabs were uncivilized people who went about unclothed and ate lizards."

One of the worst insults for Iranians is to be lumped together with the Arabs. One day during a visit to the Foreign Ministry, Hamid-Reza Asefi, the ministry spokesman, fiercely criticized Iran's presence on the State Department's list of countries that support terrorism. I told him that to some extent, the list was political, and that even Syria, considered a strategic partner in the Middle East peace process, remained on the list. How could Iran, therefore, expect to be taken off the list?

"But we're not Syria!" he exclaimed. "We're Iran!" What he seemed to mean was that Syria was a poor, tiny, artificial creation, a place like Iraq, Jordan, and the Persian Gulf states, which were created by the imperial pens and imaginations of the British and the French after World War I. How could Iran, with its glorious history, culture, and geographical importance, be put in the same category? The issue of terrorism, it seemed, was beside the point.

In 1934, the monarch Reza Shah built a modern mausoleum outside Mashad for Ferdowsi. It was a monument to nationalism as much as to the tenth-century poet, whom many Iranians credit for rescuing the Persian language from oblivion with his great epic poem, the *Shahnameh,* or *Book of Kings.* Despite efforts by some clerics early in the revolution to remove the book from bookstores, the most popular poem recited in Iran today is from Ferdowsi's epic.

Reza Shah believed that many of Iran's problems stemmed from "Arabization" and used his reign to distance Iran from the Arabs. He scrapped the lunar calendar for the Zoroastrian solar one. He encouraged people to give Persian, non-Islamic names to their children. He created an academy to de-Arabize the language and to rewrite history to stress Iran's Aryan heritage at the expense of its Islamic past. He sent archaeological teams around the country in search of Persian ruins.

Sixty-four years after Ferdowsi's tomb was built, President Khatami sought to revive the memory of the poet in a different way. Khatami used the occasion of a meeting with Iranian expatriates at the United Nations in September 1998 to talk about the Iranian national character. He served notice that even an Islamic Iran cannot mature into what it could be—a democratic republic—if it denies its Persian past, just as the Islamic revolutionaries had shown the Shah the costs of ignoring Islamic sentiments. The time had come to embrace rather than deny history. What was so dramatic about what he said was that his starting point was not the Koran, but Ferdowsi's *Book of Kings*. Khatami argued that the poem captured "a correct and beautiful image of the Iranian spirit": courtesy, respect, politeness, an aversion to war, but a willingness to fight to preserve honor.

Khatami had come a long way from where Khomeini had stood on the question of Iran's identity and history. Still, Iran's history was now more than merely the distant past, whether Persian or Islamic. Khomeini's years themselves—the years of single-minded devotion to Islam, struggle, and martyrdom—were within living memory. And in those years there had not been an aversion to war.

CHAPTER NINE

Martyrs Never Die

The distinctive characteristic of a martyr is that he charges the atmosphere with courage and zeal. He revives the spirit of valor and fortitude . . . among the people who have lost it. That is why Islam is always in need of martyrs.

— UNDATED IRANIAN HANDBOOK IN ENGLISH,
THE MARTYR

When Imam Hosein decided to leave for Kufa, some prudent members of his family tried to dissuade him. Their argument was that his action was not logical. They were right in their own way. . . . But Imam Hosein had a higher logic. His logic was that of a martyr, which is beyond the comprehension of ordinary people.

— UNDATED IRANIAN HANDBOOK IN ENGLISH,
THE MARTYR

*H*AMID RAHIMIAN lives for the dead.

As the director of the martyrs' section of the biggest necropolis in Iran, he is driven by one goal: to keep alive the memory of his fallen comrades until he can join them. They were the lucky ones, he said. They had died on the battlefield during Iran's war with Iraq and had gone to paradise.

Hamid had only been wounded. And survival means that the twenty-nine-year-old veteran is condemned, psychologically, to the living hell of waiting for his own death. He would have committed suicide had the Koran not forbidden it. "I dream of martyrdom," he told me over tea and biscuits in his small, airless, run-down office. "I am waiting for it to happen. To prepare myself, I have eliminated all personal relationships. I have no attachment to my wife or son, only to God."

Much of Hamid's life has revolved around suffering. He was only nine when the revolution triumphed. And four years later, when he was in seventh grade, he forged his birth certificate, ran away from home, and headed for the war front as a member of the *baseej* ("mobilized"), the volunteer corps drawn primarily from devout, poor families and dedicated to serving in God's war.

As Hamid's story unfolded, his body seized up as he stuttered and choked out the words. His pale face twisted in pain. "I was in a truck with twenty-one others," he said with difficulty. "We were on the road between Khorramshahr and Ahwaz. The Iraqis surrounded us with tanks. One tank hit us hard. Five of my comrades were martyred immediately. Cut into pieces. The rest of us were badly injured."

Hamid's lungs were seared and permanently scarred. His heart was damaged. Both arms and legs were badly broken. The cruel irony is that the attack came on September 9, 1988, after Iran and Iraq had signed a cease-fire ending their eight-year war. "These are my last days," Hamid told me more than a decade later. "The doctors don't have hope anymore. I know that I will die soon. That is when I'll begin my new life."

Every day for five years he has come to his office in the House of Martyrs in the center of Behesht-e Zahra, Tehran's vast cemetery, to fall under death's spell. The job pays the equivalent of $45 a month. Still, Hamid feels privileged. "I came here to work because my friends are buried here," he said. "They told me that if they died I must follow their path. The Koran says, 'Those who die for God are martyrs, and the martyrs never die. They live forever.'"

Hamid is a Shiite, and he fervently believes in the Shiite version of history, its lore and its rituals. Ayatollah Khomeini had told the Hamids of Iran that martyrdom was a perfect death, and they believed him. If they couldn't die, at least they could keep that spirit alive.

So every year, in speeches, passion plays, and processions of penance, the Shiites of Iran celebrate the ten days in which Hosein, the grandson of the Prophet Mohammad, defended his family and followers at the battle of Karbala. Every year for centuries on the anniversary of Hosein's death, men and boys like Hamid have flagellated themselves with chains and beat themselves over the head. Those at the front of the procession dress themselves in white burial shrouds and chant the story of the slaughter. In 1640, a Turkish traveler to Iran described the ceremony: "Hundreds of Hosein's devotees beat and wounded their heads, faces, and bodies with swords and knives. For the love of Imam Hosein they make their blood flow. The green grassy field becomes bloodied and looks like a field of poppies."

Under the Islamic Republic, however, the practice has come to resemble an officially condoned carnival as much as an act of religious mortification. The ceremonies are organized through neighborhood congregations called *hey-ats* and for nights beforehand participants practice their walk, their rhythm, and their chain-beating. They learn a trick to halt the movement of the chains and soften the blows. They take their practicing seriously, and since it is all in the name of religion, their wives can hardly complain. In fact, in recent years women and girls have tagged along to march and watch the spectacle—and even party.

For Shiites, the battle of Karbala is the equivalent of the passion and crucifixion of Jesus, the self-flagellation reminiscent of the medieval practice of self-mutilation, carrying of the Cross, and physical deprivation that survives in parts of the Christian world today. In recent years during Moharram, the month of mourning, Iran's authorities tried to ban the most excessive ritual in which worshippers shave their heads and carve them open with swords. As Ayatollah Khamenei said in denouncing the ritual in 1999, it "gives the impression that Shiite Muslims are superstitious and irrational."

Even so, the cult of martyrdom has deep roots in Iran's Shiite culture, and Khomeini was a master at manipulating the homegrown strain of martyrdom and its lust for sacrifice. During a sermon in Qom for Moharram in 1963 Khomeini likened the oppression of the Iranian people under the Shah's monarchy to Hosein's martyrdom. When Khomeini was arrested shortly afterward, men and women alike wrapped themselves in white funeral shrouds as symbols of their readiness to die for him.

Once the struggle for power was joined, the spilling of blood came to be embraced, not avoided. As Iran's revolution was unfolding during the Moharram ceremony in 1978, demonstrators caught in a battle with the Shah's troops smeared their hands with the blood of the victims and raised their palms toward heaven. In the months before the revolution Khomeini said, "Our movement is but a fragile plant. It needs the blood of martyrs to help it grow into a towering tree." The Black Friday Massacre in Tehran on September 8, 1978, in which hundreds of demonstrators were killed by the Shah's troops, was a key event in precipitating the downfall of the Shah. Khomeini called that day the "victory of blood over the sword."

When Khomeini returned to Iran in 1979 he had his priorities right, Hamid told me. The first thing Khomeini did was to fly by helicopter to this very cemetery to mourn the victims of Black Friday. He was hoisted onto a platform, where he raised a fist before tens of thousands of his followers. "For those of you who have given up so much for God, God must soon give you the prize," he told them.

But now, more than two decades later, Hamid was still waiting for the prize.

Hamid seemed to know every road, every monument, every grave in Behesht-e Zahra, even though it extended for miles over a vast plain off the busy highway leading out of Tehran to Qom. The cemetery had been built in the 1950s and had expanded over the years to become Tehran's principal burial ground. As one of the few public spaces in Tehran safe from attack by the security forces before the revolution, it became, in addition, a meeting place for opponents of the Shah.

Today, a sculpture of a great white hand holding a red tulip, the flower of martyrdom, beckons visitors at the entrance of the complex. Inside, men and women gather to lay wreaths, pour rosewater, and recite verses of the Koran as they caress the tombstones of their dead husbands in an effort to make contact with their spirits. The cemetery is well organized for visitors, with a playground, park benches, public toilets, a convenience store, a computer center for locating graves, a kebab restaurant and a planned Metro station.

A walk through Behesht-e Zahra is a walk through the Islamic Republic's political history. One section houses the bodies of the National Front leaders, Islamic liberal intellectuals who opposed the Shah and joined forces with Khomeini. A second section is reserved for the victims of the Shah's secret police and military during the revolution. A third is assigned to officials killed in the terrorist bombing of the headquarters of the revolution's Islamic Republic Party in 1981. The section where Hamid works houses acres of graves for the martyrs of the Iran-Iraq war.

From 1980 through 1988, when the country was at war with Iraq, the wide, tree-lined roads at Behesht-e Zahra seemed perpetually clogged with mourners. Professional flagellators-for-hire wandered about in those days, prepared with wooden-handled bunches of chains to whip across their backs and shoulders in frenzied rituals of mourning. Military musicians playing saxophones, clarinets, trumpets, and drums sometimes accompanied the caskets of particularly important martyrs. Visiting the cemetery became a form of recreation, with extended families picnicking on the graves amid the evergreens and junipers and along the canals as they watched the spectacles. Mullahs told stories about martyrdom—for pay— in singsong voices that made people cry.

On the day I met Hamid, the martyrs' section was nearly deserted. But that didn't diminish his enthusiasm. He led me through rows and rows of graves of small slabs of gray stone set into concrete. Marking each grave is a framed glass case containing both religious icons and intensely intimate mementos: Koranic texts, green banners bearing religious inscriptions, worry beads, and prayer stones, next to plastic childhood toys and figurines from wedding cakes. Some of the cases include bits of tattered and bloody clothing worn by the victims at the time of their deaths. But there is something else, startling to an American: photographs of the dead that stare back.

The war martyrs look so hopeful. And so young. The colored polyester flags that fly from the metal cases—for the Islamic Republic, for Islam, for mourning, for martyrdom, for the army, for the ready-to-die volunteers—add a macabre festive look. Hamid showed me the grave in plot twenty-six that he said sometimes gives off the smell of perfumed flowers, even though no flowers grow there. And the grave in plot twenty-seven where the spirit of Fatemeh, Mohammad's daughter, comes and cries out in the middle of the night. ("Behesht-e Zahra" means "Paradise of Zahra," one of the names given to Fatemeh.) And the grave in plot twenty-four where a mother of a martyr named Ali Derakhshani built a tiny house of green metal for herself years ago, enabling her to live above her son's grave. An empty grave nearby awaits the woman.

Hamid showed me another grave in plot twenty-four where Hosein Fahmideh, a thirteen-year-old suicide bomber, is buried. In 1981, the story goes, Fahmideh strapped a bomb to his belly, crawled under an Iraqi tank, and blew himself up. Khomeini later called the boy "our leader," adding, "The value of his little heart is greater than could be described by hundreds of tongues and hundreds of pens. . . . He drank the sweet elixir of martyrdom." In 1986, Iran celebrated his martyrdom by issuing a commemorative stamp. The occasion was the annual Universal Day of the Child.

Hamid showed me the high, wide-tiered fountain built for the martyred war dead. The fountain had once cascaded crimson-colored water dyed to look like blood. As more war dead came home, the cemetery grew bigger, so big that satellite fountains of martyrs' blood had to be built. The martyrs are "irrigating the revolutionary seed," officials liked to say. But after the war, the fountains were turned off. On the day of my visit, the main one was dry. When I asked Hamid why, he shrugged and said, "There are many things that have lost their color after twenty years. One of them is the color of the fountain. Some traitorous officials claim that the red color is a reminder of the blood shed during the war and since there is no war the fountain should not run red anymore. If it were up to me, I would build fountains in every single square in the country and fill them with red water to remind people of the sacrifices of the martyrs."

Hamid took me to the martyrs' store, where he sold cards with photos of the war dead. Some of the victims wore uniforms. Others wore civilian clothes. One young man smiled from a field of flowers. The cards had backings like stickers and could be put on the side of a car fender or the barrel of a rifle. I assumed the cards were supposed to be collected, and they did look a bit like baseball cards.

The most creative and enduring personal memento of martyrdom I have ever found in Iran was not at the martyrs' store. Walking through Tehran's main bazaar just a few weeks after the revolution, I came upon a Swiss-made wristwatch for $20 with a built-in sun sensor that allowed Ayatollah Khomeini's face to appear twice a minute. In English along the bottom of the face were the words, "Souvenir of Islamic Republic Revolution 1979." The second hand was a red splotch—a symbol of a drop of martyr's blood. More than two decades later, the watch keeps perfect time.

The Iran-Iraq war began in the fall of 1980, at a time when Saddam Hussein felt threatened by Iran's revolution and by Khomeini's appeal to the world's Muslims to rise up against their "oppressive" secular regimes in the name of Islam. Khomeini's call resonated strongly in Iraq, where the majority of the population is Shiite. "What we have done in Iran we will do again in Iraq," he declared shortly after his triumphant return in February 1979.

Iran's new revolutionary fighters launched pinprick strikes into Iraqi territory. Khomeini gave moral and financial support to outlawed Shiite groups in Iraq. In response, on September 22, 1980, Saddam Hussein launched a massive ground and air assault across the border. Within two days his troops occupied a thirty-mile-wide strip of Iranian territory. He wanted nothing less than Iraqi control over most of Iran's Arab-speaking, oil-rich province of Khuzestan, and over the Shaat al-Arab waterway that divides the two countries.

But the Iran-Iraq war was not just a dispute over boundaries. It was also a struggle for power between two despotisms, each lusting for regional supremacy. Saddam denounced Khomeini's pretensions to the leadership of the Islamic world. The role of regional leader, he declared, was his. "The Koran was written in Arabic," he claimed, "and God destined the Arabs to play a vanguard role in Islam." In Iran, paintings and rhetoric portrayed Saddam Hussein as Caliph Yazid, the general of the Sunni army that had slain Hosein at Karbala. "If you can kill Saddam before we execute him, stab him in the back," Khomeini told Iraqi Shiites. "Paralyze the economy. Stop paying taxes. This is war between Islam and blasphemy."

More important for Khomeini, the war became the glue that bound the Iranian nation—and excused the regime for demanding sacrifices of its people. When Iran drove the Iraqis back across the border in 1982, Saddam declared a unilateral cease-fire, withdrew his forces from most of Iranian territory, and called for peace. But Khomeini rebuffed Saddam's peace gesture, instead calling for his ouster and for the annexation of Iraq. Now the war became a vehicle to consolidate Khomeini's hold on power and to create an Islamic empire in the entire Persian Gulf region.

It was that sweeping goal that inspired believers like Hamid to volunteer for martyrdom. The passion play of Imam Hosein could be performed on a real battlefield every day. The cult of martyrdom prompted Khomeini to send human waves of child-martyrs with little formal military training to die on Iraqi battlefields in the name of Islam. Iran, after all, had manpower to spare. Its population was more than that of Iraq, Saudi Arabia, the other Gulf Arab states, Jordan, and Syria combined.

Hamid and others like him tied blood-red bandannas around their foreheads. On some were written the words, "Warriors of God." Others read, "Revenge for the blood of Hosein." I saw Iranian soldiers ready for battle wearing small gold keys on their uniforms where other soldiers might wear medals. They were the keys that would immediately take their souls to heaven if they should die. In some battles, soldiers carried their own funeral shrouds.

I had witnessed firsthand the religious zeal that drove men and boys like Hamid. During one tour of the southern Iraqi border after a particularly grisly battle in the early stages of the war, Iraqi victors showed me the shriveled bodies of a dozen Iranian soldiers and the crude weapons they carried. An Iraqi soldier dumped an Iranian suitcase on the ground. Out poured pocket-sized copies of the Koran, stained with blood, pictures of Imam Ali, and prayer stones inscribed with Koranic verses. The most interesting artifacts were laminated plastic cards showing Khomeini's portrait on one side and an image of Karbala on the other. Khomeini had promised to liberate Karbala. He probably didn't tell his soldiers that Karbala was over three hundred miles inside Iraq.

The end of the slaughter would not come until 1988, precipitated by the mistaken downing of a civilian Iranian plane by the USS *Vincennes* in July of that year. It was an accident, but Iran's leaders were convinced that the United States was determined to get involved in the war. And that judgment helped them to see that the war that had boosted Iran's revolution for so many years had begun to destroy it. On July 18, Khomeini accepted a United Nations cease-fire resolution, using the rhetoric of death even then. "I had promised to fight to the last drop of my blood and to my last breath," he said in a statement read on Tehran Radio that stunned the nation and the world. "Taking this decision was more deadly than taking poison. I submitted myself to God's will and drank this drink for his satisfaction."

Khomeini had reason to be bitter, for that act reversed the hopes that he had set out for his revolution. Iraq's Shiite majority would not become a satellite state of Iran. The dream of universal revolution throughout the Muslim world was dashed, replaced by "Islam in one country." After the cease-fire, banner headlines in Tehran newspapers declared, "War, War and Now Victory." But there would be no more calls to arms, no victory.

The war had lasted just one month short of eight years. Although estimates of casualties vary widely, it is believed that at least 300,000 Iranians were killed and between 600,000 and 750,000 were wounded. Another two million were uprooted from their homes. Billions of dollars were spent. The war was fought largely on Iranian territory, and sixteen of Iran's twenty-four provinces—with two thirds of its population—were targets of Iraqi bombs and missiles, including Tehran itself. The war devastated Iran's economy, causing massive losses to its infrastructure, oil industry, industrial centers, cities, and farmland.

*   *   *

By far the best way to keep the memories fresh, Hamid told me, is to watch war films in the cemetery's theater hall. On the day of my visit, we were the only people in the audience. The theater was stuffy, the films grainy and grisly. He chose one of his favorites. It was about the return of the remains of Iranian soldiers years after the war. In one scene, a widow is given the bones of her husband. She picks them up one by one and kisses them, smiling, as if in a trance. She caresses the skull and speaks to it. "Your baby child is a man now!" she cries.

In another film a group of teenage soldiers prepare for a battle. They strap on their weapons and fire artillery against the enemy. They run up hills and fire handheld weapons and machine guns from behind sandbags. Then they begin to die. In one scene, two soldiers drag the body of a wounded comrade who has lost both his legs. The camera focuses on the bloody stumps. In another, the camera zooms in on the body of a decapitated soldier propped up on sandbags. In a third, a body has been cut in two. In a fourth, a sixteen-year-old soldier with both legs sliced off screams in agony, "Allah! Allah! Allah! Allah! I die for you, Hosein! I give up my life for you!"

As we watched, Hamid wept so deeply that I wanted to reach out to console him. But I knew my touch would be rebuffed. "These are the scenes I have seen!" he moaned. "I can never come back to life. I feel martyrdom with my two hands!"

The only time Hamid smiled in the hours we spent together was when he showed me a three-minute black and white film of his unit preparing for their fateful operation the day their truck was hit. One shot showed a much younger Hamid looking shyly at the camera as he boarded a bus headed to the front.

"We gave up the best days of our lives," Hamid said. "We gave up our education. Some of us died. Some of us were wounded. Now the ideals we fought for have been buried. The new generation doesn't want us anymore. This country is becoming so materialistic. It is losing its martyrdom mentality. Even worse, there is a plot to eliminate the fighting generation."

Hamid cursed the authorities in Tehran for building cultural centers and high-rise apartment complexes instead of better graves for the martyrs and more museums in their honor.

He cursed society for forgetting the sacrifices of his generation, telling the story of how he once fell ill on the street, but was turned away from a hospital because he didn't have the money to pay.

Two Iranian women in black chadors walk past a mural in Tehran of the late Ayatollah Ruhollah Khomeini, the revolutionary leader and founder of the Islamic Republic. In the last few years, the government has made an effort to soften Khomeini's image by removing most of the stern portraits of him that once dominated the landscape. (*Agence France-Presse*)

A bride dancing with her groom at a private wedding party in Tehran. Wedding parties are still occasionally targeted by the morals police, who object to music, dancing, drinking alcohol, and mingling of the sexes, even in private. *(Alexandra Avakian/Contact Press Images)*

A table set for *Nowruz,* the Persian New Year, the beginning of thirteen days of joy surrounding the spring equinox in March. Even the most religious Iranian families set their tables with a mirror, a goldfish in a bowl, colored eggs, and seven items whose names begin with the letter "s" in Persian. *(Elaine Sciolino)*

Sakineh Ziai (second from the left), President Mohammad Khatami's mother, at a family *eftar*, the nightly ritual of breaking a dawn-to-dusk fast during the holy month of Ramadan, in the city of Yazd. Because the women and men at the *eftar* were not all close blood relatives, the women and girls did not remove their veils. *(Elaine Sciolino)*

Young men and women dancing at a private party in Tehran. Technically, they are breaking the rules that prohibit unmarried men and women from socializing. Yet there is a range of refuges from the theocracy's strict rules, from private homes to private clubs to semipublic facilities set aside for women or men. *(Dokhi Fassihian)*

Ayatollah Ruhollah Khomeini resting on a mattress in the garden of his rented house in Neauphle-le-Château, near Paris, shortly after his arrival in France in October 1978, and a few months before his triumphal return to Iran during the Islamic Revolution. *(Agence France-Presse)*

One of the most well-known posters of Iran's revolution, painted in the style of a Persian miniature. Shah Mohammad Reza Pahlavi is shown at the lower left with a broken crown and a broken sword, holding on to Uncle Sam, whose hat is decorated with the Star of David and whose shirt shows the British flag. Khomeini, Moses-like, is seen triumphant as those "martyred" by the Shah are seen floating in the sky.

Supreme Leader Ayatollah Ali Khamenei (center) confirms Mohammad Khatami, a mid-ranking cleric and head of the National Library, as the fifth president of the Islamic Republic of Iran in August 1997. Ali-Akbar Hashemi-Rafsanjani, the outgoing president, is on the left. A portrait of Ayatollah Khomeini hangs on the wall. *(Agence France-Presse)*

President Khatami, Nazila Fathi (center, in patterned headscarf) and I (at left, holding a pen and a notebook) at a graduation ceremony at the all-female Al Zahra University in Tehran. Khatami averted his eyes from the camera just before the photo was taken.

Young women shopping for makeup in an upscale cosmetics shop in Tehran. An increasing number of Iranian women are flouting the Islamic dress code by showing more hair and wearing makeup and nail polish in public. *(Jamsheed Bairami)*

Female soldiers carrying AK-47 rifles march during a military parade marking the beginning of Iran's "Sacred Military Week" in Tehran, September 1999. During the revolution and the war with Iraq in the 1980s, however, the existence of veiled and armed women— "nuns with guns," we journalists called them—was largely a myth. *(Agence France-Presse)*

Schoolgirls playing basketball. The Islamic Republic has begun to stress the importance of sports to keep women and girls healthy and busy. *(Jamsheed Bairami)*

Mary Ann Jiganti, an American tourist from Chicago, poses in front of a sign at the Homa Hotel, the finest hotel in Shiraz, that advises women to cover their heads with scarves and their bodies with loose clothing and to avoid wearing makeup inside the hotel. *(Elaine Sciolino)*

IN THE NAME OF GOD

RESPECTFUL LADIES ARE ASKED TO OBSERVE THE ISLAMIC HIJAB AND NOT TO USE THE COSMETICS IN PUBLIC.

PLEASE USE A SCARF TO COVER YOUR HAIR AND NECK.

A LONG LOOSE DRESS AND DARK STOCKINGS (OR TROUSERS).

WE WISH YOU A NICE TRIP.

HOMA HOTEL

Ayatollah Majdeddin Mahallati, one of Iran's best-known ayatollahs, walking among the roses in his garden in Shiraz. The house is a comfortable place, and I was told later by a friend from Shiraz that the fact that this high-ranking cleric had invited me, a non-Muslim woman, to join him for lunch was "the epitome of modernity." *(Alexandra Avakian/Contact Press Images)*

Iranian female tourists (in chadors at lower left) walking among the ruins at Persepolis, Iran's greatest archeological site, which dates to the time of Darius the Great in the sixth century B.C. In recent years, the Islamic Republic has tried to attract foreign tourists to Iran, touting Persepolis and the country's other historical and cultural sites. *(Staton R. Winter)*

At Tehran's vast Behesht-e Zahra cemetery, an Iranian woman mourns the death of her eighteen-year-old son who was killed during the eight-year war with Iraq. The cemetery extends for miles and has become Tehran's principal burial ground. It is well organized for visitors, with a playground, park benches, public toilets, a convenience store, a computer center for locating graves, a kebab restaurant, and a planned metro station. *(Agence France-Presse)*

Hidden from his students by a canvas screen, a male professor imparts his wisdom to female seminarians in Qom. After the lecture, the women spoke of wanting to learn the language of Islam and Islamic law, and to get paying jobs. *(Lise Sarfati/Magnum Photos)*

Young Jewish boys study Hebrew at a synagogue in Tehran. There were approximately 80,000 Jews living in Iran in 1978, the year before Khomeini's revolution; twenty years later, the number has dropped to about 30,000. The Jews of Iran are the oldest Jewish community outside Israel, and despite shrinking ranks, the community has remained the largest in any Muslim country. *(Alexandra Avakian/Contact Press Images)*

One of the last remaining anti-American murals, displayed prominently on a building on a busy street in central Tehran. Visible behind the building is the Saint Sarkis Armenian Church. There are churches in every major Iranian city and centers for Armenians scattered around the country. Before the revolution, about 250,000 Armenians lived in Iran; twenty years later the number is down to fewer than 200,000. *(Kaveh Kazemi)*

The Bahai cemetery in Shiraz after it was vandalized, the graves destroyed, following the revolution in 1979. The Islamic Republic considers Bahais to be infidels and gives them no protection under the Constitution. *(Baha'i World Centre)*

Demonstrators march through the streets carrying photos of the late Dariush Forouhar, the revolution's first Minister of Labor, and his wife Parvaneh, a writer and poet. The couple became opponents of the Islamic Republic and were stabbed to death in their Tehran home in late 1998 during a spate of murders of political dissidents and writers carried out by a "rogue" unit of the Ministry of Intelligence. *(Agence France-Presse)*

A woman chooses what to read at a newsstand. After the election of President Khatami in 1997 there was a 120 percent increase in the number of publications, for a total of more than 1200 newspapers, magazines, and journals around the country. In a crackdown in the spring of 2000, most reformist publications in Tehran were closed. *(Agence France-Presse)*

Mashallah Shamsolvaezin, editor-in-chief of the lively reformist newspaper, *Jameah*, holds up a copy of another reformist newspaper, *Khordad*, that was closed after it questioned some of the tenets of the Islamic state. In 1998 and 1999, *Jameah* was closed and reopened under a different name five times. In 2000, Shamsolvaezin was prosecuted and convicted on forgery charges and was sent to prison. *(Reuters)*

A still from the blockbuster film *Two Women* by the feminist filmmaker Tahmineh Milani, with actress Marila Zarei as Roya on the left, and Niki Karimi as Fereshteh on the right. The film tells the story of two women who had become friends years earlier in college in Tehran: Fereshteh, a poor woman trapped in a loveless marriage, and Roya, a successful career woman with a loving husband. *Two Women* became the biggest box-office hit in Iranian history.

Young, unmarried Iranian men and women breaking the rules by socializing together at a private beach on the Caspian Sea. The women are violating the law requiring them to cover their hair and to wear long, loose clothing.

Iran's Hamid Estili celebrates his team's first goal against the United States during the World Cup soccer championships in France in June 1998. Iran would go on to defeat the United States, 2–1. In Iran, millions of people poured into the highways, streets, and alleyways the moment the game ended, in a communal celebration that froze traffic, freed spirits, and cut across lines of class and gender. *(Reuters)*

Ahmad Batebi holds up the bloody shirt of a friend who had been beaten by vigilantes during the student riots in July 1999, the worst unrest in Iran since the early days of its revolution. The dramatic color photograph appeared in a number of Iranian newspapers and on the cover of *The Economist.* Later, Batebi was convicted of endangering national security and spreading anti-government propaganda and was sent to prison. His sentence: ten years. *(Reuters)*

Young men in Western-style dress hanging out. In the first two decades of the revolution, the country's population nearly doubled. Today an estimated 65 percent of the population is under the age of twenty-five. Unlike their fathers, who lived the events of the revolution, most of Iran's youth know the revolution only through their history books. (*Jamsheed Bairami*)

Gholam-Hosein Karbaschi, Tehran's popular reformist mayor, addresses the judge during his trial in 1998. He was found guilty of corruption, embezzlement, and mismanagement. The trial, which was broadcast on television, exposed the political struggles and debates raging inside the Iranian state and the arbitrariness of the judicial system itself. (*Agence France-Presse*)

The covered carpet bazaar in Shiraz. The bazaars of Iran are places of business and community centers that include mosques, public baths, religious schools, teahouses, unlit alleys, and back rooms. But the bazaar merchants are not investors looking to build the economy over the long haul. They are cash-and-carry merchants looking for quick deals. *(Christopher Boisvieux/Gamma Liaison)*

A boy casts the ballot for his father during the first round of parliamentary elections in Tehran on February 18, 2000. The contest was unwieldy, as more than 5,000 candidates ran for the 290 seats. Candidates used Western-style vote-getting techniques: paid campaign advertisements, polling, and mass mailings. In the end, reformists routed the old order, winning more than 70 percent of the seats. *(Associated Press)*

He cursed the privileged sons of high-ranking officials who drove fancy cars and carried mobile phones and even socialized openly with young women.

He cursed commercial filmmakers for presenting sanitized versions of the war. "They show soldiers clean, their hair full of gel," he said. "It's humiliating. It makes a joke of what we endured."

He cursed the United States for the "crimes" it committed over decades—in Vietnam, in Iran, in Nicaragua.

Nicaragua? I hadn't thought about Nicaragua in a long time. "What were America's crimes in Nicaragua?" I asked Hamid.

"I don't remember," he said. "But I know they were bad."

He also blamed the United States for Iraq's war with Iran. In that, at least, I found a refrain that was common among Iranians of all political leanings and all degrees of religious fervor: the United States and its Western partners wanted Saddam Hussein to go to war against Iran to keep their country weak and force its experiment with revolution to fail. Iranians found proof of that in the world's reaction to Saddam's invasion in 1980. The United States merely cautioned that it "could not condone" Iraq's seizure of Iran's province of Khuzestan. It took the United Nations Security Council more than a week to pass a resolution that urged the combatants "to refrain immediately from any further use of force." The resolution did not call for a cease-fire or for a withdrawal of Iraq's troops to its borders. And it did not threaten any military action against Iraq as it would ten years later after Iraq invaded Kuwait.

Though there is no evidence that the United States played a part in Iraq's invasion, the American tilt toward Iraq after Iran went on the offensive in 1982, and the coordination of a global arms embargo of Iran convinced Iranians that the United States had taken sides. Toward the end of the war, the United States shared intelligence with Iraq on Iranian troop strength, which the Iraqis used in their offensives. And as part of its protection of oil tankers in the Persian Gulf, the U.S. Navy sank Iran's ships, destroyed oil platforms, and captured and killed Iranian crew members. Hamid saw America's continued military presence in the Gulf as evidence of a strategy to dominate Iran.

Hamid's final curses were reserved for President Khatami, who, he felt, had abandoned the generation of the war. Khatami had not even come to visit the martyrs' graves to commemorate the twentieth anniversary of the revolution.

Khatami, in fact, was no believer in permanent sacrifice. He had even stopped groups from chanting "Death to America" during a speech he gave to tens of thousands of students at the University of Tehran in May 1998, on the first anniversary of his election as President. "In any gathering in which I am present," he said, "I would prefer there to be talk of life and not death."

But Ayatollah Khomeini's singular focus on the rhetoric of death had created another vexing problem for Khatami as well. After he assumed the presidency and began seeking better standing for Iran in the eyes of other nations, Khatami found himself struggling to close the chapter on Khomeini's call to the world's Muslims to kill the novelist Salman Rushdie. Khomeini had branded Rushdie a blasphemer for his novel *The Satanic Verses*. "I ask all Muslims of the world rapidly to execute the author and the publishers of the book, anywhere in the world, so that no one will any longer dare to offend the sacred values of Muslims," Khomeini said in a fatwa or religious ruling of February 14, 1989. Anyone who died in the process would die a martyr, Khomeini promised.

Khatami had kept silent on the Rushdie matter during his first year as President, but in September 1998 he used a breakfast meeting with journalists in New York to reverse policy. Even so, he did it so subtly that its meaning was nearly lost on those of us who attended. The announcement came in response to a question from Andrew Rosenthal, the foreign editor of *The New York Times*. Rosenthal noted that Khatami had spoken at length about the importance of understanding among nations, adding that the American people just did not understand the death sentence against Rushdie. So why didn't Khatami simply lift it?

Khatami looked annoyed. He shifted his robe and paused. Then, in a sharp tone, he said: "I was hoping and expecting that this question that has been repeatedly asked over the years would not be mentioned or asked today! In our opinion the issue of Salman Rushdie is a symbol of war between civilizations. It began by the West attacking Islam. We naturally took a defensive stand. If you are implying that we are against the freedom of thought let me state bluntly that we have no opposition to freedom of thought. . . . We don't consider insults and disrespect for a religion as thought. We should consider the Salman Rushdie case as completely finished. Imam Khomeini as an Islamic jurist gave us his opinion about this matter and many other religious leaders have given us their opinions. The Islamic Republic of Iran has announced that in practice it made no decision to act on this matter. From now on we want to push a dialogue among civilizations, not a war, and we hope we have entered this era . . ."

Andy leaned over and whispered to me, "What was that all about?" Khatami had seemed angry and defensive, not revelatory. I whispered back, "I think he made news."

Indeed, buried in Khatami's long discourse was the statement that the Rushdie affair was over. The official position of the Iranian government had long been that the decree by Ayatollah Khomeini could not be revoked, but that Iran had no intention of carrying it out. Khatami went further, suggesting that Iran wanted to put the matter behind it and that Khomeini had been expressing only a personal view as one Islamic jurist. Khatami's statement paved the way for the upgrading of relations between Iran and Britain, where Rushdie lived. The novelist himself said that he felt safer.

But was the Rushdie affair truly over? In February 1999, on the tenth anniversary of the ruling against Rushdie, more than half of the deputies in Parliament signed a statement declaring, "The verdict on Rushdie, the blasphemer, is death, both today and tomorrow, and to burn in hell for all eternity." On the eleventh anniversary, Ayatollah Hassan Saneii, the head of the 15th of Khordad Foundation, which had offered a $2.6 million reward for Rushdie's assassination, said that the sentence remained valid and would be carried out, the reward paid with interest. But then, it was widely known in Iran that the foundation was bankrupt.

For Hamid, the fatwa was not only still valid; he would have tried to carry it out himself if he were not so ill. He heeded the words not of President Khatami but of Ayatollah Khamenei, who in 1993 had called the death sentence "irreversible." "Rushdie should be and will be executed," the Supreme Leader said at the time. "It is the duty for all Muslims who have access to the mercenary to carry out the sentence." Khamenei was Hamid's hero, a "war-disabled" himself, Hamid said, because of the injuries suffered in a 1981 assassination attempt. "The leader came here and prayed in the martyrs' section for an hour," Hamid said. "He thanked us. He told us to stay on the path of the martyrs. I kissed his hand."

"Is the country going on the wrong path, then?" I asked.

"One hundred percent," Hamid replied. Then he stopped himself. "This conversation may get too political." Hamid did not want me to see his reflection in the mirror too clearly. I knew that I had pushed far enough, and backed off.

Hamid acknowledged that he was fighting on a more mundane battlefield now, to keep his job as the cemetery hired new employees with
different ideas. "The new ones are bureaucrats who just come to the office and sign papers," he complained. "They haven't seen their friends die
in a sea of their own blood."

The grisly footage in the hot auditorium had made me sick to my
stomach. I asked to be shown to the ladies' room. Hamid proudly showed
me a sign that read, "This way to the American and Israeli embassies."
That's what the toilets at the martyrs' museum are called.

"So show me to my embassy," I said.

"What do you mean?" he asked.

"The American embassy."

"You're American?" he asked in disbelief. "I didn't know. They said
you were French. I'm so, so sorry."

With much fanfare, Hamid ordered a subordinate to take down the
sign. Hamid tore it up in little bits as he led me down the stairs.

When I came back up to say goodbye, we talked about the war front
again. I told him that I had covered the war as a reporter and had also seen
the carnage, from both sides of the border, including the aftermath of a
battle in which the Iraqis had used chemical weapons against the Iranians.

"What a tragedy that you could not have found martyrdom at the
battlefield," he said.

"But I don't want to die," I protested. "My kids need me. And your
son needs you too."

"I try not to love him too much, so that he will not miss me when I
die," Hamid said of his two-year-old son, Mohammad.

"Well then, love him until you die," I said.

It was then that Hamid let down his guard. Proud like any father, he
said, "Oh, sometimes I take him to the playground. He's a great kid.
Maybe you can come to our house and meet him one day."

"Inshallah," I said, "God willing," knowing it would never happen.

Hamid then surprised me again. The man who hated and cursed
America wanted to visit. "Maybe I can take some time off and learn English," he said. "Can you help me get a passport and a visa?"

I suddenly found myself connecting with Hamid. I had gotten him to
admit he was proud of his son. Now he was talking about visiting the
United States. "Would you come?" I asked incredulously.

"Yes," he replied.

"Would you really come?"

The significance of his confession finally sunk in.

"Uh, no, no," he said. "There's too much corruption there."

But perhaps Hamid wasn't quite ready to die.

Iran came out of the war sobered, convinced of the futility of armed force as a means of settling its international conflicts. When an American-led coalition went to war against Iraq in 1991, Iran stayed out.

Keeping alive the spirit of martyrdom in the minds of the Iranian people became harder. "The major casualty of the war," wrote the Iranian-born historian and author Shahram Chubin in 1989, "has been the credibility of the Islamic Republic among its own rank and file. It will no longer be able to effectively call upon its populace for crusades and sacrifices, but will have to act more like a normal state." Some critics of the system even called for the abolition of the *baseej* volunteer corps. Within the next decade, Iran's economy was in such crisis that the government began to sell exemptions to the two years of compulsory military service. A complex sliding scale was created: a Ph.D. paid three times what a high school dropout did. Mehdi Mahdavi-Kia, a star on the national soccer team, was exempted from the draft as a reward for scoring a spectacular second-half goal in Iran's World Cup soccer victory over the United States in 1998.

To preserve what is left of the war mentality, pockets of resistance within the leadership, hard-core believers, continue to train a new generation of would-be martyrs. Every summer, hundreds of teenage boys and girls from all over the country are brought to the Bahonar Camping Center, a sprawling, beautifully landscaped estate in the mountains high above Tehran, for an all-expenses-paid week of prayers, revolutionary songs, and inspiration. Most of them are the sons and daughters of men who died in the war with Iraq.

On a recent visit, I attended a rally in a vast auditorium decorated with photos of Ayatollahs Khomeini and Khamenei. The boys sat in front, the red kerchiefs of the *baseej* around their necks. A young woman sitting next to me in the back showed me her spiral notebook. On the front, where an American teenager might tape a picture of a rock star, she had taped a photo of Khomeini.

A short, bearded middle-aged man in glasses whipped up the group's emotions. Holding up a photograph of an unnamed martyr, he shouted,

"I saw the bullets hitting his face and his body and I wanted to throw myself into the war." He told the story of a young woman who scooped up soil from the battlefront. "The soil was bloody, bloody, bloody," he sobbed. "She put it into a flower bed to help the flowers grow." He told the stories with the same long laments used by the mullahs in the mosques to encourage the faithful to weep on special days of mourning, and each reminiscence drove him and his audience to weeping. One teenage girl uttered a piercing cry. She fainted and was carried from the hall. Even the boys were sobbing now.

Sometime after the visit, I asked Khatami's chef de cabinet, Mohammad-Ali Abtahi, about the *baseej* camp and what purpose it serves. "These are the same types of people who beat their chests at the mourning rituals," he said. "But we can't expect our youth to beat their chests and mourn every day. Even if they insist on doing this we shouldn't all follow it because it leads to extremism. Joy and happiness is a part of youth too."

"But these are government-funded camps," I replied. "Why not shut them down?" He answered with a shrug. Clearly this is a part of the Islamic Republic that the President does not control. The camp represents a side of Iran that seems to have been made permanently sad and twisted, one that remains stuck in the grisly psychology of a cult of martyrdom.

Yet it is hard for me to believe this war fever can be sustained. That's because there are so many other pieces in the mosaic that is Iranian society, illustrating that flexibility and improvisation can bring renewal even after so dark a period of horror. One such discovery was a war-hero-turned-yuppie in a travel agency that catered to European and American tourists. I wasn't looking for heroes there, but one day, Taghi Aghaei found me.

Taghi is the head of an Iranian tour company named Ziggurat, which had helped to organize a tour I was taking with a group of Americans. His story unfolded over a slow-moving multicourse lunch in Isfahan.

In 1983, when he was nineteen years old and an infantryman in Khomeini's army, he was sent to the Iraqi border. One day, during a secret operation, an artillery shell exploded in front of him, sending hundreds of pieces of metal flying into the air. One piece pierced his head and became permanently embedded behind his eye. Another piece of metal sliced off his right hand. Taghi was given medals for heroism and discharged from the military. But as a believer in the call to sacrifice, he taught himself to write with his left hand and reenlisted. He wrote war propaganda pamphlets and taught recruits about the Koran.

Today, he is a forward-thinking businessman. Unlike Hamid at the cemetery, Taghi doesn't feel sorry for himself or dwell on stories from the battlefield. As a war hero, Taghi has become part of the elite and is determined to capitalize on it.

He chose a growth industry, tourism. So what if Khomeini didn't make a revolution so that people like him could make money helping foreigners have a good time in Iran? Taghi bought himself an advanced English-Persian dictionary and some language tapes. "For six months, I imprisoned myself to prepare for the entrance exam for the university," he said.

Jobs and positions for university students are held open for war veterans and the families of martyrs even if they aren't quite as good as other applicants. Taghi easily made it into Alameh Tabatabai University in Tehran, where he studied English. When Iran's state-run Tourism Organization sent a representative to the university to seek out its best student to become a first-class tour guide, Taghi was chosen. But there was the problem of the missing hand. "They said to me: 'Listen, Taghi, you can't be a tour leader,'" he recalled. "'Because of your hand. Guests want to enjoy themselves. They will see you. Maybe they will pity you.'

"Two days later was the first day of the training course. I showed up anyway. They wouldn't let me in. So I went to the general manager and told him how much I love people. I told him I could be a great tour guide. He finally relented. I loved reading all the texts about the monuments. I developed twenty different itineraries and produced a forty-two-minute film called *Iran at a Glance*. Pretty soon foreign tour operators were asking for me by name."

Taghi was promoted over and over, and in 1997 he started his own tour company. He became so successful that he ran twenty foreign tour groups in his first year and had to turn clients away.

Part of the reason for Taghi's rapid success is his special status as a war hero. And a tour operator with special status can do very well indeed. It can take weeks for an ordinary tour operator to book tickets on Iran's heavily subsidized, overbooked domestic air routes. But a certain number of seats are always reserved for war heroes. When flights are booked, Taghi can always bump other passengers. Hotels that do not give discounts to ordinary tour operators have no choice except to slash their prices for him. Restaurants open their doors when he asks. "Rules are bent," he boasted. "People always tell me, 'You defended the country so we owe it to you.' So I have an advantage."

His missing hand has become his calling card.

When I went to see Taghi in his new suite of offices in Tehran a few months later, he was expanding his business. "I was the first tour operator to start with the Americans," he bragged. He had begun to teach prospective tour operators courses like "The Art of Conducting a Tour" and "Strategic Marketing in Tourism." He offered me an assortment of fancy pastries and fresh brewed coffee, which was scarce in Iran. When I opted for tea, it came Western style with a teaspoon and a bowl of granulated sugar. Taghi knew that not many Americans take their tea the Iranian way—by clenching a sugar cube in the mouth and sipping the scalding tea through it.

After the bombast wore off, Taghi turned somber. His business was in danger of falling apart, he said, pointing to a list of two dozen tours he had scheduled for Americans in 1999—all of them canceled. America was bombing Iraq at that time, and American tourists didn't seem to know the difference between the two countries. Worse, a band of thugs had attacked a bus carrying a group of American businessmen in Tehran with stones and threats the November before.

"There is a Prophet named Ayoub, and God tested his patience," Taghi told me.

"It's Job," I said.

"Oh my God, I hope I'm not Job!" Taghi said. "They say that the destination is not important, it's the journey that counts. Like the war, they say, 'Okay, we didn't win but we fought proudly and bravely.' I love this job and I love this country. But I get frustrated. My wife pities herself and asks God why didn't she die when she was a nurse at the front. Sometimes I feel like I'm going mad."

I thought a lot about Hamid and Taghi after that. For all their differences in outlook, they have something important in common. More than a decade after the end of the war, the Hamids and the Taghis of Iran are still struggling to figure out where they fit. Were the warriors heroes or victims and dupes?

I went to the Ministry of Islamic Guidance to ask that question of Ali-Reza Shiravi, the deputy director for the foreign press. Shiravi is a believer in the system. At the age of sixteen, he stopped going to school and went on a hunger strike until his parents let him join the military. Then he watched as his comrades threw themselves over land mines in suicide missions to clear the path for soldiers in the rear. And for eight years in Iraqi prison camps, he suffered through beatings, electric shock, extremes of temperature, deprivation of food and sleep.

Shiravi said he didn't feel cheated or duped. "If you plant a cherry tree you wait a long time before it gives fruit," he said. "But once it gives its fruit it also gives other things. It freshens the air. It gives shade. It's pretty to look at. It was the same with the war. Maybe it never bore fruit. Maybe there were goals that never were reached. But the war brought us other benefits. Our children will not tell us, 'You did not defend our country.' And for a while at least, we sacrificed our needs and forgot about the materialistic aspects of life."

Shiravi had healed, but it would probably take another generation before the country would.

CHAPTER TEN

The World of Qom

Some are preoccupied with matters of religion,
And some are beset by doubt on their course of conviction;
I fear the day when a divine voice may call out:
You ignorant people, the true course is neither of your ways.

— THE *RUBÁIYÁT* OF OMAR KHAYYAM, TWELFTH-
CENTURY PERSIAN POET

God has given us all the rules of the game.
— AYATOLLAH RUHOLLAH KHOMEINI

AYATOLLAH HOSEIN-ALI MONTAZERI is the invisible man of Qom. He is never seen on the streets. He doesn't preach to the faithful. He doesn't train seminary students. Since 1989 this senior cleric has spent most of his time imprisoned in his modest home on a small street in the center of town, with a large contingent of armed security police stationed in a bulletproof trailer outside. The windows of the trailer are one-way mirrors; the police can look out, but passersby can see only a single red light bulb inside. And yet Montazeri's presence looms large over Qom, a place of pilgrimage and the center of clerical learning in Iran. From behind closed doors, he runs a kind of underground training camp for reform-minded bureaucrat-theologians, giving them religious and political support for their various causes.

As a teenager in the 1930s, Ayatollah Montazeri came to Qom from his native town of Najafabad, near Isfahan, to study with the most learned clerics of the day. It was in Qom that Montazeri became a student and close confidant of Ayatollah Khomeini, before he became one of the country's top religious figures. As a leader of the religious opposition against the Shah, Montazeri was sent to prison. After the revolution, Khomeini named him to the secret Revolutionary Council, making him one of the most powerful people in Iran.

For years Montazeri was the regime's favorite son, designated to be Khomeini's successor after his death. "The fruit of my life," was how Khomeini frequently referred to his younger charge. Montazeri also seemed more human than holy. His poor public speaking skills, his squeaky voice, and his round face and grizzled beard earned him the nickname Gorbeh Nareh, the Persian name for the cat in a cartoon serial of *Pinocchio.*

In the early years of the Islamic Republic, Montazeri was one of the architects of the clauses in the Constitution calling for rule by an Islamic jurist. On foreign policy, he advocated exporting the Iranian revolution and succeeded in channeling money, weapons, and other support to Islamic political movements around the world. He blasted Saudi Arabia as a "filthy" regime that was guilty of "colonialism and global Zionism." He routinely condemned the United States as evil, and after the USS *Vincennes* incident in 1988, he called for retaliatory attacks on American military, political, cultural, and economic installations.

But even as Montazeri railed against Iran's external enemies, he was growing uncomfortable with what he considered the revolution's excesses at home. In the late 1980s he went public with his complaints. In a series of open letters to Khomeini and other officials, Montazeri broke the code of silence that largely governs the ruling clerical elite. In doing so, he became the most important critic of the Islamic Republic.

When, for example, the judiciary, upon Khomeini's orders, punished hundreds of political opponents with swift execution, Montazeri lamented that "people in the world got the idea that our business in Iran is just murdering people." When officials blamed Iran's economic woes on foreign powers, he openly faulted government policies for creating "shortages, injustices, inflation, depressed incomes" that had paralyzed the economy. When Khomeini issued his ruling calling for the assassination of novelist Salman Rushdie, Montazeri refused to endorse it.

Qom is accustomed to theological arguments articulated behind closed doors, and if that had been all that Montazeri's tirades had amounted to, Khomeini might have tolerated them. But the clerics had now become politicians, and the arguments smacked of temporal politics.

Apparently not all the differences between the two men were ideological. There was also the case of Mehdi Hashemi, who was related to Montazeri by marriage. As a senior official in the Revolutionary Guards, Hashemi had his own foreign policy agenda, at home and in Lebanon; it was said to have included murder, sedition, and involvement in the Iran-contra scandal. Even after he was convicted of violating state security and executed in 1987, Montazeri fiercely defended him.

In March 1989, without warning, Khomeini unceremoniously stripped Montazeri of his position as designated successor. His portraits, which had hung beside those of his mentor in government offices and shop windows throughout Iran, were quickly removed. Montazeri was barred from delivering sermons or conducting public activities. Only relatives were allowed to visit him.

In accepting the dismissal, Montazeri didn't apologize to Ayatollah Khomeini. He had never wanted Khomeini's job in the first place. He asked only to be left alone as "a small teacher." Khomeini replied to Montazeri that the leadership of the Islamic Republic required "endurance more than your capacity."

At first, the dismissal seemed like a Kremlinesque purge in which a political figure simply disappears one day. But Montazeri didn't disappear. He was marginalized, but he wasn't put on trial as a traitor or sent to prison. He still had room for maneuver and remained an important player. His private classes remained popular; his followers were generous with their charitable contributions. He was, after all, a *marja,* one of the highest-ranking Shiite theologians. And he enjoyed considerable respect from the clerics of Qom, even if they disagreed with his politics.

Qom, a gloomy, dusty thousand-year-old city on the edge of Iran's great salt desert, is only ninety miles from Tehran. It might as well be nine thousand. Its main industry is producing mullahs, much as the industry of Vatican City is training priests. And like the Vatican, Qom is a sheltered, unhurried religious refuge, where clerics can debate without attention to time and without fear of interference from the state. In the Islamic Republic, Qom has assumed another role as well: it is the idea factory for a regime that seeks to regulate daily life with all the worldly tools of a modern state even as it tries to bring its people closer to God. That is the principal reason Montazeri was allowed to continue spreading his ideas, even after he had been stripped of power and liberty.

Before the revolution, Qom was a desolate place known as a center for study and worship and a producer of fine silk carpets and of *sohan,* a caramel and pistachio brittle. The more the Shah consolidated his own power, the less attention he paid to Qom; a guidebook published by his Ministry of Information and Tourism devoted just three paragraphs to the city.

Ayatollah Khomeini changed all that. His appeal was exceptionally strong in Qom, where he had lived and preached for years before he was sent into exile. In January 1978, a crowd there demonstrated against the Shah in the ayatollah's name. According to some reports, clerics and Islamic militants set up street barricades, smashed buses, halted trains, and attacked banks and shops; they were not silenced even after the police opened fire. Many Iranians came to regard what became a two-and-a-half-hour shooting spree as the opening shots of the revolution. Afterward, the regime bused thousands of factory workers and low-level government employees to Qom for a counterdemonstration in support of the Shah. But the violent crackdown sparked a cycle of mourning—and more demonstrations and violence—every forty days until, a year later, the Shah fled the country and Khomeini returned.

The first time I visited Qom I witnessed the slaughtering of a camel. It was a bright, cool, sunny day in February 1979, just a few days after the revolution, and the sacrifice was made to honor Khomeini's triumphant return after an absence of more than fourteen years. His followers made a path of red carnations for him, filled the walls with his portraits, and strung revolutionary posters and banners between minarets and lamp-posts not only in Persian, but also in Arabic, English, French, and German (for the benefit of the foreign journalists, I presumed). Khomeini had ordered that no camels were to be killed in his honor, but his followers paid no heed. The giant beast was forced on its side by a handful of men. One man swiftly slit the camel's throat with a sword. Blood spurted high into the air. The crowd praised God and smeared their hands and faces with the blood. That day, Khomeini sat in the front seat of a white Chevrolet ambulance; members of the foreign media were put on a long flatbed truck. We made our way through a shrieking crowd of clerics who chanted slogans on megaphones, soldiers who had stuck carnations in their rifles, and hundreds of thousands of people who kept running to catch up. In my chador, I slipped at one point and grabbed the arm of a young bearded Iranian assigned to help us. "Don't touch me like that!" he said. "You are in Qom."

Yes, I was in Qom.

It was in Qom that Khomeini set up his government just days after the victory of the revolution. In those heady early days, Qom seemed like the center of the universe to its residents. No longer a religious backwater, it became very much like an eighteenth-century European court where people came and went and pleaded and waited for favors. Government officials made pilgrimages by helicopter from Tehran, often several times a week, to consult Khomeini. Courtiers and security guards shielded the ayatollah from most of the supplicants. Every day thousands of people crowded behind green metal barricades at the end of the street where Khomeini lived to get a glimpse of him, usually no more than a one-minute wave from his window. Among the throng one day was a woman who told me she had come with her blind daughter all the way from Isfahan to get Khomeini's blessing, and a widow with seven children who said she had come from Mashad to ask for an increase in her pension.

After the revolution, the city emerged as an even more important Shiite pilgrimage site and the country's most authoritative center of learning. "Islam has no borders," Khomeini said, so the seminaries attracted religious scholars and students from around the world as the exportation of Iran's revolution became one of the pillars of the new Islamic system. The religious teachers of Qom were assigned the task of indoctrinating foreign students with tales about the Islamic revolution and how to duplicate it back home. During the war with Iraq, the ranks of the seminaries swelled, in part because clerical students were exempt from military service. By the turn of the century, tens of thousands of students were enrolled in the Qom theological seminaries alone.

Over the years, I have made the drive from Tehran to Qom more times than I can count: with a group of American tourists, with officials from the Ministry of Islamic Guidance, with a nephew of Ayatollah Khomeini, with Nazila. The trip has gone faster since a six-lane highway was built. But I still don't feel as if I fully understand the place. Even for many Iranians, Qom seems alien. Religion dominates the culture and the clerics don't like outsiders. I have worked for a long time with secular Iranian women who hate to go there because of the way clerics look at them. A foreigner can be spotted from miles away. I keep going back to Qom because I hope that each visit will reveal more. And indeed, it is different every time.

The distinction between what is public and what is private is drawn more starkly in Qom than in the rest of Iran; the curtain of privacy is far more tightly drawn around the clergy, making it especially difficult for an outsider to get inside. Hotels generally don't welcome women traveling on their own, and restaurants are hard to find. Qom has only one main avenue; everything important is within walking distance—the central shrine, the seminaries, even a new Islamic computer center where Koranic teachings and interpretations are on the Internet. Even so, an outsider cannot navigate without a guide. To get anything accomplished, you have to be invited; someone who belongs has to lead you down the narrow streets and do the introductions. It is especially difficult to make appointments in advance. The trick is to start out from Tehran at about 6:00 A.M., arrive at eight, and work until noon. That's when most clerics pray, eat, and nap. Most of the city shuts down until about 5:00 P.M., when work begins again.

The centerpiece of Qom is the grand, gold-domed shrine that houses the tomb of Massoumeh, the sister of Imam Reza, the eighth Imam, who died in the ninth century. Thousands of pilgrims come every day to say prayers, beg for favors, and leave wads of bills as donations. They solemnly finger the silver cage that houses Massoumeh's tomb and then touch their faces, as if her aura will somehow rub off on them.

There is an air of informality in the shrine, as in mosques, that doesn't exist in most churches or synagogues. The religious complex, like others throughout Iran, is more than simply a place of prayer; it is also a place of political mobilization. During the war with Iraq, the clerics set up enlistment centers for teenage volunteers and donation centers here where people could contribute their gold jewelry and coins to the war effort. The shrine is also a place for socializing, for getting out of the house. Women sit on the carpets and eat picnic lunches with their children. And the courtyard is known as a meeting place where the Shiite Muslim practice of *sigheh,* or temporary marriage, can be arranged by a lonely pilgrim and a woman who needs money.

Qom today is a very different place than it was at the beginning of the revolution. It boasts recreational parks and movie theaters. Most of the bookstores sell only religious books, but I have also found English-language volumes: *King Lear,* Paul Kennedy's *The Rise and Fall of the*

Great Powers, and a wide assortment of Persian-English dictionaries. Clerics drive motorbikes and some women even dare to go out on the streets in scarves and long coats, rather than black chadors.

New Koranic libraries on the Internet compete with each other to create databases for the writings of Islamic scholars, sayings of the Prophet, and Koranic interpretations. One of the libraries functions both as a research center and a producer of Islamic software. Its Web site, in Persian, English, and Arabic, includes such subject headings as "Infallible Imams" and "Shiite Geniuses." Another has transferred thousands of Koranic interpretations onto CD-ROM and onto its Web site. Sheikh Ali Korani, the director of that computer center, has acknowledged that the Internet can be either a dangerous weapon or a useful tool. "Many things have a double nature," he likes to tell visitors. "Take a knife. You can use it in the kitchen or you can use it to commit crimes."

Still, Qom remains a place where ideas of good and evil are fixed, and at times even put on public display. From time to time newspapers run small items about executions there: a thirty-one-year-old bus driver was publicly hanged after he was found guilty of raping a six-year-old girl; a married Iranian woman with children was stoned to death after she was convicted of adultery and working with a "gang of corruption."

But the illusion that time stands still in Qom is just that—an illusion. In fact, the Shiite tradition of relying on argument within the clergy keeps it bubbling with intellectual energy and political ferment. In late 1997, Ayatollah Montazeri, by then well into his seventies, did something no other senior religious leader had ever done, at least not in public. In a lecture to a group of students visiting his home, he directly attacked Ayatollah Khamenei, who he said lacked the necessary religious credentials for the job of Supreme Leader. The autocratic rule that Khamenei and his supporters exercised, Montazeri said, had made people "disgusted with the clerics."

Someone in the room recorded the lecture, and soon it was circulating clandestinely throughout Qom on cassette tapes, just as Khomeini's words had been transmitted to thousands of Iranian mosques in the months before the revolution. State-controlled radio didn't broadcast it, but the Persian-language service of the BBC did, over and over, and many Iranians monitor the BBC. I was given a copy of the lecture by an Asian diplomat. Angry rioters then attacked Montazeri's house and offices and ransacked his Koranic school before security guards used tear gas to disperse them. Khamenei branded the man who was once destined to have his job as "politically bankrupt, pathetic, and naive."

But even after that, Montazeri wasn't rendered powerless. The attack on his house was widely condemned. It had crossed that curious line that defines Iran, the line between public and private. It had violated the special boundaries held sacred in Qom. And it evoked the repression the clergy had suffered under the Shah. Even the most conservative clerics in town were appalled by such an overt attack on a *marja*. Another senior ayatollah, the usually mild-mannered Nasser Makarem-Shirazi, told visitors that even though he disagreed with what Montazeri had been arguing, Montazeri never should have been humiliated like that.

Montazeri was considered so outrageous—and so dangerous—that in mid-1999 the Special Clerical Court banned the press from even printing his photograph or mentioning his name. But Montazeri continued to get out his message through his son, through phone conversations with trusted associates and students, and through reformist newspapers that often published Montazeri's private sermons and dicta. "Despotism is despotism, whether it is imposed by the Shah or the clergy!" the independent Iranian weekly *Payam-e Hajar* quoted Montazeri as saying in 1999. He called for an independent investigation into whether Iran should restore relations with the United States, adding that even though Khomeini had called America the "Great Satan" and rejected such a move, "that ruling obviously had been temporary and could change according to economic and political conditions." He smuggled out a letter condemning the supervisory Guardian Council for abusing its power by eliminating many reformist candidates who had wanted to run in the 2000 parliamentary election.

No authority could stop Montazeri from talking, because that's what Shiite Muslim clerics are taught to do. The clerical system is a democratic, even raucous one in which students are trained to speak their minds and challenge the authority of their professors. Students choose which professor they want to follow; professors in turn develop their own followings. The art of persuasion is key. That's why sitting down with a cleric is never a short encounter. Clerics are trained to lecture in paragraph-long sentences until the listener is convinced. The process is particularly frustrating for journalists, who demand clarity, brevity, and news. It also is the Achilles heel of authoritarianism in the Islamic Republic, the reason that its reliance on an all-powerful Supreme Leader will not go unchallenged.

Even Ayatollah Khomeini had been known as too much of a talker. Talking, after all, was what had gotten him into trouble with the Shah in the first place. In 1963, Khomeini gave an angry sermon in Qom in which he railed against the Shah, branded him a puppet of the West, and called his regime "tyrannical." The Shah expelled him. Fifteen years later, in the months leading up to the revolution, Ayatollah Morteza Mottahari is said to have told Khomeini when he was still in exile in France: "You are not a cleric in Qom anymore. You are the leader of a revolution. You should not say many of the things you say. You should talk less."

The informality of the clerical system thus survives, so much so that no central authority grants theological students the authority to don a turban, a long tunic, and a cloak—or to take them off. Students decide for themselves when they think they have learned enough to dress up. Some very learned clerics never wear clerical dress; some put it on early and later decide to take it off; many clerics who have chosen other professions wear secular clothes. I once sat in on an undergraduate class in "Major Western Political Thinkers from Hobbes to Marx" at Mofid University in Qom. Most of the students were dressed in sports shirts and pants; only a few wore turbans and cloaks. I later found out that all of them were clerics.

An ex-cleric from Qom once tried to help me understand the making of a mullah. The vocation, he said, is usually passed down within a clerical or deeply religious family, although people from any class or family are eligible. In general, lower-class men receive informal basic religious training either from a family member or mentor. These clerics are called *rowzeh khan,* and are not considered religious scholars but only preachers for hire who specialize in reciting stories about the sufferings of the sacred figures of Shiism. Religious scholars must attend religious seminaries at a shrine city like Qom or Mashad and follow a strict classical curriculum that includes theology, philosophy, rhetoric, Islamic jurisprudence, logic, debate, mathematics, and Arabic. This course of study takes about two decades and eventually leads to the equivalent of a doctoral degree. High religious scholars are expected to publish original theses and specialize in specific areas of Islam. A beginning scholar is referred to as a *talabeh*; the next level is *hojjatoleslam*; the highest rank is ayatollah. A half dozen or so of the highest-ranking ayatollahs are considered *marjas.* Khomeini was one, as is Montazeri.

Unlike catholic Christianity, in which priests are ordained by higher-ranking clergy, Muslim clerics rise through a democratic process—the consensus of their peers. A cleric can't call himself an ayatollah; other people give him the title, based ostensibly on the depth of his learning and the sagacity of his writings.

Sometimes the title is handed out for political reasons, however. Ali Khamenei did not become an ayatollah until he was given the job of Supreme Leader after Khomeini's death. Sometimes the title is contested. Rafsanjani, the former President, is a *hojjatoleslam*. But some newspapers have taken to calling him ayatollah; others have not.

Titles are one thing, influence another. Within the rarefied world of theological politics that governs Qom, popularity can matter most of all. And popularity is one thing Montazeri enjoys, even after all else has been stripped from him. He has interacted with hundreds, perhaps thousands, of clerics, training them to think for themselves, just as he does. And in the religious schools in Qom and in the pages of the reformist newspapers, other clerics are doing that too.

After twenty years of mixing theological authority and temporal rule, the same ideological and generational gap that exists in Iranian society at large has begun to show up in what once was a closed community of clerics. At the time of the revolution, there were only about eighty-thousand clerics in Iran; more than twenty years later, their numbers have swelled to an estimated 600,000 or more. Many of the more established clerics have become rich off the revolution; others have become powerful politicians who hardly ever go to Qom. But many other clerics disapprove of the idea of mixing God's world with Caesar's. They want the clergy to get out of politics and business and go back to prayer. They don't know where they fit or what their role should be. Some feel they have the worst of all possible worlds: they aren't rich, they aren't respected either. And some are even more outspoken than their spiritual fathers. Emblematic of the dissatisfaction is that according to some estimates, about 70 percent of the voters in Qom supported Mohammad Khatami in the 1997 presidential election.

The ex-cleric who told me about clerical training, for example, had come to the conclusion that "clerics are nothing but 'shopkeepers' of religion," a parasitic class. "They are alien to the real message and teachings of Islam, whose goal is the moral upbringing of people," he said. "All they do is fill up people's minds and hearts with rules that have no basis in the Koran and are based in false interpretations and unsubstantiated tales." Clerics generally receive a stipend from the government, from their followers, or from their mentors. But according to the sayings of the Prophet Mohammad, the ex-cleric explained, no one should make a living from religion. He added that the only way he could hope to discover true Islam was to relinquish his turban and cloak, study religion on his own, and earn a living in the outside world. He now sells chutney at a small factory.

I never did get the chance to talk with Montazeri. During one visit to Qom, I approached his house, but the police guard outside was too intimidating. Over time, though, I did get to know another cleric, Mohammad-Ali Ayazi, a *hojjatoleslam* who considers Montazeri his mentor. A generation after the revolution, Ayazi is a driven man. He is only in his mid-forties but has been studying for thirty years, many of them under Montazeri. So he is armed with arguments about how the Islamic system has gone off course and needs to be led back to the right path. "A citizen has the right to express himself as long as it is within the framework of the law," he explained, his eyes blazing with passion. "Religion and government must be separated," Ayazi said. "Religion must be cultivated for freedom to thrive. It must not be imposed. People must accept religion freely; we do not need to impose it on people with violence and terror."

Ayazi is typical of a class of clerics, many of them young. They contend that the most important holy war in Islam is the one inside one's soul, and their mounting hostility to the conservative clerical establishment is forcing them to rethink the very meaning of the Islamic Republic and the role of religion in modern society. But Ayazi is leading his challenge from within the traditions of Shiite Islam. His life story confirms this. His father had been a cleric, as are three of his four brothers. The most glorious day in Ayazi's life, he told me, was February 11, 1979, the day the revolution triumphed. Not only was the Shah gone; the young cleric's wife gave birth that day to the first of their six children, a son.

Ayazi's life centers around study, writing, and prayer. He gets up two or three hours before sunrise to pray. He takes a brisk long hike every morning to keep himself in shape. He spends part of the morning praying at the mosque, then comes home to write. And all this before breakfast, which is served to him by his wife. The rest of the day is spent with more writing and praying, a long nap after lunch, then playing with his children and helping them with homework. Ayazi considers himself worldly. He has lived abroad—in Syria, Iraq, and Lebanon—and has traveled to Europe, Central Asia, and Africa. He works on a personal computer with a fast Internet connection, monitors the BBC's Persian-language broadcasts every day, and studies the Bible and the Torah as well as the Koran. He writes books on Koranic interpretations, political exegeses on the meaning of a civil society, and guidance on infertility and birth control. His vast library of thousands of beautifully bound books includes works in English by Erich Fromm, Raymond Aron, Harold Laski, and Karl Popper, as well as older classics by Marx, Kant, Hegel, and Adam Smith.

Ayazi stated openly that the Islamic Republic will survive only if it reforms itself from within. So I was not surprised that he also believes that the silencing of Ayatollah Montazeri is not only unjust but also threatening to the Islamic system. "What happened to Montazeri is not fair at all, absolutely not," Ayazi said, his piercing honey-colored eyes looking through me. "Montazeri is one of the pillars of the revolution. He went to prison and was tortured for the sake of this revolution. That is why he is now so critical of all the system's shortcomings. And naturally it is his right to express his ideas. Those who believe otherwise should challenge him to a debate."

Ayazi said that the popular belief that all the clerics of Qom are part of the ruling class is dead wrong. He mentioned the cases of other clerics who have been silenced for their views. According to Ayazi, they are being punished simply because they are clerics. The existence of the Special Clerical Court makes it easy for conservatives to persecute those in their midst who disagree with their views. "This court can easily target the clergy," Ayazi said. "Many secular people have said the same things these men have said but they are left alone because they are not clerics. The clergy are more oppressed than they have been in years."

This certainly was a switch. The clergy in an Islamic Republic oppressed?

"You make it sound as if you are the most oppressed class in society," I said.

"Absolutely," he replied. "Ordinary people are punished, because of crimes or wrongdoings they committed," he replied. "In our case it's different. The conservatives punish us simply to ruin our reputations. They know our influence depends on our reputations. We are definitely the most oppressed class."

Hard as it seemed to accept this statement as anything more than a self-pitying complaint, I realized that this was an ominous comment about the future of the Islamic Republic. Ayazi was warning that the ruling class was devouring itself with its internal political arguments, and in the long run such political cannibalism could threaten the very basis of the Islamic Republic itself. It was quite a moment. Here was a young cleric whose friends were in prison, whose mentor was under house arrest, saying in essence that the official interpretation of Islam that had developed under the Islamic Republic was wrong. And he was getting away with it, voicing his outrage over tea to a foreign journalist sitting in his study and preparing to tell the outside world about his intimations of doom.

But in another sense, Ayazi was tempting fate. The red lines that define allowable conduct keep moving, and with his blunt words he might cross them at any time. One of his closest friends is Mohsen Kadivar, a young university professor who also holds the rank of *hojjatoleslam,* who had been sentenced to prison for disseminating lies, defaming Islam, and disturbing public opinion in newspaper commentaries in which he even made comparisons between the Islamic Republic and the monarchy it had overthrown. "The Islamic Republic is faced with a historic catastrophe in its twentieth year of life in Iran," Kadivar wrote in a letter to his wife in May 1999 that was later described in an article in the daily newspaper *Iran.* "The main goal of the Islamic Republic was the end of absolute monarchy and the transformation to an Islamic Republic. So the return to the same conduct of absolute monarchy cannot be called an Islamic Republic."

Ayazi admitted that he expected to end up behind bars like Kadivar. Maybe Ayazi has a martyr complex; that would certainly fit with Shiite tradition. Maybe he knows that Kadivar doesn't have it so bad in prison; after all, he had used the time to write his doctoral dissertation and had even been given a furlough to defend it. Or maybe Ayazi feels that he has no choice except to further the political movement that has been started by others.

In any case, Ayazi didn't stop. He openly criticized the culture of violence that had become part of the Islamic Republic's strategy for keeping order and unity. He spoke of the existence of "secret powers" in the country that committed violent acts, including the killing of dissidents and the beating up of outspoken clerics. He denounced what he called the "tyranny" of rigid interpretations of Islam. "We must go back to the correct Islam," he said. "The Islam of 1,400 years ago is not what we mean by the correct Islam. Islam must be interpreted according to the needs of the time."

Ayazi even called for structural changes that would take power away from the Supreme Leader and the conservatives who support him and put it into the hands of reformists like President Khatami. And yet Ayazi did not advocate abolishing the institution of the Supreme Leader; he said only that the institution has to change so that whoever holds the job is accountable to the people. "The people must supervise his performance, and his power must be divided among various institutions," he said.

"Will there be a Supreme Leader ten years from now?" I asked Ayazi.

The cleric paused for a long time. "I don't know," he replied.

My chaperon from the Ministry of Islamic Guidance, Ali-Reza Haghighi, who had brought me to Ayazi's house and was doing the translating, didn't translate this last sentence. Instead, he asked the cleric, "Are you sure you want me to translate that?"

"I have no problem with what I am saying," Ayazi said calmly.

Ali-Reza grimaced, but he told me what the cleric had said.

Ultimately the concerns of Ayazi and learned religious scholars like him go beyond the restrictions imposed on Montazeri and the kind of repressive religious rule that has overtaken the Iranian political system. Their main worry is whether modern life has room for a religious establishment that insists on absolute obedience to God and on adherence to rules and customs that developed centuries ago. Many people compare their struggle to the Protestant Reformation in sixteenth-century Europe. I see it differently, as a struggle to resolve the contradictions that have been inherent in the Islamic political system from the beginning.

The challenge, of course, is to find a way to allow for differences of opinion in a system built on the assumption that statements and interpretations of the Prophet, even about minute details of everyday life, are binding until Judgment Day. Some of the clerics—a minority, I am told—simply refuse to see the need for change. Others are ready to jettison long-standing religious edicts for the sake of present-day reality. Still others, like Ayazi, clearly believe that the problems that modernity presents for the traditional interpretation of Islam add up to a fundamental reformulation. For them, religious edicts are products of human understanding and therefore devoid of inherent sacredness. An Islamic tradition that does not adapt to historical change, they argue, is alien to the very nature of the religion itself.

My visit with Ayazi introduced me to a different style of cleric—one not afraid to reveal a human side even as he explained the deep divisions between theology and politics within the clergy. That sense of seriousness and dignity is not, unfortunately, always shared by his fellow clergymen. And when they reveal their more human side, it is not always so respectful.

Part of my problem in understanding the world of Qom, in fact, is that I feel personally uneasy with clerics. I don't know exactly how to behave in their presence; in general they don't know how to deal with a professional American woman. Ayatollah Khomeini and many other clerics didn't look at me when I interviewed them, and I find the refusal of clerics to look at me disorienting. It is as if they want to make me feel unclean. Making eye contact is a basic tool of journalism as well as a natural instinct between human beings. It builds a relationship of trust. So I was relieved when the revolution softened, first after the death of Khomeini, whose stern demeanor had set the tone for a nation, and then again after the election of President Khatami, who liked to smile at both men and women.

Slowly, as my exposure to the world of Qom increased, I began to see more of the human face of the clerics. I found out that not all clerics are like Khomeini. But neither are they all like Ayazi, with his gentle, patient approach and hospitality. At a conference in Europe soon after Khatami's election, I met a senior ayatollah in his fifties who is widely regarded as a forward-looking scholar on social issues. At his request, I met him after dinner, at eleven in the evening in the garden of the hotel where we were staying. A group of Iranian musicians flown in especially for the conference played classical Persian music that would have been banned only a few years before. Our conversation was theoretical and esoteric, in part because Olivier Roy, the French scholar of Islam, joined us. We covered the landscape of political Islam: whether Islam and democracy are compatible, the doctrine of the Supreme Leader and his relationship to the most senior ayatollahs, the durability of Iran's Constitution. The ayatollah told personal stories about Khomeini—to prove how all-knowing and well-connected he was, I presumed.

"When I was with Imam Khomeini in France, a woman about fifty

years old approached me," he recalled. "She told me that she was a journalist from the Netherlands and that she had arranged to interview the
Imam. But when Imam Khomeini saw her, he said, 'I refuse to give you an
interview. You are not a journalist. You are a spy.' It turned out she was a
Jew and her husband was a rabbi."

There was nothing I could say. Should I tell the ayatollah that my husband is Jewish and that I found the anecdote offensive? Should I ask
whether it was her Jewishness that made her a spy or how Khomeini knew
she was Jewish? The ayatollah must have sensed my discomfort, so he
broke the silence. "I want to tell a joke!" he exclaimed. "A joke about sex."

He said it was a joke about a man who lived in the city of Rasht. "A
Rashti man and his wife were in bed together and the man noticed that
someone was under the bed," he said. "The husband asked his wife, 'Who
is lying under the bed?' She said she didn't know. The husband looked
and saw that it was a man lying very still. He asked his wife, 'Who is this
man who is not moving at all?' The wife explained, 'When he is under the
bed he doesn't move. When he is on the bed, he moves a lot.'"

The ayatollah guffawed. He thought his joke was very funny. His
Iranian assistant took the floor and told a joke about circumcision.

More uncomfortable than before, I moved the conversation back to a
discussion of Islam and the Islamic Republic. I told the ayatollah that I
had heard that his views on women's rights were very progressive and
asked why I had to cover my head in Iran when the Koran requires only
Muslim women to cover themselves. The rule is cultural, he explained,
not religious. "In an Islamic society a non-Muslim should observe the
rules of the society," he said. "As an Iranian, when I go to the West I observe the rules of the West." But then he confused me. "If someone does
not have Islamic dress, it is not a big sin," he added.

To explain further, he talked about gazing. "In Islam there's no ban
for a man to look at a woman, even if her head isn't covered," the ayatollah said. "What's forbidden is looking at a woman with sex on your mind.
When I look at you and we are talking like *this*, I am not committing a
sin." The ayatollah paused and looked at me.

"But if I look at you like *this*, it is a sin," he said. He leaned over close
and leered. "That way of looking corrupts me. At the University of
Tehran, most of my students are young women, and when I look at them,
I don't look at them like *this*." He leered again.

I didn't ask him if he was committing a sin with his leering. It was well past midnight and the interview was rapidly deteriorating. I excused myself and went to bed.

I learned later that after I left, the ayatollah began to recite sexually explicit tales and poetry, a kind of Islamic *Canterbury Tales*. One was a poem about an old man who was sexually obsessed with a seven-year-old girl. He watched her over the years as her body changed and her breasts developed. It was a poem of lament, as well as of missed opportunity. As her breasts got bigger, his penis got smaller. By the time she was old enough for him, he would be too old to enjoy her. A friend of mine, a serious academic from the United States who had joined the conversation after I left, was appalled. But he was also curious. "Why," he asked the ayatollah in a scholarly sounding tone, "do all of your comments reflect an obsession with sex?"

"Because I do not have any of it," the ayatollah replied.

I later asked a political science professor at the University of Tehran, who had once taught in Qom, about the ayatollah. "The clerics are the best jokers, especially in the religious schools," he explained. "When they are by themselves they feel free and start joking to each other. Even serious ones do it. When I was teaching, my students would make jokes that were so dirty they made me speechless. So much of what they study are the details of these issues." What the professor meant is that clerical students are required to study rules and interpretations of rules governing sex and personal habits including washing, urination, and defecation. There is a lot of room for dirty jokes.

Emaddedin Baghi, a former clerical student and writer who had studied for years in Qom, had a slightly different view. "The clerics are teachers," he told me. "They have a public role to play. Clerics will only show you the public side. They will not use curse words with you. They behave very differently in their private space, not because they're duplicitous, but because they play a different role there. In private they won't feel they have to censor themselves. A sense of humor exists among the clerics. They even have books of dirty jokes. Many of the jokes are very serious jokes about the teachings of Islam."

So that's it. The clerics of Qom can make jokes about Islam—and even about the Prophet himself—as long as it's done in private. What was unusual about the encounter with the joke-telling ayatollah wasn't that he cracked dirty jokes; it was that he cracked them in the presence of outsiders.

*   *   *

But Qom is not only a city of men. When I heard that there was a semi-nary exclusively for women in Qom, I thought it might provide a way to understand the place better.

Hidden behind an ornately tiled entrance in dazzling deep blue and turquoise, the Women's Seminary is a refuge of Islamic purity untouched by the ideological debate raging outside. It wasn't easy to get into the seminary, despite my letter of permission from the Ministry of Islamic Guidance and the entreaties of a female escort from the ministry. One problem was my clothing. I was wearing only a coat and head scarf, not a black chador.

"Where's your chador?" the old caretaker, a man, asked.

"Where does it say in the Koran that I have to wear a chador?" I asked in response.

"You can't go in," he said.

"I'm staying until you let me in," I said.

"You can't stand there! There are men inside! You may attract them!"

"I'm sure I won't attract anyone."

And so it went, back and forth, until the guard went back into his lit-tle guardhouse and slammed the door.

I pulled out my unofficial calling card, a color photograph of me and Ayatollah Khamenei during an interview years before. I was wearing the same black chiffon scarf with the red flowers that I had bought in Paris so long ago. "If it was good enough for the Supreme Leader, it should be good enough for the women inside," I said.

The caretaker scowled. But he opened the door.

Inside I found a simple, small classroom with unadorned walls and Koranic verses on the blackboard. Nine students clutched the folds of their black chadors under their chins with one hand and furiously took notes with the other. I also saw something I had never seen before in a classroom in Iran: the professor, a white-turbaned male cleric, lectured from behind a white canvas screen. I guess I shouldn't have been sur-prised. After all, the Koran describes how the Prophet's wives should be dealt with: "If you ask his wives for anything, speak to them from behind a curtain. This is purer for your heart and their hearts."

After the class, the women stayed behind to chat. So I asked them about issues raging in Iran at the time.

Should women be allowed to serve as judges in an Islamic Republic? One woman replied that she didn't have the knowledge to answer such a question; the others nodded in agreement.

Should women be allowed to ride bicycles? One said absolutely not; another said that only when women have more religious knowledge could they answer such a question.

Should a woman be allowed to run for President? All of them said no.

Should polygamy be allowed? Of course, they replied. A number of the students extolled the joys and the justice of polygamy when a couple is infertile. They told the story of their female professor who had been childless for years. She found her husband a second wife, who then bore children for him. The female professor now feels liberated. She still has a husband and a family life, but she can focus on her work without all the distractions that come with them. "Her husband helps her prepare her lectures," said one young woman. "And she and the second wife divide up the housework." The students couldn't have known it, but a couple of years later, the filmmaker Dariush Mehrjui would direct a powerful film called *Leila,* in which a young married woman suffering from infertility and under pressure from her mother-in-law encourages her husband to take a second wife and then feels betrayed by him.

In that classroom that day, I was incredulous. I told the class that my husband and I adopted our first child. I always try to find ways to make contact with women and I hoped the story would serve as a bridge. But adoption is not widely practiced in Iran and is not usually considered a satisfactory solution to childlessness.

"Didn't your husband want to divorce you?" one young woman asked.

Divorce just didn't come up, I replied.

For these women, polygamy was preferable—or at least that's what they told me, a foreigner.

"Aren't there problems for the first wife?" I asked.

"Maybe there might be some minor problems for her," said one thirty-two-year-old student and a mother of three children. "Maybe she'd have some psychological problems in the beginning. But they'd be minor ones. Islam takes care of it all."

On one level, the Women's Seminary is the old Qom. The women do not speak of ambitions to become great religious interpreters of Islam; rather, most of them are wives and mothers who live nearby and enjoy the use of the seminary's free day-care facility for their children. "We think a woman in Islam is a tender creature, a rose flower," the thirty-two-year-old student said. "And we should pay more attention to our roses than any other flower. The restrictions for women exist because Islam respects women."

But I always find that if I stick around long enough, other stories eventually come out. And even here in the women's restrictive world, there were signs of the ferment I found so evident among some of the clerics. The female seminarians were, in fact, rebels in their own way. It would have been a lot easier on their families if they stayed home. All the women spoke of wanting to get more education and paying jobs. They wanted to learn the language of Islam and Islamic law, which until then had been somewhat of a secret code understood only by men. The seminary was a ticket to economic freedom, or at least to a better life.

"I have a husband and a one-year-old daughter, but I want a career," said one twenty-five-year-old student. "I want to do religious research, maybe work in an institute where they interpret the Koran on the Internet."

"I want to teach religion," said a twenty-one-year-old student who had recently married. "Islam lets me decide for myself what I want to do."

Maybe these women had never had the chance to allow themselves the freedom to think for themselves. Maybe they were fighting to create space for themselves in a society that had defined a place for them. And maybe the city of clerics would be flexible enough to allow them that opportunity.

CHAPTER ELEVEN

Space for the Outsiders

O unbelievers, I will not worship what you worship
You have your religion, and I have mine

— THE KORAN, SURA 109

The Jews (may God curse them) . . . and their foreign backers are opposed
to the very foundations of Islam and wish to establish Jewish domination
throughout the world.

— AYATOLLAH RUHOLLAH KHOMEINI
IN A LECTURE IN 1970

Wait today. Tomorrow I will execute all Christians who commit crimes.

— NASSEREDIN SHAH QUOTED BY AN EYEWITNESS
DURING RIOTS IN 1848

I WAS READING THE *TEHRAN TIMES* one day when I came across an
article titled, "Views on Cleanliness of the People of Book." The *Tehran
Times* is a semi-official, very conservative English-language newspaper
under the influence of the office of the Supreme Leader. The article, citing interpretations of the Koran by important Islamic scholars, called for
tolerance, arguing that Jews and Christians are not inherently unclean,
just episodically unclean. For example, the article made the point that it
is perfectly acceptable for a Muslim to shake the hand of a Christian or a
Jew—so long as the Muslim first covers his hand with a cloth. "But if his
hand touches yours," the scholar concluded, "wash your hand."

I think about that article sometimes when Iranian officials tell me
with pride that the Islamic Republic treats its religious minorities the

same as its Muslims. Certainly Iran's long history as the home of many non-Muslim peoples makes the country different from some of its neighbors. Shortly after the revolution, Khomeini issued a fatwa that Christians and Jews are "people of the book" and therefore worthy of respect. Article 13 of the Constitution states clearly that "Zoroastrian, Jewish, and Christian Iranians are the only recognized religious minorities, who, within the limits of the law, are free to perform their religious rites and ceremonies, and to act according to their own canon in matters of personal affairs and religious education." The next article says, "All Muslims are duty-bound to treat non-Muslims in conformity with ethical norms and the principles of Islamic justice and equity, and to respect their human rights." There are designated seats in the Parliament for representatives of religious minorities—two for Armenian Christians and one each for Assyrian and Chaldean Christians, Jews, and Zoroastrians.

But the one percent of Iranians who practice religions other than Islam are considered separate and suffer to varying degrees as a result. Iran is an *Islamic* Republic; and no matter what the laws say, some Muslim writings contend that non-Muslims are too impure for a Muslim to touch. Some of the country's non-Muslims resign themselves to suffering, saying it is the normal condition of life; others find ways to keep up optimism and even to thrive, in spite of the strictures of the state.

There are degrees of discrimination. The Zoroastrians and the Christians suffer the least. Zoroastrianism is the ancient religion of Iran; Jesus Christ is revered as a prophet who predated Mohammad by more than six hundred years. The Jews come next. At the bottom of the scale are the Bahais, who are considered Islamic heretics and are subject to outright persecution. Yet the Islamic Republic requires young Christian, Zoroastrian, Jewish, and even Bahai men to fulfill two years of compulsory military service.

All conversion and proselytizing are banned, and from time to time evangelical Christian missionaries who sneak over the border and try to preach the Gospel have been put into prison. But sometimes I am surprised at how much tolerance there can be. Take the case of Arthur Blessitt and his crucifix. Blessitt, an American, was known as the "Sunset Boulevard Preacher" in the days when he ran an alcohol-free, all-night "nightclub for Jesus" on Sunset Strip in Los Angeles. But since 1969, Arthur had been obsessed by another mission: to carry a thirteen-foot-long, forty-five-pound metal cross on wheels into every country in the world before the dawn of the year 2000. Iran was one of the last places on his list. In 1998 he brought the cross into Iran in three pieces in an oversized ski bag, assembled it and carried it, Christ-like, wherever he could. When I met up with him in Persepolis, he told me that he was not trying to convert the population; he only wanted to recall Christ's suffering and death and have his picture taken with his cross in front of biblical sites like the tomb of Daniel, the Old Testament prophet, in the ancient city of Susa in southwestern Iran. The Iranian authorities viewed Blessitt as a curiosity, but they didn't arrest him. Maybe it was that he was a foreigner—one with an odd mission at that—who would soon be out of the country anyway; maybe it was that some issues involving non-Muslims are nonthreatening and can be safely ignored.

For members of religious minorities living in Iran, of course, no slack is cut. These people are left to invent ways of coping with their second-class status and avoiding the impression that they threaten the regime. Some with Muslim-sounding names choose to hide their identities as they try to maneuver more easily within the Islamic system. Others insist that the differences don't matter. Still others create two worlds—mingling in the arena of the Islamic Republic in the workplace by day and keeping with their own kind at night.

The antique shops on Ferdowsi Avenue in the heart of Tehran are owned largely by Jews and they serve all customers, just as they did in the days of the Shah. The Armenians, like other non-Muslims, are exempt from the ban on drinking alcohol and are allowed to make vodka and wine for their own personal consumption. One Armenian I know who works in an auto repair shop by day has a very lucrative side business—selling and delivering very drinkable vodka, beer, and various wines and liqueurs to non-Muslims and Muslims alike.

No matter how they feel or struggle or cope or deny, non-Muslims in Iran are different. They believe in different prophets than the Muslims do, and they worship on different days and celebrate different holidays (except for *Nowruz*, the Zoroastrian-inspired New Year that many minorities celebrate). Non-Muslims follow their own laws on marriage, divorce, and inheritance. They receive lower awards in injury and death lawsuits, but heavier punishments, than Muslims. Many members of religious minorities left Iran because of the revolution, and many of these were granted political asylum abroad after claiming religious persecution.

*   *   *

As someone who grew up Catholic, I find the statues and stained glass windows and incense and rituals of the Christian churches in Iran a familiar refuge from the omnipresence of the Islamic Republic. Armenians, by far the largest Christian group in Iran, worship in their own churches in every major Iranian city. They socialize in Armenian cultural centers, publish an Armenian-language newspaper, and run their own schools. Before the revolution, about 250,000 Armenians lived in Iran; twenty years later the number is down to fewer than 200,000. I particularly like the Saint Sarkis Church in the center of Tehran. I have no trouble finding it because it backs up against one of the last remaining anti-American murals in the capital: an American flag with skulls for the stars and missiles for the stripes and the words, "Down with U.S.A."

Before his death in 1999, Archbishop Artak Manookian, the head of the Armenian community, readily welcomed visitors like me. A native of Beirut, he wore a full beard, flowing purple robes, and an enormous gold medallion, and asked to be called "Your Eminence." Sitting behind an ornately carved mahogany desk, he would explain how good the Armenians have it in Iran. He spoke in Armenian, through an interpreter, or in barely understandable English. His Persian was pitiful, even though he had lived in Iran for forty years. To prove that his status was equal to that of the Muslim clerics in the eyes of the Islamic Republic, he once handed me a photocopy of a photo of himself with Ayatollah Khamenei. "We are like friends, very close," the Archbishop insisted.

But even the churches, schools, and cultural centers aren't complete refuges from the Islamic Republic. Next to paintings of the Christian patriarchs in the rectory's large receiving room hang photos of Ayatollahs Khomeini and Khamenei. Muslim bureaucrats administer the Armenian schools, and Armenian literature courses require government approval. Armenian girls are required to observe Islamic dress, even inside their own schools. At one point Ataollah Mohajerani, the Minister of Islamic Guidance, tried to appear ecumenical by visiting an Armenian church ceremony in Chaldaran, a remote part of western Azerbaijan province, to commemorate the martyrdom of Saints Thaddeus and Batganius. "Today I felt as if I was praying in a mosque!" he exclaimed. He apparently thought it was a compliment.

Underpinning the Islamic Republic's view of tolerance is a sometimes barely hidden belief that Islam is superior to other religions. During a visit to Washington to visit his son, Amir, Ayatollah Majdeddin
Mahallati lectured at the National Cathedral on the meaning of Jesus
Christ in Islam. He sat at a long Formica table elegantly dressed in a white
robe covered by a black gauze cloak, a white turban on his head, fingering
a polished carved wood cane. "There are twenty-five references to Jesus
Christ as the Prophet of God in the Koran," he said. "No one can be a
Muslim and not believe in the Prophethood of Jesus Christ. I doubt you
have ever heard of anyone ever being persecuted."

One American in the audience leaned over and whispered, "He certainly got that wrong." Over the years, the Islamic Republic has closed evangelical churches and arrested converts; evangelical pastors have been killed
gangland-style. But this was a polite group and no one challenged the
eminent guest. Then the ayatollah told a story about Imam Reza, the ninth-
century Shiite Muslim leader: "A young man came to Imam Reza. The
young man was a Muslim and he said to the Imam, 'My mother is a Christian. How should I treat her?' 'You should respect her even more,' Imam
Reza replied. And that phrase encouraged the mother to become a Muslim!"

So there it was. Christians are well liked. In fact, they are so well liked
that Muslims welcome their conversion. Other religions feel the same
way about people they consider heathen, of course, including a number
of Christian denominations. But none that I know of—except perhaps
the Vatican—is currently running a government.

In Iran, the impulse to convert non-Muslims still exists. One Sunday
during Lent in Tehran an Armenian Christian friend named Catherine
invited me to go with her to Mass. Just as the service was ending, a tall, thin
man in a suit walked up the center aisle, turned toward the congregation,
and held up a framed picture. It showed a portrait of Ali, the son-in-law and
cousin of the Prophet Mohammad. "You must follow Imam Ali!" the man
shouted. "Imam Ali is the way to salvation! Jesus Christ is not coming to
save you! Convert! Convert! Let the twelfth Imam save you! Convert to
Islam or go to hell!" A priest and a handful of parishioners grabbed the
man and dragged him down the long aisle to the exit. But even as he was
led away, he continued to shout about conversion and Imam Ali.

Of course, that kind of thing can happen almost anywhere, but in Iran
it resonates for the Christians in a particular way. Later, over beef schnitzel
at the nearby Armenian Club, Catherine and her thirty-four-year-old

daughter, Maria, explained that regardless of whether the Muslim intruder was crazy, the incident underscored the fact that Christians don't feel secure even in their places of worship and will always be treated as outsiders.

The Armenian Club is a refuge, a members-only club for Armenians and other Christians. A nondescript box of a building with exposed wiring and crumbling plaster, it struggles to preserve some of the elegance of better days. *The Magic Flute* plays over the stereo system. The tables are covered with salmon-colored satin cloths, the room is brightly lit by polished brass sconces and chandeliers. It is one of the few sexually integrated public spaces in Iran where women do not have to hide their hair under scarves or the shape of their bodies under long, loose-fitting clothing. For that reason, Muslims are barred from entry. I had met Catherine through Nazila, but as a Muslim, Nazila couldn't join us.

Even though Armenians can drink alcoholic beverages in the privacy of their homes, that right does not extend to the club, and Catherine didn't think the ban was such a bad thing. "When the men were allowed to drink here they'd get drunk out of their minds," she said. "It's better to keep drinking in the home."

I asked Catherine's daughter, Maria, what life was like for her. So she told me about the lashing. It had happened three years ago, but for Maria it was the defining moment of her adult life in Iran. "My colleague and I were wearing light blue coats and head scarves at work the way we always do," she recalled. "The police came and asked, 'Why are you wearing a color like that?' So I told them, 'It is the uniform for my company.' They said, 'Your scarf is fit for a discotheque.' So I asked them, 'What kind of woman would wear a scarf on her head to a discotheque?'

"They ordered us to come to a certain place for punishment. My mother tried to stay with me but they sent her away. It was a very big dirty place. The windows were painted black so no one could look in or out. There were about fifty of us sitting there from morning until night. We had to wear black chadors over our clothes.

"Finally a woman guard came in carrying a big cable in one hand and a Koran in the other. She asked if anyone was pregnant. The pregnant ones pay a fine instead of getting lashed. But the rest of us—the rest of us got lashed. One by one. We were all shouting and crying, 'Why are you doing this to us? Is this true Islam?' The guard ignored us. I was lucky. I was wearing two sweaters and a raincoat under my chador. I only got five lashes. The guard told me she didn't beat me hard because I was so thin."

Maria acknowledged her loneliness. She had led a sheltered life and years before, her parents had forbidden her to attend a far-off university because they didn't want her to live alone. Although she is beautiful, with waist-length black hair, she is unmarried, in part because she wants to marry an Armenian. Her father—divorced from her mother—is a Muslim and that has caused nothing but trouble, she said. "Some people I work with, Muslims, don't want to come to my house because they think Christians are unclean. And did you know we're considered less valuable in the eyes of the law than Muslims? It's not right. Humans are humans. It's the same body, the same blood. Who made this law and called it Islamic law?"

"Do you ever think of leaving Iran?" I asked Maria.

Catherine jumped into the conversation. "Absolutely," she said. "The U.N. will pay for our tickets as refugees. I'm going to be sixty-five. Our tickets will be coming. We'll go to America."

"I'd like to work for an airline," said Maria. "And I'm trained as a hairdresser. God knows that I believe in Him. So I'll leave my fate to Him."

In fact, two months after our lunch, the United Nations High Commissioner for Refugees arranged political asylum for Catherine and Maria and resettled them in Vienna. They had no family or friends there. They did not speak German. But Vienna was their way out, and they took it. Months later they sent me a Christmas card from Glendale, California. They were starting a new life there.

On Friday nights at the Yousefabad Synagogue in an upper-middle-class neighborhood in central Tehran, there are other believers who have put their fate into God's hands. The numbers attest to the treatment of Jews in the Islamic Republic. There were about 80,000 Jews in 1978, the year before Khomeini's revolution; twenty years later, the number had dwindled to about 30,000.

The Jews of Iran are the oldest Jewish community outside Israel. When Cyrus the Great conquered Babylonia in 539 B.C., he liberated the Jews who had been enslaved there, and many settled in Persia. Over the centuries, the Iranian Jews experienced waves of persecution and of tolerance. During a period of tolerance in the late fifteenth and the early sixteenth centuries, for example, Iranian Jews were respected winemakers, bankers, and merchants. But in the second half of the seventeenth century, Jews were branded *najes,* "unclean," and began to be persecuted as infidels. They were forced into ghettos, and banned from entering Muslim shops or homes in the belief that their presence would sully the premises. On rainy days, they were not permitted to leave their ghettos for fear that the rain would wash the impurity from their bodies onto Muslims. Jews were told that they were not real Iranians and forbidden to learn Persian. They were not allowed to testify in courts of law, even in their own defense. They were required to wear special hats and patches on their clothes. At one point Jewish women were banned from wearing chadors, putting them on the same level as prostitutes. Worst of all, some Jews were forced to convert to Islam.

The Jews endured physical attacks, rape, torture, expulsion, and murder. At times, the state held the entire Jewish community responsible for the crimes of one individual. One massacre in Tabriz in 1831 wiped out the city's entire Jewish population. However, after Reza Shah came to power in the 1920s, Jews enjoyed a greater degree of freedom. They were allowed to leave their ghettos, attend school, and practice their religion. Gradually, they created space for themselves in Iranian civic life.

Under Shah Mohammad Reza Pahlavi, the Jewish population thrived, and Israel's presence and influence in Iran increased. The Shah even opened limited diplomatic relations with Israel. Israeli and American intelligence played a role in the creation and operation of SAVAK, the Shah's secret police, and Iran remained a major supplier of oil to Israel in the 1970s, during the Arab oil embargo. In reading through classified American documents published by the militants who seized the American embassy in 1979, I came across one volume that included transcripts of verbatim conversations between senior Israeli and Iranian officials on a plan to jointly develop a missile that could have carried a nuclear warhead. The Shah, according to Richard Helms, a former American ambassador to Iran and former director of the CIA, once told the Israelis that neither Iran nor Israel should want to be alone "in a sea of Arabs."

So it was to be expected that one of the first acts of the 1979 revolution was to occupy the gray concrete Israeli trade mission in north Tehran, rip down the Israeli flag, and run off with the furniture. Even the air conditioners were unbolted and carted off. The new regime expelled the twenty-two Israeli diplomats living in Iran and handed over the building to the Palestine Liberation Organization leader, Yasir Arafat, as his "embassy." The Israeli officials took refuge in the American embassy; the Americans smuggled them out of the country on fake American passports.

The revolution's relationship with Iran's own Jews is an even more complicated matter. Certainly the antipathy for Israel hurt the Jews, and many fled. Still, Iran's Jewish community remains the largest in the Middle East outside of Israel and the largest in any Muslim country in the world. More than two decades after the Iranian revolution, Tehran has eleven functioning synagogues, some with Hebrew schools; two kosher restaurants; a Jewish hospital; a home for the elderly; a twenty-thousand-volume Jewish library; and a cemetery.

Iran's Ministry of Education runs the Hebrew schools, which are allowed to teach only the Torah and religious texts. Teaching Hebrew as a living language for everyday use—the way it is taught in and out of Israel as a pillar of Zionism—is forbidden. As in Armenian schools, the administrators of the Jewish schools are appointed by the government and with few exceptions must be Muslim. Jews can work in some government offices and state-run companies but cannot advance very far. The community's last Jewish newspaper was closed down in 1991 after it criticized the government's decision to take over the administration of Jewish schools.

One Friday night when Nazila and I visited the Yousefabad Synagogue, five hundred worshippers came to celebrate the beginning of the Sabbath. Two armed guards of the Islamic Republic stood watch at the simple entrance of green woven metal graced by the Iranian flag. Inside, women with colorful scarves covering their heads sat on the left, men in yarmulkes on the right. Intricately carved wooden doors surrounded by turquoise tiles contrasted with humble black armchairs and an old marble floor that needed a good scrubbing. A handwritten sign in Persian taped to a pillar captured the sacred and the mundane: "When reading the Torah keep silent" appeared just above "Throw the garbage in the wastebasket."

I sat with the women in the back row. Despite the solemnity of the standing and bowing and praying during the service, the women near me wanted to enjoy themselves. They chanted their prayers in Hebrew, but like many Jews who live outside Israel did not know what the words meant. Unlike the Armenian Christians, whose first language is Armenian, the first language of the Jews is Persian. The women were eager to talk to me. And talk they did, alternating between English and Persian.

"I have a son in New Jersey," a sixty-seven-year-old woman with heavy glasses whispered to me in English. "In Hackensack. His name is Eddie. I've been to America five times."

"My son lives in Connecticut," chimed in a sixty-three-year-old woman with dyed blond hair and heavy black eye makeup. "Bridgeport. Do you know Bridgeport? I lived there three years." She pulled out her address book. "This is his phone number."

The administrator of the synagogue motioned for us to stop talking. So I turned away from the group. It was no use. The woman sitting on the other side of me started talking. "My son's in Dallas," she said. "It's years that I want to go, but I can't get a visa."

As the service continued, stories of sadness trickled out: the suspicion of Jews by the Iranian authorities; the confiscation of the passports of Jews and the enormous bribes paid to get them back; the pain of not being able to visit Israel legally; the ban on telephone and mail service to Israel; the requirement that Jewish schools open on Saturdays, violating a commandment not to work on the Sabbath; the story about a member of the synagogue who had disappeared without a trace years before while trying to escape over the Pakistani border.

The women said that the repressive rules of the Islamic Republic and the relentless anti-Israeli rhetoric have made them feel even more Jewish. The synagogues have become places to meet and talk as much as to pray. "Before the revolution we went to Israel every six months," the blond woman said. "I have so many relatives there but we can't visit. My mother finally died from the sadness. The sorrow of families divided can kill us. There are hardly any young Jews in our country anymore. My son—he is very handsome. He wants to marry an American girl. Do you know any?"

Her friend in the heavy eyeglasses interrupted. "People's attitudes change toward us as soon as they find out that we're Jewish," she said. "It's impossible for a Jew to get a job. My son studied electrical engineering in the States for seven years but as soon as he writes down he's Jewish he's disqualified for jobs here. My other son got so depressed that he died of depression. I curse the revolution. It took everything from me, everything."

Maybe I was being overly sensitive, but I saw anti-Semitism under the surface in Iran wherever I looked. I saw it during a call on Fatemeh Hashemi, the daughter of former President Rafsanjani, when the conversation turned to her younger sister, Faezeh. Faezeh had recently canceled a trip to the United States. I told Fatemeh that I was disappointed, because I had planned to show her sister around *The New York Times.*

"It's better you didn't do that," Fatemeh said. "Everybody knows *The New York Times* is run by the Jews."

I saw anti-Semitism among my Iranian friends. At a gathering of a group of women at the home of my friend Nargess one evening, one woman told a joke about a Jew, a Christian, and a Muslim. Another told a joke about a Jew and a Turkish-speaking Iranian. In both jokes, the Jew was cunning, miserly, and a master merchant.

I had had it. After years of enduring comments like these, I protested. "I'm so sick and tired of these jokes about Jews," I said. "My husband is a Jew. You've got to realize how offensive these jokes are."

Nargess's sister Monir, who owns a hair salon that is one of my favorite places to visit, tried to console me. "Your husband is okay," she said. "He's not a Zionist. So it's okay that he's a Jew. My best customer is a Jew. I love the Jews. When I move back to America again, I want all my best customers to be rich Jews."

The women explained that they said nothing about Jews that they didn't say about Isfahanis, adding that Isfahanis are just as cunning and miserly as Jews.

I tried to make the point again. "Monir, you're a Turk from Azerbaijan," I said. "Everyone is always making jokes about Turks. You of all people should be sensitive to this."

"I love Turkish jokes," Nargess chimed in. "They're the best jokes in the world."

"When you were in the United States during the hostage crisis and people cursed you just because you were Iranian, wasn't that racist?" I asked.

"Not at all!" Nargess exclaimed. "They were ignorant people. And they were justified. We were burning their flag. Our culture was hurting their culture."

I couldn't win. The Islamic Republic's anti-Semitism goes deeper even than cultural stereotypes. It stems directly from interpretations of the Koran and other teachings that have been passed along for centuries. The Koran reveres the prophets of Judaism, but it also refers to the Jews of Mohammad's time as the Muslims' "worst friends." The Jews are portrayed in some interpretations and sayings as money-grubbing materialists who betrayed Moses and were responsible for the death of Jesus. That anti-Semitism was matched fourteen centuries later by Khomeini's rhetoric. "From its very inception, Islam has been afflicted by Jews," he said in a lecture in 1970. "From the very beginning, they launched their hostile activity by distorting the good name of Islam . . . by slandering and spreading lies against it."

Still, the Jews of Iran manage to maneuver in the Islamic Republic. There are some professions in which Jews are accepted—business, medicine, engineering, law. But there are limits. Jews can become lawyers but not judges; they can serve in the army but will never get promoted to a meaningful rank.

Every year during the Jewish holidays, newspapers print stories about how content the Jews of Iran are. Like this one written by the official Iranian news agency during Passover one year: "The Jewish community of Tehran, in a message issued here Wednesday, salutes the advent of Passover feasts. . . . Wishing success for the leader of the Islamic Revolution Ayatollah Ali Khamenei, President Mohammad Khatami, and the Iranian nation in the new Iranian year, the Jewish community renewed its ancient and close ties with all Iranian people."

But Iran does not recognize the existence of Israel and sees Zionist plots everywhere. One of the most prominent murals in central Tehran is a giant portrait of Fathi Shaqaqi, whom the Islamic Republic considers a hero. Shaqaqi, a leader of the Palestinian guerrilla group Islamic Jihad, was assassinated by Israeli agents in Malta in 1995 after his organization carried out a series of suicide bombings against Jewish civilians.

Leaders of the Jewish community in Iran, however, do not complain—at least not to outsiders. They have told me that the Jews have absolutely no problems making their way through the thicket of the Islamic Republic. That's what Haroun Yeshayaei, a film producer and chairman of the Central Jewish Community, said when I visited him at the dingy, depressing Jewish Community Center in central Tehran.

I sat down with Yeshayaei at a table covered by a plastic tablecloth sticky with sugar. He is a gregarious man who agreed to an interview only after the Ministry of Islamic Guidance sent him a letter authorizing him to talk. He shook my hand—he was not a Muslim, after all—and offered me tea. Yeshayaei explained that the key to survival as a Jew in Iran is to compartmentalize—to wall out the official rhetoric of hate about Zionist plots and Israeli evil. He insisted, implausibly, that life is better for Jews now than it had been in the days of the monarchy. "We have the same synagogues, the same schools, the same traditional food," he said. "Our religious life is a lot more organized than it was. The synagogues are more crowded, the people more religious. The more the Muslims got Muslim, the more the Jews got Jewish. The only thing the Jewish community has to do to is keep out of politics." And Muslims like Jews, especially Jewish doctors, he said. Even though the staff at the Jewish hospital in Tehran is entirely Jewish, more than 90 percent of the patients are Muslim.

Yeshayaei acknowledged what I had heard at the synagogue, that it is more difficult for a Jew to get a job than for a Muslim. "In this economy, it's hard for *anyone* to get a job," he said. "But especially hard for the Jews. If there is a vacant job and a Muslim and a Jew are equally qualified, the job will go to the Muslim."

He had a ready reply for every question. He likened the ban on travel to Israel to the restrictions on Iranian Muslims traveling to Saudi Arabia, which requires special government permission. "And for a while, no Iranian could go to Thailand either, because of all the prostitution there," he said.

I asked him why so many Iranian Jews want to move to the United States. "Ask any Muslim in Iran and he'll tell you he wants to go to America!" he said. "Ask half the people in the world and they'll tell you they want to live in America."

"The Jews are doing fine," Yeshayaei said. "They're mostly middle-class professionals." He reserved his bitterness for those Jews who, he said, have abandoned their country. "In Iran we don't have rich Jews anymore," he said. "They have taken their money to the States and left us miserable here. There are many, many rich Jews who left. I say this as an Iranian, not as a Jew."

Down the hall is the office of Manouchehr Eliassi, an Iranian-educated gastroenterologist and, when I met him, the designated Jewish member of Parliament. Eliassi is adamant about his Iranianness. "I'm an Iranian and I have all the same problems other Iranians have," Eliassi said. "I was born and educated here. I'm the representative of my medical business at the tax office—not as a Jew, but as a citizen. My sister lives in L.A. My brothers-in-law live in New York. One's a doctor in Queens. But my blood is in this country. Even Jews who have left the country feel this way. My sister counts the days and nights left before her visits here." Eliassi's words help to explain the tie that had kept so many Jews in Iran. For the Zoroastrians, the Armenians, the Bahais, and the Jews, the one constant the Islamic Republic can count on is that, deep down, they also feel Iranian.

His most active role in Parliament, he said, came in 1998 when he helped draft a much-debated bill to segregate medical treatment for men and women.

"So how did you vote?" I asked.

"I prefer not to tell you," he said. "Voting is done by secret ballot."

Again, it was the direct question not answered. Perhaps revealing his vote on such a sensitive issue might have aroused suspicion among his colleagues and given strength to his enemies. So I tried a different tack.

"Do you treat women patients?" I asked.

"Of course," he said.

"So I can guess how you voted."

"You guessed right."

"Then why did you help draft the bill?" I asked. He looked me in the eye and smiled. Don't cross the line, his eyes told me.

Perhaps it was this ambiguity that led the Jewish electorate to reject him for a second term in the parliamentary elections in 2000. Or perhaps it was his inability to resolve a much larger crisis within the Jewish community.

Two weeks after my meetings with Yeshayaei and Eliassi, the arrest of thirteen Jewish men and boys in Shiraz and Isfahan was disclosed. They had been accused of spying for Israel, an offense punishable by death. Seventeen Iranian Jews, including two people who were hanged in 1997, had been executed as spies since the revolution. Among those arrested in 1999 were rabbis, store clerks, an electrical worker, a perfumier, and a sixteen-year-old boy. During their confinement, they were allowed almost no contact with relatives or lawyers.

Once the arrests became public, the battle lines were drawn. Some hard-line newspapers referred to the arrested Jews as "the group of spies." But some reformist newspapers chastised the authorities, particularly Ayatollah Yazdi, then the head of the Judiciary, for calling them spies before they had even been tried. More than a year after their arrests, the trials began in closed session in a revolutionary court in Shiraz. Day after day, confessions poured out. "I was accused of spying for the benefit of Israel, and I accept the charges," said Hamid Tefileen, a thirty-year-old shoe store clerk from Shiraz and the first to testify, in a confession later broadcast on state-run television. He calmly explained that he had been recruited by Israeli intelligence during a trip to Israel in 1994 and was paid each month for working as part of a "network" that gathered and passed along "political, military, and social information" about Iran. "Israel," he added, "plays on the religious beliefs" of Jews.

Israel's government called the charges "ludicrous and barbaric"; Tefileen's confession and the ones that followed were denounced by international human rights advocates as suspect. The defense lawyers insisted that their clients' rights had not been respected and petitioned the court—unsuccessfully—to open the proceedings to the public. On one level, the trials validated those in Iran's Jewish community who felt there was no place for them in the country; on another, they highlighted an abusive judicial system in which due process and fair and open trials are not guaranteed for any Iranian citizen.

Even before the spy trials, the sporadic repression and lack of economic promise had produced a quiet desperation among many Iranian Jews. Many of those who wanted to leave, like Soviet Jews years earlier, didn't want to go to Israel; they wanted to go to America. But without family ties, that was a remote possibility. Many had no intention of leaving, although the poorest among them, like desperate people anywhere, were perfectly willing to beg for help. I discovered that by accident with Sheldon and Cynthia Katz, two American tourists from New York, at a small, poor synagogue in Isfahan in late 1998.

Isfahan was once known as *Dar-al-Yahud,* House of the Jews, and as late as the nineteenth century was home to tens of thousands of Jews. Only a few thousand at most remain today. Behind a metal door and a brick wall on a busy street corner in the center of Isfahan, the Katzes and I found the city's biggest synagogue. Unlike the main synagogues of Tehran, which are lively meeting places, even when they are down-at-the-heels, the synagogue in Isfahan is dirty and poor. We were the only visitors that day. A toothless old woman who answered the door ranted that the synagogue's caretakers had stolen her job and were determined to starve her. She grabbed at us, blocked our way, begging God for mercy and us for money.

Then a rail-thin young woman with an acne-scarred face and waist-length hair emerged from the synagogue and embraced the Katzes. I'll call her Leila. "You're Jewish! You're American!" she exclaimed. She and her sister proudly showed us around, pointing out the yarmulkes and prayer shawls, the Torah and holy books, the unlit crystal chandeliers hanging from the ceiling. She told us to ignore the old woman, who was making quite a racket with her ranting and her begging. "She's crazy," said Leila. "We take care of her, but she's crazy. Don't give her any money."

We asked Leila if she knew how we could find the old Jewish quarter of Isfahan, and she offered to take us there herself.

As we navigated the narrow streets of mud houses in the old neighborhood on the other side of town, Leila's story emerged in bits that didn't add up. She boasted that she had a good job as a secretary in a doctor's office and that Jews were treated well in Iran. She said that her family had lived in the synagogue as caretakers for fifteen years, that one of her brothers had died mysteriously two years before, when he was twenty-four, that her three other brothers had left Iran and settled in Israel.

"My dream is to move and live in Israel," she said.

That's all the Katzes needed to hear. They told Leila that they knew people in agencies in New York that could get her settled in Israel. "If you can get out of Iran we can help you go," said Cynthia, pressing her business card into the young woman's hand.

"I can't afford to leave the country," the young woman said.

"The agency will pay that too!" Cynthia insisted. "We'll help you! We'll help you!"

Nazila, who was helping with the translation, struggled to keep up as both sides competed to control the conversation. "She's asking if anyone can help her financially," Nazila said.

"Yes, we'll get her financial help," said Cynthia.

The taxi driver, a Muslim who had been quiet until then, offered his opinion. "The solution is not to leave the country," he advised the young woman. "You should stay here with your family."

Leila ignored him. But she came up with her own excuses for why a plan for her to emigrate to Israel wouldn't work. "I would have to take the family there too," she said.

"We can help your family too," said Cynthia.

"They can't go because they don't speak the language," Leila said.

"We'll get Iranian Jews to translate," Cynthia replied.

"No, it's impossible," she replied. "We don't have a phone."

"I'll have them write to you," Cynthia insisted.

Nazila finally figured out what was going on. Leila didn't have a good job, and she didn't want money to leave Iran to go to Israel. She just wanted the American visitors to give her a bit of money now, anything to ease the desperation of her everyday life.

"I'm already twenty-five," she cried. "My sister and I are the cleaners of the synagogue, so nobody wants to marry either of us. Nobody even pays us for our work. My mother is very sick and she's going blind. My father doesn't work. At first I said my dream was to go to Israel because it is so difficult to live here. But I might have a life here. I'm Iranian. And with some money, I could find a husband."

Her voice trailed off. The Katzes were speechless. Funding a young woman so that she could find a husband was not what they had in mind. But the young woman did not give up. She tugged at Nazila's sleeve as we tried to say our goodbyes.

"I need money! I need money!" she cried. "I can't leave the country. Help me with money!"

I thought of Leila's plight and how it is like the plight of so many other young people in Iran, regardless of their religion. Leila had no intention of leaving her country. She just wanted to find a good job and a good mate.

The Jews have it good compared with the Bahais, who are officially considered heretics. They are the nonpeople of Iran.

Christianity, Judaism, and Zoroastrianism can be tolerated because their origins predate Islam. But Bahaism is different. The roots of the Bahai faith date back to 1844, in the city of Shiraz, when a young Shiite Muslim named Mirza-Ali Mohammad declared himself the long-awaited Twelfth Imam. The movement that eventually emerged attracted a large following among the Shiite clergy and was suppressed by the authorities. They considered the Bahai religion heresy.

The Bahais practice a religion of peace and tolerance, avoid all political involvement, have no priests or public rituals, preach the importance of universal education, and are committed to upholding the laws of the countries in which they live. They advocate one-world government and the equality of all regardless of race or sex. They also teach that all religions are true, but that theirs, as the fulfillment of all religious prophecies, is truer.

In the eyes of many Iranian Muslims, who believe that Mohammad is the "Seal of the Prophets" and Islam the last revelation, that is apostasy. In the nineteenth century, the Bahais were given a choice: recant or die. Several thousand were executed.

Today, Iran's religious leaders—and much of the Iranian public—view the Bahais as subversives as well as heretics. As early as the 1960s, Ayatollah Khomeini referred to the Bahais as "a destructive sect," which he claimed had penetrated all areas of government and had collaborated with Israel. (The global headquarters for the Bahais is in the Israeli city of Haifa.) The Islamic Republic considers Bahais infidels and gives them no protection under the Constitution. Bahais cannot vote, but they have to pay taxes, and young Bahai men have to perform two years of compulsory military service. Their marriages are not recognized by the state, so their children are considered illegitimate.

Since Iran's revolution, more than two hundred Bahais have been executed and about eight hundred imprisoned. The Islamic state has confiscated property and businesses owned by Bahais. Many Bahais who worked as civil servants before the revolution were dismissed from their jobs and forced to repay in full the salaries and benefits earned during their careers.

The Bahais have published what they claim is an official, confidential memo signed by Ayatollah Khamenei in February 1991 and disclosing the official attitude of the Islamic Republic toward their community. The memo calls for Bahais to be treated in ways "that their progress and development shall be blocked." Specifically, it says that Bahais should be expelled from universities, prevented from attaining "positions of influence" in society, and denied employment and schooling if they identify themselves as Bahais. They are allowed access to passports, burial certificates, and work permits, the memo says, only "to the extent that it does not encourage them to be Bahais."

But Bahais believe that they are required to profess their faith, not renounce it. So the persecution of Iran's largest religious minority (there are about 350,000 Bahais in Iran and five million worldwide) is harsh, so harsh that refugee status in the West is nearly always granted to those who flee. In recent years, the Islamic authorities quietly began to ignore the rule that requires Bahais to denounce their faith before they are issued passports to leave the country. Like so many other thorny issues in the Islamic Republic, quiet abandonment has become the way out.

The Bahai community is politically active and well funded in the United States. But when I contacted some of its representatives and asked them to help arrange a meeting with Bahais in Iran, the reply was: don't bother to try; the community is under such pressure that no one will ever want to meet you. But it turned out differently once I was in Iran. A friend of the mother of a friend is a Bahai, and one day I went to see her in her office.

The woman received me warmly. She was still working, so her husband, an engineer, invited me to their home. It was the first of several meetings. A third-generation Bahai, he was surprisingly calm, even serene during our meetings, which could have landed him in prison had they been discovered. Yet, he has no fear of death, no desire to leave Iran either. "We have a proverb in Persian that says, 'There is no color beyond black,'" he said. "It means that when you are doing something you really believe in, you don't think of yourself. If someone wants to kill me, it doesn't matter."

Against all odds, the sense of being Persian was keeping this man in this country.

The engineer showed me a photocopy of a banned book published in Dallas titled *A Tribute to the Faithful, 1978–1992: The Bahai Martyrs of Iran.* It contained the stories of Iranian Bahais executed since the revolution. He gave me a running commentary, pointing out friends and relatives who had perished. "Kidnapped," "whereabouts unknown," "firing squad," "body buried unbeknownst to family," the entries read. He said that mere possession of this book could mean imprisonment and perhaps a death sentence.

The engineer told of executions denied by the authorities, even though the bodies of the victims were delivered to the families. He told how the special cemetery in Tehran reserved for Bahais had been razed, the cadavers removed and sent to unknown locations, and an Islamic cultural center built on the site. He told of hiding Bahai literature in the oven of his kitchen. He told of arrests and interrogations in which his captors knew the most intimate details of his personal and professional life. He told how his wife's passport had been confiscated four years earlier, because she had been caught at the airport with books about the Bahai faith.

September 29, 1998, was a day the engineer would remember. That was the day Iranian security officials swooped down on more than five hundred Bahai homes and office buildings in at least fourteen cities around the country, arresting dozens of Bahais and confiscating equipment, teaching materials, documents, even furniture. The raid was an attempt to halt an extraordinarily brave act of communal preservation. Bahais are passionate about, even obsessed with, educating their children. And because Bahais are banned from attending universities in Iran, the Bahai community ran the Bahai Institute of Higher Education, a makeshift secret university, from their homes, basements, and offices.

Begun on a tiny scale in 1987, the university, which was taught largely by correspondence, grew every year. Advisers from American universities provided course materials and curricula. A network of couriers smuggled in textbooks and laboratory equipment. By the time the university was shut down, dozens of volunteer faculty members had been teaching nearly one thousand students in ten areas of study, including accounting, dentistry, mathematics, computer science, and English. One hundred fifty students graduated, and many of them went on to study at universities abroad, despite the university's lack of official status. "Whenever someone wanted a class, we arranged it," said the engineer, who, like his wife, taught at the university. "We welcomed them into our home."

Then the crackdown came. "They confiscated everything they could," the engineer said. "If they went into a private house and saw a computer system, they said, 'Okay, this belongs to the university,' so they took it. If they saw a good refrigerator or a set of dining room silver, they said, 'These were used for the students,' and took them. They were thieves in the name of Islam." There was no official announcement of the closure of the Bahai university, no stories about it in Iran's increasingly lively and daring press. Within a few months, the engineer said, the university secretly started up again.

The engineer sent his only son to the Bahai university before his escape was arranged from Iran to Turkey with the help of a high-priced smuggler in Tabriz. His son spent one night on the back of a truck heading to Turkey with strangers, who all turned out to be Bahais. They walked on foot across the mountains through the next night. The smuggler handed them fake Iranian passports for Turkish customs, then put them into taxis and pointed them toward the local refugee office of the United Nations. The engineer's son telephoned his father and said, "Daddy, I'm in Turkey! And the women are not veiled here!" Months later, the son enrolled in medical school in Virginia.

The doorbell rang. I quickly put on my head scarf and tried to look normal. It was only the deliveryman with the newspapers.

I asked the engineer the same question I had asked the Christians and the Jews: do you ever think of leaving? "I will never leave this country," he said. "If someone came here and said to me, 'This is your American passport, and here is your job,' I would say 'No thank you.' I am Iranian. I love this country."

PART FOUR

Open Warfare

CHAPTER TWELVE

Dark Nights, Fear of Waves

Along with malevolence came a hundred masks
To conceal the truth and reality from all sights
— RUMI, THIRTEENTH-CENTURY PERSIAN POET

Dark nights, fear of waves, and whirlpools so overpowering
How would those standing on the shore know what we are feeling?
— HAFIZ, FOURTEENTH-CENTURY PERSIAN POET

Aʀᴀsʜ Foʀouʜᴀʀ ᴅɪsᴄovᴇʀᴇᴅ the bedsheets stained with the blood of his parents in the garbage bin behind the garden one day in the fall of 1998.

Most of his parents' papers were missing. The diaries that his father, a secular Iranian nationalist, had written for nearly forty years, along with his speeches, writings, and photographs, the documents from his political movement, his passport and identity card, even the pistol that he kept in an upstairs cupboard for protection—all were gone. Gone too were a list of names and telephone numbers of students and young people aligned with Arash's father's movement and the letters his father had received decades before from his hero and mentor, Mohammad Mossadegh, the nationalist Prime Minister overthrown in the 1953 coup. Arash saw that his mother's poetry was not there either, except for a rough, handwritten draft of a still-unfinished verse written to her husband.

At the time of sleeping
Keep your sword ready by your side
In the bend of every earthly road
Watch out for the shadows . . .

The killers of the grass and the flowers
Now wish to kill the trees
Listen to the sound of the waves
They warn against a dangerous storm.

The bedsheets had been left behind. The murderers—or perhaps the investigators who ransacked the house afterward—used them to mop up the pools of blood from the stab wounds. Why they bothered was baffling. Not to cover up the evidence. Dried, caked, purplish blood still clung stubbornly to the carpets. Not to spare the family more pain. The knowledge that someone had used his parents' sheets as cleaning rags and then tossed them carelessly into the garbage turned Arash's stomach.

Although Dariush Forouhar and his wife, Parvaneh, had few followers, the Ministry of Intelligence had kept them under twenty-four-hour surveillance for years. Yet Dariush, who was seventy when he was killed, had begun the revolution as a fervent believer. He had spent several years in the Shah's prisons for opposing the regime. He had been the Islamic Republic's first Minister of Labor, and while he was in that job thousands of people considered counterrevolutionary were purged from factories, banks, offices, schools, universities, and government agencies. But Forouhar had joined the revolution as a secular nationalist, not as an Islamic zealot, and he refused to hang photographs of Ayatollah Khomeini in his office or replace the traditional Iranian flag, with its centuries-old symbol of the lion and the sun, with the revolutionary flag with the double image of the word "Allah."

Parvaneh, Forouhar's fifty-eight-year-old wife, a poet, had unflinchingly supported his political activities. Whenever the Shah's agents hauled him off to prison, she would stand at the door of their house and sing the national anthem as loud as she could. "I will never leave you even if they cut me to pieces," she wrote to him in prison on their fifth wedding anniversary.

The crime of the Forouhars apparently had been to criticize the Islamic Republic's human rights abuses in interviews with Western radio stations that beamed Persian-language programs to Iran. That brought them to the attention of Iran's ubiquitous intelligence service. A core group of handlers visited often and warned them that they had been put under surveillance. Arash and his sister Parastou were interrogated and threatened so often that they secured berths in Germany as political refugees.

"They told me many times, 'We know everything that goes on in your house before it happens,'" said Arash. "'Anytime there is a meeting, we know who is there and what they are saying.' They were so hungry for information that they tried to turn my wife into a spy. They knew she wanted to be an actress, and they told her, 'If you cooperate with us, we'll make you a star.'"

When it came to oppression, the Forouhars were veteran victims and veteran survivors. The year before the revolution, a bomb exploded in their house, shattering the windows into thousands of pieces of razor-sharp glass and throwing Arash and his mother against the wall. The revolution didn't make their enemies go away. Early on, when Dariush was Minister of Labor, he entrusted his security to an affable bodyguard named Soleiman. Soleiman lavished affection on the Forouhar children and pledged loyalty to his boss. When Soleiman died in a motorcycle accident, the Forouhars were devastated. But when they later sifted through his belongings, they discovered from his notebooks that he had been informing on them. The elder Forouhar took it all in stride, his son recalled. "Anyone who took a job in our house—a servant, a workman, a helper—I would say to my father, 'Watch out, he's a spy,'" Arash said. "He'd say to me, 'No problem. Better we know him and know that he's a spy than fire him for someone we don't know.'"

One day in the early 1990s, when he still lived at home, Arash was trying to find his favorite station on his bedroom radio, when he recognized a familiar voice. His father was in the living room meeting with some political associates and their conversation was playing on the radio. After days of searching the house, the Forouhars found an inch-long cylindrical transponder screwed in behind an electrical wall socket in the living room. After that, Forouhar opened his conversations with a hearty, "Good morning, listeners!" He closed them by saying, "Thanks to all the listeners!"

Over the years, the Forouhars became more vocal in expressing their opposition to Iran's Islamic government. They said that the Constitution robbed people of democratic participation by putting so much power into the hands of one Supreme Leader. "Today in Iran like the past there is a stifling political atmosphere," Forouhar said in one interview with the BBC in 1989. "In the Islamic Republic . . . all of 'the nation's rights' provided for in the Constitution have been ignored." He was so critical that on the eve of the 1997 presidential election, he predicted—incorrectly—

that if Khatami were elected, the "reactionary elements of the regime" would cancel the results.

The Forouhars became increasingly fatalistic. They began to speak openly of imprisonment and even death. Still, the couple fortified the gate around their house with razor wire and put iron bars on the windows. Dariush took to carrying a gun whenever he left the house, even though it was against the law to do so. He put away his wristwatch and packed an overnight bag with a towel and a toothbrush to prepare himself for imminent arrest.

Sometime late on a Saturday night in November 1998, a year and a half after Khatami's election, the murderer or murderers walked through the front metal gate and entered the Forouhars' house. There was no forcible entry, the police report said. Much later, Mohammad Niazi, the Military Public Prosecutor of Tehran, told an interviewer that the assassins had accompanied a friend of the Forouhars to the house and that Dariush himself had let them in.

The Forouhars' pet poodle was gagged and drugged. Dariush was engaged in a lively political debate with his guests when some of them turned on him. They tied his body onto a chair and stabbed him twelve times. Parvaneh, who had been ill, was already in her nightgown in the upstairs study when she too was stabbed—more than two dozen times. The neighbors claimed they heard nothing.

The bodies were discovered the next day by friends who came for a visit. The front door of the house was unlocked. The chair holding Dariush's body had been turned toward Mecca. His wife's body lay in a pool of blood upstairs. While the visitors were there, the phone rang. There was no one on the other end of the line.

The police sealed off the home. But some time after the murder the house was ransacked, the Forouhars' papers and other possessions removed. Thousands of people attended the funeral. The Forouhars were buried in section eighty-nine of Behesht-e Zahra cemetery in plots reserved for the nationalist liberals who had opposed the Shah. "The lion and the sun are not on the flag anymore," cried an old woman, referring to the ancient symbols of the country. "They're in these two graves."

One day one of the friends who had discovered the bodies was hit by a car with no license plates as he was riding his bicycle. One night a relative who was investigating the murders on his own got an anonymous call. "This is the last warning," the voice said. "Get your nose out of this business."

Repression is the dark side of the Islamic Republic.

The Iranian revolution was made in part to throw off the suffocating political repression of the Shah's monarchy. Many of Iran's revolutionaries, including clerics like Khamenei and Rafsanjani, had spent time in the Shah's prisons, which were known for the scope and sophistication of their torture methods. According to human rights reports, those methods included beatings (particularly on the soles of the feet), rape, cigarette burns, nail extraction, sleep deprivation, electric shocks, glaring lights, solitary confinement, mock execution, near-drowning, and acid dripped into nostrils. SAVAK, the Shah's secret police, had a long arm. It kept detailed dossiers on Iranian student activists abroad, often arresting them the moment they set foot in the country.

But the revolution did not end the repression. It simply introduced a new, revolutionary form of it, based on the new regime's interpretations of Islamic law. The regime has executed people for nonpolitical crimes such as drug trafficking, gambling, homosexuality, prostitution, pimping, and adultery, as well as for murder and rape; it has also executed people for political crimes like spying, counterrevolution, and "sowing corruption on earth." Some, but not all, of the methods of torture have changed from the time of the Shah. The Islamic state has forced prisoners to spend long periods of time in coffin-like boxes and to participate in the execution of fellow inmates. The beating of the soles of the feet has also increased, because it is the form of torture that inflicts the most pain with the least evidence.

Still, repression has not had its intended effect. Iranians have been swallowing their fear and finding ways around the Islamic Republic's restrictions on individual expression and political activity. A remarkably expressive cinema and an even more outspoken press have emerged. Young people today are daring to express disagreement with the clergy's restrictions and even to show contempt for its hypocrisies. There are limits on expression, of course. But the particularly Iranian tactic of open argument, subtle deception, use of private space, and even the manipulation of social courtesies can be combined into a form of political jujitsu that turns the Islamic Republic's deepest-held principles into arguments against its most onerous restrictions. Khatami's election has been perhaps the most startling single example of this, but it did not start the process; in many ways, it was a result.

When Westerners think of repression, their first association is usually with the totalitarianism of Stalinist Russia or Mao's China, in which people were given a political line to follow with no debate allowed, and in which whole classes of perceived enemies of the state were sent off for years to gulags or reeducation camps. Perhaps some of the hard-line clerics would have liked things that way. But Iranian culture is simply too argumentative, too full of escape hatches and private corners in which dissidents can hide, both literally and intellectually. So even the hard-liners have had to adapt, leaving room at times for more than one party line and room for people to choose—even if with difficulty—among them. In addition, even when at its most rigid, the character of repression and surveillance has been episodic, rather than omniscient and pervasive.

That doesn't mean, of course, that officials with totalitarian mindsets haven't tried to clamp an iron grip on the country. There have been periods, particularly in the early years, in which the Islamic Republic has viciously suppressed its enemies, real and imagined. In 1981, for example, the regime was threatened by a campaign of terror and revenge by the opposition group known as the Mojahedin-e Khalq, or People's Holy Warriors. Created in the 1960s as an armed Islamic opposition movement against the Shah, the Mojahedin struck at targets of the state and fought in guerrilla operations that facilitated his ouster. But the Mojahedin was also avowedly socialist and was cut out of the power structure built by the ayatollahs. The group openly turned against the new regime in demonstrations that turned violent; the regime struck back mercilessly. Thousands of Mojahedin were executed in the early 1980s; more than two thousand more died in a subsequent wave of executions in 1988. From a barren salt plain on the Iraqi side of the border, Mojahedin guerrillas continue to wage an armed struggle against the Islamic state next door. Iran struggles to crush them.

In some corners of the Ministry of Intelligence a KGB mentality has developed. The ministry, which conducts both foreign and domestic surveillance, is larger than its predecessor, SAVAK, and it intrudes more into citizens' lives. While SAVAK focused on political dissidents, the intelligence service of the ayatollahs has gathered the most minute details about ordinary people.

Over the years, the Ministry of Intelligence apparently sent its assassins to an apartment in Paris to kill Shahpour Bakhtiar, who had been the Old Regime's last Prime Minister; to an apartment in Vienna to shoot to death the Kurdish leader Abdol-Rahman Ghassemlou as he negotiated an autonomy agreement for the Kurds; to a Greek restaurant in Berlin to kill other Kurdish leaders. It has placed its agents in Iranian embassies abroad, where they have shopped for weapons and plotted operations.

The ministry's primary mission has been to eliminate political dissidents at home. There has been a pattern to the way such dissidents have been treated. Usually they've been quietly arrested. Then, weeks or months later, they are paraded on state-run television recanting their anti-state activities, in detailed confessions that generally sounded more invented than real.

But repression and terror have not been constants. They come and go in waves and they have taken different forms. In 1994, after 134 members of the Writers Association signed a letter calling for an end to censorship in Iran, several of the signatories were killed or died afterward under suspicious circumstances. The next summer, the driver of a bus carrying more than twenty members of the group to a poetry conference in Armenia steered the bus toward a mountain precipice while most of the passengers were napping. When the driver tried to jump out to save himself, a passenger grabbed the wheel and steered the bus back onto the road. Again, the driver tried—without success—to run the bus off the road. This time, the bus struck a boulder.

The murder of the Forouhars in 1998 was the beginning of a new, unanticipated wave of terror that swept Tehran's literary circles, which had become emboldened by Khatami's election in the spring of 1997. Two weeks after the Forouhar killings, Mohammad Mokhtari, a member of the Writers Association, disappeared in broad daylight en route to a grocery store. Mohammad Jaffar Pouyandeh, another member of the group, disappeared en route home from his office, also in broad daylight. Their strangled bodies were found later. Another writer, Majid Sharif, was found dead in mysterious circumstances. The authorities said he died of a heart attack. A handful of other Iranian intellectuals disappeared as well.

These random murders, coming so close together, terrified people. The victims, moreover, were not the grand enemies of the revolution but merely bit players. Perhaps, some thought, the murders were meant to serve as a warning to others. "Some writers refused to walk out of their homes alone," wrote the reformist monthly *Payam-e Emrouz.* "Many writers would not sleep in the same place at night. Every intellectual in the country felt that a noose was hanging around his neck."

But fear did not mean silence. Intellectuals and an emboldened press, which had already been instrumental in the election of a reformist President—however embattled he was—had passed the point where they would accept killings by a repressive state as routine. News of the murders was spread across the front pages of the newspapers as journalists and even ordinary citizens openly criticized the specter of official terror.

One day, a stunning announcement came from an unnamed spokesman of the Ministry of Intelligence: a "rogue" unit inside the ministry was responsible for the killings. Before then, no one even knew the ministry had a spokesman, so the announcement carried at least a hint of movement toward accountability. On the other hand, the statement itself revealed little. It did not identify what it called the "irresponsible, misguided, and unruly personnel" whom it said had been arrested. It did not say who had ordered the murders. It did not promise a wholesale purge of the ministry. So instead of stopping the public outcry, the mysterious announcement only stoked it.

Then, one month later, came much more stunning news: the Minister of Intelligence, Ghorbanali Dorri-Najafabadi, had resigned. Arrests of Intelligence Ministry officials followed. One of them, Saeed Emami, turned up dead in his prison cell. The official explanation was that he had committed suicide by ingesting *vajebi,* a hair removal powder that contains arsenic, while he was alone in the bath. Intellectuals had no sympathy for this particular character, but his death suggested a grisly effort to manipulate the real story. So even this event became ammunition in the struggle for more openness. Some newspapers wrote that *vajebi* does not have the power to kill, and demanded an investigation. The leftist newspaper *Salaam* dared to publish a document that detailed Emami's efforts to clamp down on the media. The Press Court claimed that the document was top secret and shut down the paper. It was that closure, combined with consideration by Parliament of a restrictive press law, that sparked student demonstrations and widespread turmoil in July 1999.

A number of fearless journalists have told graphic stories of the mysterious deaths and disappearances of more than eighty writers, translators, poets, political activists, and ordinary citizens over the past decade. By far the most outspoken critic has been Akbar Ganji, a courageous forty-year-old muckraker whose daring columns in 1999 began to name high-ranking individuals as the ones behind the murders. An activist during the revolution, Ganji was imprisoned for three months in the late 1990s for a speech about fascism that authorities saw as an attack on the Islamic system. After his new verbal offensive, he received death threats by phone and fax.

A fierce supporter of Khatami, Ganji wrote story after story about how Intelligence Ministry operatives chose and executed their victims. He intrigued his readers by writing in code, refusing to name names but drawing attention to an "éminence grise" and "the master key" to the murders of late 1997, apparently the former Intelligence Minister Ali Fallahian. When former President Rafsanjani announced his candidacy for the 2000 Parliamentary elections, Ganji took an even more direct approach. Ganji accused him of lying when he said he knew nothing about the "arrests, mysterious killings, and slanderous television programs" under his watch. "Rafsanjani denies the truth and says no murders were committed during his term of office," Ganji wrote. He "should clearly and openly apologize to the public for the serial murders committed by gang members." Ganji added that even if Rafsanjani made it into the Parliament, the people of Iran would dismiss him as "a symbol of the past."

But Ganji's focus remained on the murders. Existing institutions, he argued, were incapable of getting to the truth and he called for the establishment of a truth commission that included members of the victims' families. "We will write, write, write until we find the truth," he told an interviewer in late 1999. A few months later, he landed in prison again, this time on charges of defaming the state.

The repression fit a pattern, not so much of full-fledged totalitarian rule as of a cyclical recurrence of revolutionary terror. Even though Iran has never quite mastered the cold efficiency of a totalitarian state, officials have not shied away from broad psychological repression. I saw this in the chilling reaction to the student demonstrations and riots in the summer of 1999. Instead of dealing with the students' demands, the Intelligence Ministry reverted to one of its old tactics: the confession. The confession is, in fact, an excellent lens through which to examine both the ambitions and the limitations of Iran's brand of repression.

The confession comes in different forms—memoirs, letters, court testimony, press conferences, debates. Probably the most interesting and revealing is the videotaped interview, extracted in prison so it can be broadcast in prime time. Such a confession would appear on a slick, magazine-like television program called *Hoviyyat* (Identity), which apparently was operated under the supervision of officials within the Intelligence Ministry. It would be used as part of a profile of a prominent intellectual, artist, or writer in order to brand the person un-Islamic and tainted by the West. Footage of Iranian royalists and enemies of the Islamic system abroad would be spliced in, implying that the groups were connected. The ultimate "mastermind" was, of course, the United States. So for good measure, the portrait of Benjamin Franklin on the hundred dollar bill would dissolve into the face of the person under attack that week.

Stage-managing a confession was an important part of its presentation. Faraj Sarkouhi, a writer and literary editor, wrote in 1997 that when he was put into prison the previous year, he had been forced to memorize texts that were prepared for him to recite in a videotaped interview. He also was beaten and subjected to intense psychological pressure. "I spent eight years in the Shah's prisons," Sarkouhi wrote. "I was arrested and imprisoned several times during his reign. But all of those eight years together could not compare in pain and distress to a mere five minutes during these forty-seven days. . . . I am a broken man."

The *Hoviyyat* program did not last long. Televised confessions had become too transparent to provoke real terror. Viewers had become more sophisticated and now saw through the claims that the regime was in permanent danger at the hands of its "enemies."

Then suddenly, during the student unrest in the summer of 1999, the confessions were back. Nazila and I had just checked into a tiny hotel in the town of Behshahr on the Caspian Sea after a long, hard day of travel and we switched on the television to relax. Instead, we saw Manouchehr Mohammadi's confession leading the news.

I have never taken Manouchehr Mohammadi very seriously. A self-appointed student leader, the young man seemed just a fast-talking self-promoter, speaking before he thought and latching on to others more serious than himself. He preached a message of fatalism, saying that a clash with the Islamic system would come sooner or later, and adding that he was willing to die for the cause. Mohammadi was in and out of jail, forever babbling about how he had just been released and how he expected to be arrested again.

Somewhere along the way Mohammadi had become the darling of the Iranian exile community. He gave interviews on Western radio stations in Persian that were broadcast back home. In the spring of 1999, he had visited the United States, participating in a panel on human rights held in Connecticut. Someone in the audience videotaped the session and sent the videocassette back home. When authorities needed to find someone to blame for the violence in 1999 and to display the consequences of such actions, they used Mohammadi.

On television that night, a deep-voiced announcer read a statement from the Ministry of Intelligence branding Mohammadi a mastermind of the unrest who had acted on foreign orders. On the screen, Mohammadi looked thinner and older than I remembered. His face was puffy and he had lost his fast-talking bravado. He admitted having had contact with outlawed political parties and holding meetings with unnamed groups and people in the United States and Turkey. The confession was undated and obviously heavily edited, which spawned rumors that it was coerced and might have been made during earlier incarcerations. I didn't doubt that he had been tortured—at the very least sleep-deprived and beaten until he was too dizzy to think of anything but saying whatever they wanted him to say and signing whatever they wanted him to sign.

One indication of what might have happened had he remained defiant was the suffering of his brother, Akbar, who was sent to Evin prison for throwing Molotov cocktails, and who decided to protest the torture he endured there in a letter to the chief of the Judiciary. "I was hit with an electric cable, hung up by a rope, and violently beaten," said the letter, which was published in a number of reformist newspapers after the Mohammadi family decided to make it public. The letter also said he had gone deaf in his right ear, lost two nails on his left foot, and suffered from kidney pain. "The prison doctor ordered me to the hospital, but up until now I have not been taken there and I continue to suffer," the letter said. It was not clear whether Akbar had been offered a chance to confess publicly. What was clear was that his only remaining legal remedy against an execution order was an appeal to Iran's religious leader, Ayatollah Khamenei.

On television that evening in Behshahr, a confession by a woman whose name was said to be Malous Radnia followed Manouchehr

Mohammadi's. Radnia looked away from the camera and swallowed hard after every few words. "I regularly gave false news to foreign media," she said. She also confessed that she had allowed a fax machine in her home to be used to disseminate information.

In the next several days, other taped confessions followed. One young man said he had been the middleman between "foreign elements" and Mohammadi. Another confessed that he and Mohammadi had tried to provoke students to riot. A few days later, a second confession of Mohammadi's was aired on television. Like the first, it appeared to have been heavily edited, but this time, a digital date was affixed, an apparent effort to prove to doubters that the confession was made after the riots. It gave new details, including the names of Mohammadi's supposed contacts in America. Mohammadi confessed that he had received money from the United States and that his group staged street fights and then put the blame on right-wing vigilante groups. The goal, he said, was to make Iran "appear to be an unstable country."

At this point the message from the confessions was clear: for those willing to believe it, there was something on which to hang the notion that the protests had originated abroad. More important, they included a warning for would-be dissidents: this could happen to you.

But in Iran, all swords seem to have double edges. Rather than stir unalloyed fear among potential dissidents, the televised confessions revived memories—and resentments—about others who had experienced such things. I discovered that at lunch one day at the home of my close friends, Farhad Behbahani and Fereshteh Farhi. I mentioned how chilling I had found Mohammadi's arrest and the confessions that followed. The talk turned to prison.

"I have a friend who spent twenty-five years in prison under the Shah," said one guest. "He was a communist. He was freed for one year with the revolution. Then the new regime put him back in prison for eight years. I asked him one day, 'How would you compare the two?' He said, 'The Shah's prisons were heaven!'"

Farhad is a British-educated chemist who now works for an engineering consulting firm. His great-grandfather, Ayatollah Abdollah Behbahani, was a leader of the constitutional movement of the early twentieth century. Farhad himself is a learned scholar of Islam. He had been a friend of the assassinated Dariush Forouhar and his wife from their days in the Freedom Movement.

"No one is safe in this country," Farhad said matter-of-factly. "Four men can come to your house at midnight. They can blindfold you and take you away. Your wife may not know for two months where you are."

I had known Farhad for years. He was speaking in general terms, but I knew he was talking about himself. In 1990, while he was working for the government-run National Iranian Oil Company, Farhad was one of ninety political activists and intellectuals who signed a letter to President Rafsanjani pointing out the deficiencies of the Islamic system and suggesting that the war with Iraq had been ended far too late. Several weeks later, Farhad and twenty-two of the signatories were arrested.

He had never talked about it to me before that day at lunch. But suddenly, he seemed to want to.

"Did they mistreat you?" I asked, not knowing how far to probe.

He laughed, and I felt as if I had asked a truly absurd question.

"Of course," he said, spitting out the words. "But after about two months it wasn't too bad. After I said what they wanted, the beatings were less brutal."

What he didn't say that afternoon he said several months later, in January 2000, in the form of a published letter to former President Rafsanjani. "Three of them grabbed me and took me to a small and dark room in the basement," Farhad wrote. "They laid me down on my chest, chained my arms and legs to the wooden bed, and began whipping my feet. The pain was so awful that I screamed, 'Oh, my God!' As though this was the moment they were waiting for, 'Haji Agha' [an interrogator] ordered my beater to pick a wooden whip labeled 'Number two.' I fainted after two lashes with it. God knows how others survived whip 'Number three.'

"Yes, Mr. Rafsanjani, this is what went on in the prisons those days."

Khatami's election three years before and the public explosion of the political debate since have left Farhad quite outspoken. That was true even the day we had lunch: he had already begun to write articles—most under his own name—in reformist newspapers and magazines that openly discussed some of the problems plaguing the Islamic system. His friends worried that he was going too far, and that he might find himself in prison again. "Do you miss the flogging?" a guest asked him. "If you do, we'll flog you and make you feel better!"

The conversation about prison ended. But Fereshteh and I talked about it—and its impact on her family—a few days later. She told me that the day after Farhad's arrest in 1990 a group of security officers came back to search the house. They took his passport and many of his writings, even his translations and textual studies of the Koran.

Titi, their fourteen-year-old daughter, had been brought up never to be afraid. She boldly told the security officers, "If one of these days my father shows up on television and says something stupid, we will know it was not his idea. My mother, I, everyone will know he was forced!"

When the men finished searching, they told Fereshteh and Titi not to mention their visit to anyone. "Why?" asked Titi. "Are you doing something wrong?"

Fereshteh was worried that perhaps she should have silenced her daughter. On the contrary, one of the men apparently felt sorry for her. Two hours later, he called to let her speak briefly to her father from the undisclosed location where he was being held.

The imprisonment changed the family's life. Some friends advised Fereshteh to censor herself on the telephone. Many of Titi's friends weren't allowed to play with her anymore. Their twelve-year-old son, Behzad, wanted to quit his swim team; it would be bad for the team, he thought. It took his coach, his mother, his grandfather, and his uncles to persuade him to keep swimming. He won six gold medals for his team that summer.

Only two months later did Fereshteh see her husband. Four men escorted her from her office one day in a Mercedes and brought her to a street where Farhad was waiting in another car. The visit lasted just five minutes. "I almost didn't recognize him," she said. "He had lost about thirty pounds. He was disoriented and didn't make sense. He told me to do whatever they asked of me."

His television confession came one night soon afterward, after he regained some weight. He said nothing extraordinary—that he had contacts outside Iran, that he had traveled to the United States, that he had seen the error of his ways. But some of his political friends couldn't understand it. Some criticized him behind his back for not being stronger. "We were used to these confessions," said Fereshteh. "From the beginning of the revolution, we saw communists who went on television to proclaim they had seen Allah's light. We never took these confessions very seriously. Whether it was this or the movie Z, it seemed the same. So my husband was the same. I said to myself, 'He must have had a good reason to do this.'"

Then after six more months in prison, Farhad was released. Now, nearly a decade later, he is writing again, with a stronger, bolder voice than ever.

The confessions after the unrest in July 1999 didn't quell the debate in the media about the nature of the Islamic state; in some ways, they intensified it. And the continuing debate proved that the authorities lacked the power to terrorize. Newspaper columnists and ordinary people started talking publicly about the absurdity of the confessions. The English-language *Iran News* ran a cartoon that showed a man standing next to a fax machine and the caption, "I have a fax machine! So I am a spy!"

"These people have been there for a long time but have now begun to talk about things in a different way," Farhad's sister-in-law, my friend Farideh Farhi, told me later. "Great leaps of bravery rarely occur in periods of absolute terror. I know it is too little and too slow but definite changes have occurred, even in the realm of terror. The kind of conversation that exists in Iran today has never existed before. Farhad takes great pleasure in this despite the fact that he knows that vestiges of a long history of terror will continue to haunt Iran for a long time to come. Cultures do not change overnight; neither do ways of conceiving politics."

Afterward, a close friend who is a political scientist at the University of Tehran said only half jokingly that he was going to send me a video of himself.

"A video?"

"I thought I'd do a video of myself saying that if I confess I have cheated on my wife and committed treason, don't believe it," he said. "It's forced. I thought I'd send it to a few of my friends."

Then he had a better idea. "Maybe I'll make two—one for my friends and one for my jailers. The one for my jailers will confess to everything. That way, they won't have to bother torturing me first. They can just put the confession on television and set me free!"

At that moment, I understood why my Iranian friends always told so many jokes, even if some of them seemed inappropriate at the time they told them. Humor is a key to survival.

I also have realized that there is not room yet for everyone to feel free in the spaces being opened by President Khatami and the other reformers. There are, for example, castoffs from the revolution, faithful believers

who were present at the creation but who have little or no place a generation later. Grayer and wiser, they refuse to abandon the revolution that
took up so much of their youth or to be engulfed by bitterness and self-
pity. Perhaps they make others uncomfortable with their presence. But
they stand steadfast, pale but persistent reminders of the ideals of the
past.

The late Houshang Golshiri, the well-known novelist, summed up
this sentiment one day when he told me: "We have no wish for another
revolution. We're looking forward to a time when we can write in peace.
We don't want to leave the country. This time, it's their turn to leave the
country. We will kill them with our pen. We will kill them with our presence."

Golshiri obviously was referring to forces opposed to change in the
Islamic Republic. Not only have many of Golshiri's books failed to win
approval from the Ministry of Islamic Guidance over the years, but in late
1998, after the Forouhars and other political and intellectual activists
were murdered, Golshiri heard that his name was on one of the master
hit lists circulating clandestinely in Tehran. He took refuge at the homes
of friends. Later, he arranged to have his new novel, *Jen Nameh*, published in Sweden rather than submit it to the censors in Iran. But he did
not leave Iran. The space belonged to him, as it had for the Forouhars and
the others who were murdered, as it does for my friend Farhad who has
survived prison. All of them have created spaces for themselves not only
behind closed doors but increasingly on public battlefields.

CHAPTER THIRTEEN

The Tom and Jerry Game

We do not know where the red lines are.

— MASHALLAH SHAMSOLVAEZIN, EDITOR OF THE NEWS-
PAPER *JAMEAH* AND ITS SUCCESSORS

*We Iranian filmmakers are like trapeze artists swinging back and forth
without a net.*

— DARIUSH MEHRJUI

To stay alive you must slay silence.

— SIMIN BEHBAHANI, TWENTIETH-CENTURY
FEMALE POET

AT THE HEART of the Islamic Republic is a contradiction so deep it
could keep theologians and political theorists in business for years:
theocracy by definition imposes religious thinking on a secular society.
Certain types of conduct and thought are not only illegal but also considered evil. So, free thought must be closed off, or at least restricted. But
Shiite Islam thrives on debate and discussion in a particularly egalitarian
style; it recognizes different interpretations and it welcomes argument, at
least among its clerical scholars, and it is not rigidly hierarchical. So freedom of thought and expression is essential to the system, at least within
the top circles of religious leadership. And if the mullahs can behave that
way among themselves in places like the holy city of Qom, how can the
rest of a modern-day society be told it cannot think and explore the
world of experience for itself?

In fact, even when the clerics exercised the tightest control on free expression in the first two decades of Islamic rule, Iranians chafed against

the limits imposed on their thinking. Of course, they have never allowed the state to crush their freedom of expression in private; but in recent years, particularly since the election of Khatami as President, Iranians have begun to converse fiercely and courageously in different forums in public. Journalists, television producers, and filmmakers have begun to push the limits of expression and debate, sometimes in the face of outright opposition and always in defiance of their own fears. And because the content of their conversations with a public hungry for more open political and cultural discourse is so provocative, it has given hope that the process will continue. By far the most astounding public conversations about the shape of society have taken place in an increasingly free press, which continues to expand public discourse despite the repeated closures of newspapers and magazines.

Events took a dramatic leap when the reformist newspaper *Jameah* published a whopping scoop just weeks after it started operating in early 1998. In a short article buried on an inside page, the newspaper reported on a closed-door meeting in Qom in which General Rahim Safavi, the head of the Revolutionary Guards, urged his commanders to silence those clerics whose promotion of democracy threatened the cult of martyrdom. "A new case of hypocrisy is taking shape with the use of mullahs' costumes," *Jameah* quoted Safavi as saying. "We must root out anti-revolutionaries wherever they are! We must use the sword to chop off the heads of some and cut out the tongues of some others! Our sword is our tongue. . . . We are seeking martyrdom!"

The article was a watershed. First of all, the newspaper had been leaked details of a top secret national security meeting of the Iranian state. These were verbatim quotes, not hearsay. If an American newspaper had published verbatim quotes from a top secret speech by, say, the Chairman of the Joint Chiefs of Staff, the Pentagon probably would have launched an investigation.

Second, the publication of the story was a daring, even dangerous act. Journalism traditionally has been a perilous profession in Iran and newspapers often censor themselves, for reasons of self-interest as well as for what they consider to be the public interest. But here was a newspaper taking on one of the most powerful people in the Iranian government by ripping open the curtain of secrecy that has shrouded Iranian politics since the revolution.

More significant than the actual story were its far-reaching ramifications. *Jameah* had set the standard for the new Iranian journalism of the Khatami era, in which newspapers play a number of roles: bearers of information, shapers of opinion, substitutes for political parties, engines for change. The conservative clerical establishment sees the new media outlets as the most subversive of its opponents.

But the impulse toward free debate hadn't started with Khatami, however much his election has done to propel it forward. Even before his election, newspapers and journals had begun to use humor, call-in questions-and-answers, and editorials written in code to question the way the country was being run. Then *Jameah* suddenly introduced a level of clarity that hadn't existed before. That clarity was certainly evident in the Safavi scoop and the debate it triggered. The general and his allies angrily responded to the *Jameah* article by accusing the journalists of having infringed the general's right to privacy and free speech—a position rich in irony and portending even more daring challenges to the official line. Unwittingly, it conceded a point most important to any journalist, namely that there is a right to free speech in the first place.

It was a sweet moment for the fearless, freewheeling pair of journalists who ran *Jameah*: Hamid-Reza Jalaeipour, the publisher and chief columnist, and Mashallah Shamsolvaezin, the editor. Jalaeipour is a bear of a man with decent English from his years as a graduate student in political sociology at the University of London. He sports a three-day growth of beard, speaks with a slight lisp, studies civil institutions, and wrote his doctoral dissertation on the "causes of continuity" in Iran's revolutionary experience. Like Khatami, he quotes the nineteenth-century French sociologist Alexis de Tocqueville more than the Koran. Even though he has never visited the United States, he sees it as a source of intellectual inspiration. "I want to see the land that de Tocqueville wrote about," he once told me. "I want to see the libraries. I want to see Princeton."

Jalaeipour also has impeccable revolutionary credentials, having learned political rebellion from his late father, a rice merchant in the bazaar who for years before the revolution had secretly visited the ayatollahs of Qom and poured money into their causes. Father and son both went to prison because of their political activities against the Shah. Two of Jalaeipour's brothers were killed in the war against Iraq. A third brother was murdered by the Mojahedin-e Khalq opposition movement. A younger sister was one of the students involved in the seizure of the American embassy in 1979. For most of the 1980s, Jalaeipour served as governor of the Kurdish city of Mahabad and then deputy governor of Kurdistan province, where the Islamic Republic carried out operations first against Kurdish rebels and later against Iraq during the war.

Shamsolvaezin had witnessed political violence firsthand when he lived in Lebanon before the revolution. In the 1980s, he was on the editorial board of *Kayhan,* an established newspaper that turned militant and supported Ayatollah Khomeini's brand of stern Islamic rule. In time Shamsolvaezin mellowed, and became convinced that reform was preferable to violent change.

For me, the offices of their newspaper have been a place of refuge. No matter how close to deadline they are, the two men have welcomed me with tea, a telephone, and the wire services—all of which are vital sustenance to a visiting reporter. If it is lunchtime, there is a hot plate of chicken kabob or *khoresht* (stew) from the newspaper's kitchen. It may have been Iranian *taarof,* the practice of polite dissembling, but Shamsolvaezin likes to tell me that he models the paper on *The New York Times* and longs for a chance to spend a week in its headquarters near Times Square.

It didn't surprise me that Jalaeipour personally took on Safavi. Writing in *Jameah* on behalf of "one martyr's family," the publisher-columnist declared that it was no longer possible to manipulate the memory of war martyrs in politics. Citing his own ill mother as representative of the changes in Iran's political landscape, Jalaeipour told Safavi that she was tired of hearing about martyrdom and a war that ended years ago. "Mr. Commander, you might be fed up with life but there is a sparkle of life in the eyes of the mother whose life was wasted during the revolution," Jalaeipour wrote. "She wants to live. She is fed up with bragging about martyrdom."

With that commentary, Jalaeipour sought to end the use of martyrdom as a political instrument in the Islamic Republic. "The language of the revolution, the language of war doesn't work anymore," he explained to me in *Jameah*'s offices. "Everyone has to learn to speak in a civil and lawful manner now." He pulled out a sheet of paper and drew a triangle on it. On the top he wrote the word "Government"; along the bottom, the word "People." He left the space in between empty. "For me, civil society means this middle part. An independent press is a big part of it."

The Judiciary didn't agree with him. The following month, a court revoked *Jameah*'s license, calling the story about Safavi's speech "distorted" and "reckless." There were other crimes as well. An exposé on prison conditions revealing that prisoners had to pay four times the market price for eggs was declared untrue. A satirical column that made fun of clerics and political figures was deemed to be an insult to the state. The newspaper had also published color photographs of everyday life that were considered "immoral": young people dancing in the streets after Iran beat the United States in the World Cup soccer competition in July 1998; middle-aged joggers looking as if they were clapping; a woman smiling broadly and wearing a colorful tribal costume.

In the past, a court's closure of a newspaper might have silenced it forever, and inhibited other publications from taking risks. But the restrictive measures that worked in traumatic times of revolution and war—ransacking offices, destroying equipment, interrogation, threats, beatings, imprisonment—no longer fit. With the election of President Khatami, the fissures in the Islamic Republic became big enough to allow for the emergence of new players, many of them would-be politicians and state-builders who found that the press was an important institution for promoting reform.

In this regard, Jalaeipour and Shamsolvaezin and their fellow journalists represent a new corps of intellectual warriors, who are using their strong revolutionary credentials to push for peaceful reform in place of violent change. They fight on a strange new battlefield where the rules keep changing as new soldiers enter the fray and their enemies prove incapable of capturing all of them. This is not Tiananmen Square, in which Chinese reformers backed down in the face of brutal, sweeping repression. For Iran's reformers, there is no turning back; the excitement is too great and the stakes are too high. "It is nothing less," said Shamsolvaezin, "than a hot test of democracy."

In a sense, the boldness is the continuation of a trend that began a century ago. Unlike most countries in the Middle East, Iran has episodically enjoyed a lively press. During the constitutional movement of the early twentieth century, 140 newspapers began publishing, most of them asking for the rule of law, justice, and a more representative form of government. In an extraordinary civics lesson and public service, one of them published proceedings of the Parliament.

The era of an independent-minded press ended with the reign of Reza Shah, whose priority was law and order, not the rule of law. It was no better under his son, Shah Mohammad Reza Pahlavi, whose heavy censorship of all forms of expression—newspapers, books, films, even fiction—worsened over the years. My friend Karim Emami, a leading literary scholar, translator, and book publisher, tells a funny (tragic, really) story about once having to destroy the entire printing of a harmless book about Marie Antoinette because the translator used the Persian word *shahbanu* for queen, not the more popular word, *malekeh.* The censors ruled that the word *shahbanu* could be used only for the present queen, not just for any queen. But maybe that wasn't the most important reason. After all, the book told the story of a king and a queen who had been executed.

The Islamic revolution was supposed to abolish censorship. One of the first posters of the revolution that I bought from a street vendor showed a dove with a flower sprouting from its head. The words, "For a Free Press!" were written across it.

But press freedom was short-lived. "I condemn the corrupt intellectuals and the poisoned pens of conspiring writers and democrats!" Khomeini declared soon after the revolution when the voices of opposition got too loud. Newspaper editors were given orders to reflect "a proper Islamic emphasis" in their pages, and for years the press remained cowed. Then slowly, in the early 1990s, publications began to take chances. The boldest was *Salaam,* a leftist daily run by a mid-ranking cleric named Mohammad Mousavi-Khoeiniha, who had achieved international notoriety in the early days of the revolution as the spiritual mentor of the militants who seized the American embassy. Like other political figures frozen out of the system by the conservative clerical establishment, Mousavi-Khoeiniha decided that the press was the most fruitful way to have an impact. *Salaam* promoted social justice and the redistribution of wealth from rich to poor. For years, its "Hello *Salaam*" column, in which ordinary people called in their questions and complaints, was the liveliest feature in the Iranian press. The first editor of *Salaam* was Abbas Abdi, one of a new breed of young revolutionaries who evolved into one of the more astute observers of Iranian politics; still, I couldn't forget that he had been one of the original hostage-takers.

I never knew whether people actually telephoned *Salaam* with their gripes, or whether the *Salaam* editors made them up. It didn't matter. The column was lively and, in the absence of opinion polls, reflected what people were grumbling about in shops, communal taxis, and the privacy of their homes. Callers complained about high prices, low salaries, hoarding, clerics who drove Mercedes. One caller said the confiscation of satellite dishes was "nothing but a ploy to distract people's attention from the country's economic problems." Another had this message for the authorities: "You never listen when the Iranian people say that we don't want hostility with the United States anymore. Do you have any statistics? In one of the anti-America demonstrations held recently, only seven hundred people showed up. That means in a big city like Tehran, there are only seven hundred anti-American people."

Jameah, even more daring, showed that the gates had been flung wide open in the struggle for control of the world of talk. The form and the outcome of the struggle became thoroughly unpredictable, in part because the political structure in Iran was becoming less monolithic. There were surprise attacks and surprise refuges. A court could shut down a newspaper one day; the Ministry of Islamic Guidance could issue a new license for it to open under a new name the next; the staff and editorial team of the shuttered newspaper could take over the license of another newspaper. The absence of complete centralized control was visible even in the world of state-controlled television. Clerical censors could demand strict adherence to a conservative line in television news, while secular producers could turn out imitations of American game shows on the entertainment side. In the movies, even as films were banned from Iranian movie theaters, the state-run Farabi Cinema Foundation allowed them to be made and shown at special screenings or to be sent abroad to compete in international film festivals.

Along the way, the struggle has pitted conservatives who, for the sake of unity and stability, are determined to preserve adherence to a strict line against reformists like Jalaeipour and Shamsolvaezin who are equally determined to open up the lines of debate and make the system more transparent and accountable. For the conservatives, too much transparency can only weaken Islamic and revolutionary values and erode the clergy's grip on power; for the reformers, democracy—and open access to good information—is the key to stability. And both sides are learning to use existing laws to their advantage. The conservatives, who control the Judiciary, obviously have more power to use—and abuse—laws, and they have done so by repeatedly closing publications and hauling off their editors and publishers to court. But the reformers are refusing to fold under the pressure; they are using both the pages of their publications and the courtrooms to challenge the way laws are interpreted.

In a sense, Khatami's election served to accelerate the effort by Iranians and some elements of their government to press for freedom, tolerance, and the rule of law. Newspapers were an important part of that process, and their success was, ironically, due in part to initiatives by the clerics to fulfill the social goals of the 1979 revolution. Literacy in Iran soared from 58 percent in 1979 to 82 percent in 1998; and the number of university graduates increased almost tenfold from 430,000 to more than four million. Khatami's election more than doubled the number of publications, for a total of more than 1,200 newspapers, magazines, and journals. At the beginning of 2000, there were more than two dozen daily papers in Tehran alone. As a deputy in Parliament in the late 1990s, Ahmad Nateq-Nouri, the brother of the former Speaker of the Parliament, complained, "Everyone who has had a fight with his mother goes and opens up a newspaper in this country!"

Readers look to newspapers less for factual information or exposés about government misdeeds than for the intense debate about the direction of the Islamic Republic. This explains why many educated Iranians would prefer to read several papers. (Some complain that it takes them two hours to read the papers every day.) I've seen people crowd around newspaper kiosks the moment papers are delivered early in the morning to check as many headlines as they can before deciding what—or whether—to buy.

The newspapers run the gamut. *Hamshahri* (Citizen), which is the mouthpiece of the mayor of Tehran and is funded by the city, focuses on local news, including announcements of social and cultural events and reviews of plays, movies, and concerts. It has the largest daily circulation—more than 400,000—in part because it has the best classified ads. *Jomhouri-ye Islami, Resalat, Kayhan,* and *Qods* spout the party line of the most conservative clerics. Before it was shut down, *Khordad,* published by former Interior Minister Abdollah Nouri, was more of a political platform for him and the reform movement than a bearer of news. The most reactionary paper is the monthly *Ya-Lessaratal Hosein,* which is run by the vigilante group, Ansar-e Hezbollah. One of its editorial positions is that vigilantes should be given arms to confront any and all anti-revolutionaries in their offices, businesses, and homes.

Jameah's approach and style was duplicated by newspapers across the country. Some, like the weekly newspaper *Sirvan* (circulation five thousand) in the Kurdish provincial capital of Sanandaj, are tiny. The paper is produced by a staff of three young men armed with one telephone line and two computers, but no e-mail or Internet connection. When I visited these journalists in mid-1999, they had been receiving repeated death threats at home from unknown opponents of their demand for more openness in the political system. They complained openly in their pages that the Islamic Republic had failed to build Kurdish cultural centers to teach their language and history and that the Khatami administration had not appointed even one Sunni Kurd (most Kurds belong to the Sunni branch of Islam) to a high government position. "If Khatami really wants a 'dialogue among civilizations,' he should start with the Kurds," Mohammad-Karim Assadbeghi, the paper's editor, told me.

Iran is not a country of independent nongovernmental organizations; the community and charitable organizations that do exist are wholly or partially controlled by the government. (The few private charitable organizations that do exist are largely apolitical.) So the main arena for independent political discourse in Iran became the newspapers. Jalaeipour once tried to form his own political party, but wasn't given a license. So he looked at *Jameah* as a substitute, an indispensable channel of communication between the people and the ruling elite, and therefore an element in the way decisions might be made more democratically. The name *Jameah*, in fact, means "Society." "It was easier to get a license to open a newspaper than a license to open a party," he once told me, "so I opened a newspaper."

With $100,000 in savings and loans, the *Jameah* team bought sophisticated computer equipment and rented a sprawling, white, California-style villa with good electrical wiring in north Tehran. Jalaeipour and Shamsolvaezin hired some of Iran's best journalists and solicited copy from some of Iran's most respected intellectuals. Within weeks of its debut in 1998, the sixteen-page paper of news, good writing, lively commentary, political cartoons, and color photographs became the boldest experiment with free speech in the course of Iran's revolution. Within six months circulation soared from 130,000 to 300,000 a day—*Jameah's* maximum printing capacity. The paper called itself "the first civil society newspaper" in Iran and sold out almost as soon as it hit the newsstands in the early mornings.

Jameah journalists wrote, under their own bylines, about many hot subjects that had been considered off the table for discussion: the weaknesses of Ayatollah Khomeini, the misuse of Islam for political purposes, torture in the prison system, the need for political dissent and relations with the United States. They also wrote about offbeat subjects, such as a student demonstration over the bad quality of drinking water. One sportswriter—a woman—once elbowed her way into a men's only soccer stadium for a story on the national team.

The paper appealed to the young. It even covered Hollywood. Rather than dwelling on tragedy and martyrdom, *Jameah* embraced the positive. On the day after Iran beat the United States in the World Cup soccer tournament, *Jameah* published a photo of the captain of the American team, Thomas Dooley, wearing the shirt of Ali Daei, the Iranian soccer star. There was even humor in its pages. When a deputy of Parliament gave a speech one day accusing *Jameah* of getting a $6 million payoff from the White House, *Jameah*'s most opinionated feature, the "Fifth Column," ostentatiously thanked President Clinton for the donation, but corrected the deputy, saying that the gift was $60 million.

Even before the court shut down *Jameah* in the summer of 1998, Jalaeipour and Shamsolvaezin were already armed with the license of another paper. Immediately after the court order was issued, several other dailies offered them their own licenses. The day after *Jameah* was closed down, the new newspaper reopened in the same headquarters, using the same printing presses, virtually the same staff and a new name, *Tous*, after the hometown of the beloved tenth-century Persian poet Ferdowsi. *Tous* lasted for five weeks before it too was closed down for "endangering national security." Jalaeipour and Shamsolvaezin were sent to prison. One cleric branded them *mohareb*—insurgents against Islam—who should be executed. It was only then that President Khatami offered a tepid show of support, inviting family members of the arrested editors for a visit. Still, he held back. "You have my sympathy, but my hands are tied," the President reportedly said. "It is unfortunate that Mr. Jalaeipour and Mr. Shamsolvaezin went so fast, that they didn't see the yellow light. They think they're living in Switzerland!"

Jalaeipour's mother didn't see it that way. She declared that the Judiciary had no right to accuse her son of weakening the country's national security. Theirs was a loyal, patriotic, and revolutionary family, she said. Then she delivered the coup de grâce. "I gave you three sons," she told the President. "You are not getting a fourth one."

It was *Saving Private Ryan*, Iranian-style. Jalaeipour and Shamsolvaezin were released.

And so it went. Every time the paper was closed, it reopened under a new name: *Aftab-e Emrouz* (Today's Sun), *Neshat* (Liveliness), *Akhbar-e Eghtesad* (Economic News), *Asr-e Azadegan* (The Age of the Free). It moved to a safer building in a more remote part of the city, installing wire mesh screens to better withstand grenade attacks.

Over dinner one evening at a conference in Cyprus, Shamsolvaezin told a group of us that he thought of himself as Jerry the mouse in the *Tom and Jerry* cartoons that had long played on Iranian television, their American origin notwithstanding. It was Ali Razini, the head of the Tehran Justice Department, who first gave Shamsolvaezin the idea during a conversation after one of the newspaper closures.

"Mr. Shamsolvaezin, how long do you intend to continue with this Tom and Jerry game?" Razini asked.

"It's up to you to decide, since you're Tom," Shamsolvaezin replied. "And it is Tom who always chases after Jerry." Then Shamsolvaezin explained to his adversary why he would lose. "You will fail, because Jerry can always run into a little hole. And like Tom, you will end up banging your head against the wall."

Eventually, Tom caught up with Jerry. In November 1999 Shamsolvaezin was put on trial on charges stemming from articles in *Neshat* that criticized capital punishment and the Islamic law of "an eye for an eye." He was also charged with forging the signature of the author of an article faxed to him from abroad, despite testimony to the contrary from the author himself. Shamsolvaezin turned the trial into a political circus, provoking a storm of criticism, some of it pretty foolish, from the conservative clerical hierarchy. (One ayatollah's comment—"Belief in equal rights for all citizens is worse than cow worship"—was my personal favorite.)

In the end, Shamsolvaezin was convicted of forgery. Outside the courtroom, Shamsolvaezin called his conviction "the price of democracy." He joked, "A few years ago intellectuals and reformists would be given capital punishment or otherwise would be physically eliminated. Now we are only getting jail terms. This is a step forward!" But he made no secret of his disappointment in President Khatami, who he believed had failed to use the authority of his office to follow through on his promises. "It was the President, after all, who had first unleashed the slogans of 'political development' and a 'civil society,'" he said. "The price for these slogans is being paid by society, not the government, and the independent newspapers are paying a large part of this price."

After Shamsolvaezin lost his appeal, he was sent to Evin prison.

Then in April 2000, *Jameah's* fifth incarnation, *Asr-e Azadegan*, was closed by the Judiciary along with sixteen other reformist publications. The publications were accused of "disparaging Islam and the religious elements of the Islamic revolution." But it seemed premature to write the obituary of a free press that had been so inventive in the past. "We are not destroyers, we are reformers," Jalaeipour said just before the crackdown. "We are in favor of making government responsive, institutionalizing the sovereignty of law and not undermining it in the name of religion, revolution, and war."

After the crackdown, Jalaeipour told Nazila, "I remain very optimistic. Even if the same newspapers do not publish, other ones will take their place. There's no turning back."

What is happening in the movies is as intellectually subversive as what is happening in the press. Iranian cinema is a world unto its own, by far the most creative expression of the Iranian imagination, so much so that it has earned a glowing international reputation. Iranian filmmakers relentlessly test the limits of what is permissible in a cultural environment still largely controlled by a rigid interpretation of Islam.

Granted, there remains an unreality about the portrayal of everyday life in Iranian films and television programs. Personal relationships are sanitized because a film, unlike real private life, is shown to men and women alike, and to them all the actors are strangers. On the screen, female characters have to keep their heads covered and hide the shape of their bodies, even in scenes of home life; they cannot dance or sing in the company of other women. Husbands and wives are not allowed to touch, and parents cannot show physical affection to their children once a daughter is nine and a son is thirteen—the legal age to get married. It is thought that such actions might inflame the passions of male viewers. Many filmmakers simply ignore the thorny issue of how to show male-female relationships by making movies about children instead.

But since the late 1980s, the Iranian cinema has quietly emerged as another public space in which the tensions, restrictions, grim reality, and simple pleasures of everyday life are laid out for all to see. Family values, sibling affection, idyllic country life, and the triumph of good over evil are not the only topics; polygamy, suicide, war, murder, mental illness, divorce, infertility, tribal oppression, unemployment, adultery, cross-dressing, social inequality, mixed-sex parties, drug addiction, wife-beating, child abuse, and poverty are all explored on the screen as well, even when they cannot be explicitly acted out.

A full-length feature film can cost less than $100,000 to make and filmmakers have found ways to raise money and get around some of the restrictions. The government-run Farabi Cinema Foundation and even the Ministry of Islamic Guidance struggle to provide funds and slip them through the cracks. Sometimes when a film is banned inside Iran, it is screened at a film festival abroad, which creates pressure on the censors to reverse themselves. Sometimes two versions of a film are made—an original for foreign distribution, a sanitized version for domestic consumption. Some filmmakers enjoy special privileges. Abbas Kiarostami, probably Iran's best-known filmmaker, often produces his films through The Institute for the Intellectual Development of Children and Young Adults, a politically tame venue. He also relegates women to the periphery, saying that he doesn't like to portray unrealistic characters in his films.

I saw the fluidity of the system one summer evening at an invitation-only screening at Tehran's House of Cinema. I was invited through Nargess, my oldest friend in Iran, who knows a lot of people in the movie business. This was no glittery Hollywood affair. The men did not wear black tie. The women were dressed in drab, loose coats with scarves covering their heads. No refreshments were served, no speeches were made, no awards were distributed. The auditorium was hot and cramped, the seats uncomfortable, the film shown on a small screen from a noisy projector.

Still, it was a special evening. The low-budget film, *Siavash*— named after a hero in Ferdowsi's epic poem, *Book of Kings*—was the first feature film by Saman Moghadam, a promising thirty-year-old screenwriter and director. The censors at the Ministry of Islamic Guidance had not approved the film, and the expectation was that they never would. But the ministry allowed the film to be shown to a select few, just this once. The director and the stars of the film were there to celebrate the special event.

The film deals with a familiar theme: the generation gap between the loyal warriors who sacrificed for the revolution and the war with Iraq, and their children who long for happy lives unburdened by the legacy their fathers left. But this film breaks a number of taboos. The hero of the film, a young composer and musician in a nine-piece rock band, plays the sort of lively music that would not be allowed in a real-life concert. Unlike most young, single Iranians, he lives alone in his own apartment, not with his family. Even more daring, he openly socializes with his girl-friend, a photojournalist who leads an independent life.

The story centers on the musician's father, who is believed to have been killed sixteen years before in the war with Iraq. The musician's mother has remarried. Suddenly, they get the news that the father is alive and on his way home. Bearded, haggard, and middle-aged, the father shows up one night at his son's concert but he doesn't reveal himself. In an apparent sign of disapproval, he crumples a small photograph of his son and storms out. But in a teary reunion, he comes to his son's rescue after the son is arrested with his girlfriend in a park. The father's vocal cords have been destroyed and he cannot speak. So the son does all the talking. "Why did you leave me alone—not for one year, but for sixteen years?" the son asks. "Didn't you think I needed a father?"

The father picks up a pen to write. "I have bad news," he writes. "I am not your father . . . I am a friend of your father. Your father was martyred two months before his release in Iraq." The film never definitively states that the man is the musician's father. That would be too transparent. But the audience just seems to know that he is.

After the screening, the audience of Tehran's beautiful people poured out into an enclosed courtyard for congratulations and conversation. I introduced myself to Moghadam, the director, who dared to shake my hand in public. "I tried to show the huge divide between the fervent be-lievers and the tired, young generation of today that wants a normal, peaceful life," he explained. "The father is just like so many others in soci-ety. He comes back from the war and expects to hear people chanting 'Death to America' and really believing it. Instead, he hears music that he thinks should be forbidden and sees ads for Coca-Cola. So he thinks his life has been for nothing. And he cannot deal with it. He's a casualty of the war. But our generation—we're the casualty of war too. And we have to find a way to deal with it."

I left the one-room cinema club buoyant. My friend Nargess, by con-trast, was enraged. "How phony!" she declared. "On the outside everyone is saying, 'Oh, what a nice movie. You should win an Oscar.' Look at that young director. On the outside, he is smiling and looking happy. But in-side, he is shivering with fear. We have an expression, 'Your hands are tied and in the mud.' That's his situation. These people are working with no hope. I feel pity for these people, pity for myself."

I was stunned. I had rarely seen Nargess so angry. I saw the film as a daring effort to expose the generational divide in Iran, play banned music, and explore the complexities of young love. And it was being shown at an officially sanctioned screening in the heart of Tehran! Nargess saw the private screening of the film as just another example of the restrictions of the Islamic Republic.

But Iran is a country of surprises, and the censors eventually approved the release of *Siavash* in Tehran's cinemas. Another surprise: the reformist daily, *Asr-e Azadegan,* run by Jalaeipour and Shamsolvaezin, panned it. The review acknowledged that the film took on forbidden subjects, but called it naive, trite, and worst of all, boring. The movie drew respectable crowds, but was by no means a smash hit.

I often think that Iranian films, which are about ordinary people leading ordinary lives, are appreciated more in the United States and Europe than in Iran. Many Iranians are too ground down by their own everyday lives to want to spend good money to watch morality tales in a movie theater. So for years, many Iranians I know have preferred to watch American videos or satellite television in the privacy of their homes. That way, outside the stern glare of the Islamic Republic, they can escape, and dream.

Still, the new Iranian cinema is a far cry from the early years of the revolution. In the last year of the Shah's reign, according to Hamid Naficy, an Iranian-born expert on Iranian movies and television, as many as 180 movie theaters were burned, demolished, or shut down as part of a cultural cleansing by the Shah's opponents. Ayatollah Khomeini hated the cinema, putting it in the same category as theater, dancing, and sexually integrated swimming.

After Khomeini returned to Iran in 1979 his revolutionary regime quickly realized the importance of film, for propaganda if not for entertainment. Movies would have to be Islamic. New rules in 1982 banned films that weakened Islamic principles, showed disturbing scenes of violence, or encouraged wickedness, corruption, and prostitution. Women were to be portrayed as modest and chaste role models, and good mothers who would raise God-fearing children. Eventually, the government produced more than 30 percent of Iranian films, subsidized film and studio facilities, and gave long-term, low-interest loans to many independent filmmakers.

In 1983, early in his decade-long tenure as Minister of Islamic Guidance, Mohammad Khatami urged filmmakers to promote "self-sacrifice, martyrdom, and revolutionary patience." A few years later he changed his mind. "Cinema is not the mosque," he said. If leisure time were to become homework, he added, "then we would have a deformed society." In a speech in the fall of 1997, shortly after he took over as President, Khatami went further. "Our cinema is a vivid and clear reflection of the greatness of our culture, people, and Islamic revolution," he said.

Eventually, directors found creative ways to deal with the strictures of Islamic filmmaking. Glances of longing replaced touching between a man and a woman. The director Dariush Mehrjui made it seem more natural for his actresses to have their heads covered at home by putting the heroine of his 1990 film *Hamoun* in a bathrobe, a bath towel wrapped around her head, as if she had just emerged from the shower, or by showing a woman doing chores around the house with a scarf holding her hair in place. In his 1996 film *Gabbeh,* Mohsen Makhmalbaf circumvented a ban on female actresses giving birth on the screen by donning a skirt and playing the role himself.

More fascinating than these distortions of reality are the intrusions of reality into film. A number of filmmakers intercut scenes of reality into fictional works, blurring the distinction between fiction and documentary; the technique confounds the censors by adding both authenticity and deniability.

In *The Lady of May,* Rakhshan Bani-Etemad's heroine, Forough, is a forty-two-year-old divorced documentary filmmaker directing a film about the model single mother. As Forough queries real-life Iranian feminists for their definition of the model mother, she struggles to decide whether she can act on her love for a male suitor and still be a good mother to her son. In an interview in the film, Shahla Lahidji, Iran's most famous real-life female publisher, tells Forough that the model mother "is the woman who blends being a mother with being a human being."

Forough also seeks out Faezeh Hashemi, the daughter of former President Rafsanjani. "In our country, the problem is the law," Hashemi says. "All the judges are men, and they don't understand the problems of women." And Mehrangiz Kar, one of the country's real-life leading divorce and child custody lawyers, says bluntly, "I don't know why the model mother has to be chosen in the first place."

I saw *The Lady of May* only because Bani-Etemad lent me a video copy of the film. It had been made years before and was shown briefly in theaters. But the censors banned it after Bani-Etemad refused to edit out the explicit way it dealt with a woman's longing—a mother's longing—

for romantic love. So *The Lady of May* sat on the shelf, seen only occasionally by her friends. And then suddenly, and without explanation, the film was released again. Such is the nature of Iranian cinema.

Eventually, as filmmakers like Majidi, Kiarostami, and Bani-Etemad took more risks—and made it past the censors—Iranians began to flock to the movies. And the movie that attracted more viewers and sparked more reaction than any other in recent memory was *Two Women,* by the feminist filmmaker Tahmineh Milani.

The film tells the story of two women who had become friends years earlier in college in Tehran: Fereshteh, a poor woman trapped in a loveless marriage; and Roya, a successful career woman with a loving husband. But in Milani's mind they are reflections of the same person—a woman as Islamic society sees her and the woman as she sees herself.

Fereshteh had been a gifted math student, until a deranged stalker threatened her, and her father took her back home to Isfahan. There, her parents pressure her to marry a man she doesn't love. Fereshteh's husband turns cruel, reneging on his promise to allow her to continue her studies, forbidding her to read books, locking the telephone so that she cannot communicate with the outside world, and accusing her of having a lover. "You should be controlled," he tells her.

Fereshteh seeks a divorce. The judge asks whether her husband stays out all night, beats her, has bad companions, or gambles. She replies that the problem is different.

"He humiliates me," she says.

"These are not good reasons," the judge declares.

The stalker resolves the problem for her. He kills the husband, leaving Fereshteh and her two children on their own. Suddenly, she doesn't know who she is. "I feel like a free bird but I don't have wings to fly," she tells her friend Roya. "I can take computer class . . . I have a lot to do . . . I must work, go to school, be the father and mother to my children."

The women in the audience cheered and clapped. *Two Women* became the biggest box office hit in Iranian history.

Afterward, I asked my Iranian friends what they thought of the film. For one female friend it sparked memories of the way her late father, as a provincial governor, granted divorces. "Men would come to our house and throw three stones over their shoulders and say, 'I divorce you once. I divorce you twice. I divorce you three times,'" she recalled. "That's all it took to divorce a woman in those days."

Another friend recalled the story of her cousin's divorce. "Her husband refused to give her a divorce," my friend said. "So she decided her best strategy was to treat him nicely and pretend that all was well. In a moment of weakness he gave her permission to travel. She left for the States with her child and never came back again."

The reaction that surprised me the most came from the fifty-seven-year-old wife of a bazaar merchant. She did not have a job outside the home. Her life had been devoted to making her husband and her son happy. "Iranian society has always been a patriarchal one," she said. "Society tells us that the man is always right and the woman is always wrong. The shadow of the man always lingers, even after he is dead. The bitter memories always stay."

Another of the best new Iranian films was *Taste of Cherry*, written and directed by Kiarostami. It was the story of Mohsen Badii, a prosperous, apparently healthy middle-aged man obsessed with suicide.

Much of the film is shot from the claustrophobic interior of Badii's Range Rover as he drives across a sunbaked lonely landscape on the outskirts of Tehran in search of someone to pay to bury him in the grave he has dug for himself in preparation for his suicide. A young cleric from Afghanistan tells him that the Koran bans suicide. A young Kurdish soldier assumes Badii's proposition is a sexual one. But an elderly taxidermist engages Badii, telling him about his own botched suicide attempt. The taxidermist says that he had once planned to hang himself from a mulberry tree, but the scent reminded him of his love for mulberries. Won't you miss the taste of cherries? he asks Badii.

In the end, I was left with the impression that Badii does indeed end his life, although the film can be interpreted differently. The film won the Palme d'Or at Cannes in 1997 and other international awards but had been shown in Iran only once—at an unauthorized screening at the University of Tehran in 1996—and would not be commercially released until the spring of 1999. What especially bothered the censors was that the film presents the act of suicide not as a sin but as a rational or at least understandable decision. "He's exhausted and can't wait for God to act," Badii says at one point about himself.

Ayatollah Khomeini had wanted films to educate the Iranian people. Certainly, *Two Women* made Iranians think about the relations between men and women and *Taste of Cherry* made people think about the wisdom of suicide, but not, I suspect, in the way the father of the revolution ever anticipated.

If the press and cinema have been bold and even subversive at times, those who disseminate information or entertain through television must walk a finer line. This medium is controlled directly by conservatives who report to the Supreme Leader. Yet even here, I have noticed a remarkable shift over the years toward material that reflects more closely what people are doing and feeling, rather than what some of the clerics would like them to do and feel. And that transformation reflects an increasingly realistic attitude on the part of the government that Iranian television has to change if it is to attract an audience.

Consider the case of my young Iranian friend Mohsen, who spends much of his day watching television. He is an importer who buys and sells industrial spare parts. Given Iran's troubled economy, he has a lot of time on his hands. So much of his social life revolves around the twenty-one-inch Sony television and VCR that he hand-carried back from Japan and gave a position of honor in his living room. Mohsen, like many other Iranians, has an illegal satellite dish that gives him access to CNN, MSNBC, the BBC, and French, Turkish, Indian, and Arab television. If he positions the dish right, he can tune in Hong Kong and Japan. I have watched *Monday Night Football* and *Larry King Live* from his living room. His wife, Lili, a graduate student, spends most of her free time buried in books in the small study of their apartment, and calls him a "TV victim." In fact, in the many years I have known the two of them, I have never been to their apartment when the television wasn't on. But these days Mohsen is an equal opportunity viewer. He divides his time between Iranian and foreign television. That's because over the years Iranian television has gotten better.

The revolutionaries' goal has always been to produce Islamically correct television. In the early days, Ayatollah Khomeini put one of his most trusted aides, Sadegh Ghotbzadeh, in charge of radio and television. Ghotbzadeh had no experience in radio and television and seemed ill-suited for the job, but he was in no position to turn it down. In its earliest days, revolutionary television served as a kind of national mobilization force, recklessly ordering all able-bodied Khomeini supporters as reinforcements to various battle scenes. Television stirred up emotions both for and against the revolution by broadcasting the show trials of the Shah's generals. Then the religious propaganda and censorship began to elicit criticism and condemnation. A young television reporter I knew back then produced an investigative story on the reopening of the vast bazaar in Tehran after months of strikes, showing that revolutionary prices were higher than pre-revolutionary ones. The story was killed. An early editorial in the now-defunct leftist *Tehran Journal* called Ghotbzadeh's censorship "worse than the Old Regime's. No reds under the camera here, please, this is an Islamic station. . . . Well, someone should tell him that the proletariat are yawning as widely as everyone else at his revolutionary broadcasts."

Leftist guerrillas who felt that they too had a stake—but no space—in the revolution staged protests outside the television headquarters. One night, when I was visiting the television studios soon after the revolution, a group of gunmen decided to attack. They called for Ghotbzadeh's death and shot at the building with machine guns and pistols for hours, knocking out as many windows as they could before they gave up and went home.

Before long, American shows like *Kojak* and *Star Trek* were replaced by revolutionary songs, speeches, poems, and prayers, repeated over and over throughout the day. Unveiled women were banned from TV screens; employees who did not share the view that an Islamic gloss was necessary for every broadcast were fired. Children's Koran-reading contests appeared. There were so many clerics on television that ordinary people dubbed it "mullahvision" and turned it off. One joke declared that Iranian television was black and white—black turban on channel one and white turban on channel two.

Simply put, revolutionary television was boring. And within a few years it proved no match for a new invention, the VCR. Before long, even ordinary people on limited incomes were saving their money to buy imported VCRs. The clerics struggled to ban trafficking in videos, labeling them "an invitation to prostitutes from the East and West to come into your living room." The campaign didn't work. And that should not have surprised the Islamic Republic. The revolution itself had been spurred on by contraband tape recordings of Khomeini's voice preaching from exile. Why should anyone think Iranians would tamely yield to a new regime's efforts to ban a new kind of tape cassette?

A lively underground business quickly grew up, selling pirated American films illegally on the streets of Tehran before they were sold legally in the United States. Because of the convenience and availability, I saw more first-run films in Tehran than I ever would have seen in the United States.

Then came satellite dishes. They were illegal but in high demand, particularly after intrepid entrepreneurs began producing them locally—which made them one-tenth the cost of foreign-made ones. Newspapers would periodically run stories of police seizures of hundreds of satellite dishes. That only made people more inventive in hiding the dishes: under foliage, elaborate covers of plastic sheeting, or camouflage tarps; in the trees; at the bottom of swimming pools; on balconies and in gardens. Even some of the most seemingly traditional families had "satellite."

Turkish television in particular built an audience with its fare of striptease dancing, violent action films, and soft porn. Then, in the summer of 1999, a massive earthquake struck Turkey, killing more than seventeen thousand people and preempting regular programming for days. "Everywhere I went in Tehran," recalled a friend who was visiting Iran at the time, "I heard complaints that the regular Turkish television shows were not being shown. One taxi driver told me, 'Okay, I can understand it for one or two days, but it's been a week of nothing but earthquake.'"

In the late 1990s, the clerics openly admitted that state-run television was second-rate. The government poured tens of millions of dollars into new programming. The result has been to make Iranian television schizophrenic. The news side is tightly controlled and largely predictable. But the entertainment division is downright avant garde.

The news side broadcasts the speeches of the Supreme Leader, the sermons of the Friday prayer leaders in Tehran, and the important debates in Parliament. The evening news is an empty ritual. For years it opened with file footage of the Iran-Iraq war and military marches. It would be as if American news began with footage of the Vietnam War and John Philip Sousa.

Whenever I visit Iran, I try to catch the English-language evening news. I watch it less for the content than for one of its anchors, an American-born woman with the unlikely name of Judy Garland who is married to an Iranian. (They met in chemistry class at the University of Oklahoma in the 1970s.) On the one hand, I find it disconcerting to hear an American voice reading Iranian propaganda. On the other hand, it is nice to know she is there every night, year after year. I have watched her as she has become more confident and loosened up a bit. She has even begun to wear makeup. Although I have never seen a strand of exposed hair, she has experimented with hoods of color—beige, brown, and blue. Sometimes I think I have detected the trace of a smile on her face.

Television still plays a blatant propaganda role for the government. I once happened to be in Isfahan with a group of American tourists on November 4, the anniversary of the seizure of the American embassy in Tehran. Except for the "Death to America" banners hanging from lampposts, there was no evidence on the streets that day that this was a particularly ominous day. But television news that evening showed angry bearded men and women draped in black chanting "Death to America" in two dozens cities and towns throughout Iran. "Today is considered 'Death to America' Day," the broadcaster announced.

My fellow tourists giggled. One said he could tell that the footage from Isfahan was fake because the protesters were wearing heavy jackets even though it had been shirtsleeve weather that day. Another noticed that some of the angry protesters were schoolkids who smiled at the camera. A third found it particularly amusing that the American flag in one bit of footage had put the stars and the stripes in the wrong place.

If Americans with only a few days' exposure to Iran can see the emptiness of the newscasts, imagine how Iranians themselves feel. I don't know a single Iranian—from any class or any part of Iran—who watches television to get the news. Politicized Iranians read the newspapers; those who can't be bothered with the newspapers listen to the Persian-language services of the BBC and Voice of America on the shortwave of their radios, just as they did before the revolution. Some prefer the Persian-language radio broadcasts beamed from Israel and France, and others the American-sponsored Radio Free Europe beamed from Prague.

And yet Iranian television's entertainment division is dramatically different. There is an appetite for programs that make people laugh. So an all-out effort has been made to attract viewers—with game shows, soap operas, call-in shows, sports events, even American films like *One Flew Over the Cuckoo's Nest* (censored and minus the closet scene). *The Fugitive* with Harrison Ford, once sold as an underground video, eventually made its way to television—with the scenes of unveiled women excised. *Jumanji* with Robin Williams was aired over and over, as was *Dances with Wolves*.

Iranian television has introduced a cooking show with a handsome male host who has become the homemakers' heartthrob. The show also has raised the consciousness of viewers, showing them that it is okay for men to cook. A channel devoted almost entirely to sports airs both sports events and call-in sports trivia shows.

For a while, the most popular television program in Iran was a slapstick sitcom about a young, educated, upper-middle-class married couple named Maryam and Ramin. They were the Iranian version of Lucy and Desi. Maryam wore brightly colored head scarves and clothing, and a shirt that covered only her hips, not a long coat that covered her ankles. She wore too much eyeliner. So did her husband, Ramin. For an hour every night she screeched at him to wash the dishes or pay the bills or compensate her for her work as a housewife. Ramin struck me as a smug know-it-all; Maryam, as irrational, emotional, childlike, and, according to her husband, always wrong. But I loved the show's novelty and its absence of religion.

Ramin and Maryam became pop culture icons. "She is the first female comedian in our country and people love her," said Shahla Sherkat, editor of the feminist magazine *Zanan,* which put Maryam on its cover. "Her character is stronger than her husband's. She's a forward, opportunistic woman who is not overpowered by a man. It's one of the first roles in which a woman is not bringing tea to her husband or washing clothes or saying, 'Yes, sir.' And it's a funny show. My daughters love it."

Then one evening, the show went off the air. No reason was given. There was a rumor that the actress who played Maryam had demanded too much money; another that conservative clerics objected to the emotional intimacy of the show. Ramin started his own talk show, interviewing people like soccer stars and social workers. It was just not the same.

Still, as Maryam's jewel-colored clothing illustrated, television characters sometimes can do things that are forbidden in real life. I flipped on television one day to find a tourist feature film about the provincial capital of Yazd. It showed a male and a female film crew on location doing amazing things together. They checked into a hotel together. Even though they had separate rooms, in real life it would be difficult to find a hotel that would have taken them. The woman called her colleague on the phone from her room, arranged for them to meet in the restaurant, and accompanied him along the streets of the city as they did their work. In real life, any of those activities could have gotten them arrested.

The sight of television and film actresses in all those colors and unusually shaped coverings sparked criticism in conservative newspapers that wanted a return to black and neutral tones. But some women wanted to know why television women were freer than women in real life. "Why can't women wear the same kind of dress on the street as women wear on television?" one reader asked in the newspaper call-in column, "Hello *Salaam.*"

While television under the revolution has always given spiritual advice on such issues as how to pray, it has also begun to give psychological guidance for social and family problems. One popular morning call-in program, *Sobh va Zendegi* (Morning and Life), often invites social workers and psychologists as guests. During one program with a female psychologist, the father of a seventeen-year-old boy called in to get some advice about how to stop his son from smoking.

"Does he exercise?" asked the psychologist.

"No," said the father.

"Does he lie?"

"Yes, and he also has a very bad temper."

"Does he sometimes take things that don't belong to him?"

"Yes."

"So, dear sir," the psychologist said, "Your son's problem is not only smoking. It's a combination of depression and anxiety. First of all, I am glad that a father is calling because most of the time it seems only the mothers are worried about their kids. Second, my advice is to be more friendly to your son. Get closer to him. Let him open himself up to you. Try to fill his time with useful activities, especially ones he wants to do, not ones you want him to do."

The psychologist asked the father whether he had ever beaten his son.

"Yes," the father replied.

"There you go," the psychologist said. "You have already done damage that will be difficult to undo."

One element that is not missing from Iranian television is moral clarity.

In its fictional serials, television has begun to deal with real-life issues, sometimes in ways that stretch reality. One of the most popular television soap operas is *The Days of Youth*, the story of everyday life for four single male students in their twenties who live in Tehran. In reality, most young people in Iran live with their parents until they get married, and the story of four guys sharing a small rented apartment made for compelling—even risqué—entertainment. One episode dealt with the problems of one student, whose rich parents disapproved of his fiancée. Another episode dealt with the fiancée's discovery of her biological mother, from whom she had been separated during air raids in the early part of the long war with Iraq. A third episode dealt with a new roommate, a heroin addict who tried to commit suicide.

The series is popular, my friends tell me, because it portrays both normal everyday life and human misery—minus all the religion. "I love this show," said my friend Nargess. "These guys sing, read love novels, and recite poetry. They help out their friends and go out with the girls they love. They deal with ugliness—drugs, prison, and bad parents."

The program also idealizes the reality of life. The characters all seem to have enough money to rent an apartment on their own, which is not generally the case. They are never shaken down or arrested by the morals police for going out with women or otherwise misbehaving. In some ways, the program reflects the way people hope life will be. At first glance, it is astonishing that the government network has allowed it to air. But consider the stiff competition from foreign-based sources. The Islamic Republic wants to satisfy a population hungry for entertainment with something other than American sitcoms and Turkish soft pornography. Iran's press and cinema are struggling to illuminate, educate, and entertain. And with the country's youth impatient for change, does the government really have a choice?

CHAPTER FOURTEEN

Night Is with Child

If we lose the hearts and minds of the young, we're finished. We cannot control them.

— ABDOLLAH NOURI, FORMER VICE PRESIDENT AND
FORMER MINISTER OF THE INTERIOR

If you were born in America, you'd be studying at Harvard or Oxford now.

— ROYA TO HER FRIEND FERESHTEH IN THE 1999
IRANIAN BLOCKBUSTER FILM *TWO WOMEN*

*T*HE YOUNG WOMAN flung off her head scarf and thrust her head out of an open window of the blue Volkswagen, her long wavy red hair flying wild in the wind. Just behind was a white police car with four officers inside. But the policemen weren't trying to stop her. They were cheering and waving at the exultant crowds lining the street, which had been driven wild by an Iranian victory over the United States—in soccer. Caught up in the patriotic fervor, the policemen were oblivious to the blatant violation of the law—a woman with an unveiled head—that was clearly in their line of vision as they drove up Africa Street, one of Tehran's busiest thoroughfares, at two in the morning.

I was standing on the sidewalk watching the events, feeling frustrated. Here was a bold, defiant demonstration of the power of the masses, and of their youth, in the face of rigid authority, and authority had backed down. Was I the only one to notice it? Wasn't there a photographer around to capture the scene?

The date was June 21, 1998, and Iran had just defeated the United States in the World Cup competition in France. In a communal celebration that froze traffic, freed spirits, and cut across lines of class and gender, millions of people poured into the highways, streets, and alleyways in cities and towns throughout Iran the moment the game ended. Not since the return of Ayatollah Khomeini in February 1979 had there been such a massive display of popular emotion.

This was a victory not just for the Islamic Republic, but for Iran. After the revolution, some clerics tried to put soccer players in long pants and others even branded the game anti-Islamic. But too many other clerics liked the game too much to suppress it. Even Ayatollah Khomeini was a soccer fan; he was said to have watched matches on television during his exile in Paris. His son Ahmad had played on a team in the holy city of Qom. In 1998, one member of Parliament went so far as to argue that soccer was important for the nation's soul, since in praying for the national team, the nation's level of religious devotion rose.

So it shouldn't have been surprising that for one glorious summer night, ordinary Iranians proved themselves capable of bursting out of their lethargy not for God, but for soccer. The frenzy, a kind of mad ecstasy, burst through the Islamic veneer that the revolution had imposed. The unveiling of the redheaded woman was only one of the revolutionary acts I saw that night.

In a dark corner on Vali Asr Avenue in the center of town, a young man positioned a twenty-gallon tank on top of his car. Through a hose attached to the tank he poured a clear liquid into paper cups and handed them out to passersby. The liquid was bootleg vodka. Old men in their eighties strolled the streets in nightshirts. One middle-aged woman waved flares and pounded on cars, ordering drivers to honk their horns and cheer. I saw women of all ages out on their balconies wearing only nightgowns and slippers.

But the night belonged to the young, and the young partied until dawn. Flags were waved, whistles blown, candies thrown, fireworks lighted, car alarms activated, soap suds sprayed. Young men and women danced in the streets to the sounds of American rock music. A dozen young men linked arms and danced, stringing the names of Iran's soccer stars into a rhyming chant. Another group of young men raised an American flag and tried to burn it, but a third group encircled them and pulled the flag to safety.

As things turned out, this was not a night to hate America. The only chant I heard about the United States was not "Death to America," but "*Iran hoorah, Amrika sourakh*" ("Iran hurray, America punctured"), a reference, I suppose, to the American team's weak defense that had made possible Iran's 2–1 victory. One Iranian woman stopped and kissed me when I told her I was an American. She assured me that Iran's victory was nothing personal. Not everyone was so sporting, however. The Supreme Leader, Ayatollah Khamenei, used the occasion to criticize the United States. "Tonight, again, the strong and arrogant opponents felt the bitter taste of defeat at your hands," he said in a message to the team. But such words were not what resonated with the crowds. In the nationwide afterglow, people told stories about the magic of that night for weeks. Some young Iranians coined a name for it: "the coming of the second revolution."

Much of the magic was the sheer subversiveness of the display of joy. This was, in itself, a revelation to the young people—and a red flag to the conservatives. Both groups know that a war is underway for the soul of Iran's new generation, and that joy is only one of youth's emotions. If so many young people could pour into the streets in celebration, they could also demonstrate in anger as well.

The ruling class doesn't seem afraid of the people who work in its shops and factories these days. It doesn't seem concerned about losing its base among the bazaar merchants. It doesn't even seem particularly fearful that it can't control dissident clerics and intellectuals. It is the youth that the authorities view with the most trepidation. At first, officials alluded to this fear sotto voce, but lately they have been shouting it out. If we don't do something to appease the youth, the ruling class in effect has been saying, the Islamic Republic will be doomed.

Thirteen months after the soccer victory, a second scene in the first act of the new "revolution" played itself out, again in the streets. But this was a darker scene, a demonstration not of joy but of rage, as Tehran's youth took to the streets to send a message that they were tired of being pushed around.

The unrest began on July 8, 1999, with a demonstration at the University of Tehran against the closing of the popular newspaper *Salaam* and against the consideration by parliament of a law that would have made it easier to prosecute journalists for what they wrote. Stones were thrown, either by plainclothes police or street vigilantes; the students reciprocated. Uniformed security forces arrived and ordered the students back to their dorms. That night, as students slept, a vigilante force of about four hundred men forced its way onto the campus and into the dorms. The men appeared to be organized, almost like a private army. They wore black trousers and white shirts and carried long rubberized green clubs of a type common among the state-supported thugs.

It was this act—the violation of the students' private space—that triggered the riots and galvanized the country. "They beat the students," Mahmoud Milani, a student who witnessed the attack, told me later. Milani had not been much of an activist, but the dormitory incident politicized him, and he emerged as one of the spokesmen for the students. "The vigilantes had clubs and chains and electric cables and broke everything they saw," Milani said. "They kicked in the doors of the rooms. The security police and riot police stood outside and let it happen. Then the riot police were ordered to attack. They came through all the buildings and beat the students. They took refrigerators and computers. They even broke public phones. They attacked the dorm of the foreign students so that Iran would be considered an anarchist country that is not stable. They threw one Pakistani student out a window. Both his legs were broken."

Shots were fired. An off-duty soldier was killed.

Vigilantes routinely invade private spaces in Iran, breaking up private parties and weddings, stopping people in cars and even on the streets. They are political thugs, not street thugs. It is assumed that they are paid, not necessarily by the Islamic Republic itself, but perhaps by a few powerful clerics whose funds come from important supporters. But the university incident was an invasion of privacy on too grand a scale even for the authorities to ignore, and they universally denounced it. The students were not mollified. Bigger demonstrations followed, and they spread to at least two dozen other cities.

As the demonstrations continued, they became more menacing. In Vali Asr Square, one of Tehran's busiest intersections, a police car and two police motorcycles were torched. I watched as riot police and security police rounded up dozens of students, beating some and forcing them into cages mounted on the backs of pickup trucks. "Filthy swine! Filthy swine!" one red-faced student screamed over and over from inside one of the cages. "Assholes! Jerks! Assholes! Jerks!" yelled another. One chador-wearing woman in the crowd cursed the clergy. "May you all be sent to burn in hell," she ranted. "Damn you all! May God rain curses on you!" I even heard chants aimed directly at Ayatollah Khamenei: *Khamenei haya kon, rahbari ro raha kon* ("Khamenei have shame, let go of the leadership"). Since the beginning of the revolution, Iranian demonstrators have had a flair for making up rhyming slogans as they went along. This one was as piercing and as dangerous as it could get.

At that point, the authorities concluded that the movement had to be stopped, no matter what. Ayatollah Khamenei himself struggled to calm the highly charged atmosphere by condemning the dormitory attack in a speech to a handpicked crowd. But he did not apologize. Rather, he blamed the United States for the unrest. The enraged students, however, were in no mood to shift the blame to the country's predictable scapegoat, and they proved their resolve the following day.

July 13 saw the worst public violence since early in the revolution. Rioters burned banks and overturned buses and police cars. Stone-throwers smashed storefront windows. Tens of thousands of onlookers climbed on rooftops and hung out of balconies and windows to watch the drama unfold. The chaos and violence closed hundreds of stores, banks, gas stations, shopping centers, office buildings, and even the vast bazaar in the south of Tehran. Security police, soldiers, anti-riot forces, Revolutionary Guards, intelligence operatives, and vigilantes fanned out from the University of Tehran north and south for miles.

Rioters of unknown identities burned police and civilian vehicles, public offices, and even the platform used for the weekly Friday prayers at the university. The violence continued into the night, with a frenzy of beatings of students, demonstrators, journalists, and bystanders. The vigilantes attacked with stones, sticks, chains, metal cables, knives, and meat cleavers as well as their traditional green batons. The cleavers reminded me of the butcher knives carried by black-clad women in the days after Khomeini's victory, when they called for revenge against the Shah's generals.

During the demonstrations, Ahmad Batebi, a student, held over his head a bloodied T-shirt for a photographer to immortalize on film. The dramatic color photograph appeared in a number of Iranian newspapers and on the cover of *The Economist.* Later, Batebi was convicted of endangering national security and spreading anti-government propaganda and was sent to prison. His sentence: ten years.

Through the commotion, I stayed on the sidelines, unobtrusive in a long black coat and a black scarf pulled tightly over my hair, wondering if I was being courageous or just foolish. I said nothing in English, and kept my few phrases of Persian to a minimum, since my accent betrays me as a foreigner. These were not days for man-on-the-street interviews. Yet the events of that day somehow did not seem like another revolution. In fact, the demonstrations showed not how close Iran was to the flowering of a second revolution, but how far.

President Khatami, whom the students had envisioned as their hero, pleaded with them to end the demonstrations. The unrest had hurt Khatami, who was caught between the students who supported him and the conservative clerics with whom he had to share power. This was not a battle worth pursuing, the President told the demonstrators. Indeed, his aides told me later that the President and many other reform leaders had feared that all-out violent street fighting could give Khatami's political opponents the ammunition to brand him weak and remove him from office. The very next day, the conservative forces turned the tables on the demonstrators by amassing crowds of their own, and it was not long before calm returned. By the time the unrest subsided, three people were dead by the official count, more by the unofficial count. Countless others were injured. Fourteen hundred people were put behind bars for inciting unrest. For the moment, the student protest movement was over.

What was clear once the excitement died down was that the students hadn't known how much power they had or exactly how much they wanted. Their demands had ranged from petty to pie-in-the-sky. One student wanted the creation of a national day of mourning in memory of the students who had been killed; another demanded a public trial for the people who had ordered and carried out the dormitory attack; another asked that the bodies of those killed be returned to the students, not their families; another would be satisfied only with the execution of those who had attacked the dorm. "Either Islam and the law, or another revolution," the students chanted, but it wasn't at all clear what a new revolution would be fought for. No one seemed to want to die so that a newspaper could reopen. If there was a common goal, it was not to abolish the Islamic system of government, but to achieve a quickening of the movement toward democracy, the rule of law, and the expansion of personal freedom. And there was a quiet understanding that summer that violence was not the way to get there, which meant that the Islamic Republic was not in jeopardy—at least not yet.

I had found one key to understanding what the youth of Tehran want a year before the unrest, in a crumbling old white stucco mansion in south Tehran. Not far from the Presidential Palace, the mansion houses a curious student commune, the Office for Fostering Unity, which wages a political battle against what it considers the excesses of Iran's clerical rule. The members live rent-free in the government-owned building, oblivious to the chipping plaster, peeling paint, exposed wiring, and absence of air-conditioning. But they enjoy telephones, computers, a fax machine, and a photocopying machine. That's all they need.

The first time I visited in 1998, I noticed that some of the old bookcases, tables, chairs, and filing cabinets didn't have a particularly Iranian look. I spotted one bookcase with a small brass plate engraved with the words *"Teheran-American School."* "Isn't this American furniture?" I asked Meysam Saidi, a twenty-eight-year-old graduate student in chemistry and one of the student leaders.

"Oh, yes," he replied, laughing. "It's the furniture from the American embassy taken by our predecessors. We're taking good care of it." I knew that the student commune drew its inspiration from the students and militants who had taken American diplomats hostage in 1979. But the presence of the furniture was unsettling. I told Saidi that perhaps he should petition the government to move into the old American embassy. "It's a pretty nice space," I joked. "Twenty-seven acres and a pool."

But where their mentors in revolutionary fervor had looked to the religious ethics of Ayatollah Khomeini for guidance, students a generation later were looking to the civic formulas of President Khatami. They had campaigned hard for him in 1997, and had embraced his message of the rule of law and the creation of a civil society, wrapping it in leftist-sounding rhetoric about social justice and equal distribution of wealth. "The most important activity of students in the last decade was the election of Mr. Khatami," Saidi explained. "He presents his ideas in beautiful language. He treats us with respect. That appeals to the youth. On the other side is a totalitarian view expressed by people who want to keep all the power in their hands. No one can claim all of Khatami's promises have been fulfilled. But the movement has begun."

And yet that movement is still being defined. The youth know what they do not want: a second revolution. They proved as much in their massive turnout in the 1997 and 2000 elections and in their decision to retreat from the streets in the summer of 1999. Slowly, they are coming to realize that with the huge youth population and a voting age of sixteen, their numbers count. And they have rejected the violent ways of their predecessors. "We will never prescribe such an action as hostage-taking of an embassy again," Saidi said. "We will make our objections known through legal ways." As for the furniture, he said, "We'll give it back when you get back your embassy someday. God willing, one day there will be relations between the two countries." In February 2000, Saidi was elected to Parliament on the reformist ticket.

Shortly after the demonstrations, I went back to the white stucco mansion. About two dozen young men who call themselves the Select Council of Sit-in Students were in charge. In a generous act of solidarity, the older student commune temporarily had turned over its headquarters to them. A handful of students ushered me into a conference room where they explained why they had taken to the streets. "Our demonstrations were different from twenty years ago," said Mahmoud Milani, the young man who had been an eyewitness to the initial invasion of the dormitories. "Twenty years ago people had one purpose: overthrowing the Shah. People today do not want another revolution. We had our revolution. We are not revolutionaries. We are reformers. We support the Constitution, as do the majority of the people."

"Supporting the Constitution" is a particularly subtle form of code. On the one hand, it implies support for the idea of religious rule, which is a safe thing to do, and on the other hand it suggests a challenge to Ayatollah Khamenei's power, which is less safe. The second point refers to the position taken by many reformers that the Constitution doesn't give Ayatollah Khamenei all the power that he enjoys in practice.

But if the students are capable of spinning such subtlety into their words, it does not necessarily follow that they have fully mastered the art of political infighting. I spotted on a bookshelf a collection of the dozens of paperback volumes published by Iranian authorities years ago that contain copies of the classified documents seized from the American embassy and their translations into Persian. Many of the most sensitive had been shredded by American diplomats in the tense moments before the seizure was complete. The occupiers painstakingly had pasted them back together.

"Have you read them?" I asked.

"Some of them," Milani said sheepishly.

"Only some of them?"

"I'm an electronics major!" he exclaimed. "I'm not in political science! I don't know about politics."

Before I left, I chided the students for not informing me of a news conference they had held the day before. "We didn't call any foreign press," one of them told me.

"Why not?" I asked. Maybe the group didn't trust the foreign media, I thought. Maybe it didn't want to be accused of conspiring with foreign plotters.

But no. These kids were politically green, isolated, even naive. Their explanation turned out to be much more mundane.

"We didn't have any of the phone numbers," the student replied. "Can you give us the phone numbers?"

And it was then that I realized just how spontaneous the unrest had been and how disorganized the student movement still is.

Just as the soccer celebration had done a year before, the street unrest in July 1999 crystallized the fundamental truth that the youth of Iran are its political future. Those in power know that to ignore their desires and aspirations is to tempt fate. It is a simple matter of demographics.

Ayatollah Khomeini had encouraged his people to breed, particularly during the war with Iraq. And breed they did. By 1986, the population growth rate was 3.2 percent per year. Realizing by then that such a large birth rate was disastrous for the economy, Iran's Health Ministry launched a nationwide campaign and introduced contraceptives—pills, condoms, IUDs, implants, tubal ligations, and vasectomies. In 1993, Parliament passed legislation withdrawing food coupons, paid maternity leave, and social welfare subsidies after the third child. Birth control classes were required before a couple could get married. Dozens of mobile teams were sent to remote parts of the country to offer free vasectomies and tubal ligations. These days, an Iranian condom factory churns out more than 70 million a year, packaged in French or English to suggest that they are imported, available in textures and flavors like mint and banana. "Islam," said Deputy Health Minister Hosein Malek-Afzali during a birth control workshop in 1995, "is a flexible religion."

But the trend had already been set. In the first two decades of the revolution, the country's population nearly doubled. And today an estimated 65 percent of the population is under the age of twenty-five. Unlike their parents, who lived through the events of the revolution, most of Iran's youth know the revolution only through their history books. Many have no particular love or hatred for the Shah, or, for that matter, for Ayatollah Khomeini.

But many of them do know the Internet—or at least know of its existence—and watch American television beamed in by satellite. Many of them just don't buy it when their leader gives speeches about the "disgustingly sick promiscuous behavior" of Western youth.

Many young people are also frustrated by the lack of economic opportunity and the continued invasion of privacy by Iran's massive security apparatus and its street thugs. They are fed up with the discrimination that is at the core of the system. Only one out of ten applicants makes it into a university, some because they are at the top of their class, some because they are well connected, some because of quotas for families of war martyrs and disabled veterans, some because they are poor but lucky.

Some students study for an entire year for the university entrance exam. Even if they pass, they can be denied entry if they fail the Islamic morality tests. That happened to a young friend of mine and her best friend. "From morning to night we studied," she recalled. "There were thousands and thousands of applicants and thirty spaces. The two of us made it. But we were disqualified. We didn't pass the test for morality. We never found out why. You cannot know how depressed I was, how much I cried. I worked so hard and they took it away."

I often think how odd it is that the first unofficial rule of ethics of the theocratic revolution is that it is acceptable—even necessary—to lie in order to survive. From the time they are in elementary school, many young people learn to live two lives, a private life inside their homes, a public life that they profess to on the outside. In public, they have to act as though their fathers and mothers love the Islamic Republic and don't drink alcohol, even when that is not true. They say they do not like Western music or satellite television even when they do. In this imaginary world, their mothers wear black chadors and pray. Their fathers wear beards and pray. They all go to the mosque together every Friday at noon.

A highly respected government official I know couldn't get his son into the school of his choice—one of the best in Tehran—because his family wasn't Islamic enough. "When my son passed the entrance exam, they called us for an interview and told my wife she'd have to wear a chador," he said. "My wife said, 'No way.' She'd wear a scarf but not a chador. A few weeks later I found out my son had been rejected, so I went to the school to find out why. They told me, 'Your son said, "I play the saxophone and my father likes music." He said your wife doesn't wear a chador.' I asked them, 'Who gave you the right to ask my kid about me?' I fought the decision for two months. I told the school, 'I'll donate two PCs to the school out of my own pocket. I'll bring in some people who can train the kids in the Internet and know how to control the access to it.' The school said no. They said they didn't want the Internet."

Undeniable truths are also shaping this generation. Young people see, for example, how important making money has become for the older generation. The sermons they hear broadcast every Friday seem nothing more than background noise without emotional resonance. Many young people believe they know how their counterparts on the outside live, because they have seen a version of it in the fantasy world created by Hollywood.

The response of the government has been to try to persuade its young to reject what others have. They have tried to wall off Iran from the rest of the world. It hasn't worked. That alternative requires too much sacrifice, too much austerity, and too little joy. The young-at-heart simply are no longer ready to die.

Jobs are scarce. Several hundred thousand young people enter the job market every year; fewer than half get jobs in an economy marked by isolation, underinvestment, unpredictable regulations, corruption, inefficiency, and overdependence on oil. Many young people are forced to defer marriage because they cannot afford the cost of a proper wedding and setting up house. In dealing with the natural restlessness of youth, other societies have a hard enough time making a "Just say no" approach work against obvious dangers like lethal drugs and sexually transmitted diseases. The ayatollahs still think they can make "Just say no" work against puppy love; and so they struggled to keep the barriers in place against socializing, holding hands in public, watching foreign television via satellite, and, of course, drinking alcohol. For twenty years, young people have been beaten up, put in jail, lashed, and forced to sign confessions about their moral misdeeds and "high" crimes—like getting caught in mixed-gender parties, being improperly dressed in public, or listening to the wrong kind of music.

The social restrictions of the Islamic Republic have begun to backfire. The ban on public dating means that more encounters between young people are taking place in private spaces. Paradoxically, it also encourages young people who might have dated casually to have sexual intercourse because an active sexual life is one way young people can rebel against the system. I know one young man who enjoys picking up young women in a particular Tehran parking lot—and sometimes ends up in bed with them.

Many young people have little hope that permanent change will come. They find their inspiration outside—in the West in general and America in particular—and in creative ways of trying to maintain dignity in confronting what they consider impossible odds. That's how Jaffar Azadi copes.

Azadi is a taxi driver and part-time mechanic in Tabriz, the capital of the northwestern Iranian province of Azerbaijan. He dresses in neatly pressed black gabardine pants and stylish sports shirts and slicks back his curly black hair. In his cab he plays the music of Dariush, the popular middle-aged Iranian-born singer who lives in exile in Los Angeles and whose music is banned in Iran.

Nazila and I found ourselves in the backseat of Azadi's taxi one afternoon and asked him about the music. "Dariush is my hero," he said. "I'm really a singer." Indeed, in the evenings, Azadi is a performer like his hero.

Azadi invited us to a chic, lace-curtained ice cream parlor in the northern part of the city, where he gave us a brief demonstration of the kind of music he sings, mostly about love and longing. He and his friends perform exclusively at weddings and private parties. Even so, singing can be a dangerous profession. Azadi's music inspires joy and a desire to move the body in unseemly ways, clearly still not acceptable in Iran, and he has been arrested many times. At one wedding reception, the police fired pistols in the air. But Azadi makes good money: $200 to $300 a wedding. More often than not, the police or the vigilantes will settle for a generous bribe and go away. In fact, he considered himself fortunate. Unlike his fellow band members, he had never been lashed with a whip.

Even though he was twenty-seven when we met in 1998, Azadi still lived with his elderly parents. And his family was so traditional that he had met his fiancée, Maryam Massoumi, through the custom of *khastehgari*, in which the family of the groom visits the home of the bride to ask her parents for her hand. "I didn't want to get married," he said. "But I knew when I met her that she was a clean woman."

"What do you mean, a clean woman?" I asked, thinking it might have something to do with hygiene. It did, but it meant something else as well.

"She is not the type to flirt with men," Azadi explained. "I told her I don't care what kind of head covering she wears, but she can't have socialized with other men." Like most residents of Tabriz, Azadi is not a Persian but a Turk, so he told me a Turkish proverb: "The man who marries a woman who has mingled with men marries a woman with a dark heart."

Although Jaffar and Maryam had signed their marriage contract and recited the Koranic marriage verses in front of a cleric, they still did not live together. They would have to wait until they had a formal ceremony and a big family party, and like many other young people in Iran, they couldn't afford it. All Azadi could think about, he said, was getting married. Politics was not on his radar screen. He voted not because he cared about who was running, he said, but because it was the only way he could get his identity card stamped to make him eligible for food ration coupons. And yet something political was bubbling underneath. "We loved the Shah," Azadi said suddenly. "But we don't like this regime. This is not true Islam. They don't practice the things they make us do."

Azadi has heard stories about how wonderful it was in the old days. In fact, for many young people, pre-revolutionary Iran has become an idealized, imaginary paradise. They ask, longingly, why they couldn't have been born back then. "That's what Dariush is good for," Azadi said. "He understands sadness, depression." What Azadi didn't seem to realize was that Dariush sang about depression and sadness during the Shah's time too.

And then, over coconut-topped strawberry sundaes in the middle of the ice cream parlor, Azadi sang softly from a song Dariush made famous years ago:

> *The year of 2000*
> *The year of silence and escape*
> *The year of running away and patience*
> *The season of the dead-end street*
> *The dark age of 2000.*

I caught up with Azadi again in the year 2000. He and his wife had been formally married and now had a baby daughter. There was not enough money for their own apartment so they all lived with his parents. Though he still could not perform legally, he was elated that the ban on many other musicians and styles of music was being eased. He and the other members of his band voted in the February parliamentary election this time to support the reformists running from Tabriz. "What's been done in Khatami's name is better than nothing," he said. "Actually, that's too negative. I see some changes. Things are getting better."

However, some children of the highest-ranking and most deeply conservative revolutionaries have turned their backs on their fathers and the values they represent. One is Ahmad Rezai. He is the son of one of the revolution's heroes, Major General Mohsen Rezai, who had been commander of the Revolutionary Guards for seventeen years, and then became the secretary of the Expediency Council, a powerful overseeing body headed by former President Rafsanjani that advises the Supreme Leader, settles Constitutional disputes, and mediates disagreements between the Parliament and the Guardian Council. When I met the young Rezai in the fall of 1998, he was twenty-three. He came to see me in my office in Washington one day, unshaven, carrying a cell phone, smiling and relaxed. He had defected to the United States a few months before, after turning up one day at the American embassy in Vienna. The CIA took over, putting him on a plane to New York, debriefing him, and giving him political asylum, he said. He hired an immigration lawyer and rented a room from a friend in Hollywood.

It is extraordinarily difficult for an outsider to penetrate the inner circle of Iran's political leaders, especially those involved with security issues. But here in front of me sat the son of one of the highest-ranking officials of the Islamic Republic. Except that the young Rezai wanted to talk less about the country's repression, and more about the repression in his own life. The CIA thought it was getting a big-time defector; it got a young man who wanted to play music and wear blue jeans.

Rezai had been groomed to be a standard-bearer of the Islamic Republic. At the age of five, he was taken by his father to visit the war front with Iraq. He accompanied his father on missions to the homes of the country's top officials, even to the home of Ayatollah Khomeini himself. Because of his father's status, Rezai led a sheltered childhood, growing up in a villa on a large compound inhabited exclusively by the families of senior Revolutionary Guards. He was not allowed to listen to music of any kind. "My mind was a complete blank," he said. "I didn't even know how a baby comes into the world."

When Rezai was nineteen, his parents sent him to study mathematics at a teachers college in Tehran. They also chose a wife for him, the daughter of a close friend of his father's. The young Rezai said he saw his wife unveiled for the first time on their wedding night. He said that life got worse after marriage. "My wife," he said, "just didn't like sex. In a way that turned out to my advantage. It gave me a reason to separate. My wife went back to her parents. I stayed alone in the apartment. I had a car. I had videos, mostly American movies. I bought a big stereo set and listened to all the cassette tapes my friends brought. But I couldn't really date or go out. Too many people knew who my father was."

Rezai had been given a governmental job as a "special inspector," which gave him, among other things, the right to stop and search any private car he wanted. But he hated the work. "I told my father, 'If you treat young people this way you're doomed,'" the young Rezai said. "But people like my father do not mingle with the people. They live within their own world."

Rezai felt trapped. So he sought refuge in the country of his videos and cassette tapes. Back in Iran, Rezai's defection was greeted with disbelief and suspicion, and it was excruciatingly humiliating for his family. His younger brother, Ali, gave interviews calling Ahmad emotionally disturbed and claiming that he had been kidnapped and brainwashed by the United States. Fatemeh Hashemi, a daughter of former President Rafsanjani, dismissed him as "unbalanced, abnormal.

"He had a car accident with his wife," Fatemeh told me. "She lost an eye. Then he just left her." Rezai had never mentioned that part of the story, and I didn't know if it was true. But more than a year later, Mohsen Rezai, the young man's father, confessed in a speech that he had been a neglectful father, and that his neglect had played a part in his son's decision to leave. During the long war with Iraq, he said, "I, like most commanders, deliberately avoided forming close emotional ties with family members in order to prevent doubt and weakness during battle." This was one confession that sounded authentic.

Jaffar Azadi and Ahmad Rezai are Iranian baby boomers, born into a generation with the power of sheer numbers but without any real outlet for rebellion or social inventiveness. So despite their demographic weight, they don't truly enjoy power. Not yet, at least. And many of the youth are in the grip of a low-level depression.

That is a frightening phenomenon for some older Iranians. Sadegh Zibakalam, a political scientist at the University of Tehran who was imprisoned during the time of the Shah, explained the generation gap this way: "My generation is not going to turn its back on the revolution because if we did, we would be like mothers saying goodbye to our children, we would be saying goodbye to our existence. But the younger generation has no attachment, no feeling for the revolution. They were just babies. When I teach the revolution in my classes, many of my students just look out the window and watch the clock for the lesson to end. They say, 'What about us? You had your revolution and your war. What's in it for us?' And I can't tell them the answer."

In the most extreme cases, depression goes far beyond singing sad songs. Nazila's sister, Golnaz, told me that one day the security guard on duty at her family's apartment complex called with gruesome news. "A body fell on the roof of your car," the guard said, as matter-of-factly as if he were announcing that the mailman had delivered a package. Golnaz went down to see for herself. There, atop her car, was the broken body of a thirty-year-old woman. Depressed, troubled, and unemployed, the woman had jumped off the balcony of the tenth-floor apartment she shared with her parents. Her skull was crushed, her limbs shattered.

Golnaz ran back to the apartment, too stunned to cry.

Two weeks later, another young woman leaped to her death, from another balcony in the same building.

Suicide has become part of everyday life in Iran, even though it is forbidden by the Koran and considered an act against the will of God. During Iran's war with Iraq, conversations were filled with stories about martyrs who had sought out death in battle to reach paradise. They are often referred to as suicide fighters in Western accounts, but in Iran their deaths aren't considered suicides. Now, however, young people were taking their lives in acts of despair. It is a phenomenon that strikes not just the children of the privileged, but the children of the poor as well.

Newspapers are filled with small items about suicide, and suicide attempts have become so common that young people have begun to talk openly about them. One summer I spent time with a nineteen-year-old young man named Arash. In the midst of our conversation, the story of a suicide attempt when he was sixteen came spilling out. His family had recently moved back to Iran from Sweden, and the adjustment from the freewheeling Scandinavian life to a place where the most mundane social activities were forbidden was too much to bear.

"I was really angry," he recalled, speaking in fluent English. "I was pissed off that my parents had brought me back to Iran. My girlfriend and all my friends were in Sweden and they kept calling and telling me to come back. In Iran, I had no friends. I couldn't speak Persian very well. I had really long hair and everyone thought I was gay or something. I locked the door to my room. I found some sleeping pills. You can find sleeping pills in every house in Iran. So I just took some. My mother came and tried to wake me up. I think she broke down the door. Then they took me to the hospital. I woke up in a hospital bed. It wasn't time for me to die."

For four years Arash's life was in limbo. He had failed the entrance exam for university two years in a row. After he refused to perform his two years of compulsory military service, his father bought his way out. But he lived at home with his parents, unable to support himself with the money he earned making pirated copies of music and films on CDs and selling them on a busy black market.

"So what do you want?" I asked him over dinner at a popular restaurant in Tehran one evening.

"I want to do normal things, like go out in shorts on a date," he said. "But it's banned. I came here the other night with my parents and they talked about how much they loved coming here before the revolution, having beer and wine to drink as they sat outside and ate a good meal. Why can't it be like that now?"

When I contacted Arash two years later, he was making plans to leave the country. He had recently married a young Iranian woman and they were moving to Sweden. He and his wife hadn't voted in the 2000 parliamentary elections. "The weather was too cold and the lines too long," he said, adding that it really didn't matter who won or lost.

The sadness of young people shows up in other ways. A young Iranian-American friend of mine who grew up in the United States but returned to Iran for a visit recently prided himself on his ability to blend in with people his age who had grown up in the country. But one day in a barbershop, the barber stated, "You recently came from abroad."

"How could you tell?" the young man asked.

"You have laughter in your eyes," the barber said. "No one at your age who has known nothing else but life in Iran has laughter in his eyes."

*   *   *

Even since Khatami's election, I have heard stories from young people about how they want more social and educational freedom, better job prospects, and most important, to be taken seriously and treated with respect. "President Khatami comes to our university, and says nice things, but he can't change anything," a student at the all-female Al Zahra University told me one day after Khatami had given a speech. "No matter what, he's still one of them. He's still a cleric. This revolution has been built wrong, like a wall where the bricks were never laid properly."

But then, I have met other young people in Iran who have succeeded in creating full lives for themselves despite the constraints of the Islamic system. Maybe it's that they've reshaped their dreams to fit the present. Maybe it's that they're old enough to have memories of the sacrifices that came with revolution and war.

I found one such woman living in a small one-room apartment, high in the mountains far away from the traffic and pollution of Tehran. When I met Nargess, who is thirty years old and holds a master's degree in political science, she was working at a governmental research institute. One roommate is a photographer who also teaches at the university, the other a photographer for state-run television. All three have lived away from home and have supported themselves for years.

Their apartment is in a crumbling building, set in a garden of mulberry trees. There is one small table and one chair, a telephone, and a small television; the only closet is filled with books. The trio share the owner's bathroom in another part of the building. I see only one mattress in the room. I have no idea what the sleeping arrangements are; I do not ask.

Nargess, a dark-haired, olive-skinned woman whose parents live far away, near Iran's eastern border, explained that at first her family had objected to her independent lifestyle. But for her, independence had come naturally. "Sure, we have a custom of living with our parents until we are married," she explained as she put a large platter of watermelon and cucumbers on the floor before us. "But my father was a fervent revolutionary. He taught me to think for myself. And I do."

Unlike so many other young women I have met, Nargess loves her work and is satisfied with her living arrangement because it affords her control over her private life. "It is as if a wind is blowing through me when I am here," she said. "Life near the mountains is very peaceful, quiet, not like Tehran. So what that it's an hour commute to work and it's a small space. Here no one cares what I do."

Still, Nargess realizes that she and her roommates are not representative of Iran's youth. "Sometimes I feel as if my goals and attachments are different from those of other people who feel so alienated from society," she said. "I really believe it when Khatami tells us that there are no saviors, that we all have to stand up and take responsibility. I do not have a high position or a high income or great expectations. Our problem we have in Iran—and it's the problem of other societies as well—is that we've lost the ability to be satisfied with what we have."

I contacted Nargess a year and a half later. She had changed jobs and was now working for a conservative newspaper. Her strategy, she explained, was "to destroy the conservative front from inside."

Indeed, many young people, like Nargess, have no intention of finding a way out of the country. They manage to live, through creativity and wit, alongside an Islamic state that has yet to figure out how to deal with them. The reformists understand the disaster that more than two decades of anti-youth policies have created, yet the conservatives hang on to rhetoric and dogma, moralizing and rejection. And it is within this context that the students' push for more democracy must be understood. They want a louder voice in their destiny, and they are getting bolder in making their demands. The older generation is also struggling to come to terms with the dreams of its young. As the youth demonstrated in the streets, their parents watched helplessly and hoped for better times, without having much sense of what that means. Sometimes it seems as if the tables have been turned, and that youth is calling the shots.

I saw this tension in the small, sweet hotel where I was staying in the summer of 1999. On the day of the riots I discovered that the hotel had been transformed into a refuge for a dozen students who had been beaten by street thugs. The hotel staff suggested that as the only foreign guest, I seek other lodging. As I was checking out, five housemaids came to say goodbye. They formed a chorus in black, reflecting variations on a theme.

"The students are saying they don't want the Supreme Leader anymore," said a small dark-skinned woman.

"What about you?" I asked.

"I don't want him either," she said. "Nobody wants him."

A second woman came running down from the balcony upstairs to tell what she had just seen. "There were two young kids!" she exclaimed. "The vigilantes beat them until they were covered in blood!"

"I'm worried about my kids," said a third woman whose three children were out on the streets that day. "Especially my twenty-year-old daughter. She's young and so angry. I can't stop her." She began to weep, and then apologized for doing it in front of me.

"I have kids who are like that too," said a fourth woman. "I don't know what to do. Yesterday I saw a young man stop a bus. He made the people get off and set it on fire. A brand-new bus!"

"It's getting just like the Shah," said the third one. "He killed people. These clergy kill people. My fear is that something's going to happen and we'll have to stop working. And I need the money to live."

Suddenly a fifth woman appeared, a young, thin woman with big gaps in her teeth. "Why do you pretend to be so miserable in front of a foreigner?" she asked. "Keep quiet!"

"This is the truth," said the mother of three. "Why should we hide it?"

Precisely. These days, the people of Iran have little incentive or desire to keep things hidden any longer. The students know it. Their parents know it. Even the government knows it.

"What do young people want?" I asked Ali-Reza Shiravi from the Ministry of Islamic Guidance one day. I wanted an official government response. I was surprised at how frank he was in his answer. "They want an end to humiliation," he said. "They want an education. They don't want others to make decisions in their names. They want social and cultural opportunities. They want modern things. They want fun. Look at what's happened with videos in this country. In the beginning of the revolution they were banned. But people didn't care. Videos became widespread. By the time the government lifted the ban it was too late. Suddenly young people feel they have been left behind. They have to catch up to reach others in a hurry. It's like the Internet. The Internet is very expensive for Iranians. But we have the Internet in our office. We offer it to the staff. So all the people come from other floors to use it. When you know there's more out there, you want more."

CHAPTER FIFTEEN

A Republic in the Making?

*The New Year is coming, and we have to clean house. There are certain
things in our house that have gathered dust. We must clean them off and
make them shine.*

— SAEED HAJJARIAN, NEWSPAPER EDITOR, AND AN AR-
CHITECT OF THE REFORM MOVEMENT, ON THE
2000 PARLIAMENTARY ELECTION CAMPAIGN

*If the charges against me are true, then God protect the Islamic Republic of
Iran. If, on the other hand, the charges are false, God protect us from our
accusers.*

— ABDOLLAH NOURI, FORMER VICE PRESIDENT AND
FORMER MINISTER OF THE INTERIOR, DURING HIS
TRIAL.

Winners have large families, but losers are orphans.

— PERSIAN PROVERB

*L*ESS THAN A WEEK before Iran's parliamentary elections in February
2000, former President Ali-Akbar Hashemi-Rafsanjani took out full-page
campaign ads and distributed two million flyers for himself in several
newspapers and through the mails. It was a desperate act. Here was one
of the country's leading clerics, a man with golden revolutionary credentials who had served for eight years as Speaker of the Parliament and for
eight more as the country's elected President. But now, he felt he had to
sell himself to the voting public.

For months, Rafsanjani had watched helplessly as his power and
prestige slipped away. The reformist press had written scathing attacks,
accusing him of having done nothing during his years in power to halt

the Intelligence Ministry's reign of terror, of needlessly prolonging the Iran-Iraq war, and of pursuing a hollow economic policy. He responded every chance he had, in Friday prayer sermons and in newspaper interviews. In an angry apologia in the newspaper *Hamshahri,* he listed his achievements, saying it was he who had laid the groundwork for Iran's new era of openness.

Rafsanjani's desperation was apparent in the photograph he chose for his ad campaign, a shot of himself, sitting under a tree with a book open on his lap and his young grandson at his side. In the West it would have been conventional. But Rafsanjani had shed his turban for this photo, making it exceptional. He recognized, in other words, that the uniform of the mullahs was no longer an automatic draw. On the contrary, it had become a liability.

When Rafsanjani decided to run at the urging of the conservative clerical establishment, he and his supporters expected him to sweep into first place in the voting in Tehran and once again become Speaker of Parliament. But the traits that served him well in another time—backroom-deal-making, cronyism, and slipperiness—no longer worked. As the campaign progressed, the electorate and the reformist newspapers pressured Rafsanjani to clarify his positions on the issues of the day. He could not remain, as he had insisted, above the fray. In the old days, he had portrayed himself as a force of moderation in a leadership of zealots. Now he suddenly looked old, gray, and behind the times. When the election was held on February 18, he squeaked in to capture the last of Tehran's thirty seats with 25.58 percent of the vote; he relinquished his seat shortly before the Parliament convened.

Since the revolution the Parliament hardly ever operated as an independent arena of power. Decisions always seemed to have been made elsewhere first, a mirror of the conflicts within Iranian society. But then ordinary Iranians hungry for a voice in government decided to ignore this reality and voted for the Parliament as if it really did have power. And in doing so, they took a serious measure of power for themselves. They also created the potential for a Parliament that might be much more independent than before.

The results of the election elated many of the reformists, who saw it as a powerful endorsement of President Khatami's policies and the means to enhance his authority to fight for further change. But the election also stiffened the spine of conservatives and opened a new phase in the ongoing struggle for the future shape of the Islamic Republic. Left unresolved were the issues of how much the new parliament would be allowed to legislate changes in Iran's political, economic, and social life and how far the conservatives would go to thwart it.

The contest itself was unwieldy, as more than 5000 candidates ran for 290 seats. Each candidate had to be approved by provincial supervisory bodies, the Ministry of the Interior, and then by the clerically dominated conservative Guardian Council. About 10 percent of the potential candidates were barred from participating because they were judged to have either rejected Iran's Islamic Constitution or lacked adequate education. Those rejected included Ibrahim Yazdi, the former Foreign Minister; Hamid-Reza Jalaeipour, the newspaper publisher; Abbas Abdi, the first editor of the banned newspaper *Salaam;* and Azam Taleghani, the woman who had tried to run for President in 1997. Even President Khatami's older sister, Fatemeh, was turned down, because she didn't have a college degree, although she was an elected member of the town council from Ardakan and headed the women's organization there. Still, the rejection rate was dramatically lower than that of the previous election in 1996, when more than 40 percent were barred.

Candidates used Western-style vote-getting techniques: paid campaign advertisements, polling, and mass mailings. They set up storefront headquarters to field phone calls, receive visitors, and distribute literature. Even though Iran has no formal political parties in the Western sense, with broad-based popular memberships and established platforms, that did not deter one of the leading reformers, the President's brother, Mohammad-Reza Khatami. The younger Khatami, an English-speaking urologist and the former Deputy Minister of Health, had nearly lost a leg while serving as a volunteer in the Iran-Iraq war. In late 1998 he founded the Islamic Iran Participation Front as a vehicle for his brother's reformist ideas, and by 2000 it functioned as an informal political party, publishing a serious issue-oriented platform and sponsoring a substantial number of candidates. Together with seventeen other reformist groups it formed the Second of Khordad Front (named after the day in 1997 when Mohammad Khatami was elected President), whose common goal was to bring about wholesale changes in the way the Parliament was run. The reformist candidates debated serious issues: personal and societal freedoms, the rule of law, the rights and duties of the entire populace to participate in the country's decision-making, Iran's rightful place in the world. The conservative side had little to say in response.

A sign of the changing atmosphere was that a candidate in the city of Karaj, west of Tehran, dared to praise Reza Shah in one of his campaign speeches, saying the autocrat had helped to modernize the country. A number of candidates in Shiraz published poems of Saadi and Hafiz—not verses of the Koran—on their campaign posters. For the first time, sex appeal played a role too. A cleric running from the western province of Loristan walked through the city with a sign that said, "Temporary marriage. Yes, temporary marriage. Free." A cleric from the city of Qazvin printed a poster of himself flanked by two beautiful, chador-clad women smiling and pointing at him. Faezeh Hashemi, an incumbent in the Parliament and the daughter of former President Rafsanjani, distributed flyers in which her legs were crossed and her chador was open, revealing a black and white polka dot coat, blue jeans, and red boots. She turned up at a political rally for the Servants of Construction, the political faction backing her and her father, and it featured music, clapping, whistling, even dancing! Some hard-liners criticized the hoopla but they couldn't quell the excitement.

Election day itself was chaotic, as 70 percent of those eligible voted—lower than the turnout in the 1997 presidential election but extraordinary for a parliamentary election. Nazila's father, Jaffar Fathi, was a typical new voter. When I spoke with him after the election and asked him if he had voted, he said, "Of course! What a silly question." Silly question? The only other time he had voted was when his younger daughter, Golnaz, had dragged him to the polls to vote in the presidential election in 1997. This time, this retired civil servant in his sixties spent hours combing the newspapers, reading the candidates' platforms, and preparing his list of thirty candidates out of a field of 861 running in Tehran. He was so proud of his list that he drafted a second copy for his daughter. He rose at dawn on election day to beat the crowds. "It was my duty," he explained.

Voting itself was not easy. In addition to choosing candidates from long lists, voters had to write in the names of their choices by hand. Polling booths were public places, full of last-minute campaigning and lively banter. People lined up for hours at mosques and schools to hand in their ballots. As in the presidential election, the country's youth and women turned out in record numbers.

In the end, reformists routed the conservatives, winning more than 70 percent of the seats. Only 20 percent of the incumbents won reelection in the first round. In Tehran, the ratio was three out of twenty-three incumbents—and all three were reformist. Of Tehran's thirty seats, twenty-nine went to candidates endorsed by the reformist front. President Khatami's brother finished first; only Rafsanjani's thirtieth-place finish prevented a clean sweep. Early in the revolution, Ayatollah Khomeini said, "Those intellectuals who say that the clergy should leave politics and go back to the mosque speak on behalf of Satan." But the voters in 2000 made clear that the mosque is where they feel the clergy belongs. Only 14 percent of the new deputies were clerics, compared to 53 percent in the first Parliament elected in 1980. And the average age of the new Parliament was more than a decade younger than the one that came before.

From the earliest days of the Islamic Republic, the idea of a legislature had been a crucial part of Iran's government. But like so many aspects of Ayatollah Khomeini's improvised revolution, it was an idea that could always be manipulated. Soon after militants seized the American embassy in November 1979, Khomeini announced that it would be up to the Parliament to decide whether and when the hostages would be released. Only the Iranian people, he said, were capable of making the monumental decision about the hostages' fate. In reality only he had the final word. But the dictum gave him latitude to divorce himself from the consequences of being either tough or accommodating, since he had officially declared the decision out of his hands.

In time, the Parliament, which is elected by popular vote every four years, has come to have the authority to draft and pass laws, to approve cabinet members, to question government officials, and to vote for their dismissal. Parliament's sessions have been open to the public, its deliberations broadcast, and its minutes published. Yet since the revolution, Parliament has hardly been independent, and despite its ostensible openness, much about its true workings remains hidden. As few as eleven members can request a closed session. Information about the political views of most members, except those from Tehran and other big cities, is limited. Parliamentary votes, moreover, have been taken by secret ballot, so unless members make speeches explaining their votes, there has been little transparency or accountability. Even then, some deputies sometimes have made speeches one way but have voted another—or have orated in Parliament simply to ratify a decision already made.

Still, whenever I visit Iran I like to monitor debates in the cavernous parliamentary chamber with its deep blue carpet, its grand chandelier, and its elaborate interiors designed by the house of Jansen in Paris. Over the years the debates have provided a window into the everyday concerns and demands of the nation. This was particularly true in the years before Khatami was elected President, before the explosion of new newspapers and magazines. Though conservatives held the majority in those days, and did what they could to keep a strict monopoly over social and political discourse, I could always count on deputies in the Parliament, particularly those from obscure villages, to speak their minds.

Deputies often have lined up to accuse the central government of failing to deliver on promises to build roads, install electrical lines, provide jobs, or rebuild areas devastated by floods and earthquakes. Nothing has been too lofty or too petty for discussion. Deputies have debated issues such as how to encourage people to eat thick bread (which has a longer shelf life than flat bread), how to develop better packing of raisins, how to decrease meat and fish imports, how to curb corruption and profiteering, how to justify having a foreign coach train Iran's national soccer team. Deputies also have taken on sweeping philosophical issues—how to interpret the words of the late Ayatollah Khomeini in present-day policymaking and how to maintain the status of the United States as the country's number one enemy.

At times the Parliament has sought to promote economic and social justice, even at the expense of landowners and businessmen; at other times it has fought to maintain the status quo. Early on, the Parliament played its role as the protector of the oppressed much more seriously than the overseeing Guardian Council thought it should. Parliament passed a law to give to the poor land that had been confiscated from large landowners. But the council vetoed the law, arguing that "private trading" in Islam was "sacrosanct." The revolutionaries in the Parliament who truly believed in the need to bridge the gap between rich and poor were criticized as people "influenced by Marxist thought."

By the 1990s, though, much of the early leftist fervor had dissipated. The process of vetting parliamentary candidates by the Guardian Council had become so heavy-handed that the Parliament came firmly under the control of the conservatives. At times the deputies seemed more interested in making points about the dominance of conservative philosophy and power than in passing laws that could be implemented. In 1999, for example, Parliament passed a law decreeing separate medical treatment for men and women, despite fierce opposition from interest groups. Women's organizations opposed the law out of fear that women would be poorly treated; doctors argued that the law was impossible to implement; reformist newspapers objected that the debate diverted the Parliament's attention from more pressing issues. Ultimately the legislation passed, but without a mechanism to enforce it. Some critics charged that the passage itself served to degrade the authority of law, since a law that was impossible to implement was a law begging to be broken.

The problem of implementing laws, in fact, has plagued the Islamic Republic from the beginning and is most apparent not in Iran's Parliament but in its judicial system. Despite its sworn mission to enforce justice according to the Islamic legal code, or the sharia, the court system in the Islamic Republic has always been politicized. Its administration has long been in the hands of conservatives who have allowed vast room for interpretation, improvisation, and abuse. However much other institutions were being remolded by the popular pressure for reform, the judicial system remained a backwater where conservatives tried to manipulate the results—with considerable success. Yet even here, pressure for change was building.

In the two years leading up to the parliamentary election, the conservatives used the judicial system to strike back at two of Khatami's important allies within the clerical-political establishment—the popular mayor of Tehran and an even more respected member of Khatami's cabinet—securing convictions that rendered them ineligible to compete in the election. But in doing so, the conservatives also ended up expanding the battle for reform, exposing the judiciary's vulnerability to public indignation and criticism. These trials made public what everyone already knew, that in Iran citizens were not guaranteed due process or fair trials and that arbitrary arrest and detention were common.

The trials also exposed deep fault lines within Iranian society and aroused deep resentments over how the courts were being used by the clerical establishment to serve its political ends. The press covered the trials critically, making themselves vehicles for expressing public outrage over the political prosecutions. And then, the voters used the parliamentary election to register another rebuke to the system—one that the clerics could no longer ignore.

The first time I ever sat through a trial in Iran was in the summer of 1979, a few months after Khomeini's return home. I had stumbled on a makeshift courtroom in a remote part of the Iranian province of Kurdistan, where the Kurds were fighting a bloody rebellion against the new regime. Khomeini sent tanks and troops to smash it. He also sent his chief prosecutor, Sheikh Sadegh Khalkhali. Prison was not an option. At the time I met Khalkhali at his temporary headquarters in the army barracks in the town of Saqqez, he was two weeks into his job and had already ordered the execution of at least seventy-eight people. Nine of these were soldiers who had refused to fire on Kurdish rebels. Nine others accused of beheading a group of Revolutionary Guards at a hospital were lined up against the hospital wall, blindfolded. The executioners tied their necks to the bars of the windows and shot them dead.

I asked Khalkhali about his mission. "I have fire in one hand and water in the other," he said. "I have to kill the killers and make peace too. I just want the killers to know I am powerful."

Khalkhali's courtroom that day was a cramped, airless, unlit room with no furnishings except dusty cushions and carpets on the floor. About twenty spectators lined the walls. The heat was so suffocating that the plump cleric removed his turban, his cloak, and his socks. He sat barefoot on the floor and picked his toes as he heard the evidence against the defendant, a thirty-two-year-old doctor accused of handing over wounded Iranian soldiers to Kurdish rebels. The doctor, unshaven and gaunt, dressed in Army fatigues, was not allowed to speak. He had no lawyer, and there were no television cameras. Khalkhali repeatedly left the room as soldiers and drivers testified about misplaced uniforms, hostages, a car that ran out of gas, an ambulance driver who didn't know how to drive, an argument over a flashlight—everything but the charges against the doctor.

I never found out if the doctor was executed or set free. In that kind of atmosphere, it might have gone either way.

For a generation, the Iranian judicial system continued to be shrouded in secrecy. It wasn't easy for outsiders to get into courtrooms, and most trials were held in closed session. But that changed in the spring of 1998 when the authorities decided to go public with a trial and televise it nationwide. In the dock was Gholam-Hosein Karbaschi, the mayor of Tehran and a close ally of President Khatami. The charge was corruption; the underlying issue was political independence. The nation was transfixed.

Karbaschi's run-in with the law had started months before, not long after Khatami had assumed the presidency. As a mayor, newspaper publisher, and head of a newly created centrist political group called the Servants of Construction, Karbaschi had been in a position to help the Khatami campaign. And help he had, mobilizing city workers on behalf of the campaign and pumping city funds directly into Khatami's campaign coffers. The conservative clerics retaliated a few months after Khatami's victory, arresting fifty-four of Karbaschi's senior aides.

Karbaschi himself was arrested in April 1998 on charges that he had misused and diverted city funds, particularly in elaborate public works projects. The arrest unleashed a storm of debate in the press about the rule of law. Abdollah Nouri, then the Minister of the Interior, complained that neither he nor President Khatami had been told the arrest was coming. But the *Tehran Times,* a conservative English-language newspaper, took the line that the Judiciary could do no wrong. "The Judiciary in Iran is based on Islamic principles and will never allow any injustice to be done to anyone," it said. Thousands of student demonstrators who supported the mayor clashed with riot police, and the specter of a sustained, large-scale, violent public protest loomed so large that Ayatollah Khamenei intervened. After eleven days of detention, he ordered Karbaschi released on bail and sent back to work.

The trial was held at the Imam Khomeini Judiciary Complex, under the eyes of Khomeini and Khamenei, staring down from fifteen-foot portraits hung at the front of the high-ceilinged main courtroom. A handwritten banner strung along one wall read, "Prayer purifies the heart." The section where an American jury might sit was reserved for dozens of reporters and photographers. Iran's state-run television placed four cameras in the courtroom. The decision to show the trial in public reflected the extent to which public pressure had become a factor in Iranian politics. The first session was shown late at night. But after numerous complaints and the realization that the public was ready to stay up all night to watch, the officials caved in and aired the trial during prime time. Sessions began with flowery salutations to the Prophet Mohammad and lengthy readings from the Koran about the swiftness and harshness of justice.

For seven sessions over nearly five weeks, the trial gripped the nation. The mayor used wit and logic, bluster and anger to fend off charges that he had embezzled millions of dollars, taken bribes, peddled influence, financed political campaigns, and misused official funds. Parents kept their children up late at night to watch the broadcasts. The testimony was aired in restaurants, teahouses, railway stations, and airport lounges. A session I attended had been postponed for five days at the request of the media-savvy mayor, who wanted to avoid a broadcast conflict with one of Iran's games in the World Cup soccer tournament.

This was not *Perry Mason* or *Law and Order*. Rather, as my friend Hosein Nosrat in the Ministry of Islamic Guidance observed, this was the Iranian version of the O.J. Simpson trial, in which the celebrity of the accused infused the trial with a disproportionate importance. And just as the lasting impact of the O.J. trial was not his guilt or innocence, but the illumination of the racial divide in America, the lasting impact of the Karbaschi trial was the exposure of the weaknesses of the Iranian political system. It quickly became clear that the trial's true purpose was not to punish corruption but to thwart Khatami's new reformist administration. The courtroom thus became an arena in which the political struggles and debates raging inside the system were there for all to see and that was the draw. The struggle had never been played out so publicly before.

The Karbaschi trial also exposed the arbitrariness of a judicial system in which the judge (a cleric chosen for his ideological commitment to the system) also serves as prosecutor, plaintiff, and jury. For a public unused to seeing political trials, the boisterous sparring between Karbaschi and the judge, Gholam-Hosein Mohseni-Ejei, raised questions about the judicial system itself. The reality was that Mohseni-Ejei, obviously confused by his multiple roles, could not stop himself from arguing with the defendant and his lawyers about the interpretation of facts, something a prosecutor would normally do. Karbaschi exploited the situation by pointing out the judge's obvious bias. Such audacity was unusual in Iranian courtrooms. But Karbaschi was an unusual defendant.

Karbaschi showed no fear. Trained as a cleric in Qom, where he studied philosophy and religion for several years, he had been imprisoned for three years in the 1970s—much of it in solitary confinement—for political activities against the Shah. After the revolution, he was appointed governor of Isfahan, where he restored the city's historical treasures and cleaned up its tourist sites. It helped that his father, a cleric, had studied under Ayatollah Khamenei and had worked for him in Qom for years.

Later, as mayor of Tehran, Karbaschi had not been afraid to make enemies. He had bulldozed apartment buildings and built office buildings without official approval, removed revolutionary graffiti from walls, planted thousands of trees, and built dozens of parks—all in the name of transforming Tehran into a city that works. He knew how to buy the loyalty of city employees by boosting their pitiful salaries with gifts and favors. Over the objections of many clerics, he built cultural centers that showed films and plays, held athletic events, and offered music lessons to young people. He started his urban renewal projects on the gritty south side, where the poor of the city live. To spread his message, he founded a newspaper, *Hamshahri,* with city money and ran it with city money. It became the largest-circulation daily in the country. He also launched a radio station, Radio Payam, which won listeners by giving regular traffic reports, and he started one of the country's first, best, and cheapest Internet providers, Neda.net.

To pay for his campaign, Karbaschi improvised perhaps a bit too much. He raised taxes and extorted money from real estate developers, who he allowed to build high-rise apartment complexes in elegant neighborhoods, only to turn around and slap a tax of more than 30 percent on their projects. He did it not for personal gain—at least not that anyone ever proved—but to raise money for the city in the absence of a coherent local tax assessment and collection system. When shopkeepers refused to paint and fix up their storefronts, Karbaschi ordered their entryways dug up and trees planted; when traffic in Tehran paralyzed the city and destroyed the air quality, he banned all traffic except for taxis and private motorists who paid the city a hefty fee; when some small factories refused to move out of the city, he cut off their water supply.

When I first met Karbaschi, three years before his trial, he was scruffily dressed in an ill-fitting jacket and trousers and unpolished shoes. His beard was unclipped; greasy bangs fell into his eyes. I told him he had earned a reputation as the most loved and the most reviled man in Tehran. "Great people in history are like that," he said, his smile showing blackened teeth. In later encounters, I noticed that he had trimmed his hair and beard and spiffed up his wardrobe, sporting well-cut suits, Calvin Klein eyeglasses, and cologne.

During his trial Karbaschi dared to turn the tables on Mohseni-Ejei, the judge. Karbaschi played the religion card, beginning each day's testimony with prayers in Arabic praising the spiritual leaders of Shiite Islam.

He explained to the judge, "I must always start everything with the words of our leaders."

"That is fine, but not here in a court of law," Mohseni-Ejei said.

"I do not think that the words of Imam Ali would be against the rules of the court," Karbaschi said at another point.

"Yes, they are," said Mohseni Ejei. "They waste time."

Karbaschi also questioned the competence of the court to try him and pointed out that the confessions against him had been coerced through pressure, threats, and even torture. Indeed, the most extraordinary testimony focused on the issue of torture in prison. Torture has always been one of the hot-button items of Iran's revolutionary experience. Even though many of Iran's top leaders had been tortured themselves as political prisoners under the Shah, the Islamic Republic was often accused by human rights groups of mistreating and torturing prisoners, though the government consistently denied such reports.

Until the Karbaschi trial, such accusations were written only in the memoirs and testimony of exiles. But now ordinary Iranians could hear about torture on national television and read about it in the newspapers: the deputy mayor who said he had been forced to stand all night on one foot and was beaten until he fainted; a second deputy mayor who said he had been beaten mercilessly with an electrical cable, deprived of food, and forced to drink from the same cup in which he urinated; a third deputy mayor who said he could hear other prisoners crying and groaning while they were being tortured; a fourth deputy mayor who said he was forced to listen to the screams of a woman being lashed and was told that the woman was his wife.

Mohseni-Ejei struggled to suppress the testimony, but it was too late; the torture taboo had been broken. More than half of the deputies in the conservative-dominated Parliament even called for an investigation after mayoral aides related tales of their mistreatment in a meeting with legislators. Ayatollah Mohammad Yazdi, then the Chief Justice, who had ordered Karbaschi's arrest in the first place, dismissed the charges as "crocodile tears." But he replaced the head of the prison system.

It became clear as the testimony unfolded that there was ample evidence that Karbaschi had exploited the lax rules of municipal management, moved money from one account to another, traded favors, encouraged poorly paid employees with bonuses and benefits, and pressured businesses to contribute to his various beautification schemes. In the end, he was found guilty of corruption, embezzlement, and mismanagement and was sentenced to five years in prison, along with a twenty-year ban on holding executive office, sixty lashes, and billions of rials in fines. The sentence was later reduced to two years' imprisonment and a ten-year ban.

But in Iran there is always room for maneuver, even in prison. The newspaper *Khordad* reported that Karbaschi had been assigned a cell with convicts imprisoned for bouncing checks and that he had told his wife he was trying to resolve the financial problems of his new friends. The hard-line daily *Qods* reported with disdain that he did not have to wear the standard prison uniform and had turned Evin into his own private office, complete with catered meals from restaurants and two mobile phones.

The photographer and cameraman Kaveh Golestan, whom I first met during the revolution when he was on assignment for *Time* magazine, took extensive footage of Karbaschi after his verdict; one clip showed a tear in his eye. "He really liked that close-up," Kaveh told me. "So he had one of his staff call me and ask for copies of the film. But they said to me, 'Golestan, there's only one tear, only one drop. Can you show it in slow motion so that we can see the tear more?'"

Even from his cell, Karbaschi seemed to be plotting a comeback. Indeed, in January 2000, Ayatollah Khamenei suddenly granted him a pardon and set him free. Karbaschi didn't even have to pay the fine. Within a few days, he was hard at work setting up another newspaper, *Ham Mihan*. He was, however, still barred from holding government office, at least for the moment.

The Karbaschi trial turned out to be a mild prelude to a much more daring and dangerous challenge to the legitimacy of the Iranian system a year later. This was the trial of Abdollah Nouri, who had served in Khatami's cabinet. He was accused of betraying the Islamic Republic, through the ideas he had expressed. Nouri had argued that pluralism was justified under the Islamic system, which meant that the Iranian people could no longer be expected to obey a single interpretation of Islam, spoon-fed to them by the conservative clergy. The reformers and the traditionalists each claimed that both God and the late Ayatollah Khomeini were on their side. The courtroom thus became the ideological battlefield for irreconcilable beliefs about the future of the Iranian theocracy.

The stakes in Nouri's trial were much higher than in Karbaschi's. Nouri was accused not of mundane financial crimes, but of treason. Moreover, Nouri was a cleric who had been a trusted lieutenant of Khomeini and the religious guide to the Revolutionary Guards early in the revolution. He had served in Parliament. He also had been Minister of the Interior and a Vice President in Khatami's cabinet until he resigned from the latter post in February 1999 in order to run in the Islamic Republic's first local elections—in which he would receive the highest number of votes in the city of Tehran. He was already being talked about as the odds-on favorite to become Speaker of Parliament in the February 2000 parliamentary election. Nouri's supporters openly called the case against him a transparent effort by his conservative enemies to sideline him.

I saw Nouri up close at the party for his departure as Minister of the Interior in the summer of 1998. The departure was not voluntary. A group in Parliament had accused him of dismissing officials who did not share his politics, appointing like-minded men and women in their place, fostering an unstable economic environment, and putting the country's security at risk by allowing student demonstrations. Since Parliament has the power to approve and remove ministers, this group introduced a resolution to strip Nouri of his office. After a day of angry debate and personal attacks, more than half of the deputies voted to oust him. But President Khatami fought back. Within hours of the vote, he named Nouri Vice President for Development and Social Affairs, a cabinet post that did not require Parliament's approval. It was hardball politics using the rule of law as a weapon.

Nouri's going-away party was unlike any I had ever attended. Thousands of people poured into the vast auditorium at the Ministry of the Interior—men on one side, women on the other. I was required to cover every bit of hair and wipe off my lipstick. There was no chitchat. There were no canapés. Just speeches and salutes to the Prophet. The audience gasped and murmured as Mayor Karbaschi, who had been on trial at the time, marched into the auditorium and sat down next to Nouri, his political ally and friend.

Nouri hardly looked like a dangerous enemy of the state. Small of build, he wore the uniform of a cleric: a turban, a cloak, and a beard. He spoke with a squeaky voice and hints of an Isfahani accent. But Nouri, like Karbaschi, was fearless. He called his dismissal "a serious warning to the Iranian people who must not assume that all is well." And he accused unnamed enemies from "the other side" of secrecy and deception against the President.

A year later, in October 1999, the "other side" took revenge, putting Nouri on trial before the Special Clerical Court. This was not an ordinary criminal court, as in Karbaschi's trial, but a powerful conservative tribunal that tried clerics for crimes against the Islamic Republic. The forty-four-page indictment accused Nouri of insulting Islam by pushing for democratic reforms that undercut the clerical monopoly on power; dishonoring Khomeini's memory by questioning the authority of the Supreme Leader; and disseminating lies to foment unrest. Articles in *Khordad,* the outspoken newspaper that Nouri published as a daily pamphlet for his cause, were used as proof that he had conspired to undermine the Islamic state. One count charged him with advocating relations with the United States, another with seeking recognition of Israel, another with drawing comparisons between the Islamic system and the monarchy. Other counts faulted his newspapers for promoting a non-Islamic way of life. Though the court banned television cameras from broadcasting the trial, it did allow the presence of print reporters, an important concession to public pressure. Until then, all proceedings of the Special Clerical Court had been held in secret.

Like Karbaschi before him, Nouri seized the occasion of the trial to turn the spotlight around and train it on his inquisitors, charging that a system without legitimacy could not survive. Never before had someone from so deep inside the establishment been so openly critical. Because of the extensive charges against him, Nouri was able systematically to lay out what had gone wrong in the Islamic system and to show precisely how the democratic elements of the Constitution had been undermined by those in power. He did all this not by attacking the Islamic Constitution, but by using specific articles of the Constitution to question the manipulation of religion by others as a means to sustain power.

Before the trial had even begun, Nouri called his indictment illegal and politically motivated. This was another Inquisition, he said. He argued that the court had no legitimacy to try him, on the grounds that when Ayatollah Khomeini created the Special Clerical Court by personal decree, the intent had been for the court to be temporary. Nouri's newspaper *Khordad* likened his situation to the trial of the Greek philosopher Socrates. The story was accompanied by an illustration of a hand clutching a bowl of hemlock. Later the text of his testimony was published, and became an immediate best-seller, under the title, *Hemlock of Reform.*

Nouri also had powerful allies within the clerical establishment. Ayatollah Jalaleddin Taheri, the Friday prayer leader from Isfahan, declared his readiness to defend Nouri in the clerical court—a powerful political signal to the judge, Mohammad Salimi, who was lower ranking and less learned. A group of sixty Islamic scholars from seminaries in Qom also threw their support behind Nouri, backing his assertion that the clerical court was illegal.

During his six-day trial, Nouri used his impressive argumentative skills to overwhelm the judge, who at one point had to remind him that he, and not the Islamic system, was on trial. "Listen," warned Judge Salimi, "the reason we convened this court is not to give the accused a platform to cross-question those who sit in judgment on him."

Nouri paid no heed. "I totally reject the court, its membership, and its competence to conduct this trial," he said. "I ask myself, what has happened to us, to our revolution, to our faith, that it has come to this, that one group of clerics can make allegations against another like this?"

He made the point that even in an Islamic Republic, times change. People change their minds. Ayatollah Khomeini himself had repeatedly done so, and others had done things against his will, Nouri said. As evidence, he cited Khomeini's insistence that Iran would never make peace with the ruling royal family of Saudi Arabia. However, Nouri pointed out, now "the government and people of Saudi Arabia are our friends and brothers." Nouri also said that in the war against Iraq, Khomeini had vowed to continue fighting "up to the very last person," but then suddenly ended the war.

No subject was off-limits. At one point he said that it was impossible to enforce the Islamic dress code for women with clubs and batons. Nouri also outlined a vision of political rule under an Islamic democracy and a vision of Islam as a forgiving and inclusive religious system. He even claimed that there was more than one way to believe. "You cannot say that religion is limited to your particular understanding of it," he said.

The impact on many ordinary Iranians was dramatic. "I learned from his trial that even though I do not pray or fast but do many other things that I am not supposed to, I can still be considered a good Muslim!" one Iranian friend told me. "What Nouri was telling me was that the only belief that is essential is belief in the Prophet and the unity of God!"

"Breathtaking," another friend called the trial. "Nouri is practically saying that the rule of the Supreme Leader is not a holy institution and that he has no special rights outside the law. No matter what becomes of Nouri, he has opened a door that will not be closed."

The jury of theologians found Nouri guilty on fifteen counts. He was sentenced to five years' imprisonment and fined. His newspaper, *Khordad*, was closed and he went to prison, but *Khordad* was later resurrected under a new name, *Fath*. The paper continued to publish Nouri's words and statements from prison. (Later, *Fath* too was closed.) The conviction barred Nouri from running for public office or holding a position in government. With the parliamentary election less than four months away, the clerics who ran the courts had now sidelined Khatami's two top lieutenants. And they did it by using the courts and the law—arbitrary and unjust though they might be.

The public debate sparked by the Karbaschi and Nouri trials echoed throughout the campaign for Parliament. It now had become clear that the conservative clerics and politicians were using the institutions of the state to keep their hold on power and to impose their will over a society no longer willing to be bullied into submission. And the people made themselves heard in the voting on February 18 and the runoff election that followed in early May. The 2000 parliamentary elections were the third consecutive victory at the polls for Khatami and his supporters: his election as President in 1997 had been followed by the 1999 municipal council elections and this victory now gave the President a commanding majority in Parliament. The conservatives' strategy had clearly backfired.

As in other elections, many of the relatives of the powerful did well. The biggest vote-getter was the President's younger brother, Mohammad-Reza. He announced after his victory that the Parliament's top priorities would be to improve the economy, increase press freedom, and speed up reforms. Second place went to Jamileh Kadivar, the wife of Ataollah Mohajerani, Khatami's Minister of Islamic Guidance and the sister of Mohsen Kadivar, the reformist cleric who was serving a prison sentence for his writings. Third place was secured by Ali-Reza Nouri, the thirty-six-year-old younger brother of Abdollah Nouri; the younger Nouri had been studying medicine in England and had never before been active in Iranian politics. Fifth place went to Hadi Khamenei, a reformist and the estranged younger brother of the Supreme Leader.

As for Rafsanjani, the clearest explanation of why he did so badly came from Hamid-Reza Jalaiepour, writing in the newspaper *Asr-e Azadegan,* the latest reincarnation of *Jameah.* The former President "did not grasp the political climate and the democratic reforms," Jalaeipour wrote. He accused Rafsanjani of relying on political tricks and his traditional sources of power, and failing to understand that the time had come for the will of the people to prevail.

Rafsanjani had once had so much power that he was given the nickname "Akbar Shah," a play on one of his first names. What was astonishing was the speed of Rafsanjani's political demise. Just as stunning was that his daughter, Faezeh, lost her seat. The same name identification that had catapulted her to second place in the 1996 contest for Parliament plummeted her to fifty-seventh place this time. Her fatal error had been to defend her father so fiercely.

A number of powerful conservatives were toppled. Former Minister of Intelligence Ali Fallahian, who had been an architect of assassinations and terror campaigns, received a scant 28,000 votes in Isfahan. His loss, the reformist daily *Sobh-e Emrouz* wrote, was "a sign of the public opinion's hatred and sensitivity toward political killings." Mohammad-Reza Bahonar, an outspoken conservative deputy from Tehran who had been at the forefront of the campaign to push Nouri from his job as Minister of the Interior, was ousted after sixteen years in Parliament. For days, he refused to believe that the conservatives had actually lost.

Ayatollah Montazeri, still under house arrest in Qom, had enough of a voice to utter his approval of the process. An enterprising reporter from the *Irish Times* went to the home of Montazeri's son, which adjoins the house of his father, and spoke to the grand ayatollah through the brick wall dividing the two buildings. "The election should be enough to stop the bad things they have been doing to this country," Montazeri was quoted as saying.

*   *   *

Well, perhaps. As ever in Iran, it was difficult to predict just how far-reaching the effects of an event might be. But one thing at least was clear. The victory of the reformers was another dramatic event that highlighted a conundrum that had confronted the revolution since its inception: whether sovereignty in an Islamic Republic is vested in clerics who claim to be God's deputies on earth or in the people. "The Islamic leaders do not have a claim on government," said the late Ayatollah Mahmoud Taleghani, in opposing Ayatollah Khomeini's strict interpretation of an Islamic system in 1979. Twenty-one years later, Taleghani was being vindicated. The people, it turned out, believed they had just as much a claim. The election had sent a clear signal that the people were determined to break the monopoly of the conservative clerical establishment, not with violence, but with the vote.

After the election, my friend Nasser Hadian, the political scientist, told me that the vote was the revenge of the outsiders. "There were groups in Iran that had been marginalized over the years—women, youth, the modern middle class," he said. "These are groups whose standard of living—culturally, politically, economically—has declined since the revolution. They have been increasingly alienated from the political system. They voted against the status quo when they elected Khatami President in 1997 and now they've done it again. For these groups, demonstrations, riots, strikes would have costs; voting is a cost-free way to register their demands for change."

Nasser said that, in a way, the reformist victory was even more important than the election of Khatami because it had proven the staying power of the reform movement. It also offered the prospect that a majority in Parliament would succeed in endorsing at least part of Khatami's drive for political and social reforms. Perhaps, Nasser said, the new Parliament would also use its authority to investigate the institutions of the state that still lay beyond its control: the foundations, the Ministry of Intelligence, the judiciary, the military. Perhaps it would pass laws making it easier for foreign firms to invest in the country. Perhaps it would use its power to fulfill its pledges to pass laws making the Iranian political system more inclusive and accountable.

But Iranian politics remains an open-ended game in which goals are tactical and reactions are based on what may happen tomorrow, not five years from now. Nasser suddenly stopped himself. He warned that the big win for the reformists signaled the beginning of a dangerous time in Iranian politics. The victory did not change the fact that, even working together, the President and the Parliament did not control many levers of power. A sustained backlash from the right was a dangerous possibility. "Many, many analysts, even secular ones, are convinced that these guys in the reform movement are moving too fast," Nasser said. "The reformers cannot pass laws by themselves. The elections have produced a large weak majority inside the Parliament without much power outside, and a small powerful minority outside the Parliament with control over the economic and political levers of power." This minority, he said, would not be likely to give up.

In addition, the Guardian Council can veto any legislation it deems un-Islamic. Any insoluble dispute between the Parliament and the Guardian Council can be resolved by the larger Expediency Council, of which Rafsanjani is still the head. "There should have been a way to keep Rafsanjani inside the tent," Nasser said. "He should never have been discredited like that. He would have made the pace of change slower, but safer. We don't have enough of a center. That makes it a dangerous time."

Indeed, after the election an article in the ultraconservative newspaper *Jebheh,* called for the police and volunteer forces to increase "their moral, social, and cultural enforcement and carry out Islamic punishments precisely, so the middle class feels fed up and believes the reformists are incompetent." The first act of revenge came swiftly. Less than a month after the parliamentary elections, Saeed Hajjarian, an intellectual pillar of Khatami's reform movement and a key organizer of the reformer's landslide victory, was shot and critically wounded by two assailants who approached on a motorcycle.

Hajjarian had made many enemies, particularly among right-wing extremists opposed to President Khatami's cultural, social, and political reforms. Having served as deputy Minister of Intelligence from 1984 to 1989, Hajjarian had first-hand knowledge of how the ministry operated. He later turned reformer, using the newspaper, *Sobh-e Emrouz,* to publish exposés of the Intelligence Ministry and its involvement in political murders over the years. The conservatives also used legal means at their disposal to forestall change before the new Parliament took power. The restrictive press law that sparked the nationwide unrest in mid-1999 was hurriedly passed. Even more serious, the Expediency Council, led by Rafsanjani, decreed that the new Parliament had no authority to investigate any institution or foundation under the purview of the Supreme Leader.

Then the conservative forces shut down reformist newspapers and magazines, arrested leading reformers, and flagrantly tampered with election results throughout the country. There was open talk of a creeping coup by the conservatives to weaken or overthrow Khatami. But these actions did not kill the reform movement. The impetus for accommodation remained strong on both sides. The goal, it seemed, was to seek some sort of equilibrium, however uneasy it might be, between the people and the theocrats.

There were even predictions that if the reformists could successfully circumvent the undemocratic elements within the Iranian political system, the outcome could have far-reaching implications not only for Iran but also for the Islamic world. The Parliamentary elections of 2000 seemed to transform the image of Iran around the world from an authoritarian, rigidly Islamic state to a vibrant political system that had proven many of its critics wrong in its ability to push for democratic change. Unlike most of the Arab Middle East, for example, Iran had shown that democratization in the region—however episodic it could be—was possible. Iranians knew it; so did their nighbors. Iraq, Syria, Libya and Egypt, for example, had long been controlled by leaders backed by the military. New monarchs took power in Jordan, Bahrain, and Morocco in 1999—after their fathers died. "In spite of the fact that it is a theocratic state ruled by a group of clerics," wrote Riad Najib Rayyes in Lebanon's *An Nahar* newspaper, Iran "has managed over the course of twenty years to nurture institutions . . . based on a mechanism of democratic competition." The London-based pan-Arab newspaper, *Al Qods al Arabi*, wrote, "To put it very simply, Iran is moving forward. We are moving too: backward."

Of course, it was possible that the conservatives would seek to snuff out the democratic movement altogether. But what an irony it would be if a generation after Iran shook the Muslim world with its revolution and its pledge to export its model of theocracy, it exported a model—however imperfect—of democracy instead.

PART FIVE

———

Dreams

CHAPTER SIXTEEN

Making Money God's Way

The mullahs have become God and the people have become poor.

— CHANT BY DEMONSTRATING STUDENTS IN TEHRAN
IN JULY 1999

*The crisis of unemployment, the crisis of recession, the crisis of inflation
and high prices, these crises can do to Iran what the United States and
world imperialism have been unable to do.*

— HASSAN GHAFURIFARD, DEPUTY FROM TEHRAN,
IN DEBATE IN PARLIAMENT, AUGUST 11, 1999

*You know what could make a killing here? Starbucks! Imagine it! There's
no alcohol here. I've got just the guy to invest in it. I'm going to talk to him
when I get back to the States.*

— DR. SHELDON KATZ, AMERICAN TOURIST AND
RETIRED NEUROLOGIST

LET ME TELL YOU a little bit about the background of Islamshahr,"
Ali-Reza Shiravi told me as we drove on a modern highway to the dusty,
crowded, impoverished town twenty-five miles south of Tehran. "It used
to belong to landowners—big and small—who grew crops and raised
cattle. But then the revolution and the war with Iraq came. The town became full of Turkish and Kurdish people from the villages near the border." That, he said, was when the economy went to pieces, shattered by
the pressure of too many refugees and too little work to sustain them.

I couldn't have asked for a better guide to Islamshahr than Shiravi.
Not only was he the deputy director of the foreign press in the Ministry
of Islamic Guidance, but he also had lived in the town for most of his life.

Even though Shiravi was only thirty-three, he was known and respected by the local officials. He had extraordinary patience; seven and a half years as a prisoner of war in Iraq had taught him that. The experience also had taught him fluent Arabic and passable English. And those skills, plus honesty and hard work, had landed him his coveted post in the ministry.

Shiravi and his wife, Massoumeh, had one child, Mohammad-Javad, a boy of eight. One child was all they could afford. But Shiravi loved what he did for a living. And his years in the prison camp had earned him double credit for his time of service in the government, which meant that he could retire with a pension in six more years. He would study law then; for the moment, he was proud to show me around his hometown.

It was July 1999, soon after the student riots had rocked the nation. Islamshahr was unaffected by them, but it had suffered through its own revolt four years before, the last time I had visited. In some ways, that revolt was a small-scale dress rehearsal for the unrest that had just come.

Islamshahr is a microcosm of the economic problems that plague Iranians—high inflation, high unemployment, high expectations. Once a small village that was a center for cattle, sheep, and crop farmers, Islamshahr has seen its population swell to 250,000 as peasants have fled the countryside and Afghans have fled their war-torn country in search of work in or near Tehran. Over time, the town has become ringed by shantytowns of houses slapped together with cement and scrap metal. Electricity service became sporadic and social services nonexistent.

In the spring of 1995, inflation hit Iran hard. One morning, the independently operated minibuses that transported day laborers to Tehran doubled their fares. The commuters revolted, blocking the roads and preventing the minibuses from leaving.

"It was the time of the Iranian New Year, when people had to have money to buy new clothes for their kids," Shiravi explained. "When workers protested the bus prices that morning, an official from the municipality came to calm them down. But he antagonized them instead. He said, 'So what that the fare has increased? You should pay it.' The number of protesters grew. They set fire to a bank. Then they moved on to Islamshahr. They set fire to another bank and then another. More people joined in. They smashed the windows of stores and burned gas stations and municipal buildings. They even attacked the Ministry of Education building."

The government rushed in anti-riot police, who fired wildly and

fought hit-and-run battles with protesters. Plainclothes intelligence officials patrolled the streets and arrested dozens of people. By the time the
riots were put down at nightfall, the streets were strewn with broken
glass, burned tires, bricks, and rubble. Several people had been killed. The
next day, hundreds of police officers lined the streets of Islamshahr as authorities bused in thousands of people to chant pro-government slogans.
The families of the dead were made to repay the police for the bullets that
had been fired. Public mourning was prohibited. No official death toll
was released.

But the bus fares came down.

When I visited Islamshahr a few weeks after those riots in 1995, an air
of fear still hung over the town. The governor refused to talk to me. An
official of a bank that had been burned pleaded with me not to ask him
questions. Most shopkeepers and residents I approached told me they
had not been in town that day. But I finally found a hotel worker who
said he had been an eyewitness to a killing. "I saw a soldier take out his
gun, point it at a man, and pull the trigger," he recalled. "The soldiers
took away the body. They cleaned up the blood right away. It was very
professional."

The owner of a fabric store told me something else. "There was nothing political about the riots," he said. "They were all because of inflation."

That last comment came back to me when I returned to Islamshahr
four years later. I arrived better prepared this time, with Shiravi and with
stamped letters of introduction from the ministry where he worked.

Our first stop was a courtesy call on the governor, Buyuk Mousavi,
whose office was in the midst of a major renovation. He told me of his
pride in the city. Islamshahr is, indeed, a town in transition. After the 1995
unrest, the central government poured in millions of dollars, in large part
to stanch dissent. Apartment blocks with electricity and running water
replaced concrete shacks. Murals of flowers and landscapes were painted
on walls. Building codes were strictly enforced. A regulation banning all
new settlements finally brought migration to an end.

Islamshahr now boasts new roads, new monuments, a conference
hall, a cultural center, a telecommunications building, an amusement
park, a university for five hundred students, and an air-conditioned
movie theater. "We don't have any problems anymore," Mousavi said.

But construction projects and agriculture have not solved the unemployment problem. The work is dirty, backbreaking and low paying.

Many of the poorest Iranians prefer unemployment, leaving the construction companies and farms to hire undocumented Afghan workers instead.

We drove past the bus stop where the trouble began in 1995. A few hundred men and boys stood idly, waiting for day work that did not come. At an open area with a long line of public telephones, dozens of young men competed to sell telephone cards for a tiny profit as they complained about their lives. "Look at all of us," said one young man in his twenties, pointing to his friends. "We're all jobless. We have nothing to do. We try to do a little bit of business here and there and we get arrested as troublemakers. That's why there are so many drug addicts here. It's the despair."

On another corner near the town's main park were three young men—a soldier in civilian clothes, a musician in jeans and a slicked-back puffy hairdo, and a paramilitary Islamic volunteer turned drug addict. "I just exist," said the musician. "I make enough to get food and shelter. I can't play my music in public. How could I ever get enough money to get married? You'll always find me here, on this corner. I wouldn't dare go to the park over there because everyone is addicted. They're all shooting heroin. As for politics, I'm like a turtle. I keep my head inside my shell."

Then it was the turn of the Islamic volunteer with the sallow complexion and yellow in his eyes. "Can I talk?" he said. "I fought forty months in the war against Iraq. When I came back the regime abandoned me." He acknowledged his addiction, which he said he supported with occasional day jobs and the charity of his friends. "The youth are becoming drug addicts," he said. "We have no freedom, no jobs, nowhere to go and have fun. So we are all addicts. The corruption is so bad that the government pays the demonstrators to chant. I know, because I used to be one of them."

Iran has a lot of drug addicts. Heroin from neighboring Afghanistan is plentiful and cheap. The official estimate is that there are as many as 1.2 million addicts among a population approaching 65 million. Sixty percent of the inmates in Iran's crowded prisons have been convicted of drug possession, dealing, or trafficking. To reduce the prison population, the judiciary has stopped jailing offenders, and instead has begun to fine and lash them and send them to outpatient clinics. Not all of the men on that corner were drug addicts. But depression was something they all understood.

"I would hang myself if I weren't so afraid," the musician said quietly.

"But suicide is against Islam," said the soldier. "And we believe in God."

There was a long, uncomfortable silence. Then the musician changed the subject. "Come to our house for lunch today!" he said.

I knew he didn't really mean it. It was an invitation that was supposed to be refused. But it was the most intimate thing he could say to me, and I thanked him over and over for the kind offer, even as I declined.

In their own way, these men are just as disaffected from the Islamic government as the student demonstrators in Tehran. They share the same desires for personal freedoms. It is just that in Islamshahr, the freedom that matters is a job. They will not rebel over the closure of a newspaper. But they might over the price of a bus ticket.

Indeed, for four hours one day in January 2000, a crowd from the slum of Chahar-Dongeh just outside Islamshahr blocked the main road, smashed the windows of a public clinic, and attacked a municipal kiosk. The crowd was protesting a decision to detach its town from Tehran (and its many social benefits) and annex it to Islamshahr. "Unfortunately the lack of attention to the problems of our residents has laid the groundwork for dissatisfaction and social protests," Governor Mousavi was quoted as saying. "We have repeatedly communicated the problem to the authorities in Tehran but our efforts have been fruitless."

So much for Islamshahr not having problems anymore.

On paper Iran is a rich country. It has 10 percent of the world's oil reserves and is the only nation with direct access to both the lucrative oil fields of the Persian Gulf and to the untapped oil reserves of the Caspian Sea. It also has the largest gas reserves in the world after Russia and sizable deposits of coal, sulfur, gold, silver, magnesium, and phosphates. Its gross domestic product is growing (although slowly) and foreign exchange reserves and foreign private investment in gas and oil development are increasing. Iran has made timely payments on its foreign debt and has a much lower debt burden than most developing countries of its size and population.

But when it comes to the economy, the Islamic Republic faces enormous obstacles. Religious ideology has hindered the country's integration into the new global economy. Structural barriers have scared away foreign investors. And traditional habits, including corruption, have inhibited the growth of a native entrepreneurial class. All of this cuts to the heart of the revolution itself, which promised not only to make Iranian society more pious, but also more equitable. That is one reason the reformers have so much political appeal; it is hard to fulfill the promises of a social revolution if the economy is in dangerous straits.

To an outsider, Iran doesn't look poor. Children don't have orange hair from severe malnutrition, as they do in parts of Pakistan and India. Beggars clog the streets, but there are no massive epidemics from bad water and there is little homelessness. Shops and restaurants have plenty of customers. Domestic airline flights, heavily subsidized, are always overbooked. The shelves of the twenty-four-hour supermarket chain are well stocked.

But there is no question that Iran's economy is in crisis. By some estimates, inflation runs as high as 40 percent and unemployment more than 30 percent. According to the World Bank, Iran's per capita income is just under $1,800, less than it was when the Shah left. Worse, the rial has been in free fall against the dollar. The dollar was worth seventy rials when the revolution overthrew the Shah in 1979. In 2000, the exchange rate was more than a hundred times higher. Officials acknowledged that they needed to create several hundred thousand new jobs each year to cope with the economic crisis, but they had no real plan to make that happen.

In making his revolution, Ayatollah Khomeini pledged to liberate the country from its dependence on oil revenues and to preserve the country's oil wealth for future generations. In Khomeini's eyes, the Shah had pumped too much oil and wasted the profits on useless weapons and grandiose projects. But Khomeini fared no better. With the exodus of foreign companies and their cadre of experts after the revolution, the government was left to develop these fields on its own, a difficult task that was further complicated by the war with Iraq, which damaged important installations in Iran's western provinces. To finance the war, Iran came to rely even more on oil as its main source of foreign exchange, leaving the country more dependent than ever on prices set by the fickle global oil market. The 1990s were devastating; oil prices, which hit $40 a barrel just after the revolution, fell to less than $10 a barrel by 1999. The government suspended most development projects, curbed imports, and rescheduled some foreign debt. When prices rose again to $34 a barrel after OPEC tightened production quotas at the turn of the century, Iran enjoyed a windfall once more. But that price fluctuation clearly has underscored the economy's unpredictability and dependence on outsiders that Khomeini had vowed to end. About 85 percent of Iran's hard currency comes from oil imports. And some of Iran's major fields, active for more than seventy years, need enormous investments if they are to maintain production.

But Iran's problems run far deeper than unpredictable commodity prices. Structurally, the economy would not make sense to either a committed capitalist or a committed socialist. The country has a centuries-old tradition of free trade and commerce, but today, 80 percent of the economy is directly or indirectly controlled by the government. The government runs all large-scale industries and mines, banking and insurance enterprises, power, utilities, radio and television, mail and telephone service, and the transportation infrastructure. This public sector is inefficiently run, top-heavy with bureaucrats, and incapable of stopping money-losing projects. Some of its decision-making defies common sense. When three of Tehran's main hospitals, for example, failed to pay their electric bills, the Ministry of Energy turned off their electricity for several hours, forcing the cancellation of surgery and wreaking havoc in the emergency rooms.

Compounding the problem is that the Islamic Republic has not resolved a basic tension that has existed from its beginning: how to balance its ideological commitment to help the *mostazafan,* the deprived ones, with a much older impulse in Persia's trading culture: making money. The government maintains massive subsidies, price controls, and foreign exchange allocations designed to placate the lower classes, but these eat up 20 percent of Iran's gross domestic product. And the subsidies on things like gasoline, bread, power, water, and transportation are not restricted to the poor; all Iranians share, regardless of need.

The government has taken some steps to confront the hard times. In fact, it has become rather creative at raising money. It sells the right to leap to the top of the long list of those seeking to make the pilgrimage to Mecca. (The Saudis have strict quotas.) It allows young men to buy their way out of the draft. It sells Treasury bonds and offers 20 percent "increase on maturity" (to keep up with the officially acknowledged rate of inflation), even though charging or paying interest is considered un-Islamic. It promotes tourism for Westerners. It even speculates on the future through bonds to investors that will be paid with tomorrow's oil revenues.

Iran began to woo back exiles with promises to return lands, homes, and businesses confiscated after the revolution, accompanied by a promise to pursue their claims. The father of a friend of mine decided to test the system to reclaim a giant piece of land, in Rasht, on which a large fruit and vegetable market had been built. After fierce court battles and enormous legal bills, the man won. The land was his. But then the city of Rasht refused to turn it over to him. And no court has forced it to do so.

Iran's economy is further hamstrung by the tension between the need for capitalist growth and the drive for piety. As part of the campaign to curb consumerism early in the revolution, advertising billboards were replaced with ones that extolled the virtues of the revolution and later the war with Iraq. Then, suddenly and without explanation, it was acceptable to advertise again. My favorite billboard was one with a double message that was mounted at one busy intersection in Tehran in 1999. It displayed alternately an advertisement for French perfume and the slogan, "Rush quickly to your prayers."

Of course, many in Iran's leadership still insist that the country's economic problems are the creation of the United States. And indeed, damaging the Iranian economy was a stated goal of U.S. policy through much of the Clinton administration. In 1995 the administration imposed a unilateral embargo, having long discouraged its allies from trading with Iran and having blocked loans through sources like the World Bank. In 1996 Clinton signed anti-terrorism legislation that imposed sanctions on foreign firms that invested more than $40 million (later reduced to $20 million) in Iran's oil and gas sector. A mild thaw came only in 1999, when America eased the embargo to allow American farmers to sell grain to the Islamic Republic and to allow Iran to buy spare parts for its aging fleet of Boeing civilian aircraft, and again in 2000 when the ban on the export of carpets and some foodstuffs to the United States was lifted.

Even so, most of the problems in the economy are attributable to the Iranian system itself, a fact that more and more Iranians have come to acknowledge. "The economic crisis can no longer be blamed on the enemy plots or the collapse in oil prices," said a 1998 article in the reformist daily newspaper *Sobh-e Emrouz.* "The problem is the country's mismanagement."

Indeed, there are few incentives for either domestic or foreign investment. Small, independent businesspeople suffer from the irrational and ever-changing rules of doing business. A middle-class Iranian woman I know who runs a small clothing factory once received permission to import a large quantity of denim from Turkey. She hired a hundred workers and signed a contract with a Turkish firm to take delivery of the fabric. Just before the delivery date, the authorities denied her the permission to import the fabric. No reason was given. She speculated that she was the victim of a broader government campaign to curb imports as a way to reduce the flow of hard currency from the country. Her company nearly went bankrupt.

Foreign firms have been wary of investing in Iran, remembering that in the aftermath of the revolution, the new regime confiscated hotels, banks, factories, farms, and countless other enterprises. The government has tried a variety of ways to woo back investors—in the late 1990s a law was adopted to guarantee the safety of investments by foreign firms—but the damage had been done. In the current global economy, with its wealth of economic opportunities, it would take a special steadiness of nerve and a special attraction to Iran to persuade foreign investors to choose it as the place to put their money. In 1999, in assigning the Islamic Republic its first credit rating, Moody's Investor Service gave it a B2, one notch below Lebanon and one notch above Russia.

One factor is that the Constitution and the laws are maddeningly vague and subject to manipulation and abuse. Confirmation of a letter of credit from an Iranian bank can require more than twenty procedures involving three ministries and five departments of the Central Bank. The Constitution mandates an economy "in accordance with Islamic principles," but fails to spell out what that means.

An Iranian economist who had been a cabinet minister under the Shah told me an illuminating story about the government's efforts to induce investment in the early 1990s. "The government told investors to build high-rise buildings because land was becoming so expensive," he said. "So a number of people connected to the regime borrowed money from the banks at low interest rates. They made tremendous amounts of money. Suddenly the leftist press started screaming about all these leeches and profiteers. The investors were brought to court. The judge ruled that many of them had earned their money illegally. Some of them ended up in prison; one was executed. All they had done was what the government encouraged them to do."

The one area where the potential for foreign investment is high, and the competition intense, is in gas and oil. Iran continues to discover new oil fields; foreign companies are vying for dozens of projects. But Iran has been slow to award the contracts—a result of bureaucratic bungling and opposition from conservative factions who still want to keep out foreign influences. When Royal Dutch/Shell signed a contract in late 1999 to invest almost $800 million in Iran's oil industry, for example, the ultra-conservative daily newspaper *Jomhouri-ye Islami* complained that the contract with the Anglo-Dutch firm will "once again allow Britain to se-cure a foothold in Iran."

Perhaps the largest, and strangest, of the structural problems in Iran's economy is the vast system of foundations, or *bonyads,* that were set up shortly after the revolution to promote broad economic justice. The *bonyads* confiscated billions of dollars in assets of the former royal family, banks, and ordinary homeowners. They even confiscated the personal belongings of some American diplomats seized as hostages in 1979.

Two decades after the revolution, the foundations are among the biggest economic complexes in the Middle East, operating as tax-exempt state-protected organizations that enjoy financial benefits, award contracts to the favored few, and confuse the distinction between public and private. The foundations, for example, can borrow money from the Central Bank at less than half the rate offered to private businesses. Most of them are the individual fiefs of powerful clerics, and their size crowds out smaller pri-vate competitors who might be more efficient, even as their corruption fuels resentment. There are foundations for the "oppressed," for housing, for refugees, for victims of the war with Iraq, for the cinema, for Islamic propaganda. One foundation administers the enormous shrine of Imam Reza in Mashad with an annual budget of $2 billion (according to some es-timates), and owns or controls much of Khorasan province.

The Foundation for the Oppressed and War Veterans, by far the largest of the *bonyads,* controls an estimated $12 billion in assets, includ-ing thousands of factories employing some 400,000 workers. Established in March 1979, just a month after the Islamic revolution, this foundation was given the responsibility of managing the land, property, and posses-sions confiscated from the Shah, his family, and the country's fifty-one largest industrialists. The foundation owns global shipping lines based in London and Athens; chemical plants, construction material factories, soybean, wheat, and cotton farms near the Caspian Sea; the former Hilton and Hyatt hotels in Tehran; Zam Zam, the country's largest soft-drink company; and thousands of apartments. It even exports nonalcoholic beer. Its subsidiaries import Japanese cars and trade crude oil through London. "We touch the life of every Iranian," Mohsen Rafiqdoust, then the head of the foundation, once told an interviewer from the *Christian Science Monitor.* He was not exaggerating.

Perhaps nowhere is the rule of law touted by President Khatami so flagrantly violated as by the foundations. They ignore laws that require them to submit their balance sheets to the court in charge of auditing. They ignore tax, tariff, and currency laws. I know a French businessman who imported spare parts for the Iranian oil industry for nearly twenty years, but when he ran afoul of one of the foundations, no threats were necessary to eliminate him from the scene. He just stopped getting visas.

The corruption in many foundations reflects a more widespread corruption in all sectors of the economy. Payoffs are needed to obtain a government contract, to get a permit or license, to get raw materials or goods through customs, to price goods in the market. Police officers openly stop motorists and pedestrians and ask for protection money. One policeman who patrols the street where a friend lives stopped her one day and said simply, "It's Friday." In other words, Friday is the weekend, the street is safe, and a reward is in order. All of this breeds a general cynicism. With about 60 percent of the economy exempt from taxation through various arrangements with the government, it is not surprising that roughly 85 percent of the population evades income tax.

Yet some of Iran's most senior clerical leaders dismiss the importance of corruption. After the arrest in 1998 of Mayor Karbaschi on corruption charges, former President Rafsanjani wondered what all the fuss was about. "Graft has always existed," he said in a sermon. "There are always people who are corrupt." But then again, the reformist press had openly accused members of Rafsanjani's family of corruption, and Karbaschi, though a reformer himself, had old ties to Rafsanjani.

I have gone looking for clues to Iran's economic predicament in Tehran's Grand Bazaar. What I have found is a hive of tradition, immensely captivating in its color and cultural roots, impressive in the spirit of its private enterprise, that is nevertheless playing a big part in stifling the country's economy. It also provides a power base for a class of politically conservative merchants.

There is permanence to the bazaar. What the British writer, traveler, and diplomat Gertrude Bell wrote in 1894 about the vast marketplace in Tehran holds true today. "The whole bazaar resounds with talk, with the cries of the mule-drivers, the tinkling bells of the caravans, and the blows of the smiths' hammers," she said. "The air is permeated with the curious smell, half musty, half aromatic, of fruits and frying meats, merchandise and crowded humanity."

The bazaar in Tehran covers a vast area in the city's oldest sector and is built on an angle to the street grid so that it can face Mecca. The six hundred shops and stalls spill out onto neighboring streets lined by crumbling buildings with wrought iron balconies dating back to the early part of the century.

Except for the carpet sellers, most of the Tehran bazaar is not geared to outsiders and especially not to tourists. Rather it is a vast shopping warehouse for wholesalers and the lower classes. I once tried to buy a few sheets of gift-wrapping paper. I was told I had to buy a hundred. It really isn't necessary for most shoppers to go to the bazaar anymore, especially since Mayor Karbaschi built twenty-four-hour chain stores throughout Tehran.

The Tehran bazaar is divided according to trade. There are streets named after the gold sellers, the shoe sellers, the fabric sellers. The narrow passageways are choked with people, not only shoppers but wizened porters pushing wide wooden carts piled high with goods, boys carrying scalding pots of tea and trays of glasses, other boys pretending to sell tea who are really selling pirated CDs and cassette tapes, men driving their motorcycles through the bazaar oblivious to the no-driving rule.

The bazaar is also a densely built community center—a maze of mosques, public baths, religious schools, teahouses, unlit alleys, and back rooms that serve as meeting places and centers of communication and discovery. I turn one corner and come upon *Timche Hajebol-doleh*, an open space lit from a hole in the beautifully tiled ceiling. I turn another and find a headquarters of the Revolutionary Guards. I turn yet another and find myself at a mosque at midday where some men pray while others carry food, mend clothes, sell cigarettes. A lone leper begs; a dervish negotiates a deal.

I went to the bazaar one day with Peyman, a charming young man who owns a small clothing manufacturing company. He knows his way around because he goes there to buy his fabric. He told me that Mayor Karbaschi had wanted to make changes in the bazaar, but the merchants don't much like change. Peyman pointed out a nearby park—not much of a park, with mangy grass and scraggly flowers. "Karbaschi tried to build a ten-story parking lot," Peyman told me. "The project started and the cement was laid. But there were objections. The *bazaari* said, 'The bazaar has been like this for a hundred years. We want to keep it that way.' Karbaschi was an outsider and they didn't want him to get a foot in here. They took their objections to their supporters in Parliament who also objected. It went all the way up to the Leader. The parking lot was stopped."

There are invisible boundaries here—of smell, of sound. And there are closed places where only the invited enter. On my trip with Peyman, I peered into small rooms behind glass doors where a group of six to eight men sat, talking. The Azeris dominate the bazaar, and much of its business is conducted in Turkish, not Persian. Instead of secret handshakes and passwords, the *bazaari* call each other *haj agha,* an honorific that combines "Mr." with the title *haji,* an assumption that the addressee has made the pilgrimage to Mecca at least once.

There are no computers in sight but plenty of abacuses and adding machines. There are no female merchants either. In Tehran's bazaar, women have only one role. "It's tradition," Peyman said. "Women can shop but they cannot sell."

We stopped at the stall of a young fabric merchant named Shahin, who asked us to sit and served us tea. His grandfather had been a bazaar merchant, and his father's stall was nearby. Shahin called himself a "new *bazaari.*" He didn't pray; he didn't believe in the superstitions that governed the *bazaari* world. "Don't misplace anything on Wednesdays or Sundays," Shahin said mockingly. "Otherwise you will not sell them. Always cut fabric on Mondays."

I asked Shahin why there were no computers in any of the stalls. Superstition, it turned out, had nothing to do with it.

"*Bazaari* are afraid of tax collectors," he said. "*Bazaari* will do anything to avoid taxes. Sometimes people have big offices upstairs. That's where they hide their computers. They don't want the tax collectors to see them. We want to have everything as simple and as old as possible. People with mobile phones hide them in a drawer.

"We have an expression in the bazaar. You have five fingers but you have to hide one of them. Show only four fingers. We always say that business is bad. There's always a recession. If people don't think your business is bad, they may give you the evil eye and make your business bad. There's always the fear that if one businessman is too successful the others will unite against him."

In a taxi on the way home, Peyman asked me what I thought of the *bazaari*. Then he answered his own question. "I hate the *bazaari*. They have very cushy jobs. I'm a producer. I make things. I have to buy the buttons, the zippers, the cloth, the thread. I have to employ seamstresses. I create jobs for others. In my workshop I support at least ten people and their families. Under the law, I can't fire them if they don't perform. All the *bazaari* do is buy and sell. They don't put things in the ground to grow. They don't pay taxes. Every time the rial loses its value, *bazaari* hoard their goods. But they make a lot of money. If they invested their money in production, things would change. It would build strong pillars for the economy. But they're just middlemen. Buy and sell. Sell and buy. That's all they do."

Peyman had put his finger on one of the reasons why Iran's economy doesn't grow. The *bazaari* aren't investors looking to build the country over the long haul. They are cash-and-carry merchants looking for quick deals. They finance most private industry at interest rates of 7 percent per month. The government allows them to import goods at special exchange rates. Traditional in their business habits, they don't computerize or trade on the Internet, or they hide the fact that they do so. Religious, the *bazaari* have had a close alliance with the clerics since the nineteenth century. The money that many *bazaari* gave to the mosques and their decision to shut down in the months before the revolution were critical for Ayatollah Khomeini's success. They continue to support some of the country's key clerics, and in turn those clerics protect the interests of the bazaar.

In the end, all of this economic irrationality has hurt the middle class the most. The rich and the politically connected have done just fine, accumulating wealth through trading and real estate and currency speculation; the poor have benefited from the revolution's massive subsidies, better access to education and housing and building projects. But for the middle class, living standards have deteriorated. I just needed to look at Nazila's family to see that. Her father, a retired government official, had studied in England and later lived abroad, as had many middle-class professionals. But when the time came to send Nazila and her sister, Golnaz, to college, there was only enough money to send them to local universities.

In that atmosphere, survival has become the mark of success for the middle class. I am close to a woman whose entire family was in one way or another involved in government service at the time of the Shah. Most of them lost their jobs or chose to resign their positions after the revolution. So they reinvented themselves as small entrepreneurs: an oil company scientist and researcher went to work for a private medical laboratory and later managed to help found a medical laboratory; a naval officer became the owner of a furniture store; his wife, a homemaker, helped in the lean years by setting up a thriving home-based business making and selling clothes; an engineer founded his own contracting business.

My friend Abdol-Karim managed to survive in a different way—by working *with* the Islamic Republic. A gregarious man of sixty with a big nose, big smile, big mustache, and big Rolex watch, he isn't a classic *bazaari,* tied to one product and hiding his money. But he is a trader, an import-export merchant, buying from Japan, South Korea, China, Europe, even the United States, and selling whatever the market wants. He circumvents the American embargo by moving goods through subsidiaries in Toronto and Dubai. He can get a top-of-the line GE Profile refrigerator for $3,500, a hefty sum, but not unrealistic in Iran for a well-made status symbol. Peyman would not approve of him, because he is a trader who turns a profit, not an investor who helps create jobs and self-sufficiency.

Over lunch one day in the comfortable apartment he shares with his wife, Abdol-Karim recalled the day he stood on the roof of a building in what he still calls "Eisenhower Square" (the revolution renamed it *Azadi* or Freedom Square), when Khomeini came home. "I said to myself, 'From this day on, I won't have to bribe anyone anymore.' The next time I was at customs, I told the officer to get my goods without a bribe, and he did. But within only three months, things changed. They were exactly like they were before." The new government confiscated Abdol-Karim's share in a bank and a factory. He lost about $600,000. It took years to rebuild his business.

Abdol-Karim made friends with people in the ministries, particularly in the Ministry of Defense, and in the foundations. One of his specialties was finding American-made spare parts for military vehicles and equipment from third countries. (He said he drew the line at selling American-made parts for weapons. He spends about three months a year in the

United States and has no intention of landing in an American prison.) He boasted that a deal that would take a government office six months takes him only three days. Still, he can't compete with the foundations. He pays taxes; they don't. They have access to low-interest bank loans; he doesn't.

I asked him why he didn't move to the United States, where he had family. "I love doing business over there," he said. "People keep their promises in business. But it's too far away. Too lonesome. They still need my expertise here. I'm needed. And I have family here. I get homesick for the Eastern way of life."

His wife, who had been silent for much of the lunch, suddenly piped up. "I go crazy in the States after only ten days," she said. "I even miss the grocery store on the corner. I feel easy here, peaceful. I even love the weather. I just don't feel that way there."

Easy? Peaceful? In a country where you never know when you might be stopped on the street by a thug telling you to fix your head scarf? But Abdol-Karim's life is an ordinary, nonpolitical, and family-centered one. For him, at least, business isn't bad. He and his wife are in good health. And they own a small house on the Caspian coast just a block from the sea, in a country they love.

They have, in short, survived. It is because of people like Abdol-Karim that the country limps along. It is also because of people like him—traders, not investors—that the economy doesn't grow.

In addition to survivors, Iran still has dreamers. Hosein Sabet is one. He is building an Iranian Disneyland. Or maybe I should say Wonderland, because he is trying to make Iran a tourists' paradise. And the effort, once you take a close look, just gets curiouser and curiouser.

Sabet is thin, tanned, fit, and long-haired. He is clean-shaven, wears un-Islamic short-sleeved shirts unbuttoned one button too many, and he shook my hand.

"Sabet was well born," he said of himself over pastries and tea in the white-walled, modernistic headquarters of the Sabet Organization, which looks out over the Persian Gulf. "His grandfather owned vast estates; his father had been a wealthy tea merchant.

"Since I was a child I had three dreams: to become a businessman, a helicopter pilot, and a magician. I have become all three." He entered the tourist business by building an empire of seven hotels in the Canary Islands that catered to German tourists. Years later, he said, his late mother came to him in a dream and said, "Build a bridge and go back to Iran." He decided to go home. He went to Kish, an island off the southern coast of Iran lined with sterile, air-conditioned, glass-and-marble duty-free shopping centers. He bought two hundred acres that included a partially built luxury hotel from the time of the Shah, which he redesigned with the help of Spanish and British architects to look like a modern-day Persepolis. He uprooted ten thousand palm trees and ten thousand evergreens from the mainland and transplanted them. He brought in hundreds of tons of soil. He built a water desalination system. When U.S. sanctions prevented him from buying the American-made aquarium-quality glass he needed, he hired European technicians to manufacture it in Germany. He designed a butterfly enclave and giant volcano exhibit, a rain forest with hundreds of exotic birds. He built international restaurants representing the cuisine of different countries. There would be no showgirls or alcohol at his nightclub, but there would be laser and water shows.

Sabet wanted to attract what he called "high-class Iranians." "High-class tourists" from the Gulf countries would come next, then Europeans, and finally, Americans. "I have left behind the Canary Islands to build my own country!" he said with glee. "This is going to be the first step toward opening up the country."

Sabet was not the first to see bizarre potential in this ninety-square-mile island. It had been inhabited mainly by fishermen and pearl divers when the Shah decided to turn it into an exclusive paradise retreat for himself and his privileged guests in the 1970s. Thousands of villas were built; branches of Europe's fanciest shops followed. A government advertising campaign for the Gulf Arabs touted it as a suitable vacation spot closer to home than the French Riviera.

Then, after the revolutionaries swept in, they established Kish as one of three duty-free islands. Today the clerics see it as an ideal place for foreign investors, and in 1999, Iran's Parliament passed laws allowing banks and insurance companies to open there. Money is exchanged openly at the black market rate. The tough mainland labor laws do not apply, and foreigners can be hired easily. In fact, foreigners—even Americans—do not need visas to visit.

Kish is also a tourist spot; if one believes the official Iranian estimates, the island receives between 500,000 and 800,000 visitors a year.

The Shah's palace has become a shopping mall. There is a stadium for horse racing and a sports complex where women can play tennis on segregated courts. Kish is just far enough from the mainland to be out of the stern gaze of the conservative ayatollahs, and there are no morality police. Men and women ride bicycles side by side.

I stayed at the Shayan Hotel, which had been built by the Shah. Its cosmopolitan self-image was reflected in the clocks behind the reception desk: they told the time in London, Washington, D.C., the United Arab Emirates, Canberra, Beijing, Moscow, Tokyo, and Tehran. But this was still the Islamic Republic. The swimming pool was empty; the beer in the minibar, nonalcoholic.

Apparently there are ways around some of the strictures, but not for an American journalist who might expose them. When my businessman friend Abdol-Karim checked into a Kish hotel, he was offered a clandestine bottle of Red Label scotch for $50; he settled for a $32 bottle of Russian vodka, which was quietly delivered to his room. He discovered his television was linked to an officially banned satellite. Three porn channels were blocked, but for a generous tip the concierge unblocked them. The concierge also asked him if he wanted female company for the night. Being a good family man, he politely declined.

I walked into what had once been the Shah's casino and I couldn't believe that I was still in Iran. It looked like the lounges from my childhood on the West Side of Buffalo—a red-lacquered bar, velvet-covered couches, tiny white lights hanging from the ceiling, and odd-shaped tables. The bar was closed, but in an adjoining room men were playing pool at a half dozen tables. Gambling is forbidden in Iran. And here in a public lounge men were actually betting good money on the game.

Then I heard a clanging noise: three old slot machines from the time of the Shah. The stakes were not high—the machine took fifty-rial coins. At the time of the Shah the coin had been worth about seventy cents. Now it was worth less than a penny. But there was a man with a roll of them, feeding the machine, over and over, watching the little oranges and lemons and cherries roll before him. He didn't stop until he won. And then a huge smile filled his face.

At dinner at a local seafood restaurant, I was surprised again. A trio sang Old Regime songs banned by the revolution. "I'm proud of your beautiful body," went one lyric. "You beautiful flower, you with the golden hair, you force the world to fall in love with you. Why don't you dance?"

I visited duty-free shops in Kish but didn't do much shopping. The marble-halled malls with overhead fluorescent lighting just don't have the magic of the covered bazaars. People come for the cheap goods, things like a Chinese-made Minnie Mouse playing an accordion, televisions, vacuum cleaners, three-inch-soled Sketcher shoes imported from Egypt, eye creams from Paris, pirated American videos like *Flubber* and *Space Jam.*

Hosein Sabet acknowledged that his investment in Kish was a huge risk. "The worst thing that happens is that no one comes to my hotel and I sleep in a different room every night," he told me. "If no one comes to see my dolphins, I get to play with them all by myself. I have buried my heart in my country. I have to be in love to do this."

With this kind of sentimentality, I thought, how can any businessman ever make money? And what American tourist is going to pay top dollar to go to a difficult-to-reach beach resort where women have to cover their heads and bodies, where there is no alcohol, where there is nothing to see of historic interest, and little to do at night?

But then I thought about just how daring—and how important—Sabet's gamble is. He understands that the era of blaming outsiders for one's misfortunes is over and that only if people like him take risks will the economy recover. It is one thing to express love for one's country, as so many Iranians do, but quite another to pour a lifetime of savings into it. The problem is that Iran has very few Sabets.

CHAPTER SEVENTEEN

The Center of the Universe

I am a man who has come from the East. . . . I represent a great and renowned nation whose civilization began tens of centuries ago.

— PRESIDENT MOHAMMAD KHATAMI AT THE UNITED
NATIONS ON SEPTEMBER 21, 1998

Iran is an international outlaw.

— SECRETARY OF STATE WARREN CHRISTOPHER AT A
CONGRESSIONAL HEARING ON JULY 29, 1994

One of the most wonderful places in all of human history, one of the most important places culturally in all of human history.

— PRESIDENT CLINTON DESCRIBING IRAN AT A
FUND-RAISER HOSTED BY IRANIAN-AMERICANS ON
MARCH 4, 2000

AMERICANS, IT IS OFTEN SAID, have too little sense of history, and the people of the Middle East too much. Where people in the Middle East carry around every past misfortune as a burden to be redeemed or avenged, Americans are constantly shucking off the past in favor of the present. This difference in outlook is one reason Americans and Iranians have arrived at the beginning of the twenty-first century so profoundly suspicious of each other.

I wonder how many Americans know that the first real confrontation between Harry Truman and Joseph Stalin after World War II was not over Korea or Czechoslovakia or Berlin. It was over the Iranian province of Azerbaijan. The year was 1946. Stalin was determined to keep his troops in that corner of northwestern Iran, where they had been posted during World War II to ensure the Red Army's lifeline to Allied supplies.

Truman demanded their withdrawal. Iran, meanwhile, relied on the skilled diplomatic maneuvering of its Prime Minister, Ahmad Qavam, to resolve the crisis. That combination of American and Iranian diplomacy persuaded Stalin to back down.

The incident was a coming of age for the United States, which previously had left the matter of Iran to its ally Great Britain. But Britain was now too weak to engage in the kind of game required to block the ambitions of the Soviet Union. The power play in Azerbaijan became an early and important chapter in American efforts to contain Moscow and block its path to the oil and trade routes of the Persian Gulf. Ever after, the Iranian-Soviet border at Azerbaijan was a red line in American eyes, beyond which Soviet influence could not be allowed to extend.

And that, in turn, put the United States foursquare behind the rule of the Shah, who would in time come to be perceived in Iran as an American puppet. So when a popular Iranian nationalist named Mohammad Mossadegh became Prime Minister and nationalized Iran's oil industry in the early 1950s and the United States began to worry that he might open Iran to Soviet influence, the United States—together with Britain—decreed that he would have to go. The Shah was restored to full power, and for the next quarter century the people of Iran were left with an autocratic ruler, who was intent on Westernizing the country even at the expense of its Shiite traditions, and on maintaining close political and military ties to successive American administrations.

None of this history is lost on Iranians. And of course the official post-revolutionary rhetoric has guaranteed that this history remains alive to this day as a source of political mobilization. But little of it has ever resonated for the American people. For that reason, Americans have been puzzled, even shocked, by the depth of official Iranian hostility toward the United States over the last twenty years, and Iranians have been incredulous that Americans don't understand it.

This chasm of misunderstanding with the United States is without doubt the most important feature on the landscape of Iran's relationship with the rest of the world in the past two decades, if only because the United States is such a powerful figure in the globe's politics and economy. The troubled relationship with Washington has isolated Iran diplomatically and culturally, kept it from developing economically, shaped its efforts to make alliances, even dictated how it ended the most disastrous of its wars.

And that is ironic, because for many centuries Iranians have thought of themselves, not the Americans, as the ones whose travails and accomplishments provide a lesson for the world. The country at "the center of the universe" is how Graham Fuller of the Rand Corporation described Iran's view of itself in a 1991 book of the same name. The term is taken from one of the many titles the nineteenth-century Shahs gave themselves. It also reflects the Iranian sense of superiority, based on an ancient and glorious history.

But Fuller made another observation about Iranians' self-image, and it too is critical for Americans who want to understand Iran today. Memories of conquest and cultural grandeur coexist with the memory of subjugation by Greeks, Arabs, Turks, Afghans, Russians, and others, and this has produced a "nagging sense of inferiority," in Fuller's words. The result, he pointed out, is a world view and an interpretation of power he described as "a subtle labyrinthine approach to politics" that is consistent with the Shiite sense that history is a tale of suffering and injustice. In this view, Fuller explained, "Events never have simple explanations, but rather reflect the existence of unseen political forces at work behind the scenes manipulating reality."

The combination of Iranian pride and sense of grievance was certainly evident among the leaders of the revolution, who sought to spread the word throughout the Muslim world that Iran's model of politicized Islam, with Khomeini as its standard-bearer, was the wave of the future. The model adopted in Iran, they felt, could light the way for all of Islam in overcoming the shame of Western exploitation and disrespect. So intent were they to avenge past wrongs that they overlooked the crucial fact that the eighty-five percent of the world's Muslims who are Sunnis would never be likely to follow the lead of a group of Shiite ayatollahs with their own peculiar version of Islamic rule. It has taken twenty years, and plenty of bitter experience, for reality to intrude on that notion.

Even today, Iranians in all walks of life express contradictory feelings about their country's place in the world. Over the centuries, revolutions, popular revolts, and nationalizations have been made in the name of throwing off the yoke of foreign powers, with the predictable result of dictatorship at home followed by renewed accommodation with those same powers. Many Iranians have come to believe that a cycle of dictatorship and chaos, subjugation and revolt, is inevitable and that democratic rule is impossible.

But today, another interpretation may be in the making: Iran, especially since the election of Mohammad Khatami in 1997, may be finding
a way to break the cycle of dictatorship and chaos. Many Iranians hope
that their country may one day be able to build a place for itself in the
world based not on a remembered great past or an imagined great future,
but on a realistic understanding of global politics and of how countries
balance their national interests. "Our goal in the twenty-first century is
not to find new enemies, but to turn enemies into neutrals and neutrals
into friends," Deputy Foreign Minister Mohammad-Javad Zarif told me
during a visit to New York in March 2000. An American-educated political scientist who lived in the United States for fifteen years, Zarif has always taken the long view. "We don't expect enemies to become friends
overnight. After all, as a country with a very old civilization, we tend to
look at diplomacy in terms of decades, not days."

Iran has been both blessed and cursed with a strong national identity,
bountiful natural resources, a strategic location, and an ancient intellectual and cultural tradition. It lies between the oil fields of the Persian Gulf
and the Caspian Sea, with the power of Russia to the north and the riches
of India to the east. If after World War II the Americans saw Iran as the
first place where Russian power had to be stopped, the British before
them had seen it as a way station on the path to India. For most of the
century, Iran also served as a balance against Arab power in the Middle
East. Its theological institutions have played an important role in maintaining the influence of Shiism in parts of the Islamic world. Since 1979 it
has been the most dramatic illustration of the Islamic political revival
that has aroused Muslims from Algeria to the corners of Indonesia.

I am often asked why the United States should care about Iran. After
all, for a generation, the United States has gotten along just fine in the region—it has even fought and won a war—without relations with Iran.
My first response is: Look at a map. Iran shares borders with Iraq, against
which it fought an eight-year war; with Pakistan, which exploded a nuclear device close to Iran's border in May 1998; with Afghanistan, which
rules through terror with a strict fundamentalist version of Islam; with
Turkey, whose secular government disapproves of Iran's theocratic state
and has problems with its own Islamic opposition; and with three former
Soviet republics: Armenia, Azerbaijan, and Turkmenistan. This is not a

stable neighborhood and any outbreak of hostilities would threaten important U.S. interests.

My second response is that Iran is an intellectual giant of the Middle East and of the Muslim world. Its struggle to reconcile Islamic principles with its people's yearning for freedom reverberates far beyond its borders. Its experimentation with elements of democracy makes it a potential model for those Muslim nations that have more authoritarian governments. Strange as it sounds, the country that Americans have feared so much is potentially a strong partner in ways that are not yet fully appreciated—including the adaptation of representative government to the Islamic world.

Too often the United States government has treated Iran simplistically—either like an unruly child to be ignored, or an international criminal to be punished. Perhaps a more appropriate and more profitable approach would begin with a recognition of how strongly Iranians feel about their nation. In a sense they are like New Yorkers—or, for that matter, Americans in general. They bicker and fight with each other, but when an outsider dares to attack them, they close ranks and proclaim their superiority. Despite the conflicts and fault lines, an Iranian would rather be Iranian than anything else. If there is any doubt of this simple fact, just ask any Iranian what he or she thinks of the suggestion of calling the Persian Gulf the "Arabian Gulf" or simply the "Gulf."

I heard this from the two sisters who could have emigrated to the United States but decided to run an aerobics studio in Tehran instead. I heard this from the feminist lawyer, Mehrangiz Kar, who was both frustrated and energized by her battles for women in court. I heard this from the Bahai engineer whose family had suffered so much persecution at the hands of the Islamic Republic. I heard this from my political scientist friend Farideh Farhi, who lived in the United States but longed for summer, when she could take her children back home. I even heard it from Nazila. "I could never imagine making my life outside Iran," she told me once when I asked her why she did not move away for good. "My parents are there. My husband's parents are there. I can't even pass an Iranian restaurant or hear Iranian music when I'm on vacation and not get nostalgic for home."

Sometimes that love of country came across as self-centeredness. I saw that in January 1998, when President Khatami gave an interview to CNN in which he suggested that cultural exchanges were a way to break down the mistrust between the United States and Iran. His aides expected a high-level response, nothing less than a nationally televised speech by President Clinton from the Oval Office. But that was the same week Americans first heard about the President's affair with Monica Lewinsky, and I tried to explain that Iran was not high on the President's agenda just then. Iranian officials were flabbergasted. How, they wondered, could President Clinton's personal life be more important than a gesture of friendship from the President of Iran?

I saw it again later that month when Secretary of State Madeleine Albright told an interviewer from *USA Today* that she did not envision going to Iran "in the near future or medium or distant future." I was in Iran at the time, and I don't think I have ever seen so many Iranians—officials, intellectuals, taxi drivers—so united in their dismay. They could understand when an American Secretary of State called Iran a rogue state or a supporter of terrorism. Name-calling, after all, was part of politics. But how could she not want to visit Iran, the land of the ancient ruins of Persepolis and the mystical poetry of Hafiz?

Mr. Salimi, my driver, wanted me to bring Albright a volume of Hafiz poetry and some pistachio nuts and dried fruits as a peace offering. Taghi Aghaie, the war-hero-turned-travel-agent, offered to prepare a package of travel materials, including a copy of his forty-two-minute promotional videocassette. "I'll show her the country myself, and I'll do it for free," he said. "It's my duty. She has to see it for herself."

This sense of Iranianness has withstood even the test of revolution. At first, the prospect of Islamic rule sparked ethnic rebellions across the country. Overnight, the new regime was confronted with unrest among the Turks in Azerbaijan, the Baluchis in Baluchistan, the Arabs in Khuzestan, and the Kurds in Kurdistan. Ayatollah Khomeini suppressed the rebellions one by one through political guile and military force, and then used the war with Iraq to solidify a sense of nationalism and loyalty to the Iranian state. Once Iran and Iraq were at war, ethnic and religious minorities including Kurds, Arabs, Armenians, Jews, and even Bahais were fighting and dying for their country, Iran. When I traveled through Iranian Kurdistan in 1979, I often came upon Kurds determined to unite with their ethnic brethren from Turkey, Syria, Iraq, and parts of the former Soviet Union to create a new nation called Kurdistan. Twenty years later, the Iranian Kurds I met had a different agenda—to pressure the Iranian government to reward them with factories and other economic projects and to allow them to expand their national culture within the boundaries of Iran.

But if pride runs strong, so does a highly developed sense of victimhood. The revolution made the Iranian people masters of their destiny, but it did not eradicate that feeling of victimization. The United States, above all, is still seen as a self-interested manipulator, the hidden hand responsible for Iran's problems or capable of solving them. When misfortunes have no logical explanation, they can always be blamed on the CIA. (This is a role previously ascribed to British intelligence, and in some quarters the British are still considered to be behind every disaster, problem, plot, and powerful institution, including the CIA itself.)

The conservative clerics drummed this anti-American view into the populace from the pulpit at the University of Tehran every Friday. America was to blame for Iran's crippled economy, the fall of Iran's currency, the moral corruption of the youth, the promotion of Zionism, the bolstering of Israel's status around the world.

In the eyes of Iranian officials, the ultimate proof of America's evil intentions was an effort by the U.S. Congress in 1995 to give the CIA $20 million to carry out a covert program to undermine the Iranian government. Though the funding effort was reported in the American press, the money was never appropriated or spent, because President Clinton never authorized the program and Congress never passed it into law. Even so, many Iranians continue to believe that the CIA is carrying it out. American officials have not publicly denied the existence of the program since they are not permitted to talk about "covert" operations. And even if American officials issued a denial, would the Iranians believe it?

Even the Shah in his final days in power showed signs of suspicion and distrust. In May 1978, he asked former Vice President Nelson Rockefeller, who was visiting Iran, whether "the Americans and the Russians have divided the world between them." Riots that would culminate in the Shah's overthrow had begun a few months before; a coup in Afghanistan had just put a communist faction in power. The Shah couldn't believe that events like these were not orchestrated. And sometimes I still hear from Iranian friends the question, "Why did the United States put Khomeini in power?"

I have seen this sentiment over and over in my travels to Iran. At a women-only dinner party at the home of my close friend Nargess in the summer of 1999, when talk turned to the impeachment trial of Bill Clinton, the group had a lot of sympathy for the President and none for Monica Lewinsky. But not for the reasons I would have thought.

"She was a Zionist spy sent by Israel to discredit Clinton," said Nargess's sister Monir, a forty-year-old hairdresser who had once lived in the United States. "It was a conspiracy by Mossad [the Israeli intelligence agency] to ruin Clinton because he was too pro-Palestinian."

"Don't you think she loved him?" I asked.

All the women laughed, and Nargess, who had also lived in the United States, jumped into the conversation. "I suppose you think that the death of Princess Diana was accidental too!" she exclaimed.

When I said that I thought it was, she replied, "Ha! I knew it. Don't you know that Diana was planning to convert to Islam and marry an Arab? They wouldn't stand for it."

"Who's they?" I asked.

"The British," said Nargess. "The British decide everything—even which governments rise and fall."

"I suppose you think the crash of John Kennedy Jr.'s plane was not an accident either," I said.

That statement really set the group to laughing. "The Kennedys are Democrats," said Nargess. "Even though they're rich, they're loved by ordinary people. They all have to be exterminated. JFK Jr. was the last one. He was about ready to announce he wanted to run for President. They had to stop him."

"Who's they?" I asked again.

"The ones who control everything, the ones behind the curtain," said Nargess. "The ones who run the world economy and world politics."

"But who are they?"

"We don't know who they are," Nargess replied. "How could we? They're behind the curtain."

Iran's place in the world, of course, involves more than simply its relationship with the United States, but the Iranians themselves have not figured out what their role should be. The era of "Death to America" may be over, but what comes in its place is a matter of intense debate. Iran has built a web of political and commercial relationships with other countries and regions to serve its interests, and these relationships reveal a more pragmatic and less ideologically driven nation than was the case early in the revolution.

Perhaps the most dramatic example of Iranian realpolitik involves its old enemy, Iraq. Iran and Iraq remain the two strongest and most battle-tested powers in the Persian Gulf, and they still engage in border skirmishes and name-calling. But ever since the 1991 Gulf War against Iraq, Iran's overriding policy has been one of restraint. It did not rush to the aid of Iraq's Kurdish and Shiite rebels in the aftermath of the war. Instead, it remained quiescent as the United States retained forces in the region and enforced no-fly zones over much of Iraq's airspace.

More recently, Iran has supported Security Council resolutions requiring Iraq to comply with inspections of its military installations, and it watched from the sidelines in the late 1990s as U.S. bombs damaged Iraq's remaining military capabilities. At the same time, Iranian pilgrims have begun to take organized, carefully policed tours to Shiite shrines in Iraq even as the slow exchange of remaining prisoners of the Iran-Iraq war continues. In fact, the two countries maintain diplomatic relations with embassies and chargés d'affaires in each other's capitals. "We are condemned to be neighbors," Iran's Foreign Minister Kamal Kharrazi once said of Iraq, meaning that Iran has to figure out a way to coexist with whatever regime is in power in Baghdad.

Iran has also had to face the reality that its revolution has failed to make it the leader in the Muslim world. So Iran has pushed ahead in building relationships with its Persian Gulf neighbors, particularly Saudi Arabia. In a classic display of balance-of-power politics, Iran and Saudi Arabia, OPEC's largest oil producers, have shaped a more normal relationship around their common interests—stabilizing oil prices and containing Iraq. That effort accelerated in December 1997 when Crown Prince Abdullah met President Khatami in Tehran at the quadrennial summit of the world's Islamic countries. This was "the start of a new era in relations between the two big countries of the region," Khatami told Abdullah.

It's not that the Saudis have any illusions that Iran has abandoned its long-term goal of dominance in the Gulf. But for the sake of regional security, the Saudis cannot afford a hostile Iran. One example of Saudi accommodation may be its response to the terrorist bombing that destroyed Khobar Towers, the American military barracks outside Dhahran, Saudi Arabia, in June 1996, killing nineteen American servicemen. U.S. officials have said publicly that they suspect an Iranian link to the bombing but they have never been able to prove their case. Some

American intelligence officials have speculated that the Saudis will squelch any evidence of such a link if Iran, in exchange, ends its support for Saudi dissidents.

Iran has also emphasized diplomacy over force in its relationship with the Taliban regime in Afghanistan. To the Iranians, the Taliban—a Sunni Muslim movement that follows an extreme, repressive version of Islamic law—are backward peasants who have given Muslims a bad name. Iran may require its women to cover their heads and bodies, but at least they can vote, pursue careers, and participate in society. In Afghanistan women cannot work and must cover their faces and most girls are not allowed to go to school. "A disgrace to Islam," was the way Kharrazi characterized Taliban rule.

The Islamic Republic (in loose collaboration with Russia) has supplied other Afghan factions with weapons, money, and logistical support, and by late 1998, Iran and Afghanistan seemed to be on the brink of war. But in the end, cool heads prevailed. If the entire Soviet military could not tame Afghanistan, the thinking went in Tehran, how could Iran hope to do so? Iran withdrew the troops it had sent to the border, and the crisis dissipated.

Outside its immediate neighborhood, the strains in Iran's relationships with vast swaths of the world have receded in recent years. It has, for example, forged partnerships with both China and Russia. Russia is helping Iran complete construction of a nuclear power plant at Bushehr on the Persian Gulf, over American objections, and has broken a pledge to the United States to stop selling Iran goods, services, and technology that could help Iran develop weapons of mass destruction or ballistic missiles. China has remained a key supplier of weapons to the Islamic Republic, although it has ended its nuclear cooperation; Iran, in turn, has begun to help China meet its growing energy needs with oil exports.

Iran has also built a mosaic of political and commercial relationships with Europe. A $2 billion deal between the Iranian government and the French company Total (together with Russia's Gazprom and Malaysia's Petronas) in September 1997 was particularly problematic because the U.S. Congress had passed legislation requiring sanctions on foreign companies that invested more than $20 million in Iran's energy sector. The legislation infuriated European governments, and in May 1998 President Clinton waived the sanctions against the companies. After assassinations in Europe of Iranian opponents of the Islamic Republic abated, relations between Iran and Europe warmed even more.

That development has left both Europeans and Iranians free to explore political and economic cooperation. At the beginning of the twenty-first century, European officials and corporations are positioning themselves for possible business deals and distancing themselves from American policy. "Iran has the capability to take on the role of a leader in the region," said Italy's Foreign Minister, Lamberto Dini, when he visited Iran in March 2000. "We want Iran to be the center of stability in the region."

Iran even restored relations with its longtime foe, Britain, in 1999, an outgrowth of assurances by the Iranian government that it had no intention of carrying out Khomeini's order to assassinate the novelist Salman Rushdie. Iran has benefited as well from the extraordinary public efforts by President Khatami to reshape Iran's image. On a trip to Italy in 1999, Khatami proved himself a master of the photo opportunity as he pitched his call for a "dialogue among civilizations." He went to the Vatican as a man of religion, to Florence as a man of learning, to Rome as a man of politics. He posed with the Pope, with scholars, and with the Prime Minister. During a trip to France later that year, Khatami asked to visit the Pantheon, the secular temple to the great men and women of France. After laying sprays of red and white carnations before the tombs of Jean-Jacques Rousseau, Emile Zola, Victor Hugo, and Marie and Pierre Curie, Khatami climbed to the dome of the Pantheon, where he set in motion Foucault's pendulum, the scientific instrument that a century and a half before had proved that the earth rotates on its axis.

To say that Khatami is open to some Western ideas about democracy and modern science, however, is to draw only part of the picture. It does not explain why the chasm with America remains so deep.

One difficulty is obvious: American officials, having been burned before, remain wary of the possibility that Khatami will prove unable to restrain the conservative forces still arrayed against him—forces that may have lost popular support but that still have great resources of power and money. They include clerics allied with Ayatollah Khamenei, bazaar merchants who resist reform, and Islamic foundations that control so much of Iran's economy. Still, when it comes to America, the extent to which Khatami and Khamenei sustain a mutually dependent relationship is important to remember. They may differ in their views of the United States, but there is no sign that these differences are deep enough to cause a permanent rupture between them.

Americans also must reckon with a deeply ambivalent Iranian attitude about America, one that does not fit into a predictable equation about when to expect goodwill. It is shaped by experiences both good and bad with the United States, and it springs from Iranians' unique sense of who they are.

In the eyes of many Iranians, America is a country of both dreams and demons. It is hated, admired, idealized, and challenged, sometimes simultaneously. There is not one view of the United States; there are several, operating on different levels.

In many ways, the Iranian view of the United States remains colored by Iran's lingering resentment over America's conduct during the Iran-Iraq war. Officially, particularly in the beginning, the United States took the position that both sides should stop the slaughter. Unofficially, many officials agreed with a sentiment expressed best by former Secretary of State Henry Kissinger: "Too bad they can't both lose." Once Iran went on the offensive in 1982, the United States tilted toward Iraq. From then on, nothing could convince the Iranians that America's motives were anything but hostile. Their worst fears seemed to be confirmed when the USS *Vincennes* shot down an Iran Air passenger plane in 1988. The United States claimed it was a terrible accident and years later paid compensation to the families of the victims. But the warship's commander and crew were not punished; the commander was given the Legion of Merit for "exceptionally meritorious conduct" during the period of his command; the anti-air warfare officer was granted two Navy commendation medals for his service on the ship; the crew were given combat-action ribbons for their tour in dangerous waters.

Another grievance, which cuts across all classes and all political persuasions, involves America's use of economic weapons against Iran. Particularly galling for the Iranians are sanctions that prevent American and other foreign firms from investing in projects that would benefit Iran; the blockage of loans from the World Bank and the International Monetary Fund; and the slowness in litigating the remaining cases of Iranian financial disputes against the United States. At times America has justified such steps by saying that it was punishing Iran for "unacceptable behavior," including the use of terrorism and the development of ballistic missiles and weapons of mass destruction. But this phrase drives some of my

Iranian friends crazy. Who are the Americans, my friends ask, to go around criticizing others for bad behavior, as if they are obstreperous children?

Related to this grievance is a deep resentment over the issue of Caspian Sea oil and gas, and over who will build and control the pipelines that will transport oil and gas to market. Iran has bridled at American efforts to shut it out of the pipeline sweepstakes by signing an agreement with Turkey, Azerbaijan, Georgia, and Turkmenistan to build a pipeline to the Mediterranean port of Ceyhan, in southern Turkey. Iranian officials argue that Iran is the logical export route, and that if the Turkish route is completed, its impact will bolster Iran's neighbors economically at Iran's expense for decades to come.

Iran and the United States are also separated by a gulf of distrust over relations with Israel. The Islamic Republic does not accept Israel's right to exist. Iran has given substantial amounts of money and weapons to the Lebanese Shiite militia Hezbollah, which has long been active in armed attacks on Israeli military and civilian targets in southern Lebanon and northern Israel. Iran has provided political, financial, and perhaps military support to the Palestinian movements Hamas and Palestinian Islamic Jihad, whose mission is to sabotage peace between Israel and the Palestinians. Because resolution of the Arab-Israeli conflict has for decades been one of the highest foreign policy priorities of American administrations—and certainly will be for future administrations—no other issue is higher on America's agenda vis-à-vis Iran. Yet if there is one position on which both President Khatami and Ayatollah Khamenei agree, it is that Israel is an aggressive, racist enemy. Still, there may be room even here for maneuver. Khatami has met with the PLO leader Yasir Arafat and is on record as saying that Iran would accept any settlement acceptable to the Palestinians, even though Ayatollah Khamenei has called Arafat a "traitor and an idiot" and demanded the annihilation of Israel.

Complicating matters is that both Israel and Iran regard the other as a military threat. Israel is concerned about Iran's development of ballistic missiles and is convinced that Iran is determined to become a nuclear power; Iran fears Israel's military capability, its presumed nuclear arsenal and its military relationships with the United States and Turkey. Iran's hostility to Israel extends to the smallest issues. Contact between Iranians and Israelis is regarded as so dreadful that when two wrestlers from Iran's national team drew Israelis as opponents in an international competition in Colorado in March 2000, the Iranians called in sick and forfeited the matches.

Yet from time to time, there have been unconfirmed reports in the Iranian and Israeli press about business contacts, like the one in the November 22, 1999, issue of the Israeli daily *Yediot Aharanot* that disclosed an agreement in principle between Israeli businessmen and representatives of Iran's Ministry of Agriculture for Iran to buy seeds for fruits and vegetables through a German middleman. A disapproving article in the conservative Iranian daily *Jomhuri-ye-Islami* in July 1999 reported that Israeli-made burglar alarms had become popular in Tehran.

A great many Iranians believe that politics ought not to get in the way of doing business, and that the United States can be a reliable business partner. So what if America wants to humiliate Iran, the argument goes, let's be practical. America is the key to Iran's prosperity and to its entry into the global economy.

The most active proponent of this view has been Ali-Akbar Hashemi-Rafsanjani, the merchant-turned-state-builder who served as Iran's President from 1989 to 1997. In 1986, when Rafsanjani was Speaker of Parliament, a Beirut newspaper broke the story about secret American arms sales to Iran—with Israeli complicity—to help free several American hostages being held in Lebanon. The Reagan administration was ridiculed for claiming it had found Iranian "moderates" among the uniformly hostile leadership of the Islamic Republic. If the revelations were an embarrassment for the Reagan administration, they were potentially even more explosive for the Iranians. But when Rafsanjani faced the nation at Friday prayers that very day, he adroitly dismissed the whole affair as strictly business. Iran had bought the weapons to fight the war with Iraq, he said, but had rebuffed the political overtures of the American envoys. He even joked about the chocolate cake (from a kosher bakery in Israel) that the envoys had brought as a gesture of friendship. Iranian security men, Rafsanjani quipped, "got hungry and ate the cake." A master of concealment, he didn't bother to tell the faithful that he himself had been deeply involved in the arms-for-hostages initiative.

A few years later, as President, Rafsanjani once again tried to get some business going. In early 1995, he quietly signed off on a multibillion-dollar deal with Conoco, an American oil company, to develop oil and gas fields in Iran. Shortly afterward, Warren Christopher, who was then Secretary of State, learned of the pending deal through a newspaper article. Stunned that the negotiating had been going on without his knowledge, and humiliated that his former law firm was representing Conoco, Christopher recused himself from policy decisions but made no secret of his firm opposition to the deal, which President Clinton quickly canceled. Once again, Rafsanjani was angry. He later told Peter Jennings of ABC News that the deal was intended as a "message to the United States" that even without diplomatic relations, the two countries could at least work together to make money. The message, he said, "was not correctly understood."

Or perhaps it was, and Rafsanjani was the one who didn't quite get the drift. The point of Clinton's sanctions policy was that until there was a political opening, commercial contacts were unacceptable. Once again, Iranian thinking and American thinking were at cross purposes.

It is no exaggeration to say that when it comes to Iran, the United States is still dealing with the fallout from the hostage crisis of 1979–81. The images of that time—the crowds chanting "Death to America," the blindfolded hostages being paraded before the news cameras, the wreckage of the failed military mission to rescue the hostages—remain embedded in the consciousness of America; Iran's strident rhetoric has reinforced the idea that Iran was America's most implacable and uncompromising foe.

If there was a moment when Americans began thinking of Iran as a place only of veils and terrorists, the hostage crisis was it. And later, Americans were given new reason to equate the words "Iran" and "terrorism." In Beirut in April 1983, Shiite extremists blew up the American embassy, killing more than sixty people inside; six months later, suicide bombers destroyed an American military compound in Beirut, killing 241 American servicemen. In both cases, the bombers were believed to have had links to Iran. For years Iranian-backed extremists held American and other Western hostages in Lebanon, including, most notably, the Associated Press journalist Terry Anderson. Finally, in September 1991, after the hostages had outlived their political usefulness and Iran was eager to improve its international standing in the aftermath of the Persian Gulf war, Iran reportedly paid the kidnappers between $1 million and $2 million for the release of each hostage.

Americans have also been suspicious of the steps taken by the Islamic Republic to rebuild its military arsenal in the years since the end of the Iran-Iraq war. Tanks and fighter aircraft are simply too expensive. So Iran has improvised, focusing on its navy more than its army and air force. It has bought Kilo-class submarines from the Russians and cruise missiles from the Chinese that give it the capability to challenge the American naval presence in the Persian Gulf. With Russian help, it is also actively developing an eight-hundred-mile ballistic missile that could attack Israel, Saudi Arabia, and Turkey. Iranian officials insist that they need to develop their conventional capability in order to stabilize their borders, to deter Iraq and Israel from attack, and to project influence over the Persian Gulf.

The United States is particularly determined to prevent Iran from developing a nuclear capability. An Iranian interest in nuclear weapons would be easy to understand, given that Pakistan, Iran's neighbor to the east, has tested a nuclear weapon; that Iraq, Iran's neighbor to the west, came close to building one before the Gulf War and may still intend to build one; and that Israel is widely assumed to possess nuclear weapons. The consensus among policymakers and intelligence officials in Washington is that Iran is continuing to buy sophisticated equipment that serves no civilian purpose and can only be part of a nuclear weapons program. Iranian officials repeatedly and vigorously deny assertions that the country is seeking nuclear weapons. And they particularly resent Washington's attempts to slow down their civilian nuclear power program.

Because Iran's nuclear energy program doesn't make obvious sense, it is easy to see why Washington is suspicious. Iran has two partially built nuclear reactors near Bushehr on the shores of the Persian Gulf that are frozen in time. For the Iranians, the enormous steel and concrete structures represent what might have been and what might be, a symbol of their legal right to develop nuclear energy and of their potential to become a great regional power. For the Americans, they represent a means for Iran to gain expertise that could be used in a nuclear weapons program. I visited the site in 1995 and it struck me quite differently: as an Iranian Chernobyl in the making.

Earlier that year, the Russians had signed a contract to complete the reactors, which were started by the Germans under the Shah and were damaged by the Iraqis during the Iran-Iraq war. On the day of my visit, I asked my host about the gaping holes in the inner dome of the less-damaged structure. "Blisters," he replied, waving his arm as if to swat away flies. "It's nothing." I'm no engineer, but they looked pretty bad to me.

Complicating progress on the site is that the Germans, bowing to American pressure, had withheld the blueprints, making it difficult to fit 1,000-megawatt Russian-made reactors and turbines into a structure intended for German-designed 1,200-megawatt reactors—sort of like putting a Zil motor and body onto a Mercedes chassis. I've joked that if the United States truly wanted to shut down the reactor site, it could mount a covert operation that would send boats filled with environmental activists up and down the Persian Gulf with bullhorns predicting nuclear catastrophe.

As much as America has wanted to punish Iran for its provocations, the U.S. government has never lost its appreciation of the Islamic Republic's value as a potential partner on the eastern flank of the Arab world. Even as successive administrations demonized and isolated the country, they also took stabs at engaging and rewarding it, dreaming of pulling it back into an orbit where the United States could deal with it again. But for twenty years all those efforts failed, sometimes ludicrously, leaving Iran the Bermuda triangle of American foreign policy.

Ronald Reagan secretly sold weapons to Iran in a vain effort to help free the American hostages held in Lebanon, even as he vowed never to negotiate with terrorists. George Bush expressed a simple policy, "Goodwill begets goodwill," leaving the door open for dialogue and promising to reward Iran for "good behavior." His enthusiasm backfired on him one day, when he eagerly picked up an Oval Office telephone to talk with a man he thought was President Rafsanjani. It was a hoax.

Bill Clinton took a more confrontational position, choosing to view Iran as a reflection of its openly belligerent neighbor, Iraq. His policy was even given a name: "dual containment." But to call it a policy is to dignify its haphazard and off-the-cuff genesis. Not long ago, I asked Martin Indyk, the creator of the "dual containment" concept during the time he was Assistant Secretary of State in charge of the Middle East, whether he ever regretted uttering the two words. "No, it was a very good slogan, and you suggested it, actually," he replied. Me?

In fact, in 1993, very early in the Clinton administration, I had written an article for *The New York Times* on the emerging yet unarticulated American policy toward Iran and Iraq. The administration, I wrote, "argues that neither regime should be strengthened and that each should be dealt with as a separate problem—a sort of parallel containment. Framing the policy in that way leaves the unfortunate impression that Iraq is less and Iran is more of an enemy and that parallel containment may be just a reworked version of old-fashioned power balancing."

Shortly after my analysis appeared, Indyk gave a speech laying out American policy goals in the Persian Gulf. He called the Clinton administration's new approach to Iran and Iraq "dual containment." My wording—"parallel containment"—would have been bad enough, since I had intended it as a deliberate effort to point out the weakness of the policy. But "dual containment" was an even more unfortunate phrase. It seemed to equate the two countries, and it raised the question: was Iran really as dangerous as Iraq, a nation that had overrun a tiny neighbor; used poison gas against its own citizens; fought a major war that united the West, most of the Arab world, and Israel against it; and refused to abide by United Nations resolutions regarding weapons of mass destruction? Still, the slogan stuck, even though it became an object of wide criticism among experts on the Middle East, and was quietly dropped by many—but not all—in the Clinton administration in the late 1990s.

After Khatami's election in 1997, Clinton took small, politically safe steps to make amends. He called Iran a "great civilization" and said that it was not normal that the two countries did not have diplomatic relations. He asked Iran to begin an official dialogue. In April 1999, Clinton even acknowledged Iran's historical grievances, saying, "Iran, because of its enormous geopolitical importance over time, has been the subject of quite a lot of abuse from various Western nations. And I think sometimes it's quite important to tell people, look, you have a right to be angry at something my country or my culture or others that are generally allied with us today did to you fifty or sixty or one hundred or 150 years ago." The Clinton administration also eased sanctions slightly, allowing Iran to import food and later to export carpets, caviar, dried fruit, and pistachios.

This could be a start, but at the same time the United States may be asking Iran to do more than it can be expected to do given its unsettled political situation. Scarred by recent history, fearful of a backlash in Congress, wary of Iranians who look like "moderates," the United States has told Iran that the way to an improvement in relations is through an authoritative, official dialogue. But the Iranian way of negotiating has been to maintain room for maneuver, to keep things in the shadows, to conduct important business in private.

Yet for all the misunderstandings and missed opportunities by the leaders of both countries, many Iranians have their own private view of America, a view that I have often found compelling and that gives me hope that if the United States made concrete gestures to resolve specific problems, those gestures would not be rebuffed. The great majority of Iranians I have met retain an unabashed affection and admiration for the country they call "The Fortune Land." Iranian demonstrators might still occasionally burn the American flag, but an audience watching *Primary Colors* during a film festival in Tehran cheered when the American flag filled the screen. There are so many marriages arranged with Iranian-born men who have become naturalized American citizens that one joke going around Tehran is that Iran's biggest export is not its oil or its carpets but its women.

Other Iranians find a different way to articulate the lure of America. "The United States is the last station on the train, the highest rung on the ladder," said my friend Monir, the hairdresser. "When I lived in the United States and went to apply for my Social Security card, all the nations of the world were represented in the waiting room. We all got equal treatment. When I went to register as a hairdresser, they told me I needed a hundred hours of training. I proved that I had years of experience. So they calculated my experience and said, 'Okay, you get so many points for this and so many for that.' And they gave me my license. I didn't have to know anyone important. I didn't have to bribe anyone. It's a country of laws where everyone is equal before the law."

Such positive feelings toward the United States are rejected by the conservatives. In 1962, the writer Jalal Al-e Ahmad first identified what he called the cultural "illness" that had stricken the cities and towns of Iran, and in the process he invented a concept that I cite frequently: "Westoxication." It is even harder for a Westerner to translate Al-e Ahmad's Persian word—*gharbzadegi*—than it is to pronounce it. Westoxication probably expresses it best. Ayatollah Khomeini loved the concept and used it often in his sermons.

But the conservatives are not the only ones who hold power in Iran today, and there are strong signals that a struggle is underway to bring Iran into a new understanding of its place in the world. Indeed, a principal reason for the failure of previous efforts to improve relations with America has been the sense that it was impossible to tell who was really in charge in Iran. When the landslide for Khatami as President was followed by a landslide for reformist legislators associated with him, it did not change the fact that conservative clerics could still veto efforts to establish the rule of law and improve relations with the West. But at least the elections of 1997 and 2000 have now made it clear where the population stands and which politicians can count on popular support. With "rule of law" a watchword for the reformists, an argument is gaining currency in Iran for warmer ties to democracies around the world, especially if such ties will bring the country into the global marketplace.

The reformists in Iran are thus beginning to adopt a more nuanced and dispassionate view of America, saying that if it is in Iran's national interest to develop a relationship with the United States, so be it. After all, the United States and Iran share a number of significant interests: opposition to a rearmed Iraq, opposition to the excesses of the Taliban in Afghanistan, the desire for a secure Persian Gulf, an eagerness to control the flow of drugs from Afghanistan.

In the last few years, it has become more acceptable for Iranians to discuss publicly the possibility of improving relations with the United States and to criticize the long-held belief in conspiracies. There is even an expression these days with which to ridicule old thinking: *tavahom-e tote-eh* or "imagining of conspiracy." This view was on display during the unrest in July 1999, when commentators began to challenge the official line that the United States was the hidden hand behind the demonstrations and riots. "Why do we accuse the foreign enemy, instead of acknowledging the truth and finding our own weakness?" asked an editorial in the reformist newspaper *Khordad.* "Do we have a foreign enemy that is so strong that it managed to penetrate and riot even in the most central streets of Tehran?"

A small pro-reform newspaper, *Iran-e Vij,* argued that two decades of hostile relations with the United States had made Iran the loser. "For twenty years our nation has repeatedly and at every occasion shouted 'Death to America,'" it said. "In practice, our national currency has lost its value hundreds of times over . . . and Iran has been turned into a major debtor in the world. Surely, this hasn't been the aim of our struggle against the United States."

Even the state-run demonstrations in front of the former American embassy in Tehran and in cities and towns around the country on the anniversary of the embassy occupation have lost their fervor over the years; the crowds have shrunk and the chants of "Death to America" have grown weaker. On November 4, 1998, the nineteenth anniversary, Mohsen Rezai, the Secretary of the Expediency Council and the former commander of the Revolutionary Guards, proclaimed, "It's not possible to reconcile with the United States," only to have a group of schoolboys in the back of the crowd chant back, "It's possible. It's possible."

Then after Secretary of State Madeleine Albright's speech in March 2000 announcing that the United States would allow the import of some Iranian goods and acknowledging past errors in U.S. policy toward Iran, Rezai softened his line. He called the speech "a new chapter" in U.S-Iranian relations and predicted major developments in the coming year.

Two decades on, even the hostage-takers have mellowed. Abbas Abdi, one of the masterminds of the embassy seizure, no longer marches in street demonstrations, condones violence, or justifies the violation of international law as part of the natural process of revolution. He calls himself a democrat and advocates a civil society, freedom of speech, due process of law, and the formation of political parties. He believes that Iran must focus on its national interests, not on what others say it should and shouldn't do. Iran, he says, is strong enough to deal with the United States, even if the interests of the United States do not coincide with those of a potentially more democratic Iran.

Abdi now runs a consulting and research firm near the University of Tehran. As the editor of the leftist newspaper *Salaam* in its early days, he wrote articles critical of Iran's conservatives and of the corruption of the giant foundations and called for the creation of institutions to bolster democratic reform. In 1993, his editorials, sharply critical of the clerics' undemocratic ways, landed him in prison—and solitary confinement— for eight months. "I am always asked how I have changed," he said in November 1999, in a speech to mark the twentieth anniversary of the hostage seizure. "Well, I am older now. Young people don't care so much about the costs of their political actions." And older people, he added, tend to weigh the risks against the benefits.

But that doesn't mean that Abdi is naive about what it will take before Iran and America kiss and make up. I found that out when I later met Abdi at a conference in Cyprus. He gave a long speech that laid out why American policy toward Iran was misguided. But Abdi added an interesting twist. He said that American policy toward Iran had been much softer in the 1980s, a tense decade of Cold War and terrorist activity, than it was in the more quiescent and reformist 1990s. This, he said, proved that any further gesture of friendship by Iran would lead not to reciprocity but to even more pressure by the United States. After the first round of parliamentary elections in February 2000, Abdi offered an even tougher assessment. Iran had become too democratic and open for the United States, he said. "Americans prefer to negotiate with an undemocratic system behind closed doors so that they can take advantage," he was quoted as saying in the reformist daily *Asr-e Azadegan.* "This is impossible in a democratic system because as soon as such negotiations take place, the press would report them."

And yet my experiences in Iran over more than twenty years tell me that the Iranians will not be content to leave matters at an impasse. They remain masters of improvisation, masters of making room for themselves even within the most rigid and restrictive rules of conduct.

Perhaps there are more surprises in store. Just as one day Iran freed the hostages, just as one day Iran ended the war with Iraq, so one day Iran may find a way to restore some sort of relationship with the United States—if America is willing to listen. "Iranians have a strange habit," said Michael Metrinko, who lived for years in Iran as a Peace Corps volunteer and diplomat and suffered as one of the American hostages. "They'll call you after you haven't spoken in months and say, 'Why haven't you called?' One day, the Iranian government will wake up and say, 'Why haven't you established relations with us?' And we'll wonder what the hell is going on."

When I shared this comment in early 2000 with Mohammad-Javad Zarif, the Deputy Foreign Minister, he had a different take on it. "Your friend has it backward," he said. "I hope one day the American government will wake up and say, 'Why haven't we understood the political realities in Iran?'

"Look at it this way," he added. "The United States and Iran are playing a long card game. The United States has most of the cards. We discarded our rhetoric card when Khatami reached out and called for a dialogue among civilizations. The United States discarded its rhetoric card when it abandoned its negative tone toward us. Now the United States wants to keep the rest of its cards but wants us to discard all of ours. It wants us to open a dialogue while it still is keeping a number of sanctions against us. We're saying, 'You can't keep all your cards. It's not in our interest and it's not in your interest.'"

"So is there a winner in this card game?" I asked.

"There are losers," Zarif replied. "The American people."

He paused for a moment, then added, "The Iranian people too."

The Bride Has Gone to Pick Flowers

Do not be sad, my dear, winter will soon be over.
The spring will come, the rice will be put out, and everything will grow.
We shall be happy together, my dear, we shall be happy then.

— TRADITIONAL SONG FROM THE CITY OF RASHT

Have patience, and I'll make halvah for you from unripe grapes.

— PERSIAN PROVERB

AT A CONFERENCE on Iran in Cyprus in the summer of 1999, I asked a panel of Iranian scholars a straightforward question: would an Islamic Republic and the office of the Supreme Leader exist ten years from now?

The panelists—and the audience—bobbed and weaved. I was asking a question that was much too direct. I knew it myself, but we had been talking around the issue for two days and I wanted to get it squarely on the table. No one answered the question. Next to me sat Rasoul Asghari, an Iranian journalist who at the time worked for the newspaper *Entekhab*. Rasoul leaned over and whispered in Persian, "The bride has gone to pick flowers."

The people sitting around us laughed out loud.

When an Iranian couple gets married, the person officiating at the wedding—usually a cleric—asks the bride whether she agrees to marry the groom. The bride stays silent, but the wedding guests answer the question for her. "The bride has gone to pick flowers," they say in unison. The question is asked a second time, and a second time the guests give the same answer. Only after the question is asked a third time does the bride respond affirmatively to a cheering crowd.

Rasoul's response was a very Iranian one. Don't ask such a direct question, he was saying. This is an open-ended process and we don't know the answer. Even if we know the answer, it is unwise to tell you. So let it go. Keep things in the shadows. Improvise. This is the time for the bride to pick flowers.

Rasoul was also saying something important about navigating in the Islamic Republic. Resist the impulse to make predictions. In a fluid society like Iran, predictions are dangerous. First, they are likely to be wrong. Second, if they are made at the wrong time, they may alter the course of events in a way that sabotages the desired outcome. So even Iranians who live and breathe politics every day don't make them.

That's hard for us Americans to understand. Predicting the future lies at the core of American politics. Plotting long-term strategies keeps armies of analysts occupied in the bowels of the Pentagon and the CIA. Take away predictions and where would American pollsters and pundits be?

But I will resist the temptation to make predictions. I cannot say that Iran is destined to be an Islamic democracy; I cannot forecast the demise of the Islamic Republic. All I can do is point to what I've learned in writing about Iran for more than twenty years.

I've learned that it is impossible to talk about a monolithic Iranian "regime" any longer; the struggle for the country's future is far too intense for that. Today there is no unified leadership or all-powerful governmental superstructure that makes and executes all decisions. Rather, power is dispersed among and even within many competing power centers, with varying agendas and methods of operation and degrees of authority. Even as I write, alliances are shifting. Players are adapting. Coalitions are building.

I've learned that democracy is being born at the grassroots level and that Iran today is more democratic than at any time in its history. The era of exclusionary politics that has dominated Iranian life since the beginning of the revolution, when Khomeini and his lieutenants marginalized all those who did not adhere to their vision of an Islamic state, is over. The slogan "Iran for all Iranians" adopted by the reformists during the parliamentary elections of 2000 is the ultimate symbol of that trend. It means that Iranians who don't believe in the Supreme Leader, Iranians who are not religious, Iranians who left the country years before—all have a place, however limited, in their country. Granted, there is no roadmap for how to get there. But recognition of the need to get there has become part of everyday politics.

But I also have learned that Iran remains a country of cultural apartheid, where people are punished for their lifestyles as well as their crimes. It is still a place with a dark side, where unpredictable repression and vengeful acts of violence are carried out by sometimes unknown power centers intent on remaining in the shadows and keeping themselves in control and the population at bay.

And while I do not dare predict the outcome of this struggle, I have a sense of just how fundamental it is. It could change the mirror Iranian leaders hold up for the world (and for their own citizens) to see them in; it could mark the passage from centuries-old habits of intrigue and suspicion into a more modern trust in openness and rational give-and-take.

In a sense politicians like Mohammad Khatami have challenged the practice of ruling through a splintered, dazzling, but ultimately mystifying mosaic of mirrors. Their goals are, above all, transparency, coherence, and predictability. These concepts take a number of other names in Iran today—the rule of law, democratic freedoms, easing of social restrictions, accountability—concepts that in the West are taken for granted as the critical tools of a just society, a modern economy, and a trustworthy foreign policy. In Iran, however, achieving them would signal a transformation, because the image of how and why the state does what it does would, at last, be easier to understand.

I have learned that the key to understanding the Islamic Republic is to get to know the people of the country—behind their closed doors. This is a country with a population and a history too complex to remain confined in a revolutionary mold forever. Most Iranians I know have no intention of abandoning the place of their birth. My friend Mina at the aerobics studio in Tehran put it best: "If a thief comes into your house, what do you do? Do you leave or do you stay? It's still your house. You stay. If you have a retarded child, what do you do? It's your child. You love it."

Finally, I have learned that the Iranian revolution still hasn't run its course. It took some scholars of the French Revolution two centuries to finally declare that revolution dead. Many of the battles fought in the Islamic Republic today are the unfinished battles begun during the revolution's early days. There is energy to fight these battles, but not to foment another revolution. One was enough.

＊　　＊　　＊

Ehsan Naraghi, an Iranian intellectual and sociologist, got it right in his 1991 memoirs, *From Palace to Prison*. Caught up in the revolution's brutal power struggle in the early 1980s, Naraghi was thrown into Tehran's formidable Evin prison, where he was beaten, threatened with death, and allowed almost no contact with his family until he was released nearly three years later for lack of evidence.

In one of his many moving stories of prison survival, Naraghi explains how a kind prison guard allowed him and his fellow inmates to use an oil stove to make tea and even to cook. On Thursday evenings, when many of the prison staff left for a day at home, Naraghi made omelets for his cellmates. "The secret was to use the whole range of ingredients at our disposal: potatoes, tomatoes, onions, and even apples and dates," he wrote.

"A useful rule was never to turn away food offered by the prison administration but instead to try to improve it. For example, once a week our supper ration was a kind of stew. It was inedible in itself, but the ingredients were not of bad quality if taken separately. So we would take the carrots from the stew and recook the potatoes and meat on the oil stove, adding a few onions and some tomato sauce which we could buy at our small prison cooperative. In this way the stew would be transformed into a completely different meal for our collective. Then there were the awful kidney beans, which the prisoners refused to eat. . . . I was quite happy to use the rejected beans and to fry them with a 'white sauce.' They were consumed with delight by everyone." Naraghi said he was such a good cook that some of the prison guards sometimes hung around to eat dinner with them.

When his politically radical cellmates congratulated him on his innovative cooking, Naraghi replied, "Unlike you, I am not a revolutionary, and I don't advocate that we reject everything and start again from scratch. Instead I try to improve what I have, using the ingredients at my disposal. But this is precisely the kind of reformist approach that fills you with horror."

And it is that reformist approach that just might allow the Islamic Republic to survive. Of course, it might not work out that way. Demographics and economics may combine to spark an explosion of incalculable force—of instability, civil unrest, popular revolt, or anarchy that could in turn produce a new era of repression.

But in the twenty-first century, many Iranian officials, politicians, women, clerics, journalists, filmmakers, intellectuals, entrepreneurs, and young people throughout the country are trying to do what Naraghi did with his oil stove in his prison compound: improve what they have, based on the ingredients at their disposal. Starting again from scratch is not an option for them. One revolution in a lifetime is enough, they say. Now is the time to pick flowers—and to plant more.

Acknowledgments

AND NOW FOR the fun part.

This book has been a long time coming. I first wanted to write a book on Iran in 1982, when I was the Edward R. Murrow Fellow at the Council on Foreign Relations in New York. But the time was not right. The United States had not recovered from the trauma of the hostage crisis. So I put away my notebooks and my letters of rejection from publishers and moved on to other things.

I couldn't kick the Iran habit. I kept going back to the country until, in 1998, I decided I had no choice except to write this book.

When it comes to writing, I play tennis, not solitaire. I can't play alone. I need to bounce ideas off friends, colleagues, and family. Even my pre-adolescent daughters read my leads and edit my copy. So I can honestly say that writing this book has been a process that would never have been started or finished without the help, friendship, and love of others.

I first must thank the editors of *The New York Times*. Joseph Lelyveld, the executive editor, and Bill Keller, the managing editor, generously gave me time off from the paper to write this book. They both truly understood that the passion I had for the subject would not subside until the book was written. Joe shared with me some of his own wisdom about successful book writing: write early and leave time for revision; don't fret about breaking news; write for yourself, not an imaginary audience.

Michael Oreskes, the Washington bureau chief, helped me throughout the process both as an editor and a friend, cutting through red tape, urging me on, and heeding every call for help. R. W. Apple Jr. has been a marvelous mentor since I first met him on the streets of Tehran during the revolution. Andrew Rosenthal, the foreign editor, was supportive in ways I will always cherish. Andy, his predecessor, Bernard Gwertzman, and Jack Rosenthal, Adam Moss, and Gerald Marzorati of *The New York Times Magazine* sent me on several assignments to Iran that convinced me that the time was right to write this book. Kyle Crichton, my editor at the magazine, helped me look at my material on Iran in a new way. Nancy Newhouse encouraged me to write a personal story for the Travel section on touring Iran with a group of American tourists. Jill Abramson, the Washington editor, helped me to think strategically about my material. William Schmidt, whom I have known since we worked together in the Chicago bureau of *Newsweek* in the mid-1970s, was on my side throughout the process.

This book was written with the help of fellowships and grants from various institutions. The Woodrow Wilson International Center for Scholars hosted me as a Public Policy Fellow. I call Robert S. Litwak a magician; he knows why. Lee H. Hamilton, Michael Van Dusen, Samuel F. Wells Jr., and Bahman Amini all made me feel part of the Wilson family.

The United States Institute of Peace hosted me as a Senior Fellow after that, giving me a marvelous collegial atmosphere in which to work. Richard H. Solomon let me do my own thing; Jon B. Alterman shared his wonderful insights on the Middle East; John Crist and Sally Blair cut through the bureaucratic thicket; Kerry O'Donnell tried to teach me how not to break the rules. I owe a very special thanks to Joseph L. Klaits, who was always full of ideas and helpful analysis, even though we did at times end up discussing a mutual passion: eighteenth-century France.

Open Society Institute provided me with a generous writing grant. I thank George Soros, Aryeh Neier, Gara LaMarche, Anthony Richter, Leigh Hallingby, and particularly Gail Goodman.

My friends were always there for me, even when I was at my most difficult.

I felt that I'd never get the book done. But I had my wonderful friend Robin Toner to tell me day after day, "You've never missed a deadline," and "Play to your strengths."

I felt cranky and irritable. But I had Carol Giacomo to get me to laugh, reminding me that no matter what, I had my health.

I felt that I didn't have enough to say. But I had Johanna Neuman to tell me, "Stop reporting. You have enough to fill three books."

I felt daunted by writing in a personal voice, saying, "I feel as if I'm a small landscape painter pretending to be Jackson Pollock." But I had

Joyce Seltzer to tell me, "Do you think that's better than being a Pollock pretending to be a small landscape painter?"

I also had Jonathan Randal to tell me war stories and fill me with good cheer, as he has done since he first introduced me to Iranian politics in Paris twenty-two years ago. I had Tony Clifton, my *Newsweek* colleague during the Iranian revolution and the hostage crisis, as a constant friend with whom I could communicate in shorthand. I had Isadore Seltzer to share with me his artistic vision and his strategies for dealing with 4:00 A.M. bursts of angst and energy. And I had Judi Brown to take me swimming and to Costco when she knew I needed a break.

There are two friends whom I must single out for special thanks. Farideh Farhi and I became friends in Iran almost as soon as we met—after recovering from a very heated public argument about the motives of American journalists working in Iran. While I was writing the book, Farideh and I were in contact daily, sometimes several times a day. She read every word of this manuscript—parts of it many times. She patiently filled in gaps, offered insights, corrected mistakes, and helped reorganize chapters. She pressed me to push on when I had no energy left. And she gave new meaning to the words of Eleanor Roosevelt: "Argue the other side with a friend until you have found the answer to every point which might be brought up against you."

Marc Charney, a gifted *New York Times* editor and a wonderful friend, spent endless evenings and weekends reading the manuscript. Just as important as his creative instincts were his generosity, encouragement, and wonderful sense of humor. I cherish our long talks—about totalitarianism and Azerbaijan, jazz and poetry.

There are other friends and colleagues who read all or part of the manuscript and provided support. Haleh Esfandiari is never too busy for her friends, and she offered constant and deep friendship as well as sound editorial judgment, often well into the night. Her husband, Shaul Bakhash, shared information and guidance on Iran as he has for nearly twenty years. Jahangir Amuzegar patiently answered my endless questions. Wade Greene was crucial in getting the project off the ground. Robert Pear, as with my previous book on Iraq, offered encouragement and saved me from making several mistakes. Sarah Weissman, with her sharp eye and her determination, helped locate and choose photographs.

Others who gave freely of their time, expertise, and editorial and strategic advice along the way include Gary Sick, Houchang Chehabi, Jeff

Gerth, Ahmad S. Moussalli, Tariq Fatemi, Michael Metrinko, Robert H. Pelletreau, John Limbert, Ken Simonson, Geoffrey Kemp, Judith Kipper, Steven C. Fairbanks, Suzanne Maloney, Julia Nanay, and Eliz Sanasarian.

I was blessed with a great editor. Paul Golob is smart, tough, and funny. He spouts poetry and baseball metaphors. He constantly urged me to write and write again, to tear up chapters and reorder the book—all in the name of excellence. He is a rarity in the book publishing industry: an editor who edits every line. Then, Rachel Klayman, who picked up the project after Paul left the Free Press, enthusiastically carried it to the finish line. And Gypsy da Silva, my copy editor at Simon & Schuster who lived in Iran long ago, corrected my transliterations as she got me giggling with her colorful Persian slang.

Andrew Wylie, my literary agent, gave me crucial advice at every point along the way, calling me Mother's Day morning and Thanksgiving evening and sending me e-mails from far-flung places like a beach in St. John and a hotel room in Milan. At one crisis point, he ordered me to put my notebooks into a file cabinet and write from my gut.

I also enjoyed working with a number of people who helped with research. Chris Holbrook brought balance to the project; he'd work hard during the week and do a triathalon on the weekend. Sara Borodin brought enormous energy, intelligence, and good cheer. Kelci Gershon brought extraordinary research skills and common sense. Dokhi Fassihian shared her insights as a young Iranian-American who had lived in Iran. Naghmeh Sohrabi, Jeffrey Ross, and Vida Ghaffari cheerfully carried out impossible assignments. Monica Borkowski of *The New York Times* helped locate Web sites, sources, and documents. Alys Yablon of the Free Press helped resolve numerous editorial and technical issues. In addition, the Middle East Institute generously allowed me the use of its marvelous library.

I am not a technical person, but I enjoyed the support of *The New York Times*'s Washington bureau team of specialists. Ronald Skarzenski, Clifton Meadows, and Von Aulston went into action when a "worm" attacked my system and started eating my files. Ron spent countless evenings troubleshooting with patience and ease. Cliff got me to laugh.

In Iran, I was helped by a number of officials. Mohammad-Ali Abtahi, the chef de cabinet of President Khatami, spent long hours with me. Hosein Nosrat, Ali-Reza Shiravi, Ali-Reza Haghighi, and the staff at the Ministry of Islamic Guidance and Culture went to extraordinary lengths to help arrange interviews and trips and occasionally get me out of trouble. They were available to help at all hours and on weekends. Fatemeh and Faezeh Hashemi introduced me to a side of Iranian life I otherwise never would have known.

There are a number of Iranian friends with whom I worked in Iran who educated me about the country and welcomed me into their homes. Nazila Fathi, *The New York Times* stringer, is truly in a class of her own. I met Nazila in 1992, when she was just out of college, and we began to work together closely three years later. We have traveled to all parts of Iran together, and she never quit until the task at hand was finished. I marvel at her patience, kindness, sense of humor, and pursuit of journalistic excellence. Nazila, Babak Pasha, her husband, Golnaz Fathi, her sister, and Jaffar Fathi, her father, are like family. Nazila and I worked with Hadi Salimi, a loyal and courageous driver and friend who was there whenever we needed him to take us on our next adventure.

Farhad Behbahani and Fereshteh Farhi opened up their home and their hearts to me, inviting me to spend time with their family and friends. Nahid Hosseinpour, whom I have known since she started working with *The New York Times* during the revolution, is as loyal a friend as I could ever hope to have. Over the years Goli Emami welcomed me with tea and sweets, wisdom and one-liners whenever I turned up on her doorstep; her learned and patient husband, Karim Emami, shared his wisdom on history, literature, language, and culture, and brought precision and clarity to the manuscript. Nasser Hadian, his wife, Shirin Parvini, and their daughter, Tahereh, shared their stories and hospitality. Amir Mahallati showed me Shiraz and introduced me to Persian poetry. Abdol-Reza Houshang Mahdavi filled me with history. Jamsheed Bairami, a gifted photographer, led me to magical hidden places throughout the country. Christophe de Roquefeuil and Kianouche Dorranie of Agence France-Presse warmly welcomed me to their bureau whenever I visited and shared their time and insights.

There are other Iranians who helped me at times during this project and prefer to remain nameless. To them, my deepest thanks.

There is one Iranian friend whom I cannot thank: Elahe Samii, who worked with me in Iran in the 1980s at great personal risk, eventually escaping through Turkey and settling in Europe. Her free spirit and positive attitude made covering Iran in those difficult days bearable and fun. She was killed in the crash of Swissair Flight 111 off Nova Scotia in September 1998.

Acknowledgments

The most constant and important support came from my family. Some writers need to get away from family members to work; I needed to be with them. I mostly wrote from home, which meant that every day after my daughters got home from school, I got to hear their stories and share in their day over tea and cookies.

Alessandra gave me a translucent red stone to rub to relieve stress and plastered notes of support on my computer. My favorite was, "I love my Mom a lot, and I hope she gets her book done on time or even a little early."

Gabriela needed to have a hands-on role, helping to collate and number pages and order and print chapters. She was full of tough questions (How do women get their hair done if they have to wear head scarves? Do women have to wear head scarves when they have sex?).

My mother, Jeannette Sciolino, and my mother-in-law, Sondra Brown, were there for my daughters at crucial times. Our baby-sitter, Wilna Papenfus, and before and after her, Katharina Björkström, gave them daily love and support.

Most important, there was my husband, Andrew Plump. Andy understood from the start how important the project was for me. He helped me formulate the concept and structure of the book, read the chapters over and over with his lawyerly precision, and stayed up late with me when the deadlines came. He was a single parent when I went off to Iran for weeks at a time. He remains my best editor and my best friend.

This book would not have been written had it not been for Maynard Parker, the editor of *Newsweek,* who died of cancer in October 1998. It was Maynard who took a chance on a female reporter still in her twenties with only a few months' experience as a foreign correspondent and put her on a plane to Iran with Ayatollah Khomeini in 1979. It was Maynard who gave her impossible assignments and sent her to remote places and never lost faith in her. And she did what she was told, and more, because she knew that he had done it all himself, once upon a time. This book is for him.

Chronology of Events

February 1921   Reza Pahlavi, an army colonel, carries out a coup d'état against the constitutional government of Iran.

December 1925   Reza Pahlavi is voted king by a Constituent Assembly appointed by Parliament, marking the beginning of the Pahlavi dynasty. He is thereafter known as Reza Shah.

August–September 1941 During World War II, British and Soviet troops invade Iran to secure a supply route to Russia, to safeguard oil installations, and to keep the country out of pro-German hands. Three weeks later, Britain and the Soviet Union force Reza Shah to abdicate in favor of his son, Mohammad Reza Pahlavi.

May 1946   Soviet troops withdraw from the Iranian province of Azerbaijan under pressure from the United States in what is considered the first crisis of the Cold War.

April 1951   Mohammad Mossadegh is appointed Prime Minister and proceeds to nationalize the British dominated oil industry.

August 1953   The Central Intelligence Agency and British intelligence carry out a coup d'état to oust Mossadegh and restore to power the Shah who had recently fled Iran.

June 1963   Ayatollah Ruhollah Khomeini, an influential cleric living in Qom, gives a scathing speech in which refers to the Shah as a "miserable wretch" and accuses him of violating his oath to defend Islam and the Constitution. Khomeini is arrested and imprisoned two days later, inciting demonstrations, which are crushed by security forces.

November 1964	Ayatollah Khomeini is exiled to Turkey; a year later he settles in Najaf, Iraq.
October 1973	The Organization of Petroleum Exporting Countries, of which Iran is a member, announces an embargo on oil shipments to the West in response to the Arab-Israeli War of that year. The embargo lasts for several months and precipitates the world's first energy crisis.
January 1978	Theology students and their sympathizers riot in the holy city of Qom, igniting mourning ceremonies and unrest in dozens of cities.
September 1978	Government troops fire on demonstrators on a day that comes to be known as Black Friday. Martial law is declared.
October 1978	At the Shah's request, Iraq's President Saddam Hussein expels Ayatollah Khomeini. The exiled Iranian cleric is refused entry to Kuwait and chooses to relocate temporarily in France.
December 31, 1978	President Jimmy Carter visits Tehran and in a toast to the Shah on New Year's Eve calls Iran an "island of stability" in the Persian Gulf.
January 16, 1979	Amid massive demonstrations, crippling strikes and rioting, the Shah and his family flee Iran, leaving the country in the hands of a caretaker government led by Prime Minister Shahpour Bakhtiar.
February 1, 1979	Ayatollah Khomeini returns triumphantly to Iran.

February 11, 1979	After two days of clashes between government troops and pro-Khomeini demonstrators, the army's Supreme Council declares neutrality in the crisis and orders troops back to their barracks. The Bakhtiar government falls and the revolution triumphs.
February 14, 1979	Militants briefly seize the American embassy in Tehran. It is liberated after a few hours.
October 22, 1979	The Shah enters the United States for cancer treatment, over the objection of Iran's revolutionary government.
November 4, 1979	Islamic militants again seize the American embassy in Tehran and take dozens of Americans hostage.
December 3, 1979	The Constitution of the Islamic Republic of Iran is ratified in a national referendum, codifying the concept of *Velayat-e faghih,* or rule of the Islamic jurist.
April 24, 1980	An American military mission to rescue the hostages is aborted after three of the eight helicopters involved are put out of action by technical problems. In the evacuation, a helicopter collides with a C-130 transport plane. Eight servicemen are killed.
July 27, 1980	The Shah dies of cancer, in Egypt.
September 22, 1980	Iraq invades Iran, the start of the Iran-Iraq War.
November 4, 1980	On the anniversary of the embassy seizure, Jimmy Carter is defeated for reelection by Ronald Reagan.
January 20, 1981	After 444 days in captivity, the American hostages in Tehran are released minutes after Reagan takes the oath of office as U.S. President.
October 1981	Ali Khamenei is elected President of Iran.
November 1984	The United States and Iraq reestablish diplomatic relations, which had been severed after the 1967 Arab-Israeli war.

1984–1985	Militant Islamic groups with suspected ties to Iran take American and other Western hostages in Lebanon.
November 1985	Ayatollah Hosein-Ali Montazeri is designated as Ayatollah Khomeini's eventual successor as Supreme Leader.
November 1986	The Iran-Contra scandal comes to light, revealing a covert program by the Reagan White House to finance the anti-Sandinista rebels in Nicaragua with profits from illegal arms sales to Iran.
July 3, 1988	The American naval warship USS *Vincennes* accidentally shoots down a civilian Iran Air plane over the Persian Gulf, killing all 290 people on board.
July 18, 1988	Ayatollah Khomeini accepts a Security Council resolution calling for a cease-fire ending the Iran-Iraq War.
February 14, 1989	Ayatollah Khomeini issues a fatwa branding novelist Salman Rushdie a blasphemer for his novel *The Satanic Verses* and calls for his assassination. An Iranian foundation offers a $2.6 million reward to the executioner.
March 1989	Because of his outspokenness in criticizing the regime, Ayatollah Montazeri loses his designation as the successor to Ayatollah Khomeini.
June 3, 1989	Ayatollah Khomeini dies. The Assembly of Experts quickly convenes and appoints Ali Khamenei as the Supreme Leader's temporary successor.
July 1989	Khamenei is confirmed as the new Supreme Leader. Ali-Akbar Hashemi-Rafsanjani, the Speaker of the Parliament, is elected President.
August 2, 1990	Iraq invades Kuwait. The United States organizes a military coalition against Iraq and moves troops to staging areas in Saudi Arabia.

January 17, 1991	The Gulf War begins with air strikes against targets in Iraq, which is followed in February by a 100-hour invasion.
February 27, 1991	Four days after ground troops are sent into Kuwait and Iraq, President George Bush proclaims victory, ending the Gulf War.
August 1991	Former Prime Minister Bakhtiar, now an opposition leader in exile, is assassinated in Paris, apparently by Iranian government agents.
December 1991	Terry Anderson, the last American hostage held in Lebanon, is released.
April 1995	President Bill Clinton announces a U.S. trade embargo on Iran and blocks the American oil company Conoco from moving forward on a $1 billion contract to develop oil fields in Iran.
August 1996	Congress passes the Iran-Libya Sanctions Act (ILSA), which imposes sanctions on foreign companies investing more than $40 million (later reduced to $20 million) in Iran's energy sector.
May 23, 1997	Mohammad Khatami is elected President in a landslide upset victory over the clerical establishment's favored candidate, Ali-Akbar Nateq-Nouri.
January 7, 1998	In an interview with CNN, President Khatami proposes cultural exchanges as a way to break down "the wall of mistrust" between Iran and the United States. But he rules out an official government-to-government dialogue, saying there is no need for political ties with Washington.
January 31, 1998	The first issue of the lively newspaper *Jameah* appears on newsstands.
May 1998	The Clinton Administration waives sanctions as required by ILSA on three foreign firms, Total of France, Gazprom of Russia, and Petronas of Malaysia.

June 17, 1998	Secretary of State Madeline Albright calls for the United States and Iran to develop a "roadmap" for eventual normalization of relations.
June 21, 1998	The United States faces Iran in a World Cup soccer match in Lyon, France; Iran defeats the United States 2–1.
June–July 1998	Gholam-Hosein Karbaschi, the reformist mayor of Tehran, is put on trial for corruption, embezzlement, and mismanagement. He is sentenced to two years' imprisonment.
July 22, 1998	Iran successfully tests the Shehab-3, a medium-range missile with a range of about 800 miles, capable of hitting Israel, Turkey, and most of Saudi Arabia.
September 22, 1998	President Khatami, in a news conference in New York, calls the Rushdie affair "finished" and declares that Iran has no intention of carrying out Ayatollah Khomeini's fatwa. The statement paves the way for the upgrading of relations and the exchange of ambassadors between Iran and Britain in 1999.
October 31, 1998	Radio Free Iran/Radio Liberty begins broadcasting from Prague in the Czech Republic.
November 22, 1998	Dariush Forouhar and his wife Parvaneh are found stabbed to death in their home, as part of a wave of murders of dissident writers and intellectuals by a "rogue" cell in the Ministry of Information.
February–March 1999	The Iranian government arrests thirteen Iranian Jews on charges of spying for Israel.
February 26, 1999	Iranians vote in the first local elections ever held in the country. Reformist candidates win nationwide.
April 12, 1999	President Clinton says in a speech that Iran has a right to be angry at the West, having "been the subject of quite a lot of abuse from various Western nations."

June 7, 1999	The leftist daily newpaper *Salaam* is banned for "attempting to create turmoil and instability."
July 8, 1999	In response to the closing of *Salaam* and a restrictive press law in consideration in parliament, widespread student demonstrations begin. That night, student dormitories at the University of Tehran are attacked by vigilantes and state security forces. The unrest lasts six days before the government restores order.
July 27, 1999	The United States lifts a ban on sales of food, medicine, and medical equipment to Iran.
October–November 1999	Abdollah Nouri, former Vice President and a former Minister of the Interior in Khatami's administration, is put on trial and convicted of heresy for publishing "anti-Islamic" articles in his newspaper *Khordad*. He is sentenced to five years' imprisonment and barred from running for public office or holding a position in government.
December 4, 1999	The United States, citing concerns over airline passenger safety, announces a decision to allow Boeing to sell spare parts to Iran for its aging civilian fleet.
February 18, 2000	More than 5,000 candidates run for 290 seats in parliamentary elections. Reform candidates easily win a majority in the first round.
March 17, 2000	Secretary of State Albright announces the easing of sanctions on nonoil exports from Iran, including carpets, pistachios, and caviar. She also acknowledges—without apologizing—American errors in past dealings with Iran, including the CIA-led coup in 1953 and the American tilt toward Iraq during its war against Iran.
April 2000	The Judiciary shuts down seventeen reformist newspapers and magazines on

	charges that they published material that "disparaged Islam."
May 5, 2000	The second round of parliamentary elections is held, with reform candidates again winning a clear majority.
July 1, 2000	Ten Jews and two Muslims are found guilty, following a trial in Shiraz, of spying for Israel and sentenced to prison terms of two to thirteen years.

Bibliography

BOOKS

Abdi, Abbas. *Ghodrat, Ghanoon, Farhang (Power, Law, Culture).* Tehran: Tarheh No, 1998.

Abrahamian, Ervand. *Iran Between Two Revolutions.* Princeton, N.J.: Princeton University Press, 1982.

———. *Khomeinism: Essays on the Islamic Republic.* London: I.B. Tauris, 1993.

———. *Tortured Confessions: Prisons and Public Recantations in Modern Iran.* Berkeley: University of California Press, 1999.

Afkhami, Mahnaz, and Erika Friedl, eds. *In the Eye of the Storm: Women in Post-Revolutionary Iran.* Syracuse: Syracuse University Press, 1994.

Afkhami, Mahnaz, and Haleh Vaziri. *Claiming Our Rights: A Manual for Women's Human Rights Education in Muslim Societies.* Bethesda: Sisterhood Is Global Institute, 1996.

Akbar, Fatollah. *The Eye of an Ant: Persian Proverbs and Poems.* Bethesda: Iran Books, 1995.

Al-e Ahmad, Jalal. *Plagued by the West (Gharbzadegi).* Translated by Paul Sprachman. New York: Caravan Books, 1982.

Amanat, Abbas. *Pivot of the Universe: Nasir al-Din Shah Qajar and the Iranian Monarchy, 1831–1896.* Berkeley: University of California Press, 1997.

Amirahmadi, Hooshang. *Revolution and Economic Transition: The Iranian Experience.* Albany: State University of New York Press, 1990.

Amuzegar, Jahangir. *The Dynamics of the Iranian Revolution: The Pahlavis' Triumph and Tragedy.* Albany: State University of New York Press, 1991.

———. *Iran's Economy Under the Islamic Republic.* London: I.B. Tauris, 1997.

Arberry, A.J. *Shiraz: Persian City of Saints and Poets.* Norman: University of Oklahoma Press, 1960.

Arjomand, Said Amir. *The Turban for the Crown: The Islamic Revolution in Iran.* Oxford: Oxford University Press, 1988.

Bakhash, Shaul. *The Reign of the Ayatollahs: Iran and the Islamic Revolution.* New York: Basic Books, 1990.

Bibliography

Baktiari, Bahman. *Parliamentary Politics in Revolutionary Iran: The Institutionalization of Factional Politics.* Gainesville: University Press of Florida, 1996.

Bani-Sadr, Abol-Hassan. *My Turn to Speak: Iran, the Revolution, and Secret Deals with the U.S.* New York: Brassey's (U.S.), 1991.

Baraheni, Reza. *The Crowned Cannibals: Writings on Repression in Iran.* New York: Vintage, 1977.

Barks, Coleman. *Feeling the Shoulder of the Lion: Poetry and Teaching Stories of Rumi.* Vermont: Threshold Books, 1991.

Bayat, Asef. *Street Politics: Poor People's Movements in Iran.* New York: Columbia University Press, 1997.

Bell, Gertrude. *The Hafez Poems of Gertrude Bell.* Bethesda: Iranbooks, 1995.

———. *Persian Pictures.* London: Ernest Benn, 1947.

Beny, Roloff. *Persia: Bridge of Turquoise.* London: Thames and Hudson, 1975.

Bill, James A. *The Eagle and the Lion: The Tragedy of American-Iranian Relations.* New Haven: Yale University Press, 1988.

Boroujerdi, Mehrzad. *Iranian Intellectuals and the West: The Tormented Triumph of Nativism.* Syracuse: Syracuse University Press, 1996.

Brinton, Crane. *The Anatomy of Revolution.* New York: Vintage, 1965.

Brooks, Geraldine. *Nine Parts of Desire: The Hidden World of Islamic Women.* New York: Doubleday, 1997.

Brown, Edward Granville. *A Year Amongst the Persians.* London: Century Publishing, 1984.

Byron, Robert. *The Road to Oxiana.* London: Macmillan, 1937.

Carter, Jimmy. *Keeping Faith: Memoirs of a President.* New York: Bantam, 1982.

Chardin, Sir John. *Travels in Persia, 1673–1677.* New York: Dover Publications, 1988.

Christopher, Warren et al. *American Hostages in Iran: The Conduct of Crisis.* New Haven: Yale University Press, 1985.

Chubin, Shahram, and Charles Tripp. *Iran and Iraq at War.* Boulder: Westview Press, 1988.

Chubin, Shahram. *Iran's National Security Policy: Capabilities, Intentions and Impact.* Washington, D.C.: Carnegie Endowment for International Peace, 1994.

Clawson, Patrick, Michael Eisenstadt, Eliyahu Kanovsky, and David Menashri. *Iran Under Khatami: A Political, Economic, and Military Assessment.* Washington, D.C.: Washington Institute for Near East Policy, 1998.

The Constitution of the Islamic Republic of Iran. Translated by Masouduzzafar. Tehran: Pars Associates, 1980.

———. *Amendments Made to the Constitution.* Tehran: Pars Associates, undated.

Cooper, Roger. *Death Plus Ten Years.* London: HarperCollins, 1993.

Cordesman, Anthony H. *The Iran-Iraq War and Western Security, 1984–87: Strategic Implications and Policy Options.* London: Jane's Publishing, 1987.

———. *The Lessons of Modern War, Volume II: The Iran-Iraq War.* Boulder: Westview Press, 1990.

Bibliography

Cottam, Richard W. *Nationalism in Iran.* Pittsburgh: University of Pittsburgh Press, 1964.

Curzon, George Nathaniel. *Persia and the Persian Question.* London: Longmans, Green, 1892. Two volumes.

Davis, Dick. *Borrowed Ware: Medieval Persian Epigrams.* Washington, D.C.: Mage Publishers, 1997.

Eisenstadt, Michael. *Iranian Military Power: Capabilities and Intentions.* Washington, D.C.: Washington Institute for Near East Policy, 1996.

Esfandiari, Haleh. *Reconstructed Lives: Women and Iran's Islamic Revolution.* Washington, D.C.: Woodrow Wilson Center Press, 1997.

Eslami, Kambiz, ed. *Iran and Iranian Studies: Essays in Honor of Iraj Afshar.* Princeton: Zagros Press, 1998.

Fall of a Centre of Deceit. Tehran: Islamic Propagation Organisation, undated.

Faramarzi, M.T. *A Travel Guide to Iran.* Tehran: Yassaman Publications, 1997.

Farmanfarmaian, Manucher, and Roxane Farmanfarmaian. *Blood and Oil: Memoirs of a Persian Prince.* New York: Random House, 1997.

Farman Farmaian, Sattareh, with Dona Munker. *Daughter of Persia: A Woman's Journey from Her Father's Harem Through the Islamic Revolution.* New York: Crown, 1992.

Farsoun, Samih K., and Mehrdad Mashayekhi, eds. *Iran: Political Culture in the Islamic Republic.* London: Routledge, 1992.

Ferdowsi, Abol-Qasem. *The Tragedy of Sohrab and Rostam: From the Persian National Epic, the Shahname of Abol-Qasem Ferdowsi.* Translated by Jerome W. Clinton. Seattle: University of Washington Press, 1987.

Fuller, Graham E. *The "Center of the Universe": The Geopolitics of Iran.* Boulder: Westview Press, 1991.

Graham, Robert. *Iran: The Illusion of Power.* New York: St. Martin's, 1979.

Haeri, Shahla. *Law of Desire: Temporary Marriage in Shi'i Iran.* Syracuse: Syracuse University Press, 1989.

Harnack, Curtis. *Persian Lions, Persian Lambs: An American's Odyssey in Iran.* Ames: Iowa State University Press, 1981.

Harney, Desmond. *The Priest and the King: An Eyewitness Account of the Iranian Revolution.* London: I.B. Tauris, 1998.

Helms, Cynthia. *An Ambassador's Wife in Iran.* New York: Dodd, Mead, 1981.

Hureau, Jean. *Iran Today.* Paris: Editions Jeune Afrique, 1975.

Imam Khomeini and November 4th (Aban 13). By the Muslim Students in the Line of the Imam, Ministry of Islamic Guidance, 1982.

Iran, A Country Study. Washington, D.C.: Library of Congress, Federal Research Division, 1989.

Iskandar, Kai Ka'us Ibn, Prince of Gurgan. *A Mirror for Princes.* Translated and republished by Reuben Levy. London: Cresset Press, 1951.

Jalaeipour, Hamid-Reza. *Pas Az Dovomeh Khordad: Negahi Jameahshenakhti be Jonbesh-e Madani-e Iran (After the Second of Khordad: A Sociological Study of Civil Movements in Iran).* Tehran: Kavir, 1999.

Bibliography

Jalal al-Din Rumi, Maulana. *The Essential Rumi.* Translated by Coleman Barks with John Moyne. New York: HarperCollins, 1995.

Jerome, Carole. *The Man in the Mirror: A True Inside Story of Revolution, Love, and Treachery in Iran.* London: Unwin Hyman, 1987.

Kaplan, Robert D. *The Ends of the Earth: A Journey at the Dawn of the 21st Century.* New York: Random House, 1996.

Kapuscinski, Ryszard. *Shah of Shahs.* New York: Vintage, 1985.

Keddie, Nikki R. *Religion and Politics in Iran.* New Haven: Yale University Press, 1983.

———. *Roots of Revolution: An Interpretive History of Modern Iran.* New Haven: Yale University Press, 1983.

Kemp, Geoffrey. *America and Iran: Road Maps and Realism.* Washington, D.C.: Nixon Center, 1998.

———. *Forever Enemies? American Policy and the Islamic Republic of Iran.* Washington D.C.: Carnegie Endowment for International Peace, 1994.

Kennedy, Moorhead, *The Ayatollah in the Cathedral: Reflections of a Hostage.* New York: Hill & Wang, 1986.

Khatami, Mohammad. *Az Donyayeh Shahr ta Shahreh Donya. (From the World of the City to the City of the World)* Tehran: Nashreh Ney 1997 (third edition).

———. *Bimeh Moj (Fear of Waves).* Tehran: Simayeh Javan, 1993.

———. *Hope and Challenge: The Iranian President Speaks.* Binghamton: Institute of Global Cultural Studies, Binghamton University, 1997.

———. *Islam, Liberty, and Development.* Binghamton: Institute of Global Cultural Studies, Binghamton University, 1998.

Khomeini, Ruhollah. *A Clarification of Questions.* Translated by J. Borujerdi. Boulder: Westview Press, 1984.

———. *Imam's Final Discourse.* Tehran: Ministry of Islamic Guidance and Culture, 1989.

———. *Islam and Revolution: Writings and Declarations of Imam Khomeini.* Translated and annotated by Hamid Algar. Berkeley: Mizan Press, 1981.

———. *The Jardinière of Love: Eight Odes Composed by Hazrat Imam Khomeini.* Tehran: Institute for Compilation and Publication of the Works of Imam Khomeini, 1994.

———. *Sayings of the Ayatollah Khomeini: Political, Philosophical, Social, and Religious.* New York: Bantam, 1980.

———. *Selected Messages and Speeches of Imam Khomeini (From Oct. 1980 to Jan. 1982).* Tehran: Ministry of Islamic Guidance and Culture, 1982.

The Koran. Translated with Notes by N.J. Dawood. London: Penguin, 1997.

Lewis, Bernard. *The Political Language of Islam.* Chicago: University of Chicago Press, 1988.

Mazaheri, Ali Akbar. *Youth and Spouse Selection.* Qom: Ansariyan Publications, 1995.

McGhee, George. *Envoy to the Middle East: Adventures in Diplomacy.* New York: Harper & Row, 1969.

Bibliography

McManus, Doyle. *Free At Last!: The Complete Story of the Hostages' 444-Day Ordeal and the Secret Negotiations to Set Them Free.* New York: New American Library, 1981.

Mernissi, Fatima. *Islam and Democracy: Fear of the Modern World.* Translated by Mary Jo Lakeland. Reading, Penn.: Addison-Wesley, 1992.

Meskoob, Shahrokh. *Iranian Nationality and the Persian Language.* Washington, D.C.: Mage Publishers, 1992.

Milani, Abbas. *Tales of Two Cities: A Persian Memoir.* Washington, D.C.: Mage Publishers, 1996.

Milani, Farzaneh. *Veils and Words: The Emerging Voices of Iranian Women Writers.* London: I.B. Tauris, 1992.

Montazam, Mir Ali Asghar. *The Life and Times of Ayatollah Khomeini.* London: Anglo-European Publishing, 1994.

Morier, James. *The Adventures of Hajji Baba of Ispahan.* London: George C. Harrap, 1948.

Mortimer, Edward. *Faith and Power: The Politics of Islam.* New York: Random House, 1982.

Morvarid, Younes, ed. *Dadgah-e Melli: Az did-e Moardom va Matbouat (National Court: Views of People and the Press).* Tehran: Vahedi, 1998.

Mottahedeh, Roy. *The Mantle of the Prophet: Religion and Politics in Iran.* New York: Simon and Schuster, 1985.

Mutahhary, M. *The Martyr.* Tehran: Great Islamic Library, undated.

Naipaul, V. S. *Among the Believers: An Islamic Journey.* London: Penguin, 1981.

———. *Beyond Belief: Islamic Excursions Among the Converted People.* New York: Random House, 1998.

Naraghi, Ehsan. *From Palace to Prison: Inside the Iranian Revolution.* Chicago: Ivan R. Dee, 1994.

Niloofari, P. *Persian Folk Songs,* edited by P. Niloofari and translated by A. Aryanpur, and M. Aryanpur. Tehran, 1971.

Nouri, Abdollah. *Showkaraneh Eslah (Hemlock of Reform).* Tehran: Tarheh No, 1999.

O'Donnell, Terence. *Garden of the Brave in War: Recollections of Iran.* Chicago: University of Chicago Press, 1980.

Pahlavi, Mohammad Reza. *Answer to History.* New York: Stein and Day, 1980.

———. *Mission for My Country.* London: Hutchinson, 1961.

Paidar, Parvin. *Women and the Political Process in Twentieth-Century Iran.* Cambridge: Cambridge University Press, 1995.

Parsons, Sir Anthony. *The Pride and The Fall: Iran, 1974–1979.* London: Jonathan Cape, 1984.

Pope, Arthur Upham. *Introducing Persian Architecture.* Tehran: Soroush Press, 1969.

Ramazani, R. K. *Revolutionary Iran: Challenge and Response in the Middle East.* Baltimore: Johns Hopkins University Press, 1986.

Randal, Jonathan C. *After Such Knowledge, What Forgiveness? My Encounters with Kurdistan.* New York: Farrar, Straus and Giroux, 1997.

Rizvi, Sayyid Muhammad. *Marriage and Morals in Islam.* Qom: Ansariyan Publications, 1990.

Roosevelt, Kermit. *Countercoup: The Struggle for the Control of Iran.* New York: McGraw-Hill, 1979.

Ross, Sir Denison E., and Eileen Power, eds. *Sir Anthony Sherley and His Persian Adventures.* London: George Routledge & Sons, 1933.

Roy, Olivier. *The Failure of Political Islam.* Cambridge: Harvard University Press, 1994.

Rubin, Barry. *Paved with Good Intentions: The American Experience in Iran.* New York: Penguin, 1991.

Rushdie, Salman. *The Satanic Verses.* New York: Viking, 1988.

Sackville-West, Vita. *Passenger to Teheran.* London: Hogarth Press, 1926.

St. Vincent, David. *Iran: A Travel Survival Kit.* Berkeley: Lonely Planet Publications, 1992.

Schirazi, Asghar. *Constitution of Iran: Politics and the State in the Islamic Republic.* Translated by John O'Kane. London: I.B Tauris, 1997.

Shawcross, William. *The Shah's Last Ride: The Fate of an Ally.* New York: Simon and Schuster, 1988.

Sheil, Lady Mary. *Glimpses of Life and Manners in Persia.* New York: Arno, 1973.

Shirley, Edward. *Know Thine Enemy: A Spy's Journey into Revolutionary Iran.* New York: Farrar, Straus and Giroux, 1997.

Shuster, W. Morgan. *The Strangling of Persia.* Washington, D.C.: Mage Publications, 1987.

Sick, Gary. *All Fall Down: America's Fateful Encounter with Iran.* New York: Random House, 1985.

Simpson, John. *Behind Iranian Lines: Travels Through Revolutionary Iran and the Persian Past.* London: Robson Books, 1988.

———. *Inside Iran: Life Under Khomeini's Regime.* New York: St. Martin's, 1988.

Simpson, John and Tira Shubart. *Lifting the Veil: Life in Revolutionary Iran.* London: Hodder and Stoughton, 1995.

Stark, Freya, *The Valley of the Assassins, and Other Persian Travels.* London: Messrs. Wyman & Sons, 1934.

Stevens, Roger. *The Land of the Great Sophy.* London: Methuen, 1971.

Sullivan, William H. *Mission to Iran.* New York: W.W. Norton, 1981.

Tocqueville, Alexis de. *Democracy in America.* New York: New American Library, 1956.

———. *The Old Regime and the French Revolution.* Translated by Stuart Gilbert. Garden City: Doubleday, 1955.

The World Bank. *Entering the 21st Century: The World Development Report, 1999/2000.* Oxford: Oxford University Press, 2000.

———. *World Development Indicators.* The World Bank, 1999

Wright, Sir Denis. *The Persians Amongst the English.* London: I.B. Tauris, 1985.

Wright, Robin. *In the Name of God: The Khomeini Decade.* New York: Simon and Schuster, 1989.

———. *The Last Great Revolution: Turmoil and Transformation in Iran.* New York: Alfred A. Knopf, 2000.

Bibliography

Zibakalam, Sadegh. *Ma Chegouneh Ma Shodim (How Did We Become We?)*. Tehran: Rozaneh, 1995.

Zonis, Marvin. *Majestic Failure: The Fall of the Shah*. Chicago: University of Chicago Press, 1991.

———. *The Political Elite of Iran*. Princeton: Princeton University Press, 1971.

ARTICLES

Ajami, Fouad. "The Impossible Revolution." *Foreign Affairs* 67 (January 1989): 135–55.

Bakhash, Shaul. "Iran's Remarkable Election." *Journal of Democracy* 9 (January 1998): 80–94.

———. "Iran's Unlikely President." *The New York Review of Books* (Nov. 5, 1998): 47–51.

———. "Letter from an Iranian Prisoner." *The New York Review of Books* (April 10, 1997): 52–53.

———. "Prisoners of the Ayatollah." *The New York Review of Books* (August 11, 1994): 42–45.

———. "The Revolution Against Itself." *The New York Review of Books* (November 18, 1982): 19–26.

———. "What Khomeini Did." *The New York Review of Books* (July 20, 1989): 16–19.

Chubin, Shahram. "Iran's Strategic Predicament." *The Middle East Journal* 54 (Winter 2000): 10–24.

Khomeini, Ruhollah. "Five Mystical Ghazals by the Ayatollah Khomeini." *Iranian Studies* 30 (Summer/Fall, 1997): 272–76.

Matin-Asgari, Afshin. "Abdolkarim Soroush and the Secularization of Islamic Thought in Iran." *Iranian Studies* 30 (Winter/Spring 1997): 95–116.

Index

Index

Index

homosexuality, 106, 130
Hosein, Imam, 38, 39, 173–74, 178
House of Cinema, 261–62
House of Martyrs, 172–73, 184
Hoviyyat (identity), 242
humor, 206, 220, 247, 251, 271
Hussein, King of Jordan, 47
Hussein, Saddam, *see* Saddam Hussein

Imam:
    eighth, 195
    meaning of title, 16, 38
    twelfth, 39, 60, 226
Imam Khomeini Judiciary Complex, 302
India, 322, 339
Indyk, Martin, 352–53
inflation, 318, 322
informants, 99–100, 106–7
Information and Tourism Ministry, 193
inheritance, 115, 127, 147, 212
intellectuals, 42, 64, 76, 78
    freedom of expression and, 249–73
    in opposition to Shah, 175
    political repression of, 239–48
Intelligence Ministry, 20, 24, 77, 100, 234,
        241, 242, 243, 295, 311, 312
    reach of, 238–39
    "rogue" killings scandal and, 240
Inter-Continental Hotel, *see* Laleh Inter-
        Continental Hotel
Interior Ministry, 66, 77, 296, 307
International Monetary Fund, 347
International Women's Day, 146–47
Internet, 22, 195, 196, 201, 257, 283, 284, 293,
        304
invitations, 29, 68–69, 321
Iran:
    ancient battles still being fought in,
        38–39
    Arab countries and, 43
    author's arrival in, 11–14, 140–41
    author's twelve rules for coping in,
        28–45
    chronology of events in, 370–77
    climate and topography of, 36–37
    as combination of Persia and Islamic
        Republic, 36–38
    credit rating of, 325

derivation of word, 42
ethnic and language groups of, 36, 213,
        341
fluidity of rules in, 30–32, 64–65, 94, 96,
        137–38, 142, 253
history of democracy and pluralism in,
        71
international role of, 343–46
Islam brought to, 169
national identity of, 36, 43, 84, 157,
        169–71, 222–23, 228, 230, 338, 339,
        340–42, 347, 361
1953 coup in, 43, 52, 233
1979 revolution in, *see* revolution, Iran-
        ian
nuclear power program of, 34, 345,
        351–25
political prospects of, 312–14, 339,
        359–63
population of, 15, 36, 39–40, 178, 282
power struggle in, 354–55, 360
religious groups of, 38, 210–30, 341
self-image of, 338, 341
strategic location of, 339
terror and assassination in, 40–42
as theocracy, *see* Islamic Republic
U.S. visitors in, 2, 4, 45
younger generation of, 40, 74, 78, 94,
        129, 200, 226, 237, 261–63, 272–73,
        274–93, 312, 320–21; *see also* student
        demonstrations of 1999
see also Persia
Iran, 202
Iran Air, 11–12
    Vincennes attack and, 45, 179, 191, 347
Iran at a Glance, 187
Iran-e Vij, 355
"*Iran hoorah, Amrika sourakh,*" 275–76
Iran-Iraq war, 31, 39, 40, 63, 74, 85, 114, 136,
        137, 154, 163, 164–65, 172–79, 194, 195,
        245, 251, 252, 261, 262, 269, 287–89,
        295, 296, 309, 318, 320, 326, 337, 339,
        341, 344, 351
    burial place for martyrs of, 56, 172–73,
        175–77, 180, 181, 184
    casualties in, 179
    ending of, 173, 179, 357
    events of, 177–79

Index

Index

Index

Persia, 14–15, 26, 36, 153, 157, 161–62, 165, 167, 169, 170, 216, 323
   history of, 42–43
Persia and the Persian Question (Curzon), 33, 127
Persian Gulf, 42, 45, 181, 321, 337, 339, 340, 344, 345, 353, 355
Persian Gulf states, 170, 178
Persian language, 36, 42, 43, 83, 84, 112, 116, 158, 159, 169, 196, 201, 213, 217, 218, 234, 270, 279, 329
pesh merga, 41
Petronas, 345
photographs, "immoral," 253
Picasso, Pablo, 146
pilgrims, 127, 194, 195, 323
pistachios, 164
pluralism, 306–7
poetry, 6, 102, 154–61, 167, 170, 297
politeness, truth and, 34–36, 252
   see also taarof
political assassinations, 41–42
   of Dariush and Parvaneh Forouhar, 233–37, 248
   of intellectuals, 239–40
political parties, 71–72, 76, 243, 257, 296
political refugees, 216, 227, 234, 287
pollution, 16, 116, 153, 154
polygamy, 114, 122–23, 208
Pony Express, 43
porrou, 118
Postal Service, U.S., 43
Pouyandeh, Mohammad Jaffar, 239
presidency of Iran, 72, 73, 78, 84, 208
   Taleghani's candidacy and, 112–13, 114, 296
Presidential Palace, 81, 82
Press Court, 240
private space, 6, 68, 93–108, 195, 237, 263
   alcohol and, 102–4, 283
   beauty salons as, 104–5
   behavior in, 27, 29, 96, 99, 283–84
   indeterminate definition of, 94, 96
   intrusions into, 98, 100, 107–8, 197, 276–77
   invitations to, 29

   as refuge from Islamic Republic, 93–94, 95–96
   see also homes
prostitution, 122, 126–29, 217, 222

Qavam, Ahmad, 337
Qazvin, 112
Qods, 256, 306
Qom, 36, 44, 53, 77, 80, 85, 110, 111, 112, 127, 136, 137, 138, 154, 174, 175, 190–209, 249, 250, 251, 275, 303, 304, 309, 311
   Khomeini's house in, 65, 194
   layout of, 195
   location of, 192
   Montazeri's house attacked in, 196–97
   Montazeri under house arrest in, 190–92
   number of clerics in, 199
   as private place, 194–95
   roles of, 192–93, 194
   seminaries of, 194, 207–9
   women in, 194–95, 196, 204, 207–9

Rabbani, Burhanuddin, 139
Rabbani, Hamideh, 139–40
Rabii, Amir-Hosein, 54, 61
radio, 53, 56, 73, 270
Radio France, 14
Radio Free Europe, 270
Radio Payam, 304
Radnia, Malous, 243–44
Rafiqdoust, Mohsen, 327
Rafsanjani, Ali-Akbar Hashemi-, 23, 76, 77, 118, 121, 128, 139, 143, 219, 237, 245, 264, 287, 288, 297, 313–14, 327, 352
   author interview with, 164
   background of, 164, 294
   clerical rank of, 199
   Conoco oil deal and, 349–50
   Persepolis rehabilitated under, 164–65
   pragmatic political style of, 164
   in 2000 election, 241, 294–95, 298, 311
Rafsanjan Pistachio Producers' Cooperative, 164
Rahimian, Hamid, 172–73, 175–77, 178, 180–81, 183–85, 188
rajol, 112–13
Ramadan, 68, 107

Index

Randal, Jonathan, 48
Rand Corporation, 338
rape, 115
Rasouli (waiter), 19–20
Rayyes, Riad Najib, 314
Razini, Ali, 259
Reagan administration, arms-for-hostages
    deal and, 41, 349, 352
religious minorities, 210–30
    see also Bahais; Christians in Iran; Jews
    in Iran; Zoroastrians
Resalat, 256
revolution, Iranian, 4–5, 17, 18, 30, 39,
    46–67, 81, 86, 88, 110, 119, 166, 168,
    171, 177, 191, 200, 212, 237, 251, 261,
    298, 322, 341, 342
    abolition of censorship as aim of, 254
    events of, 57–61, 174, 193
    and Khomeini's return from exile,
       46–47, 54–57
    ongoing nature of, 361
    younger generation's relationship to,
       280–81, 289, 291
Revolutionary Council, 30, 85, 164, 191
Revolutionary Guards, 14, 73, 85, 192, 250,
    287, 288, 301, 307, 328, 356
Reza, Imam, 195, 214, 326
Rezai, Ahmad, 287–88
Rezai, Ali, 288
Rezai, Mohsen, 287, 288, 356
rial, 322, 330, 334, 342
Rockefeller, Nelson, 342
Roosevelt, Kermit, 52
Rosenthal, Andrew, 182–83
roupoush, 95, 135–36
rowzeh khan, 198
Roy, Olivier, 204
Royal Dutch/Shell, 326
Rubáiyát (Khayyam), 93, 160, 190
rule of law, 76, 88, 109, 128, 129, 130, 253,
    279, 296, 302, 327, 355
Rumi, 233
Rushdie, Salman, 182–83, 191, 346
Russia, 88, 137, 321, 325, 339, 345, 351
    see also Soviet Union

Saadi, 154–55, 156, 157, 297
Sabbath, 219

Sabet, Hosein, 332–33, 335
Sabet Organization, 332
Sackville-West, Vita, 6
Saddam Hussein, 48, 99, 177–78, 181
Sadeghi, Zohreh, 70, 80, 143
Safavi, Rahim, 250, 251, 252
Saidi, Meysam, 280–81
Saint Sarkis Church, 213
Salaam, 77, 240, 254–55, 276, 296, 356
Salimi, Hadi, 14, 16, 141, 159–60, 341
Salimi, Mohammad, 309
Sanandaj, 23, 29, 256
Saneii, Ayatollah Hassan, 183
Saqafi, Khadija, 134
Sarkouhi, Faraj, 242
Satanic Verses, The (Rushdie), 182
satellite dishes, 2, 44, 99, 255, 263, 267, 269,
    283, 334
Saudi Arabia, 4, 72, 112, 132, 178, 191, 222,
    309, 323, 344–45, 351
SAVAK, 217, 237, 238–39
sayyid, 39
Second of Khordad Front, 296
secret police, 4
    of Shah, 56, 175, 217, 237, 238–39
    see also Intelligence Ministry
Security Council, 344
Select Council of Sit-In Students, 281
Servants of Construction, 76, 297, 302
Seyed Hosseini, Reza, 159
Shaat al-Arab waterway, 178
shahbanu, 254
Shahed (Witness) shop, 13
Shahnameh (*Book of Kings*) (Ferdowsi),
    170, 171, 261
Shah of Iran, historical titles of, 46,
    338
Shamsolvaezin, Mashallah, 144, 249,
    251, 252, 253, 255, 258, 259–60,
    263
Shaqaqi, Fathi, 221
sharia, *see* Islamic law
Shariat-Madari, Ayatollah Kazem, 137
Sharif, Majid, 239
Shayan Hotel, 334
Sheil, Lady and Sir Justin, 26
Sherkat, Shahla, 121–23, 271
Shiite Center, 60